ALSO BY MICHAEL SHNAYERSON

Irwin Shaw, a Biography

THE CAR
THAT COULD

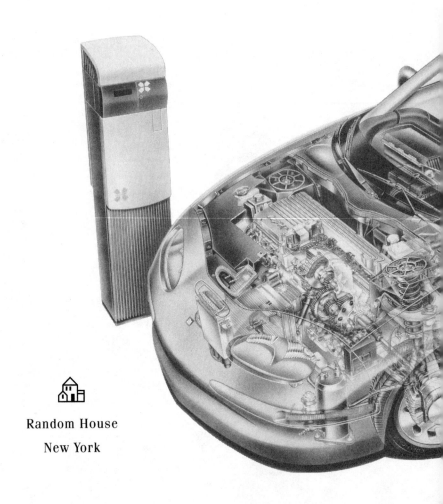

Random House
New York

MICHAEL SHNAYERSON

》》》 》》》 》》》

THE CAR
THAT COULD

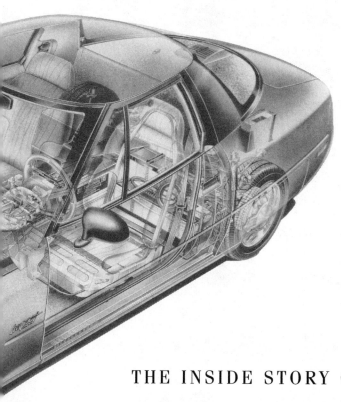

THE INSIDE STORY OF
GM'S REVOLUTIONARY
ELECTRIC VEHICLE

Title page illustration courtesy General Motors

Library of Congress Cataloging-in-Publication Data
Shnayerson, Michael.
The car that could: the inside story of GM's
revolutionary electric vehicle / Michael Shnayerson.
p.   cm.
Includes index.
ISBN 0-679-42105-X (hardcover)
1. EV1 automobile.   2. General Motors Corporation—History.
I. Title.
TL215.E92S53   1996   629.22′93—dc20   96-5557

Random House website address: http://www.randomhouse.com/

Printed in the United States of America on acid-free paper
2 4 6 8 9 7 5 3
First Edition
Book design by Victoria Wong

For my father

"All the electric runabouts I ever saw, while they were very nice cars, didn't seem to go very fast or very far. . . ."

—*Tom Swift and His Electric Runabout,* 1910

Acknowledgments

)))

This book was made possible by the willingness of Kenneth Baker, the first manager of GM's electric vehicle program, to meet with me back in June 1992 to discuss it. In fact, I wouldn't have been able to set up that meeting without Jean Crocker, then the program's public-affairs chief, who was open-minded enough to imagine there might be some good in having a reporter track a GM car program from the inside for the first time in the company's history. I am deeply grateful to both for allowing me unlimited access to the program, and for letting me write this book without any editorial interference.

As I accumulated the 275 interviews that form the basis of this book, I relied especially on a handful of the program's top engineers who sat for more than a dozen lengthy interviews each. Ken Baker was one; the others were Jim Ellis, Jon Bereisa, and John Williams. To all four, heartfelt thanks. I am also grateful to Robert Purcell, the business planner who became the program's manager in March 1994. Purcell agreed to inherit this odd reportorial arrangement, and sat for several interviews; he turned out to be a real student of GM culture and history whose insights enriched the book.

Chief among others who sat for multiple interviews and provided critical perspectives were Robert Stempel, GM's ex-chairman, and Stanford Ovshinsky, whose advanced battery technology impressed Stempel enough to become the inventor's ally in trying to get the battery to market. Thanks also to John Wallace and Jean Mallebay-Vacqueur, of Ford's and Chrysler's electric vehicle programs respectively, who granted me lengthy and spirited interviews. Harry King of Hughes tutored me on EV electronics; Bruce Zemke, an engineer on the GM program whose breadth of knowledge is unusually wide, spent long hours on the phone helping me understand technical concepts and correcting errors. For any errors that remain, of course, I am entirely to blame.

For one or more interviews, my thanks to Tom Austin, Bob Bish, Pat Bouchard, Richard Bowman, John Brogan, Alec Brooks, Linda Carpalucci, Joe Caves, Al Chesnes, Tiny Chickensky, George Claypole, Alan Cocconi, David Cole, Kevin Crowner, Malcolm Currie, John Dabels, Richard Daskivich, Ron Dasner, Mike Davis, Subhash Dhar, Jeff Dickenson, Dave DiPietro, Ron Dork, John Dunlap III, Lynne Edgerton, Tom Everhart, Andrew Farah, Daniel Fessler, Mike Fetcenko, Marty Freedman, Mike Gage, Alex Gherlan, Paul Gifford, Marvin Goldberger, David Goldstein, Jason Grumet, Janet Hathaway, Rami Helmy, John Hepke, Stan Horky, Paul Huzzard, Chuck Imbrecht, Stephan Iscoe, Mike Iwanowicz, Frank Jamieson, Arianna Kalian, Robert Kiessel, Harry King, Richard Klimisch, Al Laubenstein, Sam Leonard, Mike Liedtke, Tom Lobkovich, Joe LoGrasso, Paul MacCready, Mike Magiera, Rich Marks, Tim McCann, Sean McNamara, Joe Mercurio, Maureen Midgley, Dave Modisette, Barre Morris, Freeman Nelson, Stan Pewoski, Bill Pine, Gus Plascencia, Pam Pudar, Ben Pusheck, Latham Redding, Lloyd Reuss, Michael Riezenman, Wally Rippel, Clive Roberts, Don Runkle, Tom Ruster, Pete Savagian, Randy Schwarz, Frank Schweibold, Jananne Sharpless, William Shepard, Roger Smith, Bob Thompson, Robin Vidas, Roy Visser, Gary Wahl, Bill Way, John White, Howard Wilson, Diane Wittenberg, Gary Witzenburg, James Worden, Bob Wragg, Bill Wylam, Larry Zahner.

Robert Loomis, my editor at Random House, had the confidence to chance this book in the first place, and the perspicacity to see the bones of a real story within the morass of pages he first received; on nearly every page of several drafts, his polite but pointed queries ("Boring?") helped me produce a publishable work. Thanks to Graydon Carter, editor-in-chief of *Vanity Fair*, for his patience and support throughout; thanks also to Tom Wallace, editor of *Condé Nast Traveler*.

Thanks, above all, to my wife, Cheryl Merser.

Prologue

))))

As this book appears, a more important product will be rolling off an assembly line in the factory town of Lansing, Michigan. To the untutored eye, it will seem General Motors's latest effort at a two-seat sports car, and that is, in a sense, what it will be: a small, sleek teardrop, as bold and sassy in its inaugural edition as the first Corvettes of more than thirty years ago.

When its wheels start to turn, the difference between it and sports cars of the past will be dramatically, surreally apparent.

Aside from the slither of tire tread on pavement, this car will be silent. It will have no engine, because it doesn't need one. It will have no tailpipe, because it has no tailpipe emissions. It will be, in fact, the first modern, factory-produced, from-the-ground-up electric vehicle in the world, inspiring by its example the most profound change in automotive transportation since the internal-combustion engine.

That such innovation should emerge from General Motors is almost more astounding than the car itself. For more than two decades, the world's largest corporation exhibited all the symptoms of an enterprise past its prime. Bloated and befuddled, stagnant and resistant to change, it turned out ever more lackluster products, steadily losing market share to its domestic rivals, to Europe, to Japan, while stubbornly fighting the expense of every technological change to make its cars safer and cleaner until it had no choice. How could GM, of all companies, be so radical as to try electric cars?

But corporations, like countries, are comprised of individuals, and not all think the same way. At GM, nearly a decade ago, a few observed the gasoline engine being refined to a state of near perfection yet still polluting. They noted the world's population of people and cars growing at alarming speed.

They thought that if a truly clean car could be devised, the company, as well as its customers, might profit. It helped, of course, that one of those individuals was the chairman.

As much as with anyone, the story of GM's development of EV1 begins with Roger Smith, the largely discredited captain of the corporate ship through the 1980s. It was Smith who, fascinated by future technology, sanctioned the concept solar car that led to a concept electric vehicle. It was Smith, impulsive to a fault, who publicly declared on Earth Day, 1990, to the horror of his adjutants, that GM would produce the vehicle—known then by the unseemly name of Impact—and so encouraged California regulators to build a mandate on his boast, requiring the seven largest carmakers to sell "zero-emission vehicles" in 1998. With that, the chairman promptly retired, leaving others to figure out how a one-of-a-kind fiberglass model might be transformed into a crashworthy, fully producible, market-ready electric vehicle. Say what one would about Smith, no one would deny him this: the man knew when to leave.

Despite firm support from Smith's successor, Robert Stempel, over the next two years the Impact program was clearly imperiled by the most dramatic losses in GM's eight decades. Its technological challenges and costs, the uncertainty of its market, the lack of necessary infrastructure, not to mention the utter mystery of when the company might hope to get a return on its investment—all these doubts about Impact grew inexorably as the company's fortunes declined. Understandably, if with a trace of paranoia, Impact's engineers came to see their program as a rogue cell in the corporate immune system. Their mission, as they saw it, was to do whatever they could to evade the white blood cells that sought to destroy them.

The end seemed to come in December 1992, not long after the boardroom revolt that replaced Stempel and his loyalists with new men and ordered new, harsh cuts amid fears, not voiced since 1920, that GM might actually go broke. The EV program, an obvious target, was taken off its track to production, its platform of 400 engineers reduced by two-thirds, the surviving third assigned to make a Tucker-like fleet of fifty handbuilt prototype Impacts that might, at least, teach the company more about EVs, as electric vehicles were called, for the next time around. To the outside world, and to most of GM's engineers as well, Impact seemed all but dead.

How Impact's engineers then initiated secret talks with Ford and Chrysler to consider a Big Three EV consortium, how those talks led instead to GM's renewed determination to do Impact on its own, and how the program was restarted under wraps even as GM publicly decried the EV mandate make for a car story unlike any other in the history of Detroit. The bones of it are object lessons in how, within behemoth GM, innovation at last prevailed, inspiring and, perhaps, redirecting the company.

Technically, as a growing number of automotive journalists have proclaimed, the rechristened EV1 is a rousing triumph. It is not merely the best electric car yet made; it is the best-engineered small car in General Motors's history. Whether or not it will succeed is quite another question. Will an initial market materialize for a high-priced electric car with significant range and recharging limitations? Will the car's high production costs dip quickly enough to make EVs appealing to a wider market? Will those limitations of range and recharging be quickly enough eased by innovation to make a market grow? Will an infrastructure of charging stations rise soon enough to make a difference, and will government be able to help, even as politicians push to reduce its social responsibilities?

If EV1 succeeds, it will restore to GM a long-lost luster as the world's leader in automotive technology, and lead it farther into the future than any of its managers, until recently, considered possible—into a twenty-first century of hybrids and ultralights and hydrogen fuel cells, in which the internal-combustion engine comes to seem as antique as a Gutenberg press. If, on the other hand, EV1 fails, it will bring more than ignominy and a multimillion-dollar write-off to a company just getting back on its feet. It will also mar, if not ruin, the electric vehicle market for other manufacturers, and render the very notion of EVs misbegotten, with the EV1 consigned a place beside the Edsel.

This is a story of engineers, and of a dream made real. Behind it, though, is a backdrop of politics. The prospect of a modern electric car, during the years this story recounts, caused deep and bitter conflict at the state and federal level between those who wanted EVs in the world—to help the environment, to free America from foreign oil, to spur economic growth—and those who, for various reasons, did not. The crucible of EV politics in those years was the California mandate, inspired by Impact and then, ironically, attacked by GM, as well as Ford, Chrysler, and America's oil companies. To the carmakers and oil companies who spent so many millions of dollars to thwart it, the mandate's demise as this book goes to press is great news—proof of their view that government should never try to mandate invention, but rather let the forces of competition and market demand induce it as they will.

That news provokes an editorial comment that is, I hope, one of the few this book contains. To me, it seems clear that the mandate, by forcing the world's largest carmakers to start the hard R&D march to electric vehicles at a time when none but GM wished to do so, has been a triumph of social policy as important to the betterment of this country in its day as the Clean Air Act was a generation ago. Quite literally, it has jumpstarted the future of automotive transportation, and in doing so shown, in an age of political selfishness and cynicism, that government can, on occasion, offer enlightened leadership.

I should also mention here that General Motors in no way compensated me for the writing of this book. I asked, as a journalist, to spend as much time visiting the EV program as I liked, to be able to interview its engineers freely, and to write my story as I saw it. GM, rather to my surprise, agreed. The company's only condition was that it be allowed to review a final manuscript to correct factual inaccuracies and to delete any confidential details pertaining to future car programs.

The company proved as good as its word. This book is the result.

North Haven, New York
January 1996

Contents

))))

THE CAR
THAT COULD

A Dubious Offer

))))

He couldn't figure it out.

"What does he want?"

"Didn't say."

The call had come from Lloyd Reuss's office. Reuss wanted to see him the next day. Early—7:30 A.M. Ken Baker looked at the message slip a moment, then called back. "Vivian," he asked Reuss's secretary, "why does Lloyd want to see me?"

Vivian said she couldn't say.

"Oh come on, Vivian," Baker exclaimed. "The new president of General Motors doesn't call and say he wants to see you out of the kindness of his heart!"

"Just don't worry," Vivian told him.

Right.

In fact, Baker had no *reason* to worry. On this June morning of 1990 he was doing fine. Not as well as he might have hoped after twenty-one years at GM as a high-potential engineer, but high-pots, as they were called by the company—their careers tracked and nurtured, their fondest hopes stoked— tended to develop outsize ambitions, and Baker knew he could be unrealis- tic. At forty-two, he was an upper-middle manager in CPC—the half of North American Operations that comprised Chevrolet, Pontiac, and GM's Canada business—with one foot in advanced engineering, the other in service. The advanced engineering he liked; he got to oversee the designs of cars three and four years out. The service, which had been thrust upon him, was a bore. You didn't ascend from service to the pantheon of GM vice presidents—the fifty or so who ruled the company of 750,000. Of all the reasons Reuss might want to see him, naming him a vice president was almost certainly not one of them.

Reuss might more likely intend to give Baker, at last, a car program to manage: to oversee a team of hundreds bringing a model from dream to gleam, as the saying had it, from artist's sketch to production. *That* was how an engineer became a vice president. Certainly Baker had the intellect and experience for the job. But image, in GM's executive ranks, was just as important, and Baker knew his had a couple of dents. For one, his résumé lacked heft. Most high-pot engineers at GM had a master's degree in their field, if not also an M.B.A.; Baker had only a B.A. from tiny Clarkson College. Then there was his appearance.

Baker was handsome in a clean-cut, vaguely patrician way, with dark hair turning silver at the temples, and an attractive air of command. He tended to brood, and could radiate a bristling sense of competitiveness, which he felt, and for which he was known. But he could also brighten as he recounted some amusing incident with the pleasure of a real storyteller, and when he did, he looked boyishly winning. His problem had been his weight. A compulsive eater feeding dark anxieties, at one point he had ballooned to over 300 pounds. It wasn't easy finding stylish clothes in a size fifty-eight, and he knew his superiors must have wondered, consciously or not, how a man who let himself go to such an extent could impose control over a car program.

But if not to give him a program, why *did* Reuss want to see him?

An appointment with Reuss meant a trip from the campus-like Tech Center in suburban Warren, where most GM engineers worked, to the corporate headquarters in downtown Detroit: the lonely building on West Grand Avenue, ringed by urban blight. A GM executive needed to walk just two blocks from this stolid bastion of a bygone era to enter a ghetto with rundown tenements, bodegas, and open, abandoned lots. None ever did. The finance types who worked here every day drove with all doors locked from their homes in Bloomfield Hills, parked in the guarded garage across the street, then used a basement tunnel or the fourth-floor skyway, their shoes never touching the pavement outside. This was the great irony of Detroit: the car business had brought generations of southern blacks and poor immigrants to its factories to build cars that propelled white executives to the suburbs, leaving the city to die of neglect.

Within the building, a mustiness prevailed. The visitors' check-in room was large but almost bare. In the adjoining cafeteria, tired black waitresses dispensed plates of watery food onto plastic trays, and poured coffee into old, automat-style mugs. Too few people seemed to pass through the high, wide corridors, to wait for the gilded elevator doors to open. Here, two years before, filmmaker Michael Moore had arrived, camera rolling, in a vain effort to get past the hall guards and up to the fourteenth floor, where he hoped to interview chairman Roger Smith for his scabrous documentary *Roger and Me*, about GM's recent factory closings. Smith and his top officers remained on fourteen—a show of faith in the city, they might have said, but also, increasingly, a symbol of how distant they had become from GM's day-to-day business in Warren. A few minutes before the appointed hour, Baker rode up to fourteen, trying to quell his jitters.

Immutable as the corridors seemed that day, change was in the air. After a decade as chairman, Roger Smith had announced he would retire, and named as his successor his number two man, Robert Stempel. In the broadest sense, GM executives were either finance guys or car guys. Smith was a finance guy, Stempel was a car guy, and that, however doggedly the new chairman planned to pursue his predecessor's course, was bound to make a difference. A tall, garrulous engineer who'd headed the team that invented the catalytic converter, Stempel was as comfortable talking to mechanics as top officers, unpretentious, and widely liked.

A general feeling of disappointment, however, had greeted the news that Lloyd Reuss, a fellow engineer, would step up to replace Stempel as president. Reuss's record was a good deal less exemplary than Stempel's: over the years, he'd earned a reputation for rising out of each program he managed just before his mistakes came home to roost. His promotion also meant two car guys at the top. To have the finance guys excluded from the top tier, at a time of sharply dwindling profits and market share, seemed unwise. But Stempel had insisted that Reuss be his deputy, and GM's notoriously complacent board members had acquiesced, though not without signaling their reluctance by stripping Reuss of the president's traditional second title as chief operating officer.

Smith had set August 1 as his retirement date. Until then, however, he felt empowered to rule as freely as he had throughout his tenure. It was, in fact, one of his last bold acts, taken utterly on his own, that had resulted in Baker's appearance on the fourteenth floor this morning and his arrival at Reuss's office, where he found the president-to-be accompanied by Bob Schultz, one of two newly named vice chairmen.

"Good *Lord*, Ken," Schultz exclaimed in genuine shock. "What happened?"

"What do you mean, Bob?" Baker deadpanned.

"I mean . . . is that really *you?*"

Schultz hadn't seen Baker for some time, and Reuss hadn't thought to tell him the news.

Baker had lost 140 pounds.

He was, quite simply, a man transformed: lean, fit, and dressed in a sleek Italian suit, size forty, with a wonderfully garish tie. "Did it in thirty weeks," he told his astonished colleague.

"But—but how?" spluttered Schultz.

"I just decided," Baker said coolly, "that life is not a dress rehearsal."

A midlife alarm had been sounding for some time. But then, that spring, Baker's mother had died. Not long after, he'd gone in for a medical checkup. How old was Baker's son, the doctor had asked. Ten years old, Baker replied. If Baker did nothing about his weight, the doctor declared, he might not live long enough to see his son graduate from high school. Baker had gotten the message.

Now it was Baker's turn to be surprised, and not altogether pleasantly.

"You know Roger's really committed to that electric car," Reuss said casually. "How'd you like to do it?"

Reuss looked, as usual, salesman slick, every dark hair in place, features as sharply drawn as the lines of his perfectly tailored suits. This was a man who reveled in image. Invariably, his French cuffs were set off by large gold links that showed the insignia of one of the divisions where he'd worked; today, it was the fleur-de-lis of Cadillac. His massive wood desk was clutter-free. Behind him, on either side, were silver-framed pictures of himself with various American presidents. Baker was among those who genuinely liked Reuss, and saw a soul behind the salesman's mask, but Baker's was not a majority view.

"Electric cars . . ." Baker swallowed hard. "Gee," he said wryly, "didn't I do that once before?"

There was a knock on the door, and Baker looked back to see Stempel leaning in. "Just wanted to add my voice to Lloyd's," the chairman-to-be said. "You *are* the man for the job."

Perhaps, Baker thought later, he should have expected this. He knew that almost two years before, Smith, urged on by Stempel, had agreed to have GM pay a small California R&D firm to design and build a concept electric car. Letting outsiders do that for GM was remarkable in itself. That the outsiders were mostly young, ardent environmentalists led by a visionary who talked of solving America's problems with a three-dollar-a-gallon gasoline tax—that was more so. No one, though, had expected the kind of reaction Smith got when he introduced the car at the Los Angeles auto show in January 1990. Smith himself had been so surprised and exhilarated by the acclaim that he had gone on, against the pleas of all his advisors, to hold an Earth Day news conference at the Washington Press Club to declare that GM would actually produce this thing.

How GM would produce it was Baker's next career challenge, Reuss explained with his salesman's smile—if he agreed to accept it.

Baker felt flattered, but wary. In the late 1970s, he'd let himself be talked into heading up GM's last electric vehicle venture: the ill-fated Electrovette. With OPEC prices high and Jimmy Carter bartering for hostages in Iran, the time had seemed right for electric cars that might start to wean America from

Middle Eastern oil. The Electrovette—a converted Chevette—ran on zinc nickel oxide batteries with a DC motor. Zinc was proclaimed to be the answer: it had greater energy density than lead, so it gave the Chevette twice the range of lead acid batteries, and a way had been found to keep zinc from deteriorating after relatively few recharges.

It was a great plan, except that the batteries cost far more than lead acid, and more range still meant at most 100 miles. This was also before the new age of automotive electronics; the car had a mechanical-electrical control system that made for lots of arcing, energy loss, and unreliability. When oil prices dropped, the Electrovette died a quiet death at the demo stage, and Baker came to feel that the years spent on a loser were a career-stalling embarrassment. It was a suspicion confirmed by the company's next triennial gathering of senior managers at the Greenbrier resort in White Sulphur Springs, West Virginia. Baker had been invited to the previous triennial; that next time, he didn't make the cut.

"I have to think about it a bit," Baker said frankly to his superiors. "I don't know that I want to go back to electric cars."

"Talk to Don," Reuss advised. "He really wants you to do this."

That was Baker's other concern.

Baker would still be reporting directly to a vice president, as he was in his current post, rather than becoming a vice president himself. But he would also have a "dotted line," as GM jargon had it, to Donald L. Runkle.

Runkle.

For two days, Baker pondered the pros and cons. Runkle was a worry, but perhaps Reuss would keep him from meddling too much. The electric car was a gamble, but it was, after all, a car program, and Baker would manage it. Maybe he could turn it to advantage. If he could just believe that GM would follow through this time, it would also be a chance to prove electric vehicles could work after all: to vindicate his first stab at them, to write a page of automotive history, to help create the first new *kind* of car since the early twentieth century. A car that would have no engine, no gasoline, no exhaust. A car that would help the world.

But if he failed again? Two strikes on EVs and he would be out—out of the running, at least, for a vice presidency.

Finally he called Reuss. "Okay, Lloyd," he said, feeling his future shift with the words, "I'm your man."

In fact, Baker was an obvious choice to head a risky program that would demand invention on schedule. His EV experience was the least of it, though it helped; as important, he'd stayed involved in advanced engineering as cars were transformed, throughout the eighties, by complex computer controllers. Both Stempel and Reuss saw in him, too, a natural leader, confident enough to enjoy the role, good at exhorting those around him, remembering names, offering praise. Baker was, as it happened, also a deeply emotional man with a sensitive ego, given to highs and lows, easily hurt; a man who felt each small defeat with great intensity. If he had been a car, Baker would have been a convertible roadster, moving fast, open to the elements, with only the weakest shock absorbers to absorb the occasional bumps.

Don Runkle would have been, perhaps, a Cadillac. Lean, cool, controlled, moving smoothly up the corporate ranks, he was one of the few executives in Detroit who displayed not only technical capability but talent as a writer and public speaker. So frequently had Runkle appeared in the press, and with such panache, that he was rumored to have his own public relations man.

Both from small towns and modest backgrounds, both competitive and very smart, Baker and Runkle had been thrown together at Buick in the early eighties and immediately become rivals. Runkle would speculate with friends as to which man was likelier to rise faster in the ranks; Baker would do the same. Over time, Runkle's two master's degrees—the second from MIT—seemed to give him an edge. Stalled in service, Baker had had to endure Runkle's ascension to the pantheon of vice presidents. And not just to any VP slot, but to head the advanced engineering staffs—AES—at the Tech Center in Warren.

It was in Runkle's spacious VP office at the Tech Center that Baker heard more about his new assignment. As head of AES, Runkle had helped oversee the California skunkworks, as secret projects were called, for the concept electric car. He understood, now that Smith had said the car would be produced, that it would require its own program at the Tech Center, and its own full-time program manager. Baker, Runkle averred, had been his own first choice. Baker had his doubts about that, but he tried to listen with an open mind as Runkle described the challenge as he saw it.

To Runkle, the fact that the car was electric was almost secondary. He felt passionately that GM had to foster independent programs—give them all they needed to make cars on their own, as if they were separate lines of business. Not surprisingly, his vision featured a starring role for his own advanced engineering staff. New cars might start, he theorized, within a single launch center that AES would oversee. They could be nurtured there, away from the finance guys who always tried to get a new car program to use leftover parts from old programs, away from engineers afraid to try new ideas, away from all the politics that had plagued GM cars in the past. Then, when their designs were set, they could be shifted back to the various divisions—badged, as the carmakers put it, as Buicks or Pontiacs or Chevrolets.

The electric car, Runkle felt, could be the launch center's test project.

Baker wondered aloud if the program would really be large enough to serve as a test case. How many cars would be produced?

That wasn't clear yet, Runkle felt. Perhaps, at most, 25,000 cars a year—a far cry from conventional programs, which produced ten times that many. But Baker shouldn't be put off by that. The smallness of the program would be an important test, too. For decades, the world's biggest company had done everything big, producing every new car by the hundreds of thousands, priding itself on the profits that came from such economies of scale. But the world was changing. The loyal GM customer was gone, driven away by too many years of bland, mediocre GM cars, drawn by the craftsmanship of Japanese cars better manufactured on far smaller scales. The talk now was of flexible manufacturing, with shorter assembly lines and smaller factories. These, in turn, would demand less capital investment, so that profits could be made by producing far fewer cars; as the market changed, GM could change more quickly with it.

Runkle was especially eager to use the electric car as a test of systems engineering, the corporate religion GM had discovered when it bought Hughes Aircraft four years before. Traditionally, a GM car started out in the design studio. Drawings were thrown "over the wall" to engineers, who created the guts of the car as best as they could within those specs; they in turn threw their work over the next wall to manufacturing.

For the electric car, all three factions—design, engineering, manufacturing—might sit together at the start, with each team clarifying its needs to the others. Technical requirements and targets, spelled out in excruciating detail, could be put on paper and bound together in fat, black three-ring binders— all before a single part was made. Systems engineering had worked brilliantly at Hughes for satellites and fighter planes. The question now was whether it could be used to make a car.

As far as Runkle could see, Baker had no choice. Though the concept electric car could be changed and improved upon, its basic dilemma was fixed. It had 843 pounds of lead acid batteries instead of a gas tank; each of those pounds contained about 16 watt hours of energy. The energy density of gasoline when used in cars was 5,000 *watt hours per pound*.* Put another way, those batteries packed the energy equivalent of a bit more than a gallon of gasoline.† Perhaps better batteries would come along, but Baker shouldn't

---

* In fact, the energy density of gasoline is more like 35,000 watt hours per pound, but a gas car wastes as much as 85 percent of its energy through combustion heat, sticky rubber tires, the friction and heat from braking, and bad aerodynamics.

† A gallon of gasoline weighs about 6 pounds. If each pound of gas contains 5,000 watt hours of unwasted energy, then a gallon has six times 5,000 watt hours, or 30,000 watt hours. That's a little more than twice the watt hours of an 843-pound battery pack with 16 watt hours per pound— $843 \times 16 = 13,488$—which would suggest that the batteries together had the energy equivalent of half a gallon of gas. However, Impact had been made so much lighter and more energy efficient than a gas car that it squeezed three times as much range from the energy it had. Thus it had, in effect, the energy equivalent of a gallon and a half of gasoline stored in its battery pack.

count on it. He had to make the EV energy efficient to a degree that no car had ever been made before. The skunkworks team claimed its one-of-a-kind car had a range of 120 miles, but this was a car with none of the amenities a real car would need. It wasn't even crashworthy. Somehow, Baker would have to make it so, and make it saleable, while preserving, if not increasing, its range. Systems engineering, Runkle thought, could help him do that.

But the car couldn't merely get to market. It had to be *first* to market: the first mass-produced electric car of modern times. And when it did, laden with brand-new technology, it had to cost no more than an ordinary gas car, or else no one but a few rich Hollywood environmentalists would buy it.

What Baker was being asked to do, he realized, was not unlike being asked to produce the world's first laptop computer, but also to make it, at the same time, as cheap, and as efficient, as laptops a decade down the line.

On a warm summer day, Baker went out to the Tech Center's test track for his first look at the car he was to inherit. The track, a mile long, was an elongated figure eight. With him were his first senior staff picks—the chiefs, as they would be called.

In the far loop of the track rested a low-slung, silver sports car. Beside it stood a young man with thick, unruly black hair and glasses, a plaid shirt, faded jeans, and sneakers. He slid in behind the driver's seat, and then the car began to roll toward the waiting engineers. Baker had known what to expect, but still he was amazed. The car was absolutely silent.

Only as the car drew up did the chiefs hear the noise of tire tread on the macadam, and a faint whine from the gears. The young man got out and looked with a mix of pride and sullenness at the GM executives in their dress shirts and ties. He was a member of the California R&D team. His name was Alan Cocconi. He was the one who had designed the most complex part of this electric show car, the inverter that changed the batteries' DC current into AC current for the two motors that turned the front wheels. Cocconi had built the inverter himself, first on his computer screen, then by soldering every one of more than 5,000 parts to various circuit boards. It was as if a musician had composed a symphony, then built the piano to play it. The engineers regarded him with awe, curiosity, and wariness.

The car was smaller than it appeared in pictures, a low-lying lozenge about the size of a Mazda Miata. In its curves, and the way it seemed to hug the ground, it was, as the engineers put it, very aero. For a handbuilt show car it also looked unusually sleek, its silver paint so well applied that its body appeared to be aluminum rather than mere fiberglass.

One by one, the engineers drove the show car up the track and back, with Cocconi in the passenger seat. Baker was impressed by how roomy the car felt as he slid inside. He turned the key, pressed the accelerator, and—*whoosh*—

the car leapt eerily forward. Baker felt as if he were in a glider. But as he rounded the turn, he felt the car pitch out. There was no suspension to speak of; there was no chassis development. And there was that gear noise — a whine that rose and fell as the gears of the two motors at the front wheels were engaged. With a car that had no engine to muffle them, those sounds would be hard to get out.

As the last of the engineers was rounding the track, Runkle joined the chiefs and asked if he, too, could drive the car. Of course, Baker said, startled. Of course.

Runkle had driven a lot of concept cars, so he knew to expect a rough ride, but this thing was *harsh*. All it did well was accelerate in a straight line. And when he pressed the brakes, he could feel how cheesy they were: low-weight motorcycle calipers that would never do for a production vehicle.

A lot of time would be needed to develop this strange contraption. But to Baker he emphasized the positive. "This'll be tough," he said when he emerged from the car. "But the greatest challenge was getting it to this point. It *can* be done, you know."

Baker nodded, but his own ride had made him wonder. Transforming an electric show car — a one-of-a-kind model — into an assembly line product *might* be possible. Then again, it might not. Baker looked over at Runkle, trying to read his face. Was this a trap? Had Runkle chosen him knowing he'd fail?

Time and Again

))))

The vision of a practical electric car had floated like a poltergeist through the upper echelons of GM for decades. Billy Durant, GM's founder, was still buying up every available maker of horseless carriages in Michigan and beyond to make his unwieldy empire even bigger when the company, in 1912, produced an electric-powered truck. No thought was given at the time to the salubrious effects of electric vehicles on the air; the air was clean. The plan, instead, was to challenge gas-powered trucks. By then, as it turned out, the internal-combustion engine had all but ended the first golden era of the electric automobile.

Inventors had tinkered with battery-run cars since the 1840s, but the golden era, and the struggle for dominance between gas- and electric-powered cars, had begun in earnest at noon on June 11, 1895. That was when twenty-two horseless carriages set off from Versailles along France's poplar-bordered Route Nationale, headed from Paris to Bordeaux and back, for a widely publicized round-trip race of more than 700 miles. Most were fueled by gasoline, a few by steam, two by lead acid batteries. Charles Jeantaud, a Parisian carriage maker, drove an electric-powered surrey all the way to Bordeaux, exchanging battery packs along the way at prearranged stops; had he not suffered a hot rear bearing, he might have finished the course. Camille Jentzy's bullet-shaped "La Jamais Contente" took an early lead at 65 miles per hour, but discharged its batteries in less than an hour. Eight gasoline-powered and one steam-powered car made it back to the finish line; the winning car, gasoline fueled, rolled to the finish in 48 hours and 48 minutes, having traveled at an average speed of 14.4 miles per hour.

Though the race made clear their limited range, electrics were soon being produced with great success, particularly in America. Gas cars were loud, smoke-belching brutes whose cranks could snap up and knock a man senseless. Besides, they had *gas*, stored in tanks, right under a driver's seat. "You can't get people to sit on an explosion," observed Colonel Albert Pope, the largest maker of electric cars of the late 1890s. Steam cars were prone to explosions, too. Electrics were silent and clean, they had no cranks, and they ran slowly but reliably on city streets, which made them especially appealing to women—wealthy women whose husbands could buy them an electric for the small fortune of $3,000 so that they could more comfortably view the great houses of Newport, or shop along Broadway's Miracle Mile. Playing to that market, carmakers outfitted their newest models with running boards for liveried footmen, leather and brocade interiors, and cut-glass flower vases.

The electrics' range—few went more than 50 miles on a charge—grew more annoying as roads began to extend from the cities and touring became the new American adventure. Spare cans of fuel could be stowed aboard a gas car; electrics were too fragile for dirt roads, there was nowhere to plug them in, and recharging took a whole day. Touring was also very much a male endeavor, and the roar of gas cars, their ruggedness, even the challenge of cranking them were part of the sport. Advertisements for electrics stressed their appeal to women, and for this reason too, men eschewed them.

Still, for some time the outcome was unclear. In 1900, more electrics were sold in America than gas-powered cars. Despite the vogue for the latter, electrics were widely assumed to be the car of the future—as soon as their range problems could be resolved. So confident was Thomas Edison of their potential superiority that at the peak of his success, in his early fifties, he devoted a decade of his life and most of his fortune to a search for more effective battery elements than lead and acid. The nickel and iron pairing he settled on failed in cars, but led to the nickel and cadmium batteries in universal use today in flashlights and a hundred other devices.

In retrospect, the race was lost in 1908 when Henry Ford's Model T rolled off the first automotive assembly line at a working man's price of $850. Overnight, the Model T created a vast new market. Until 1912, electrics held their own smaller, high-end market. That year, though, Charles "Boss" Kettering's electric starter replaced Cadillac's crank. As its use spread to other models, even rich ladies found gas cars preferable to electrics. One by one, the electric carmakers of the day—Woods, Baker, Studebaker, Columbia, and others—sold their last models, mostly to stubborn dowagers who used them to ride in elegant silence the private roads of their great estates. As for GM's electric truck, sold with either lead acid or Edison's nickel-and-iron batteries, it was pulled out of production in 1916.

As old electrics languished in museums, the gas-powered automobile had a more profound effect on the world than any other invention of the twentieth century. Airplanes, telephones, and television might seem greater marvels, but the car redefined society itself. In America, it transformed established East Coast cities; forced a national network of roads; created suburbia; shaped the newer cities of the West; moved goods; accounted for 40 percent of the gross national product with a matrix of materials and processes unrivaled in their number and complexity; employed one in seven citizens and, not least, gave Americans most of their greatest pleasures: mobility, speed, fast food, drive-ins, the promise of freedom, and backseat romance.

By the late 1960s, though, smog had entered the language and settled ominously over America's cities, and automobiles were to blame for two-thirds of it. Over the next two decades, cars became nearly 95 percent cleaner, due to increasingly stringent state and federal standards. Yet ever more of them took to the roads, so that gains in air quality began to seem ephemeral while the country's addiction to foreign oil grew with alarming implications. In Southern California, where smog was at its worst, engineers, policy makers, and politicians struggled with how to resolve the dilemma. In January 1987, a few were startled to get help from a man who seemed more a part of the problem than the solution.

The inter-office envelope sent from Roger Smith's office in Detroit one early January day in 1987 to Howard Wilson, a vice president at GM-owned Hughes Aircraft in Los Angeles, contained an invitation passed along from Australia. No note was appended to it, not even a scrawled word or two to indicate how Smith might feel about the enclosed. But Wilson would have warmed to it however it arrived.

The invitation was to join a first-time race across Australia, from north to south, Darwin to Adelaide, by purely solar-powered cars. While solar cars might never find a practical use — not even the most efficient solar cells imaginable would ever generate enough electricity to power a two-ton pickup — the race might show that the future for *electric* cars, designed more efficiently from what could be learned on solar cars, and packed with enough batteries to propel themselves without benefit of the sun, could be closer to a reality than most of the world imagined.

Close to retirement, Wilson was one of those rare older men who delight in the future, envisioning technological marvels without seeming to worry that they themselves might not be there to witness them. A solar car race intrigued him; it might also help him do the job he'd volunteered to take on eighteen months before when General Motors bought Hughes Aircraft from the Howard Hughes Medical Institute for $5.7 billion. Despite Roger Smith's boast of the deal as a "lulu," GM's latest acquisition had come under harsh scrutiny from analysts and shareholders who asked what GM could gain by buying Hughes just as the aerospace industry was declining. Smith talked excitedly of space-age technology that might be transferred to automobiles, but no such transfer yet seemed apparent between a military contractor that spent billions on a single satellite, and a company that made cars by the millions. That was the job that Hughes's chairman and CEO Malcolm Currie had given Wilson: to see where the transfers might be.

A handmade solar car would be a far cry from putting Hughes technology into a new Chevrolet. But it would send the right signal, send it fast, and cost relatively little. Of course, GM's top executives would have to be assured a GM-Hughes solar car could *win*. Wilson thought he could make a pretty good case for optimism. Hughes made solar cell panels for satellites; no other company in the world knew the technology better. A lot of work, too, had been done at Hughes with batteries. Not with the everyday, lead acid variety, but with high-energy silver zinc packs. Silver zinc was too expensive and short-lived a battery pairing to be a serious prospect for cars, but for one very light car, in one six-day race, it might do the trick.

What Wilson needed was a skunkworks—a small, dedicated team outside the walls of either GM or Hughes that would know how to design and build a solar car, get it to the race on time, and win. One name kept coming up as Wilson checked around: AeroVironment, a small R&D firm in the San Gabriel valley founded by Paul MacCready.

Among engineers, MacCready was legend, a modern-day Wright brother and Leonardo da Vinci in one unassuming package. A Cal Techie whose fascination with aerodynamics had at one point pushed him to become the world's soaring champion, MacCready in 1977 had designed the *Gossamer Condor*, a pilot-pedaled flying machine of aluminum tubing, balsa wood, piano wire, and space-age plastic wrap, and sent it into the air to win an international prize for sustained human-powered flight. Two years later, a pilot had pedaled MacCready's *Gossamer Albatross* across the English Channel; in 1981, his sun-powered *Solar Challenger* had flown back the other way. By then, MacCready had been named Engineer of the Century by the American Society of Mechanical Engineers. As it turned out, one of MacCready's best young engineers, Alec Brooks, had toyed with entering the Australian race himself, but realized he hadn't the funds to pursue it. He was *very* interested. And so was MacCready.

Emboldened, Wilson flew to Detroit one day in early March. Lloyd Reuss, as newly named head of North American car operations, was the man he had to win over. Brimming with enthusiasm, Wilson made his pitch. Reuss listened, said little, sat back, and frowned. "I don't see what a car race in Australia has to do with selling cars in the United States," he said. He was afraid GM would have to pass.

As Wilson left, chagrined, he noticed Bob Stempel at his desk in the adjacent office. Stempel had just been promoted to executive vice president of Truck and Bus, a title that included GM's overseas business. Perhaps, thought Wilson, GM's Australian operation, Holdens, might find more reason to back a solar car. Blithely, he asked if Stempel had a couple of minutes to spare, slipped in, and shut the door behind him. Fifteen minutes later, he emerged with Stempel's approval to spend $75,000 on a three-week feasibility study.

What, he wondered later, might have happened if Stempel had been away on business that day? Nothing, he felt, at least nothing in the manner and timing of what did happen. No Sunraycer, no Impact, no California mandate, no worldwide race to build electric cars.

Paul MacCready was the first to say he knew nothing about the auto industry in March 1987. Nor, for that matter, did any of the young engineering zealots he gathered to consider Wilson's challenge in the glass-walled offices of AeroVironment. But whatever design they chose would have more in common with MacCready's human-powered flying machines than anything out of Detroit. Like them, it would have to be as lightweight and aerodynamic as possible to make the greatest use of a modest energy source. Almost none of the materials used on a gas car would have any relevance here; all would be too heavy. Nor would any of the vehicle shapes that the team began to consider bear any similarity to standard automobiles.

Alec Brooks, assigned to head up the study, shared MacCready's love of aerodynamics and energy-efficient vehicles. A slightly built, intense introvert with two degrees in civil engineering, he had graduated from building model airplanes to sailplanes and extra-light bicycles. Brooks was MacCready's protégé. There were those who would say the two even looked like father and son, each so diffident, so cerebral, daydreaming in theoretical abstractions but building their visions as vehicles that rode, or flew, or in the case of Brooks's *Flying Fish*, skimmed pedal driven across the waves as the world's fastest human-powered watercraft.

Brooks knew that in the short history of solar cars, most had relied on some form of direct-current motor to channel the sun's energy to the wheels. The sun's energy was converted by solar cells into direct-current electricity that could be stored in a battery and simply passed to the motor as needed. But DC motors used so-called brushes—bits of carbon on either side of a copper cylinder called a commutator—that created friction, limited motor speed, and led to wear and tear.

Newer alternating-current motors did away with the brushes and commutator. Instead, current could be fed by electronic switches: no friction, far greater speed. AC motors were also lighter than their DC counterparts. The catch was that the DC current from the batteries had to be inverted, or "chopped," into alternating current for the motor. Whether an inverter could be made to do this for a solar car was unclear. Inverters to date were heavy things that sat on factory floors and enabled robots or machine tools to operate at variable speeds by supplying them with variable amounts of AC. A few small inverters had been attempted for electric cars—an engineer at GM named Paul Agarwal had made one in the 1960s for an EV called the Electrovair. But electronics then had been crude and too expensive, and Agarwal had given up in disgust. Brooks needed a new perspective, from some young, brash engineer not afraid to think creatively. For that, he knew just whom to call.

Brooks had first met Alan Cocconi at Cal Tech, where the two spent much of their time in the university workshop, Brooks building human-powered motion machines, Cocconi crafting ever more ambitious, remote-controlled planes. As a student, Cocconi had earned mediocre grades. After college, he had worked as a freelance consultant in analog electronics,* acquiring neither fame nor wealth. Yet among the engineers of AeroVironment, Cocconi's was the mind to match. In analog electronics he seemed to have no equal. In any other field of engineering, all he needed was a bit of time to quiz the resident experts before getting up to speed. He wasn't a team player, and to Brooks's annoyance, would not be persuaded to join AeroVironment full-time, or even to take an office there. But as a freelancer, he was willing to help.

Cocconi thought he could design a DC to AC inverter light enough for Sunraycer. He thought he could make it work in reverse, too, to employ a nifty concept called regenerative braking. When the driver took his foot off the accelerator and the wheels began to slow, they would feed mechanical energy back into the motor, which now turned in reverse, acting as a generator. The generator would send the energy as AC electricity back through the inverter, which reformed it as DC and stored it in the battery pack. Regen, as the engineers called it, thus recouped energy even while acting as a brake. Sunraycer would need front disc brakes as well, but most of the braking could be regen.

On March 26, Brooks, MacCready, and Wilson went to Detroit to present their design for a solar car utterly unlike the awkward, flat-panel-on-wheels kind that had dominated solar races of the past. Theirs was teardrop-shaped, which made it far more aerodynamic, with a Cocconi invention called a peak

---

* In analog electronics, input and output signals are continuously variable, unlike digital electronics, in which all electrical signals are expressed by some combination of zeros and ones. Stereo speakers use analog electronics because music constantly varies; Cocconi's remote-controlled planes were analog because of the planes' varying altitude and speed. Digital electronics are most commonly used in computers.

power tracker that enabled the car's batteries and motor to draw optimum power from even those solar cells not fully exposed to the sun.

Bob Stempel, whose vote would decide the matter, had a revealing reaction to it. To him, the strongest appeal of the Sunraycer project was as a teaching tool. Why not make two cars, he suggested, one for the race, one as backup; twice as many schoolchildren could see it when the race was done. Brooks breathed a sigh of relief. *That* was the kind of question he wanted to hear.

When the twenty-three entries rolled off at the starting gun through the streets of Darwin on November 1, Sunraycer almost immediately took the lead with a speed of 60 miles per hour and never surrendered it. By the sixth day, as Sunraycer streaked across the finish line in Adelaide, it could claim to have had no breakdowns other than the fully expected stops for three flat tires. Indeed, MacCready would conclude that the car's one design flaw was too *few* flats. If the team had used tires with thinner tread, he reckoned, the diminished rolling friction would have shaved an hour from Sunraycer's finishing time of 44 hours and 54 minutes, more than compensating for a half dozen more tire-changing stops of about two minutes each. Such were the modest regrets in a nearly perfect race, run at an average speed of 41.6 miles per hour and bisecting a continent on the energy equivalent of five gallons of gasoline.

Sunraycer lent a sheen of technological daring to a carmaker widely viewed as stodgy. It toured hundreds of schools before finding a permanent place in the Smithsonian Institute. And that, given the unfeasibility of ever producing a practical solar car, was that, as far as most GM officers were concerned. To AeroVironment's young engineers, however, Sunraycer was merely the prelude, the test that could lead to the larger project GM might be induced to fund while the good feelings glowed: a concept electric car.

What AeroVironment's Alec Brooks had in mind was a sporty two-seater built from the ground up to be lighter and more nimble than any electric vehicle of the past. A car that could use a more powerful version of the solar car's inverter and AC motor, and accommodate a battery pack that had the *power* to propel a lifesized electric vehicle as fast or faster than a gas-powered car, as well as the *energy* to make it go more than 100 miles.* Brooks already knew an EV could be designed to be far more efficient than a gas car—using

---

* Power and energy are two distinct, measurable properties of any kind of battery. Power denotes how much current can be pulled from the battery at any given instant, and thus governs an electric vehicle's acceleration and speed. Energy denotes how much electricity a battery contains over time—how long it can generate current until it's completely discharged—and so defines an electric vehicle's range. Brooks's goal of 100-mile range was defined by the apparent energy limitations of lead acid batteries; it was, at least, twice that of golden era electrics.

90 percent of its energy, versus a gas car's 15–25 percent. Because it had no engine, and had far fewer moving parts, it also would need far less maintenance: no oil changes or tune-ups, no broken hoses or radiators to refill. And powered by electronics and an electric motor, its life might be far longer than a gas car's—perhaps ten or twenty years. Brooks, for one, had no doubts about his ultimate goal: to prove that EVs of the future could be not only cleaner than gas cars but in most respects better; even, some day, *cheaper.*

In early 1988, Wilson and Brooks flew to Michigan to float the idea they had taken to calling Project Santana, for the Santa Ana winds which blow smog out of the Los Angeles basin. They saw it as a potential skunkworks, to be kept secret from all but those who had to know. That way, if it failed, GM wouldn't be publicly embarrassed. Next to Stempel, the most important ally to recruit was Don Runkle, who had helped oversee Sunraycer from Detroit. When Brooks explained that he hoped to make an electric vehicle that accelerated from 0–60 miles per hour in eight seconds, Runkle's eyes lit up.

"Now *that* would throw down the gauntlet, wouldn't it?" Runkle said. "No little incremental gains, just flat out for double or triple the mark." Even if the car remained a one-time experiment, it would still silence the cynics who jeered that EVs would never perform better than golf carts. How would Brooks get the drag coefficient down, Runkle wanted to know? How would he shave the tires' rolling resistance? The Californians talked and, with a growing sense of excitement, Runkle listened.

Runkle was the one who told Wilson and Brooks, perhaps a bit cavalierly, to talk to Baker to learn what they could from his ill-fated effort to launch the Electrovette. The man they met for dinner was huge, dressed in an extra-wide pinstripe suit. He told them about the day he took a GM vice president for a test ride in an Electrovette prototype. "Transmission got stuck," Baker said, wincing at the memory. "I had to walk a mile and a half back to the office with this VP cussing me out the whole time." He didn't miss EVs at all.

Still, Baker understood how critical recent advances in electronics might be, and offered to serve as an informal advisor. He told the California engineers why they should design their car with a tunnel of batteries down the middle, rather than packaging them in the rear. He explained why front-wheel drive would let them do more with regen braking than rear-wheel drive. Privately, he was intrigued that Runkle had sent them to him. If Runkle thought he was going to shunt Baker off to GM's next hapless stab at EVs, he should think again. Baker had lost enough career mileage as it was. He didn't need to make the same mistake twice.

Baker and Runkle agreed that Brooks was right to go with lead acid batteries. If the point of this project was to prove that EVs were feasible, lead acid was still the only practical, producible battery pairing around. In government and university labs around the country, battery developers were still playing with Baker's old nemesis, zinc. They were also playing with nickel-based batteries, and sodium sulfur, with lithium polymer and lithium ion and a hundred other pairings. All looked promising. All *had* looked promising for ten or twenty years. All claimed lifetimes of 1,000 cycles—1,000 times they could be discharged down to 20 percent of their capacity—and amazing energy, and even better power. All remained one-of-a-kind temptations, made by hand at mind-boggling cost, seemingly as far from production and a commercial market as cold fusion.

Lead acid worked, it was cheap, and a lead acid–powered EV could, in theory, go very fast indeed. Unfortunately, the science of lead acid batteries had progressed hardly at all since 1859, when Gaston Plante immersed lead plates in diluted sulfuric acid and proved he could conduct current repeatedly through them. Plante had positively charged one of his plates, making it lead oxide. The other was simply lead, which had a negative charge. His breakthrough was to create a flow of electrons from the negative plate, up out of the battery as electricity, then to feed the flow back into the battery, making the world's first rechargeable, or secondary, battery. Lead acid was *reliable*. But the chemistry of how it charged and discharged had seemed to defy improvement ever since.

In a gas car, at least, the chemistry of lead acid had long since ceased to be an issue. A gas car used only one battery, the battery was used only for an instant, and its current was quickly replenished by the generator that pulled energy from the engine and turned it back into electricity. In an electric vehicle, however, far greater demands were made of batteries. Instead of just starting an engine, they had to keep the car running. By the end of a 50-mile ride, they were deeply, if not entirely, discharged, which caused enormous stress to the electrodes and might quickly destroy them. Theoretically, an EV could cost far less to operate than a gas car: about 2.2 cents per mile in electricity, rather than 5 or 6 cents per mile for a gas-fueled car. But those savings would go out the window if an EV's battery pack proved short-lived.*

Then there was the problem of gas. A flooded lead acid battery—one that used a liquid electrolyte of water and acid to conduct its electrons—released, as it discharged, hydrogen molecules that fizzed up like Alka-Seltzer bubbles and emerged as gas. A bit of space had to be allowed for that gas in the battery above the plates; and after some time, as the gas kept escaping, the battery's water, of which the hydrogen was one element, diminished and had to be replaced. Not long ago, drivers had had to water their batteries every few thousand miles. Now batteries were advertised as maintenance-free. In fact, the

---

* Given the fluctuations of electricity rates and gas prices, such comparisons were necessarily averaged; the disparity might actually be wider, because gas cars cost at least $600 a year to maintain, while EVs would cost almost nothing.

process was simply occurring at a much slower rate, so that the battery would not have to be opened during its "life" as a starter battery in a car.

Not so the batteries in an EV. Drastically discharged as they were, time after time, they also gave off more hydrogen and oxygen than starter batteries, and so had to be watered. Bob Bish, the battery expert from GM-owned Delco Remy who flew out to meet with Brooks and his team, explained that every EV battery engineer had experimented with automatic watering systems. They were, as Bish put it, a plumber's nightmare, freezing in winter, getting gunked up with acid. Electric cars had to have maintenance-free batteries, and with flooded lead acid that just wasn't possible.

There was an answer, but it hadn't been tried with electric cars, and remained in a fairly experimental stage. This was the gas recombinant battery. It was still lead acid, but instead of using a flooded liquid electrolyte, the electrolyte was absorbed into sponge-like glass and fiber mats between its plates. The recombinant battery no longer required any space above the plates for the gas to vent and the liquid electrolyte to reform. That meant batteries could be more densely packed and take up less space. A good thing, Bish realized when he studied Brooks's specs. Brooks wanted 900 pounds of batteries to give the car the acceleration and speed he wanted; Bish ran some figures and saw he could only fit 843 pounds in the space allotted.

Bish still had no idea if recombinant batteries would *work* in an electric car, or if they did, whether they would work reliably over time. He did know that even in theory there was only one way to pack thirty-two batteries with enough power to get the car from 0–60 in eight seconds. Bish had to devise the densest lead acid battery the world had ever seen.

On a hot July day in 1988, Brooks and Wilson flew to Detroit to deliver presentations to all the top executives who would judge whether to fund the secret Santana Project. This was the summer so unremittingly hot it seemed apocalyptic. The greenhouse effect seemed all too real, the world all too fragile. Yet within his chairman's office, Roger Smith told his fellow officers he thought GM should pass on the project. Sunraycer had already provided all the PR GM needed in that department; why fund another one-of-a-kind car that wouldn't be produced?

Fervently, in the ensuing weeks, Stempel and vice chairman Don Atwood worked on him. Atwood, who at Delco Systems had helped design an early version of the inertial navigation system used on Apollo spacecraft, was especially persuasive; the electronics would work, he said, and eventually their cost would come down. Finally, in September, Smith gave the project his reluctant blessing, along with a budget of some $3 million and a fifteen-month deadline.

Now, around the AeroVironment team, the supporting cast changed. Hughes all but dropped out because the car would have no solar panels and because the one chunk of electronics it might need created, the inverter, Cocconi insisted on doing himself. Delco Remy, based in Indiana, became a new player because of the batteries. So did—with no small amount of resulting tension—GM's Advanced Concepts Center in nearby Newbury Park, California, to design the electric car's body.

The ACC was set up out in car-crazy California for the express purpose of encouraging its designers to shuck Rust Belt convention and indulge their creative muses. To Brooks's dismay, the very notion of an electric car fired the designers with visions of swooping curves and futuristic grilles. They sounded almost New Age-y as they spoke of design in terms of *feeling;* first came the feeling, then the shape. Aerodynamics, as far as Brooks could see, played no part in their designs at all.

First the ACC designers drew up a car that had wheels in huge protruding pods. Then they tried one with a long pointed tail. They tried rocket ship looks and barracuda looks. They made a cockpit that looked like that of a fighter plane. The one that most shocked Brooks had only two wheels—down the middle—with airplane-like landing struts on either side. For each design the GM designers made a small-scale clay model and tested its drag coefficient in the wind tunnel of nearby Cal Tech.* Brooks's goal for the car was 0.19, a drag similar to that of an F-16 fighter jet. Invariably, the studio's designs came in way above that.

Disgusted, the AeroVironment team began working up covert designs of its own. When the GM studio designers learned of the counterdesigns they grew so outraged that Don Runkle was forced to fly out to California to shake up the troops. There would *not* be two cars, he declared. There would be either one, agreed upon by both sides, or none. Runkle told Brooks that the AeroVironment designs looked terrible. But he agreed the car would have to have a better drag coefficient than any of the studio's designs to date.

With that, the design team glumly set about making the best of Brooks's aerodynamic demands and came up with the most successful design yet: a teardrop that did score 0.19. Its bottom lay only 5 inches from the ground and was sheathed by a bellypan like a turtle's that helped sweep onrushing air past it. Bellypans were hardly high tech, but carmakers had never used them before; with no premium on efficiency, they simply hadn't bothered. The pan could also be completely sealed because the car had no exhaust pipe. Above, air split by the car flowed smoothly along a sharply tapered rear, made possible because the rear wheels were set nine inches closer together than the front ones.

---

* Drag coefficient is the measure of how a moving object is affected by the air it's moving through. The lower the measure, the less affected the object is. In other words, the lower the measure, the more streamlined, or aerodynamic, it is. An average gas car has a drag coefficient between 0.35 and 0.4; Sunraycer's drag had been a mere 0.12, but no electric car, carrying a drivetrain bound to enlarge its shape, could be *that* aerodynamic.

Cocconi, meanwhile, worked obsessively at home, month after month, designing and building the car's inverter—its electronic heart. Technically, he was building two inverters, one for each 50-kilowatt motor—the prospect of constructing a single 100-kilowatt inverter had daunted even him—though the two would be packaged in one attaché-like case. In a sense, these were simply scaled-up versions of Sunraycer's inverter. But in addition to handling far more power to push a far heavier car, they had to be capable of instant fluctuations of current as the car sped up or slowed down. The solar car, by contrast, ran mostly at the cruising speed it could achieve by gleaning maximum power from the sun.* Though Cocconi was using standard electronic processes and parts—a computer to design his maze-like circuit boards, then resistors, capacitors, and other electronic pieces he attached to the boards himself—no one had ever devised such an intricate yet compact and lightweight inverter before. When it was done, his one-of-a-kind case would weigh all of 61 pounds.

Cocconi labored over the inverter alone in a mustard-yellow ranch house on a middle-class suburban street in Glendora, a short drive from AeroVironment in the San Gabriel valley. From the street, the house appeared no different from its neighbors, though the proliferation of yellowing supermarket circulars by the front door suggested an absentminded resident within. Through the back door, which Cocconi favored, lay a sunroom filled with circuit boards, its bookcases crammed with electronic parts, its ceiling hung with model planes and helicopters. The sweat work was done back in the shed, where Cocconi kept two milling machines, a lathe, and a bending brake, among other heavy machinery, mostly to bend and cut metal.

The comforts of ordinary homes held no more interest for Cocconi than the lifestyle they embellished. His living room was bare but for a stereo on the floor and two racing bikes; every Sunday that the weather permitted he rode ten miles uphill into the San Gabriel mountains, as intense and independent at play as he was at work. No real meal had likely ever been cooked in his narrow, gloomy kitchen. Forced eventually to tear himself away from his computer, Cocconi would sate his hunger with a can of sardines, his mind on his work as he ate at a dingy, formica-topped table that also accommodated a small black-and-white television. He had a girlfriend, but in his personal life, as with his work, he seemed to need a strong measure of independence. He was clearly too absorbed to be lonely; he seemed too absorbed to lead any other life but the one he was leading in this small house, navigating the boundaries of analog electronics—a life of the mind for which he had been

---

* Each motor was three phase, so each inverter had three switching stations, each with 48 semiconductor transistors. Six "smart poles," as Cocconi called them; 288 transistors in all. The smart poles switched a 320-volt system of current 20,000 times a *second*.

prepared, to an unusual degree, since childhood, as the son of not one, but two, nuclear scientists.

By the time Cocconi brought his case over to AeroVironment, there was a car to look at, its curves captured in fiberglass body panels. Brooks and his team had agreed on fiberglass because the car was, after all, merely a proof-of-concept vehicle. But they wanted the fiberglass to have the contours, the feel, and even the weight of spot-welded aluminum. Aluminum body panels, the designers felt, were what a real electric vehicle would have some day.

Wally Rippel, a longtime EV advocate and friend of the AeroVironment team, worked freelance with a local motor house to design the induction motor and gears. At Delco Remy, Bish and a partner, Terry Poorman, froze battery cases and plates to 0 degrees Fahrenheit, then chilled electrolyte mats down to 40 degrees before sliding them between the plates.* The car that AeroVironment called Santana was coming together, but its schedule of creation had slipped precipitously. In July 1989, Brooks reported to Runkle that he would need more than five months to finish the job. He was in for a surprise. Roger Smith, the car's greatest skeptic, had grown so excited by its progress reports that he'd decided to unveil it at the L.A. auto show in early January.

This was not, among his colleagues, a popular decision.

Did Smith realize, they asked weakly, what effect such an introduction might have on the harebrained California regulators? If GM said an electric car could be done, why, the regulators might make them do it, failing to appreciate, as usual, the difference between a proof-of-concept vehicle and a fully productionized car. Besides, why share the project's hard-won technological secrets? One after another of the car's enthusiastic supporters counseled Smith to keep Project Santana a secret, at least for a while. Stempel. Reuss. Runkle. Atwood. Cheerfully, Smith waved away their fears. "Most engineers would still be working on the 1971 Chevrolet if someone hadn't grabbed it away from them," he explained later. "I just figured it was time to get this thing out of the chute."

So began the real crunch, night after late night. The car's fiberglass frame and body were hand assembled, part by part. Molds for the car's windows were sent to the Pennsylvania supplier that would make them—then sent back again and again by Federal Express as Brooks discovered just how complex windows could be. First they failed to fit. Then, when he set them in their door frames, rolled them halfway down, and shut the doors, they broke. One night, Brooks broke four side windows and gave up. The Santana would simply make do with fixed glass.

---

* By chilling the acid, Bish and Poorman could slow its reactions and slide the mats into narrow spaces between plates before the mats could expand. The narrower the space between the plates, the denser the battery; the denser the battery, the more power it contained; the more power it contained, the more speed and acceleration it would provide.

At 1:00 A.M. on the morning of November 28, 1989, a strange sight rolled out of a back entrance of the AeroVironment building into a dark alley. A doorless shell of raw green fiberglass on wheels, it rolled with a slight whine, but no engine noise, to the end of the alley and back. It wasn't a car yet. But its batteries and inverter and motor all worked. Thrilled, the engineers took turns whipping around the parking lot with squeals of burning rubber. Every time it took off, the car pinned the delighted driver against his seat. A gas engine took a few long seconds to reach its peak power. This thing flew forward as fast as the current could reach the wheels, which was to say, *instantly*.

As soon as its doors were affixed, the car was taken by flatbed truck to GM's desert proving grounds in Mesa, Arizona. It weighed in at a remarkably light 2,200 pounds, including its 843 pounds of batteries. On the track, it jumped from 0–60 in 7.9 seconds—faster than such sporty gas cars as a Mazda Miata or Nissan 300 ZX—and quickly reached 75 miles per hour, the top speed allowed by its controller software. On a highway range test, it went 124 miles at 55 miles per hour; on an *urban* range test, one with lots of stopping and starting to simulate city traffic, it did nearly as well. That was extraordinary. A gas car had at least a 300-mile range on the open road. In the city, however, its range was sharply diminished as it idled at stops and used extra fuel to accelerate. Slowing, the Santana car recouped energy from its regen braking. Stopped, it consumed no energy at all.

The show car's windows remained fixed, its suspension and handling were terrible, and it lacked amenities and such safety features as air bags. Despite these and other drawbacks, it *worked*. A paint crew sanded the car and gave it a first coat of silver, making it look that much more real so a video could be made the next day for the L.A. auto show. As it was rolled out in front of the camera, a GM PR man stopped the action and pointed to the license plate the AeroVironment team had added to its rear bumper. "The Future Is Electric," the plate announced. "That'll have to go," the PR man declared. "It's too strong a statement."

The young engineers were taken aback. Did GM believe in electric cars, or didn't it?

On January 3, 1990, after two weeks of intensive sanding and repainting, the now sleekly silver show car was brought to Hughes corporate headquarters in Los Angeles where Roger Smith was to introduce it to journalists as a preview to the auto show. The backdrop was chosen to disprove critics who still claimed Hughes an awkward fit with GM, but the Hughes executives were somewhat embarrassed about that: Hughes had contributed nothing to the car.

During the car's transformation from ugly duckling to shiny show car, its name, along with its color, had changed. In the course of a routine copyright check, GM's lawyers had discovered that Santana was registered in Europe as a Volkswagen model. The AeroVironment team came up with alternatives, including, from Cocconi, "Escape," an acronym for Electric Sports Car and Pollution Eliminator. None was accepted.

Either Chuck Jordan, the GM vice president of design, or Don Runkle, both up at the Tech Center, came up with the name GM adopted—the credit, or blame, was never clearly attached to one or the other. Brooks and the rest of the AeroVironment team were dismayed by the choice, but there was no time to appeal it. The car was now the Impact, for the impact it would have on the world—a name that with its obvious double entendre immediately robbed the homely Edsel and hapless Studebaker of their distinction as the worst names in the history of automobiles. The next night, Johnny Carson would become the first, but by no means last, to ridicule the choice. "What next," Carson asked, "the Ford Whiplash?"

An hour before the event, Roger Smith and his retinue swept into the Hughes basement for the chairman's first look at the show car. Smith was delighted by it, but declined Brooks's invitation to give it a test spin around the basement. "I'm sure it'll be fine," he declared.

Brooks swallowed hard. The Impact did take a little getting used to; the regen braking would feel new. What if Smith got confused at the wheel and floored the wrong pedal? "Sir, perhaps you should just give it a whirl," Brooks suggested.

Smith seemed taken aback, but then shrugged and slid in behind the wheel. With Brooks in the passenger seat, he drove around the basement a minute or two. "What's that sound?" he said suspiciously.

Brooks listened. There *was* some sort of scraping sound.

"You'll get that fixed by showtime, right?" Smith said.

As soon as Smith and the others had left, Brooks slid under the car. The sound seemed to be coming from under the front wheels, but no obvious suspect presented itself. Hurriedly, a pit crew of mechanics jacked up the car and pulled off the wheels. Nothing. Only when the wheels were replaced did a mechanic notice one of the aluminum disc brakes rubbing against a tire. With a Swiss army knife he set to filing the disc. By the time Smith reappeared, the disc no longer rubbed.

The Hughes press conference was a great success—especially for Smith, who dominated it. The next day, the chairman appeared with the car at the L.A. auto show and again basked in the glow of public excitement. Never mind that the car was as far from being production-ready as a child's plastic model, that its very appearance as an aluminum car was an illusion, that it remained too unrefined for reporters to drive. After another tough year of dwindling market share and closing factories, Smith seemed almost intoxicated by all the approbation.

To the minds of the AeroVironment engineers, Smith also seemed to feel that GM had wrought this wondrous toy with only the barest assist from some unnamed R&D firm. Wally Rippel, for one, was shocked by the video accompanying the display. No credit was given to AeroVironment. The "GM engineers" shown in their white lab coats at the Tech Center were actors. The test-track scenes in Mesa showed other white-coated engineers who were actually Brooks and Cocconi, induced by the filmmakers to act as unnamed GMers; Cocconi's role involved holding a stopwatch as the car roared by.

MacCready, taking the long view, reasoned that in making electric vehicles seem real, Impact had hastened the arrival of real alternative vehicles by five years. Who cared if GM took most of the credit? Fortuitously, too, AeroVironment would be granted a long-term contract from GM to conduct an ongoing skunkworks of future automobiles. In fact, MacCready was less interested now in electrics than in hybrids, which might offset the limited range of their battery packs with a small engine as a second source of power. Though the engine, presumably powered by some fossil fuel, would keep the hybrid from being entirely emission-free, its small size would make it nearly so, and the much increased range would make it, MacCready thought, a far more practical car of the future than the electric. With Impact, he'd really just wanted to show how fuel economy could be dramatically improved with very lightweight structures.

But Smith was too dazzled by the flashbulbs to let Impact go at that.

Starting from Scratch

))))

Every morning now, Ken Baker's alarm clock woke him at 4:45 A.M. His wife groaned and went back to sleep, but Baker forced himself to the basement. There, in a windowless workout room, he flailed away for an hour on an exercise machine that worked both his arms and legs. Baker never missed a morning. He felt he had no choice. Without exercise, the weight would come back.

Most months of the year, the Michigan sky was dark at 7:00 A.M. when Baker left the house, for here at the western edge of the eastern time zone day broke nearly an hour later than on the Atlantic coast, so that a gloom appeared to linger across the flat land. Usually he drove whatever new GM model he was testing; every three months or 3,000 miles executives on or above the company's eighth level of hierarchy still received a different new car to try. PEP, it was called cheerily: product evaluation program.

On warm summer mornings, though, Baker sometimes took his cherished red 1962 Corvette to work. The car had been in fairly good shape when he bought it not long ago, but when one electrical problem led to another, he'd finally ripped out the harnesses and put in new wiring himself. He'd even taken the brakes apart, cleaned them piece by piece with a die grinder and wire brush, then put the whole brake assembly back together. He loved the car, and he loved fixing it. Old Corvettes, with their swashbuckling curves and snarling power, evoked the glory days when GM all but owned the market with its yearly style changes, before the rollercoaster ride through boom-and-bust times, before onerous environmental standards, before Japan. Roger Smith, as it happened, drove a '59.

From Baker's home in Bloomfield Hills, the drive down Interstate 75 South to the Tech Center in Warren took twenty minutes without traffic. But there was always traffic. By 7:00 A.M. the highway was thick with cars, all just nudging along, as factory workers joined executives in the dark ride to work, each driver alone in his sealed, temperature-controlled vessel. In the state that made cars, there was no mass transportation, aside from buses for the poor. Most mornings, as a result, Baker's drive took him up to an hour.

The Tech Center occupied a broad swath of former farmland in a worn-out suburb that had served, three decades before, as one of Detroit's first bed-room communities. On every side now the Tech Center was bordered by heavily trafficked boulevards and the detritus of car culture: strip malls, fast food restaurants, motels, and car washes. Hidden beyond were streets of mod-est, brick-walled houses, each with its postage stamp of lawn, each with an American-made car—never a foreign-made—in the driveway. The suburb of Warren had no center, except, perhaps, the guarded Tech Center. At arbi-trary lines, it merely ended.

Within the Tech Center's surrounding chain-link fence and scrim of leafy trees, through one of the security gates on each side where visitors checked in, lay an oasis of open space. The center's low-lying buildings were set off by broad greenswards and by two rectangular man-made lakes. A flock of Canada geese had taken up residence on the lakes, befouling the surrounding sidewalks, but the center benefited from a touch of anarchy. Otherwise, a stern sense of order prevailed. The buildings, designed forty years ago by architect Eero Saarinen and distinguished from each other mainly by end walls of blue- or red-painted brick, were austere, the grounds still but for the passing of cars and the occasional clump of earnest engi-neers striding from one meeting to the next. The Tech Center looked all business, and it was.

Baker's new office was in Engineering South, where an ever-changing cast of engineers from one car line or another came in to work up new designs. To *sandbox*, as the jargon had it. Beyond the lobby guard and waiting area with torn leather chairs was a hangar that ran the length of the building, lined on either side with bays where mechanics worked on cars. Upstairs were two wide floors of cubicles and corridors. If the engineers succeeded, their proj-ects would be moved out to Buick, or Cadillac, or one of the other of GM's seven car divisions, and made part of a future production program. If they failed, the engineers left anyway, to make room for the next team of hopefuls. Baker strode past the Eng South building guard by 8:00 A.M., flashing his em-ployee badge, then walked briskly down the long corridor beside the bays. Es-chewing the elevator, he ran up the back stairs to the third floor: a last bit of exercise to keep the weight off.

At the moment, the third floor was nearly unoccupied, awaiting Baker's team. The cubicles in the open middle area were bare. The small private offices that lined the surrounding walls were empty but for gray metal desks and chairs. Baker's office at one far corner had, in addition to these institutional issues, a small round table and sofa and a cluster of framed inspirational sayings that Baker had chosen to hang on the walls. "The person who says it can't be done should not interfere with those who are doing it," read one. "Whatever you vividly imagine, ardently desire, sincerely believe and enthusiastically act upon," read another, "must inevitably come to pass."

By now, Baker knew he needed all the inspiration he could get. Runkle — and Reuss and Schultz and Stempel — had acted as if the Impact program was a little experiment in bureaucratic *process*. The car itself? A piece of cake. Those brainy futurists in California had already done the hard work. The car existed. It *drove*. The new electronics were in place. So were the new lightweight materials. And for batteries, the car used plain old, dependable lead acid. All Baker had to do was change the frame and body from fiberglass to aluminum, throw in some heat and air-conditioning, maybe power windows and a CD player, and send it off to production. Surely it was easier than starting a new car from scratch.

Less than a month into his new job, Baker realized how glib that assessment was. Even on its own terms, the show car fell short. At GM's proving grounds in Milford, 50 miles west of Warren, a young test engineer named Marty Freedman drove it out along the straightaways and curves of the links-like course. He found its range woefully short of the 120 miles claimed by AeroVironment, the range reported faithfully in every one of the hundreds of news stories written about the car after the L.A. auto show. The AeroVironment range as configured was real, but the news stories failed to mention that the car's side mirrors had been removed, its windows and doors and body seams taped, that the seals had been cut off bearings to reduce even that bit of drag.

More important, the stories failed to mention that the regen braking had been cranked so high that on level ground the car would nearly stop as soon as the driver let up on the accelerator; on steep downhills, of course, the high regen recouped that much more energy, yielding that much more range. And the car had been driven until its pack was 100 percent discharged, punishment no battery could repeatedly sustain. At Milford, in real driving conditions, with the regen adjusted and the pack taken down to 80 percent depth of discharge, the car's range was more like 70 miles. On a sunny day. A *windless* sunny day. A windless sunny day on which the driver chose not to use the heater or cooling fan.

On a cold rainy night, passengers in a gas car were warmed by the engine's heat, channeled as needed through air ducts. A gas car's windshield wipers, headlights, and other electrical devices played off the engine, too; the engine powered the alternator that sent them current. Neither Impact, nor any other electric car, would have it so easy. The heat that Impact's inverter, batteries, and motors threw off was insignificant. The AeroVironment team had used a small heat pump, reasoning, logically enough, that Impact would be driven only in Southern California. They had allowed for headlights and a few other electrical devices. But all these drew current directly from the batteries' precious store. One of the show car's batteries was set aside just for this; an electronic controller meted out current as needed. Unfortunately, it generated about 30 watts—only enough power to light five or six Christmas tree bulbs.

A better heating and air-conditioning system, Baker saw, would have to be installed in a production car, especially if it was ever to be driven on even a winter day in Southern California. And what if such expected luxuries as power windows and steering, a radio, and a tape player were added? How much current would be left to run the car on a chilly night for 30 miles, let alone 120?

Impact's radical aerodynamics had helped give it the range it did have, and stirred much excitement from the press, but here were Baker's next problems. How practical was a car that sat 5 inches from the ground? The first speed bump it met would be its last. From hard experience, GM set a minimum of 8 inches ground clearance for all its cars—measured with two adult passengers *in* the car, not with the car sitting empty. And what about water? If the car went through a puddle of any depth, water might slosh through the car's air-cooling inlets and short out the inverter, or seep into the batteries through the pack's not-too-well-sealed tunnel. Having the rear wheels narrower than the front ones was clever, but how would the car go through a car wash? These were the kind of considerations, like power windows and steering, at which AeroVironment's young Turks scoffed. But a production car had to take them into account.

No surprise, at least, about the car's fiberglass frame and body: they would have to be replaced, likely by aluminum. But that was easier to say than do. Light as aluminum was, it was still heavier than fiberglass. It was also far more brittle than steel when welded, and far more expensive; not by chance had carmakers shunned it in the past. The tubular frame—the car's skeleton— would need to be rethought, and the whole car would need to be strengthened, a lot, to make it crashworthy. All this would add mass, which meant more work for the batteries to do, and thus less range.

Then there was the car's propulsion system. The electronics on the show car had cost $100,000. Somehow, that cost would have to come down to about one-fiftieth of that. But the electronics would also have to work—consistently, day to day, year to year, for the life of the car. So far, Freedman, the young test engineer, was finding that every twenty hours or so, one of the inverter's power switches—its so-called MOSFETs—would blow, taking a whole string along with it and shorting out the car.

Freedman's specialty was acoustics; what he heard driving the show car depressed him thoroughly. At first, the car did seem eerily quiet. But that irksome whine rose as the car began to roll, then hovered somewhere in the higher reaches of audibility even as the car hit cruising speeds. This was the noise of ordinary gears, masked on a gas car by the thrum of the engine. The gears could, perhaps, be more tightly meshed. But eliminating the gear noise altogether would be a monumental effort. It was ironic, thought Freedman. Acoustics had become a sort of final frontier in car design of late, and here was Impact, the car of the future, with acoustics somewhere between bad and miserable.

So far, Baker had a staff of one; if he'd wanted, he could have blamed that one for getting him into this mess. After the L.A. auto show, John Williams was the engineer who had led a secret task force to determine if the concept car could be produced. Williams had done his best, analyzing the electronics, traveling around the country to visit would-be aluminum suppliers and the like. In the end, he and Runkle, to whom he reported, had had to make a decision based less on information than on instinct. The car could be made. Whether it could be made well enough and inexpensively enough to find a market, no one could say. Like any new technology, it faced the Catch-22 of innovation. Until a wide market emerged, the car's hardware likely would remain unrefined and overpriced. But until the hardware improved, why would a market appear?

Williams and Runkle had told GM's board they thought the gamble worth taking. A market would emerge eventually, and GM should establish a leadership position in it, both for the environmental benefits EVs could provide and—ultimately—for profit. At the same time, the task force had strongly advised that GM keep its production plans private—to go black, as they put it. Williams had a motto for it. "Hardware," he liked to say, "before hoopla."

Roger Smith, acting entirely on instinct, had ignored the recommendation. On the other hand, he'd sanctioned the program. And while Williams knew, from having talked with them, how likely the California regulators were to take their cue from Smith's announcement, it was also true that a risky program like Impact felt far more protected within the company for having the chairman's public imprimatur.

Baker and Williams were old friends, in part because they were so different from each other. Williams had never competed with Baker; he seemed never to have competed with anyone. Mild mannered, affable, with a slight frame and dark goatee, he looked more like a village minister than a GM career man. In fact, he took an active role in his local Catholic church and lived north of the suburbs in the more rural setting of Lake Orion with his second wife, Maggie. Yet of all the engineers who would join the program, Williams would be drawn into the fiercest confrontations to protect fundamental facts from being distorted. That would have surprised him to know, in the summer of 1990, though his new job, now that the program had begun, was to be its long-range planner. Already he had begun devising large display charts of lines and boxes and acronyms to try to control the mind-boggling complexities of a GM car program. The so-called *four-phase* process had been divined by studying the methods of affiliated carmakers, principally the GM-Toyota partnership called NUMMI, in California, and GM's Opel operation in Europe; it was just now being adapted to the company's U.S. operations, so that in this regard, too, Impact would be a test case.

Until Baker had a senior staff, there wasn't much he could do. He spent his first weeks calling around the corporation, searching for candidates. One of his earliest hires was chief of propulsion, the program's most technically challenging job. For that, he had no second choice.

Baker had known Jon Bereisa since the two worked together on the Electrovette. A tall, heavyset man in his mid-forties, Bereisa was a brilliant engineer who spoke so quickly, and with such enthusiasm, that a layman had no hope of following him as he riffed on about why IGBTs were better than MOSFETs. He was a rarity at GM, a polymath who knew engines and motors, but also computers and semiconductors, and one who liked nothing better than taking on seemingly impossible tasks.

Bereisa would be responsible for the batteries, the motors, the inverter between them, and later also the charger—a whole new system of powering a car, incredibly delicate and complex, which he would not merely have to design but produce in the two years Baker was budgeting for the program. This was, as Bereisa would not be shy to observe, like inventing a new gas-powered car, the engine within it, and the gas pump that fueled it, all at the same time.

Bereisa could seem bossy, and more than one engineer in the program would soon be left muttering darkly about his managerial style. He didn't listen, didn't delegate; really, he didn't manage at all. What he did was focus his extraordinary intelligence on the challenges at hand, and go at them with an all-consuming, almost boyish passion, pushing aside any opinions that got in his way. To Baker, at least, he showed deference; the two were also close friends. Baker knew, however, that he needed a chief engineer, an overall number-two man, both because Bereisa would have his hands full with propulsion, and because even Baker saw the limits of Bereisa's managerial skills. His choice said a lot about him—and about Jim Ellis.

Ellis was tall, laconic, and low-key, but he held a few firm opinions about how the program should be managed and they didn't include having Baker and Bereisa rule as a pair of benevolent despots. Those opinions had been formed in the late seventies, when Ellis was named the *first* program manager of the ill-fated Electrovette. He had understood his mission was to design a real production electric car with no compromises. The executive to whom he reported was the very embodiment of autocratic management. He thought the Electrovette a misbegotten notion, and told Ellis not to aim for production; just knock out a fast demo, he said, and the corporation would put it out of its misery. Ellis insisted on doing a more thorough, time-consuming design. Upper management got restless, and Ellis was replaced—by Baker.

Ellis had felt no resentment toward his successor. After a few backwater years, he had gone on to work for Baker at CPC as chief engineer of the successful Corsica/Beretta car program. But he had also read deeply in the somewhat dry literature of management theory and developed strong opinions about it.

Invariably, when Ellis began to articulate his views, he reached for a pen and drew two pyramids. The first was right side up, with the manager/leader occupying the top echelon, then his middle managers, then the factory workers. The second pyramid was upside down. Now the leader, from his point at the bottom, *supported* his middle managers, who in turn supported the workers. The workers, in the inverted pyramid, were the most important figures. They were the ones who would build the car.

Baker and Bereisa felt they knew how to begin making Impact real. They wanted to make the decisions and pass them down for release engineers to carry out. Ellis didn't want that. He wanted teams of release engineers to design the car themselves, system by system, limited only by certain parameters—of mass and cost and basic function—set by senior staff down in their pyramid point below. He wanted every engineer to voice opinions, take responsibility, and be accountable. He wanted the design to flow *up*.

Often in the weeks after Ellis's arrival, Baker and Bereisa would reach an engineering decision, and Ellis, tensely, would confront them. "I'm the engineering director, and you're the program manager," he would tell Baker. "You deal with the business issues; I deal with the car issues." Baker got angry, but he also understood that Ellis was probably right. And if he hadn't wanted a strong number two, he wouldn't have hired Ellis in the first place.

A technology as novel as Impact's, Baker felt, demanded engineers who felt a real excitement about electric cars. To weed out the careerists, Baker declared that no one joining the Impact program would get either a raise *or* a promotion. And in no case would corporate GM move bodies into the program against their will. Everyone, in one sense or another, would be a volunteer.

Baker brought a lot of passion to his pitching—he was committed now, not only corporately but emotionally; he no longer had a choice. One by one the engineers he wanted agreed to join. To be sought out by a new program manager was flattering, and a downturn in the market had helped loosen a few prospects from their programs. But there was more to it than that. Engineers who thrilled to the intricacies of internal-combustion engines also knew the stakes. They knew cars had to be cleaner. Especially to those who had always been drawn to advanced engineering, the technological challenge of creating a completely clean car—a car, at least, that itself produced no emissions—was compelling. It was exciting. So was the notion of curbing America's thirst for foreign oil. If anyone doubted the importance of that, here was Saddam Hussein attacking Kuwait, and President Bush drawing lines in the sand.

Randy Schwarz, a rangy manufacturing engineer who might have passed for Sam Shepard, got a call from Baker on a Friday afternoon. Baker had heard Schwarz was the best young manufacturing engineer at GM. He'd also heard that Schwarz had accepted a transfer to Japan. Would he join Impact as its manufacturing chief instead? Schwarz told Baker the moving van was coming on Monday, that he and his wife would be flying off that day. They'd already been to Japan once, and rented an apartment. Besides, the Japan job was a real step up. Doggedly, Baker went on about how important Impact could be. Schwarz asked for twenty-four hours to decide. Twenty-four hours later, he called to accept.

Of the more junior hires, nearly all came from Runkle's realm of advanced engineering, some just a year or two out of graduate school, working on experimental builds until they could join a real program. What they brought, along with freshly earned degrees, was a sense of mission. They were engineers, not activists, but they did care deeply about the environment. The older engineers would be impressed by their eagerness to work long hours, less so by the arrogance they sometimes displayed despite their lack of experience in bringing a car to life.

One of the first of the eager young engineers to arrive was Tom Lobkovich, a second-generation GMer. At Runkle's AES he had led a team designing the structures—the skeletons—of futuristic concept cars. Lobkovich loved structure. It didn't bother him that no one in the outside world ever saw the structure of a car, much less thought about it, or made a buying decision based on it. Structure, he felt, defined and expressed a car's essential character. It was the car's soul. Disciplined, with a brisk, almost military air that belied his youthful blond hair and mustache, Lobkovich had the tensile strength and durability of a structure himself. In a sense, by arriving as early as he did on the platform and defining the structure he thought Impact should have before the rest of the car came together, he would seem to make its soul his own.

By August, when he joined the platform, bringing his own AES structures team with him, Lobkovich had already decided that Impact's structure—not merely its body panels—should be aluminum. Never mind that cars for ninety years had had steel frames, that aluminum had its problems, that a car filled with batteries might strain an aluminum frame. Lobkovich wasn't worried about the risks. Aluminum would work, he was convinced. Aluminum was the only way to go.

Of the fifteen or twenty first hires that fall, most were men. For that matter, most were white Anglo-Saxon Protestant men who shook hands vigorously, made pleasantries in a flat, midwestern cadence by the communal coffee machine, and drove home at the end of the day in their company cars to wives and young children. There was, perhaps, no industry left in America quite so dominated by white Protestant males except, perhaps, the CIA.* When the program swelled at year's end to several hundred, a few black faces would appear, and if one looked *very* hard, one might find a Jew. But perhaps not two. As for women, one could count on one hand the number in GM's higher ranks. On the Impact program, however, more than a few began to appear: smart, strong engineers as thoroughly enamored of the mechanics of cars as their male counterparts.

One of the first to arrive was Arianna Kalian. Half-Armenian, half-Italian, with short black hair and olive skin, she had grown up in Manhattan playing the oboe and English horn. A keen interest in math and science had made her curious about how cars worked; viscerally, she'd been drawn to racing. At local tracks, she had worked as a pit crew member in timing and scoring—on night shifts, when the work was easier for a teenage girl to get—and eventually done the same for Daytona teams. By then, she'd graduated from New York's best public school, Stuyvesant, and majored in mechanical engineering at Cooper Union. As a GM intern, she worked in the Corvette body group and came to appreciate how complex a challenge body structure was; every squeak and rattle suggested a whole array of interlinked problems. At AES, she had worked under Lobkovich, then come to Impact as part of his team. Her job would be making the car crashworthy. One look at the show car and she saw what *that* would mean: redesigning, and extending, the whole front end.

As the process of hiring went on, Baker was pleased to realize he did have the power to hire whom he chose. He had expected the dotted line that led to Don Runkle to bring strong advice, and for Runkle to feel that the program was still, in some ineluctable way, his to direct. Two or three times Runkle made suggestions that Baker ignored, and when they were brought up again, a certain tension hung in the air. Generally, he held back. For both men, it was an oddly gratifying experience to be aligned, to share the goal of wanting

---

* GM, for the record, objects to this characterization, and says it aggressively pursues diversity in its hiring policies.

Impact to succeed. Baker would hardly have acknowledged it to his old rival, but he was almost beginning to *like* Runkle.

When he drove home, Baker could look out over the flat suburban landscape at dusk, over the inelegant patchwork of glass towers and subdivisions and minimalls and imagine the farms that had once thrived here. He came from a farming town; his father had grown up on a farm.

The town was Auburn, New York, at the northern tip of Owasco Lake, in the state's Fingerlakes region—about as rural as one could get east of Detroit. Baker's mother was a generation removed from farm life. She had two master's degrees, and taught elementary school and music. She had met her husband when he came home on leave from the marines. His military service done, he took a line worker's job at a nearby plant that made locomotive parts, and kept that job his whole working life.

Baker had grown up an only child and was indulged, particularly by his mother, in his curiosity with how things worked. He went to Clarkson, in the northern reach of the state, to be an engineer. In his senior year he married a sorority girl from a nearby teacher's college, the same one his mother had attended. Rosetta Cardino was a lively, dark-haired math whiz. In the summer of 1969, as the Woodstock festival was convening downstate, Baker and his bride headed west for Michigan—a young American couple untouched by drugs, Jimi Hendrix, or the antiwar movement—where Baker had been offered the job of his dreams as a test engineer at Buick, and where Rosetta hoped to teach. Baker had grown up in Buicks, his family squarely in the midrange between Chevrolets and Cadillacs. The very idea that a small-town boy who'd rebuilt lawn mower motors could work at General Motors was breathtaking. "I'm going to need a tuxedo," Baker told his new bride. "Because this is the auto industry. This is where it happens."

Until the mid-eighties, Baker had worked in Flint, where Buick was still based, and lived in Grand Blanc, a suburb favored by Flint's white-collar workers. Grand Blanc was a great place to raise kids, everyone agreed, with its nice new subdivisions, and for the Bakers, who soon had a daughter and son, that was key. But Grand Blanc and Flint were a long drive northwest of the Tech Center. And the Bakers were worlds away from Bloomfield Hills, where GM's top executives lived. When Baker was transferred to the Tech Center in 1986, he told friends the commute from Grand Blanc had become too onerous. But he didn't move his family to one of the upper-middle-class suburbs near Warren. He made straight for Bloomfield Hills—*west* of Woodward.

Woodward Avenue was the dividing line in a town that measured status by the inch. To the east lay homes more comfortable than grand, and then subdivisions, and then humbler subdivisions. West of Woodward rolled the town's eponymous hills, in whose laps nestled gated Tudor mansions, and around which snaked tree-lined roads that led to half a dozen lakes. There were subdivisions in Bloomfield Hills, too, but of large new houses, often set off in the mock-Tudor style that was oddly and inexplicably popular in suburban Michigan. In one of the newest and finest of these, the Bakers bought a cul-de-sac lot and built a spacious house.

From his back patio, when he sat out with a glass of wine after work, Baker could look in any direction and see the home of some high-level car executive. Next door was Bob Eaton, then the president of GM-Europe, later to become Lee Iacocca's successor at Chrysler; the price of Eaton's rise would be a guard booth manned twenty-four hours a day outside his house in response to threats from union dissidents. Arv Mueller's rolling back lawn swept up toward the patio from the opposite side like an emerald tide. Mueller, Baker's boss at CPC, would soon become a vice president and general manager of the entire Tech Center; he was a mentor and friend. In one house down the street lived Jack Smith, GM's future chairman. Soon, into another, would move GM's prospective worldwide purchasing chief, Ignacio Lopez.

Powerful as they were, the executives were all bound by a strict neighborhood covenant of rules. Lawns had to be closely cropped, cars kept in garages, garbage cans put out only at precise collection times. One reckless homeowner up the street had gotten it into his head to remove his lawn altogether and install a southwestern desert look, complete with rocks and cacti. The keepers of the covenant had come down on him like avenging angels and made him revert to grass.

The new house had strained the Bakers' finances considerably, but Baker was deeply proud of it, and felt, as overextended new homeowners will, that it would pull him up to its level soon enough. Now it might be about to do that—if he could just get Impact to market.

Fighting for Turf

))))

As program manager, Baker could hire whom he chose, shape the program as he liked, and overrule his chief engineer on design changes whenever he chose. That was a lot of leeway. It was a lot of power. Yet over the heart of the car—the batteries and inverter and motor that made up its powertrain—neither he nor his propulsion chief, Jon Bereisa, had much control at all. Not only might the powertrain's parts be unproducible; the teams in charge of them were states away, disinclined to do Baker's bidding and distracted, anyway, by their own bitter efforts to discredit one another.

In the months to come, scores of outside suppliers would be lined up to make parts for Impact, from tires to steering wheels to cupholders. Scores more would be hired to make parts for *those* parts. In most cases, bids would be solicited, comparable offers weighed, outside sources as likely chosen as those within GM.

Not so for the car's powertrain.

At General Motors, the powertrain of any car—from the starter battery and engine to the transmission and motor—had been supplied traditionally by divisions and wholly owned subsidiaries, princes within the realm. The princes didn't merely have dibs. They had letters of charter, signed by GM's top executives. Delco Remy *would* do all batteries and motors and alternators for GM cars. Delco Electronics *would* do all radios and electronic controllers. Staying in-house theoretically kept costs down and offered more sources of profit. It also gave the corporation more control over the process of putting a car together. Of course, in-house suppliers could get complacent. And when the market subsided, every boat tethered to GM subsided with it.

Charters harked back to the glory days when GM ruled the world. Now the world and GM were at a standoff, and the world was winning. In the global marketplace, a motor from China was likely to be cheaper and just as well made as its Rust Belt counterpart. Even final assembly might now be done beyond American borders, by nonunion workers in Mexico. Both Ford and Chrysler were relying ever more on outside suppliers. At GM, the empire lived on, but its princes sensed how soon it might end and clung that much more fiercely to their corporate monopolies.

Baker had seen what he was up against in his first week on the job when he sat in on a tense meeting called by Bob Schultz and William Hoglund—then vice president in charge of the company's in-house suppliers, the Automotive Components Group (ACG)—at the GM building downtown. Delco Remy's cantankerous battery chief, Bill Wylam, was there, up from Anderson, Indiana. So was Delco Electronics's Al Laubenstein, a former aerospace engineer; DE was based near Remy in Indiana, in the automotive boondock of Kokomo. There, too, was Harry King, a senior radar systems engineer from Hughes's original compound in Culver City, California. At issue was who would take on which part of the powertrain.

The princes had come to a peace of their own some weeks before over pizza and beer in a motel room near the Detroit Metro Airport. Neither of the Delcos liked dealing Hughes in at all; they felt they could handle the powertrain on their own, and would have, if Hughes had not become their new stepbrother. They also felt threatened; perhaps the world's premier aerospace company would try to scoop up all of GM's automotive electronics. Grudgingly, they had agreed that Hughes could do *some* work on the inverter, using controllers and power switches supplied by Delco Electronics, but that Remy would do part of the inverter, too. When Harry King had suggested Hughes do a smaller, subsidiary inverter that fed DC current to the car's headlights, radio, and the like, Wylam had dug in his heels. "That does what the alternator does on a gas car," he said. "We do alternators. We do twelve-volt power. That's *ours.*" Remy of course would do the batteries and motor too; they were *charter* products. Hughes could do the car's offboard battery charger however, since GM had never done such a thing before, and no charter existed for it.

Angrily, Schultz and Hoglund scrapped the princes' pact and imposed their own. Impact was Hughes's chance to show, at last, how useful it could be to GM. It needed more of a role. Hughes would start by creating about fifty replicas of Alan Cocconi's inverter, using power switches and controllers from DE. If it did the job well, it would go on to make inverters for the production car. Remy would do the car's batteries and motor, and it could keep the smaller 12-volt inverter, but no more.

All three suppliers left the meeting disgruntled. King thought Hughes should have gotten both inverters. Laubenstein was appalled that Delco Elec-

tronics was to be a second-tier supplier to first-tier Hughes; by GM's strict pro-
tocol, that meant he had to *report* to Hughes, which had no experience with
cars. For Wylam, who saw EV powertrains as nothing less than Delco Remy's
future, the verdict was a stinging setback. But not a final one. Though no one
else at the meeting would share his recollection, Wylam felt sure he heard
Hoglund say the inverter decision applied only to Impact. As far as Wylam
was concerned, that left Remy free to develop EV powertrains for future GM
electric cars. Or for any other customer it could line up. "Hey," Wylam would
say with a confident grin. "It's every man for himself."

The meeting, like the Munich Pact, had been called to define a peace. All
too soon, it would lead to war.

Back in Culver City, Hughes's Harry King, a gentle and professorial engineer not far from retirement, met warily with the AeroVironment team to
start replicating the inverter. Cocconi, he'd heard, could be particularly difficult, and abhorred Hughes because of its military defense work. To King's
surprise, Cocconi proved at first patient and cooperative, and seemed privately pleased to be given a pass to enter the top secret facility at will. But
even with his help, the inverter was a nightmare.

Cocconi, it turned out, had made notes only for about 2 percent of his one-
of-a-kind inverter as he created it at home. The Hughes engineers were reduced to taking pictures of his work and trying to use the pictures as
diagrams. To "reverse engineer" the box, as they put it. The circuit boards
were extremely difficult to map, much less reproduce, and manufacturing
them seemed impossible. Most complex were the transistor switches that
made the inverter work—the heart of the heart of the car, switching DC current from the batteries to AC for the motors. The transistors were both the
boon and bane of Cocconi's design.

Each of Cocconi's switches was a cluster of new electronic transistors
called MOSFETs, a clumsy acronym that was, at least, easier to remember
than the words it stood for: metal oxide semi-conductor field effect transistor.
He wasn't the first person to use them. He *was* the first to use them in devising an electronic inverter that could switch enough DC current to AC to
power a car, yet be small enough to fit *in* the car. But while MOSFETs
worked well for a one-of-a-kind breakthrough like Cocconi's, producing
MOSFET-based inverters was quite another matter.

To King, the problems seemed inherent in the MOSFETs' size and con-
struction. A MOSFET was about the size of a postage stamp. It contained
one inscribed silicon chip wrapped in plastic, about ⅛ to ¼ inch square. Only
so much current could be passed through each MOSFET, due to the limits
in chip size imposed by the delicate process of creating silicon. So Cocconi
had strung MOSFETs together in four rows of twelve to make a switch he
called a smart pole: Forty-eight MOSFETs in each switch, six switches alto-

gether, 288 MOSFETs. All well and good. But if one of the 288 MOSFETs failed, a chain reaction ensued. A row of twelve would short out, causing the whole inverter to conk out amid the smell of burning plastic.

King never did quite figure out why a new transistor happened along just when it did to replace the MOSFETs. It wasn't in response to Hughes's need, or for that matter, anyone else's. As King put it, it was sort of a solution looking for a problem. The new transistor was called an IGBT—which stood, even less memorably, for insulated gate bipolar transistor. The Japanese had begun to use them in elevators, but so far there weren't many calls for transistors that so compactly switched such huge currents.

The IGBT was a beautifully compressed piece of solid state circuitry about the size of a package of cigarettes. It contained four silicon chips, rather than one, and each was itself as large as a postage stamp: the greater the area of silicon, the more current the transistor could handle. Because the pack didn't need the connecting wires that a clump of MOSFETs did, there were fewer parts and less chance the whole thing would fail. It was the difference between a string of Christmas lights, where any one light's failure would short out the string, and a single floodlight. More light, more reliability. A single IGBT, at this stage of development, replaced twenty-four MOSFETs; soon, it would replace twice that many. Cocconi's inverter, the Hughes engineers were finding, had some 7,000 parts in all, including the nuts and bolts. To build just one took eight man-weeks and hundreds of thousands of dollars. IGBTs, at least, were a step in the right direction.

Cocconi would have used IGBTs on the show car if they'd been available. But now he was wedded to MOSFETs. He told the Hughes engineers that MOSFETs could be improved, and not to go with IGBTs; it bothered him intensely to imagine a bunch of aerospace engineers messing up his elegant creation. The engineers, after comparing MOSFETs to IGBTs, disagreed. MOSFETs would never be as reliable as IGBTs. So King's team went with MOSFETs for the first batch of fifty inverters. Without telling Cocconi, they started a separate group to make inverters with IGBTs.

Switches were an inverter's heart, but a brain was needed, too, because switches couldn't think for themselves. They needed a controller—a computer, really, with commands imbedded in its memory circuits to open and close the switches thousands of times a second—to orchestrate the flow of electricity back and forth. Cocconi had a controller, built right into the attaché case that held the inverter. But its electronics were analog, rather than digital. The drawback to analog's variability was that its circuits tended to drift, and its signals to wander, necessitating frequent adjustments; the ones and zeros of digital circuits, once set, remained set. As far as the Hughes engineers were concerned, it was time to bring the controller into the digital age.

As the engineers made their suggestions, Cocconi began to simmer. He had assumed *he* would design the production inverter, and that the Hughes team would simply carry out his vision. Now he realized the Hughes engineers had their own ideas and were going to pursue them whether he liked it or not. Perhaps, not coincidentally, his opinion of their skills grew darker. Often, he said later, he was appalled by the level of incompetence he found at Hughes, especially among the assemblers.

Cocconi didn't explode at King, or stalk off in a huff. He just stopped coming around, and when King left messages, Cocconi somehow failed to call back.

One day that September, Baker flew to Culver City to check in on Hughes's inverter team. The first replicas were coming together slowly. Still, Baker was pleased—until he met with Harry King's boss, a tall, decorous Georgian named Freeman Nelson.

Nelson told Baker he hadn't minded having a few of his radar systems engineers detached to do the Cocconi replicas. It was a short job that would bring Hughes $3 million, and if it helped show Hughes was useful to its new parent, all the better. But Nelson wanted no part of the production inverter. If GM asked him to do it, he would decline. If forced, he would do whatever he could to minimize his team's involvement.

Baker was stunned. The inverter was already proving so complex that, privately, he felt only Hughes could see it through. Why would Nelson want to turn down the work?

"GM politics," Nelson said bluntly.

In the months after its purchase of Hughes in 1985, Nelson related, GM had been embarrassed enough by the scornful reactions to demand that every division of Hughes do something to show how useful it could be to its new parent. Nelson, as head of radar systems, had decided to adapt a head-up display, of the sort devised to help fighter pilots by projecting dashboard information on the cockpit windshield electronically so they could avoid looking down and risking a loss of concentration. When Nelson's team presented it to great corporate acclaim, Delco Electronics stepped forward. Now that the head-up was judged a success, DE would manufacture it. DE, after all, did all the electronics for GM cars. That was its charter.

So Hughes was expected to design new products for GM, then meekly hand them over to DE? What incentive was there in that? "We're both relatives in the GM family," Nelson told Baker of Hughes and DE. "But DE is a relative by blood. We're just a relative by marriage."

There was, to be sure, some posturing on Nelson's part. Hughes's fondest hope was to be "systems responsible" for the whole propulsion system: to build the inverter, then put it together with the batteries and motor and ship the works off to some GM factory in California where the cars could be assembled. Neither Baker nor anyone else at GM took that plan seriously. The point was to get Hughes into GM's car business, not set it up as an EV manufacturer on its own. Stubbornly, he kept on until the older man seemed to relent.

"I'll do it under one condition," Nelson said at last.

"What?"

"If I have your guarantee that if we are competitive, we will not lose this later by reason of turf."

Baker thought hard for a moment. Hadn't Reuss and Runkle told him to be a strong program manager? Wasn't this exactly what they meant? "Okay," Baker said. "I'll give you my word. Do you want it in writing?"

"No," Nelson said. "We'll just shake on it. Your word is good enough."

Despite Baker's assurances, suspicions grew on all sides. Many at Hughes were sure DE would steal the inverter as soon as Impact went into production, and that Remy would do whatever it could to make Hughes look bad so it could do the inverter itself. The whispers had already begun: that Hughes only understood high-cost, low-volume production, that it wouldn't have a clue as to how to make parts competitively for a consumer car, let alone one as challenging as the Impact. DE's engineers, meanwhile, worried that Hughes—DE's boss, in effect—would seek power switches and controllers from outside suppliers and freeze DE out altogether. As for Wylam over at Delco Remy, he suspected Hughes's talk of being "systems responsible" for the powertrain was merely a prelude to freezing Remy out, too, by using batteries and motors from some outside supplier.

The two Delcos were, in a sense, allies against Hughes. But their enmity for each other went back decades. In name and blood, they were corporate brothers, set 50 miles apart among the farms and dirt roads of central Indiana. But as with many siblings, some of that blood was bad. Delco Remy dated from the early days of automobiles: Frank and Perry Remy, who had a car parts shop in Anderson, had joined forces in 1916 with Charles "Boss" Kettering, whose Dayton Engineering Laboratories were called Delco. Soon after GM bought both in 1920, Kettering's lab was moved to Detroit and the Remy operation began making batteries and motors for all GM cars. Remy then made some of the first car radios, but to the enduring indignation of its engineers, was not allowed to keep them. Instead, GM saw fit in 1936 to create Delco Radio as a separate enterprise. From that hybrid had grown Delco Electronics.

In the late seventies the copper spinners of Delco Remy, as motor winders were deprecatingly known, had been dealt a greater injustice. They had produced the first electronic microprocessor to be used in a car, one that controlled the firing of spark plugs to make engines run better. For Remy, a whole new world seemed to open up. But it was not to be Remy's world. Once again, GM took the business away and plunked it down in Kokomo. Before long, DE was making computers for controlled fuel injection that replaced carburetors, computers for transmissions, for heat and air-conditioning systems, and for dashboard diagnostics. Within two years, every GM car—7 million of them—had computer controllers, and DE made them all.

Remy hadn't merely lost a new market. It was losing its old ones. Mechanical parts—the breaker and points in ignition systems, for example—were being replaced by electronics, so DE did them. Remy made alternators, but the voltage regulators in them were electronic, so DE did them, too. Remy still made motors, but Asia made them more cheaply. Remy still made batteries, but without much profit. All the while, DE had grown.

More and more, Remy was looking like a company whose time had passed. Wylam knew that, and was resisting it fiercely. If he could position Remy to make EV powertrains at the start of this new automotive era, to outmaneuver Hughes *and* DE, the company would thrive once again.

If he didn't, it would almost certainly die.

On October 4, the wary factions—both Delcos and Hughes—met for a first major conclave at Culver City. Presiding was Jon Bereisa, Impact's new propulsion chief. For the nearly 100 engineers gathered in a large Hughes conference room, Bereisa *was* GM: big, bearish, and not at all bashful about throwing his weight around. By now, the princes knew that neither Hughes nor the Delcos would be "systems responsible" for the powertrain. That power would remain with GM itself—with the Impact platform and therefore, as far as the 100 engineers of the outlying fiefdoms were concerned, with Jon Bereisa.

"This may upset you," Bereisa told his fractious brood. "But I *am* going to be the boss. In fact, I'm going to be an absolute tyrant. I have all the goddamn money, and none of you has any recourse. I don't care where you go, whatever level; go to the chairman! You're going to get the same damn answer, and if you want to hear it from his lips I'll make the call for you.

"The second thing," Bereisa said, "is that you're not going to get around me technically. You're not going to wiffle up some conjured excuse that will be dressed up with all these red-colored lights and parsley, and sell me a bunch of rotten meat in the case. It just isn't going to work."

Alan Cocconi, there too with AeroVironment's Alec Brooks, listened to Bereisa with barely veiled disdain. He knew all about the propulsion chief. At Cal Tech, Cocconi had been selected as a GM scholar, one of a handful of engineering students around the country to be awarded full tuition for two years in return for working the summers in between at some GM facility in advanced development. His first summer he'd landed at a GM-owned Delco Electronics outpost in Santa Barbara, California. His boss, as it happened, was Bereisa.

Both brilliant, both proud and strong willed, the two men, a generation apart, circled each other that summer with wary respect but also resentment, testing each other at every turn. Perhaps inevitably, resentment won out. Cocconi came to view Bereisa as an ethical and corporate sellout, willing to work on DE aerospace projects for the military, squandering his talents for job security and a big paycheck. To Bereisa, who accommodated Cocconi by assigning him to non-military work, the younger man was the worst sort of maverick—a closed-form solution unto himself, as Bereisa put it, who would never be able to work with others for the common good, but instead spend his life lighting candles under bushel baskets, then running off to let others deal with the consequences. Under Bereisa's indignation one could hear a faint strain of self-pity and regret. The inverter needed enormous refinement; it might not be producible at all. But it remained one man's one-of-a-kind tour de force achievement, and Bereisa was not that man.

Cocconi had no desire to work for Bereisa again, but then, none of the young AeroVironment engineers felt much like staying on. Thrilled at first by GM's decision to produce their creation—their wildest dream come true— they had come to realize what that really meant. The car wasn't theirs anymore. It *belonged* to GM—after all, the company had paid for it—and when the young engineers finished teaching GM what they'd done, their roles would end. Had they possessed any corporate ambition, they might have asked Baker for jobs on the program, joined GM, and ridden the car into the showroom. None of them did.

Worse, they now saw what GM would do to their elegant exercise in energy efficiency. GM would make it a *car*. A luxury car, with all the extras: power windows, power mirrors, power locks. This was exactly what Impact wasn't about; it violated the whole concept. True, they admitted in the daylong meeting at Hughes, the inverter needed a little cleaning up. But then why not take the car right to production? If GM really cared about electric cars, it could get Impact to market within twenty-four months. Perhaps this whole effort was a sham.

Pete Savagian, a young member of Harry King's inverter team, wasn't the only Hughes engineer in the audience who felt the Impact show car itself was something of a sham. Not only was the range clearly exaggerated; the inverter's power level seemed overstated. Savagian told the group that based on making the first dozen replicates by hand of Cocconi's inverter, he and his team had had MOSFETs fail on them routinely, especially when subjected to warm weather. As for the "smart pole" clusters of MOSFETs, they were merely tricky mechanical assemblies with a couple of low-tech circuit boards soldered on. A *bad* assembly done six times, and a headache to build. How was Hughes supposed to get labor down to the three or four hours GM expected—and produce inverters for $2,000 each? Savagian had no idea.

For Cocconi, that autumn was a time of bitter reflection. As far as he was concerned, the car AeroVironment invented was dead, its best ideas bastardized and discarded by Hughes and GM. Dropping the MOSFETs in the inverter was the least of it. The AeroVironment team had painted the concept car silver to show its body should be aluminum. The engineer in charge of exterior panels at GM had informed them bluntly that aluminum would be too easily dented and too expensive; the body would be plastic panels. AeroVironment had air cooled the car's electronics because fans were simpler and lighter than liquid cooling, and wasn't simplicity the whole idea? But the GM team had said air cooling wouldn't be adequate. Most insulting, Hughes and GM had agreed not to adapt Cocconi's onboard charger.

Cocconi had designed a charger that used the inverter's circuitry—simplicity itself. That way, a driver could recharge merely by plugging a cord from the wall into a socket on the car. But Hughes's engineers had found that Cocconi's charger tripped the ground fault interruptors of nearby wall sockets. Also, the charger itself added mass, which cut into range.

The answer, it seemed to Hughes, was obvious: take the charger offboard. Now the engineers would have the freedom to design a system that was both safe by Underwriters Laboratory standards and could be coded and packaged more easily.

Cocconi was furious. He felt with time he could easily devise an onboard charger that avoided tripping the ground fault interruptors. Why squander the economy of a design that used existing parts? The reason, Cocconi felt, was that Hughes wanted to corner a new market in offboard chargers. Make people buy something they don't need and charge a lot of money for it, he scoffed. Capitalism at work.

One day in January, Cocconi walked into Alec Brooks's office at AeroVironment and said he was quitting. He'd been paid well enough that he didn't have to worry about money for a while, and he wanted to clear his mind. He filled a backpack with a few essentials, got on his racing bike, and with no idea of what his next job would be, rode out into the California desert.

A Nemesis
Known as CARB

))))

Lines were being drawn, turf established, power defined. Yet even as the factions vied, their world was being affected for better or worse by a force beyond their control.

In a brown-brick building in Sacramento, not far from California's domed statehouse and gardens, the ten members of a bland-sounding government agency called the California Air Resources Board concluded two days of hearings in September 1990 by issuing a thick packet of tedious decrees about future car emissions standards, filled with dry statistics and jargon, that contained one absolutely radical page.

CARB, as the agency was widely known, ruled that in 1998, each of the seven major carmakers—GM, Ford, and Chrysler in the U.S., Honda, Toyota, Nissan, and Mazda in Japan—would make 2 percent of its fleet emission free. In 2001, the bar would raise to 5 percent, then to 10 percent in 2003.* The carmakers could do this any way they pleased, though, as the regulators noted, only one way seemed feasible so soon: electric vehicles. The regulators knew EVs could be done, they added blithely, because GM had said as much.

Sam Leonard had been expecting that.

Leonard was Mr. Emissions at GM. He was the one who went off to do battle with the Environmental Protection Agency in Washington, or CARB in Sacramento, armed with statistics showing the advances GM's engineers might hope to make in the next few years and what was beyond their reach.

---

* In 2003, smaller carmakers such as Volkswagen, BMW, and Mitsubishi would be forced to offer emission-free cars as well.

Inevitably, he testified that GM could do less than the regulators hoped, then fed his numbers to auto lobbyists and lawyers who might abet his campaign of persuasion. Inevitably, the regulations were passed. The game, as he put it, was not to win; Leonard never won. The game was to forestall, to buy the time GM needed to develop technology to meet the next regs and keep factories operating in the meanwhile.

Until now.

That Leonard should appear before CARB this time and meekly endorse what would soon be known simply as The Mandate was not, in truth, a sign of new faith on his part in the efficacy of environmental regulation. As a college student in the seventies, Leonard had been influenced for life by *Atlas Shrugged*, the massive Ayn Rand novel whose protagonist invents a pollution-free automotive engine but refuses to give it to a society so constricted by government regulations; instead, he forms his own utopian, regulation-free community in the mountains where individuals such as he can thrive. A bit of Ayn Rand served Leonard well in his job as director of environmental activities for GM. He didn't just fight regulation because it was his job. He *believed*.

Leonard endorsed the mandate because he had no choice: with his own company saying EVs could be done, he could hardly say they couldn't. He endorsed it cheerfully because CARB had made two concessions in return. For the first time, cleaner gas would be mandated along with cleaner cars, which only made sense: put garbage in, as Leonard liked to say, and garbage came out. Privately, Leonard also felt this would keep other states from following California's lead. As important, CARB would hold a biennial technical review of EV progress to see if EVs were evolving fast enough to justify keeping the mandate in place. Based on two decades of experience, Leonard thought the chances of EV R&D conforming to CARB's schedule were absolutely nill.

Behind his big, paper-strewn desk, Leonard looked the very embodiment of Detroit's seeming indifference toward the environment. Considerably overweight, he was also a heavy smoker, and as he rattled off numbers, he filled his office with a blue cloud of his own emissions. But his story of what had really happened between regulators and Detroit from 1968 to the radical document of September 28, 1990, was instructive.

Leonard admitted the car companies had fought new clean-air standards time and again, claimed they couldn't meet them—emissions impossible—only to meet them after all. But the car companies hadn't met them, he would point out, not when the regulators ruled they must. The technology hadn't been there. And so deadlines had been missed, compromises reached, until the carmakers had inched into compliance—pretty much when they'd said they could. "Matter of fact," Leonard would say with grim satisfaction,

"Ninety-three was the first model year we ever built a model certified to seventy-five standards."

CARB, the dreaded acronym, had come into being in 1968, before the advent of any national standards. This was no case of California trend surfing: the state's air was worse than that of all forty-nine other states *combined*. The mountain ranges that backed California's shoreline kept warm air from being swept inland, creating stagnant air masses that grew ever fouler as cars and trucks issued pollutants into them. CARB was sanctioned by a Republican governor and made a watchdog, with broad powers to dictate standards to Detroit as well as to refineries and other in-state pollution sources.

So unhealthy was California's air that in 1970, when the Clean Air Act was passed with the goal of imposing national standards, CARB was allowed to remain as it was, a power unto itself, answerable to no one but the governor, who appointed its members and could, if provoked, replace them. Leonard understood the need for CARB. But over time, he felt, the watchdog had grown into a bear.

Take hydrocarbons, Leonard suggested. Along with nitrogen oxides, hydrocarbons were the main ingredients of smog. The first gains had been the easiest to obtain, the cheapest, and the most dramatic. An uncontrolled car in 1960 spewed about 18 grams per mile of hydrocarbons. Of that, 4 grams came from evaporation of fuel sitting in the tank and being fed through the carburetor to the engine, 4 from the engine itself, and 10 from the tailpipe. Thirty years later, a host of innovations from fuel injection to catalytic converters had reduced hydrocarbons to less than half a gram. Half of *one* gram. Each innovation had been harder to achieve, and more expensive, adding more than $1,000 in all to the retail cost of a new car. Yet CARB wanted hydrocarbons down from .50 to .062 gram per mile. That was the goal behind its hearings of September 1990. And the story with nitrogen oxide — and, for that matter, carbon monoxide — was about the same.

The further cuts to be phased in over the next fifteen years were so tiny, felt Leonard, that they would make virtually no difference to California air quality. What was more, they were utopian: some vehicles would always malfunction, so that anything below .15, say, would be impossible to achieve.

The fact was, Leonard argued, that cars were now incredibly clean. So why did CARB keep making more demands? Because Detroit was the easiest target. All CARB had to do was point a finger at the big bad car business and declare it do the now nearly impossible task of squeezing out those infinitesimal improvements at costs that couldn't be passed on to car buyers. Politically, it was always popular; economically, it passed the buck. But you could take all the cars of the last five years out of California, as Leonard liked to put it, and still have a growing pollution problem. Because CARB wouldn't take on the real emissions culprits of the nineties.

Leonard ticked them off one by one. The oil refineries. The fossil-fuel plants. The old "clunker" cars that provided as much as 80 percent of all auto emissions but which the state refused to subject to stricter inspection tests because that was politically unpalatable. For that matter, why not put a huge tax on gasoline and use the money to discourage long trips, encourage car pooling, and fund mass transportation and other air quality control measures? On that, Leonard and die-hard environmentalists came full circle and met. But voters would rebel, and in the meantime California, along with the thirty other states that had federally unsuitable air quality, had to show continuing improvement or face the loss of hundreds of millions of dollars a year in federal highway funds. So CARB held hearings, Leonard testified, and the standards rose and rose.

Jan Sharpless conceded that Leonard had his points. But CARB's chairperson had to wonder what carmakers, left alone those last two decades, would have done on their own to improve the cleanliness of cars. Any change that didn't directly improve sales was a change to be resisted. Change was expensive. Change was hard. It stood to reason they would hate the agency that made them change, and say it went too far.

The carmakers had always complained that CARB, in California, had no sympathy for their business in Detroit. They observed that its ten members included an agriculturalist, a medical expert, county supervisors, but not one automotive engineer. That the chairperson who had more power over them than anyone else in America was a woman *may* not have added to their frustration. That she was tough and unyielding certainly did.

In newspaper pictures, Jananne Sharpless looked just as the carmakers thought she might: stern, with short, schoolmarmish hair. A tree hugger, no doubt. An environmental extremist. But this was far from the case. At forty-five, Sharpless was a Republican appointee who had grown up in Sacramento and worked her way up through local committees; only by chance had she come to work on environmental issues. Unmarried, active in her local Presbyterian church, she had chaired CARB for five years and, being a conscientious public servant with an appetite for the grind of government, plunged herself into the minutiae of long-term health studies, the numbing analyses of diesel fuel toxics. To her delight the dry reports had augured dramatic change.

Though carmakers might not believe it, Sharpless bore no animus toward Detroit. She had pushed her fellow CARB members to draft the mandate because she felt she had no choice. The state had missed CARB's deadlines on clean air; it had missed the less stringent federal deadlines as well and might, as Leonard observed, lose federal highway money as a result. A Republican governor was under more pressure to act than a Democrat would have been;

Democrats were assumed to be environmentally minded and got a free ride. So acute a problem was air quality in California that it allied a broad array of interests, including big business, which had had to take expensive measures to clean smokestacks and other industrial pollution sources and wanted to share the burden of compliance.

Sharpless had heard Leonard's panaceas before, and remained skeptical of them at best. Cash for clunkers sounded great—especially for the car companies, because it might move more new cars. But clunkers were either vintage cars whose owners wished to keep them, or truly dilapidated heaps whose owners were too poor to replace them with new models. Besides, the worst polluting cars were not always the oldest; sometimes they were newer but malfunctioning cars. Stricter—better yet, *centralized*—inspection and maintenance would certainly help, but every state in the union was up against local service stations that took in easy fees from the system as it was and had proved a feisty special interest; soon a few northeast states would try a centralized system and learn just how unpopular it could be among gas station owners and customers alike. A gas tax? Politically, it was even less possible to push through, and anyway it wouldn't improve auto emissions. Mass transportation? Fine, if anyone wanted to use it: as of 1990, only 4 percent of American commuters did, and that number was dwindling in all but the most concentrated urban areas where driving and parking were out of the question.

As for the gains that might be won by the mandate, Leonard was flat wrong, Sharpless felt, to speak so dismissively of them. This was a case where a technology fix, as the jargon had it, might not only be easier than a social fix, but more effective.

For all the improvements in hydrocarbons, for example, California still had more of them than any other urban area in America, and vehicles still produced about half of them, along with much of smog's nitrogen oxide, as well as carbon monoxide. Cleaner cars had alleviated some of the smog in the L.A. basin, but soon it would worsen again as the state's population grew from 29 million in 1990 to a projected 40 million in 2005. Already the number of cars in the state was far greater than the number of people and growing far faster than the population rate: in little more than a decade, the 74 million cars registered in California in 1974 had more than *doubled*. Surreally, the California Energy Commission estimated that to accommodate the growing number of cars, by the year 2010 the state would have to expand its freeways by twenty to forty lanes *each*. Without such measures, the average freeway speed in California would drop, it was estimated, to 11 miles per hour, with nearly 50 percent of all automotive travel a snarl of bumper-to-bumper traffic. The lower the speeds the more polluting even clean cars would become as their engines' efficiency decreased. Even the most minute emissions from that many more vehicles, using that much more gas, threatened the state's very survival.

California's paucity of mass transportation was certainly one reason for the thickening traffic. But other factors were at play. Rising real estate costs forced workers to live ever farther from their jobs so that they drove 65 percent more miles than they had twenty years before. Two-income families generally needed two cars; the sharp decline of nuclear families meant more people living alone, each with his or her car. Gas was plentiful and cheap—so much so that Americans were falling in love with Jeeps and other so-called sport utility vehicles that consumed half again as much gas as ordinary cars. For all these reasons, and for the traffic that resulted, the state simply had to adopt higher emissions standards. And higher standards *would* help.

Electric vehicles had no smog-forming tailpipe emissions, so they defined the highest standards yet imaginable. But there were other reasons Sharpless and her board had called for them. One was that gas cars, as clean as they might become, would always emit carbon dioxide.

In modest amounts, of course, carbon dioxide helped sustain the planet. But too much carbon dioxide blocked long-wave sunlight as it radiated back from earth into the atmosphere and, by most scientists' reckoning, exacerbated this greenhouse effect enough to cause global warming. A 1990 study would conclude that as much as 96 percent of excess greenhouse gases were carbon dioxide, and that to avoid a planet-threatening increase in temperature as much as 80 percent of man-made carbon dioxide would have to be eliminated. Cars in America, it was reckoned, contributed 25 percent of the country's man-made carbon dioxide: it was an unavoidable chemical byproduct created when fossil fuels were burned. Greenhouse warming as a concept still had its skeptics, but why ignore the prospect when steps might be taken to avoid it?

CARB's job was to make the air cleaner. But that fall the escalating Gulf War offered a graphic example of the other great benefit electric vehicles might provide—one the regulators could hardly ignore.

By 1990, America's cars, trucks, and buses required roughly 8 million barrels of oil a day, about half of the country's overall consumption. In the last decade, transportation's share had increased even as other major shares—buildings, industry, power plants—declined. Oil had come to account, indeed, for nearly half of America's $110 billion trade deficit. Yet the federal government continued to subsidize its producers with tax breaks and to refrain from imposing taxes that might encourage and finance mass transportation and other social benefits—the sort of taxes that brought the pump price of gasoline in Europe to four dollars or more a gallon. Tens of billions of dollars more went yearly to maintain U.S. military strength in the Mideast and guarantee the unrestricted flow of oil. Major oil spills, of course, required costly cleanups as well, never mind the environmental costs.

Oil was expensive in subtle ways and increasingly less plentiful as well. Oil industry lobbyists liked to suggest that vast new reserves lay under northern Russia and Alaska, among other places. Even if those existed, the lobbyists themselves estimated that the world's reserves would last at least forty more years at current consumption levels; they offered this figure as reassurance. But the world's population was due to grow from 8 to 12 billion by 2010, and Third World countries such as China and India would be likely in that time to trade in some of their rickshaws and bicycles for cars, leading to increased demands, the prospect of shortages, and the inevitable conflicts that shortages would bring.

For all these reasons, the regulators asked: wouldn't electric vehicles help?

As a result of its two-day review, CARB proposed a schedule of escalating emissions standards—and proliferating acronyms. In the 1994 model year, 10 percent of gas cars sold in California would have to be TLEVs—transitional low emission vehicles—much cleaner than the rest. By 1997, 25 percent of cars sold would be LEVs—cleaner still—while 2 percent would be ULEVs (ultra low emission vehicles), virtually emission free. Then would come the radical demand of 2 percent emission-free cars in 1998.

It was worth pointing out, and Leonard would be only one of legions of frustrated auto lobbyists to do so, that with its EV mandate CARB was departing in the most remarkable way from its own history and, for that matter, the history of American public policy. Past CARB edicts had applied to all cars at once: a buyer couldn't choose between a car that had a catalytic converter and one that didn't. Much as carmarkers would groan and motorheads mourn the passing of an era, all new cars were still equally burdened. Requiring just 2 percent of all cars to be ZEVs in 1998 was an acknowledgment of how new and uncertain the technology was. But the phase-in approach meant that for the first time consumers would be able to choose between cleaner cars with new technology that almost certainly carried a premium, and conventional cars that might emit a few invisible pollutants but also cost less. Detroit would come to call it a *sales* mandate. CARB could mandate the production of electric vehicles. It couldn't require anyone to *buy* them.

There was no point, Leonard figured, in telling CARB that a sales mandate might bring huge losses to the carmakers and also turn people against electrics if the cars weren't good enough yet. Or that mandating electrics to appear so soon would have the perverse effect of forcing carmakers to lock in technology that wasn't effective yet, thus keeping them from following a more natural learning curve. Or that by insisting on *zero* emissions, they were blocking development of hybrids that seemed the more logical next step from gas cars, with far greater range than electrics and *almost* no emissions. Why should they listen to any of this when they'd heard Roger Smith say GM would build the car? So with a sigh, Leonard had bowed to the inevitable.

Much later, Robert Stempel would bridle at the suggestion that the mandate had been, on balance, a bold and wise move. The mandate, he would say, was a mistake, brought on by GM's error in going public with the Impact. But then he would laugh. "If there was one good thing about Roger's announcement," he would say, "the date is on the calendar. *We did it before.* And CARB didn't know shit about electric vehicles."

Framing the Picture

))))

The mandate would come to matter—a lot—to Baker and his team. At the time, it seemed to mean almost nothing. Perhaps it would silence critics within the corporation—legislation had a way of doing that—but Baker had all the support he needed from GM's new chairman and president. Anyway, the mandate's timetable would, he hoped, be irrelevant to him: by the schedule he was drafting, the first production Impacts would be out by September 1993. If anything, the mandate might work against him by forcing six other carmakers to play the EV game, too. But then, GM held a strong lead.

Baker's greater concern was more immediate. He'd rounded out his senior staff: seven men with very different skills from different corners of the company. But the chiefs had no blueprint for the car they hoped to build. They had a show car, but its shortcomings were such that it would have to be thoroughly recast. They had to start by establishing the car's broadest goals: what it would do, what it cost, what it would be. Those goals, in turn, could best be set by understanding the car's market.

That was a problem.

For almost a century, new cars had evolved from old cars, and old cars had markets that could be defined in comforting ways. Impact had no history. It had no market. It was defined, at this point, by its seeming limitation as a warm-weather car—more particularly, given the mandate's distant deadline, as a California car.

One day that fall, the chiefs flew out to Los Angeles to soak up what they could of California ethos. For most, L.A. was a strange, forbidding place, as different from the suburbs of Detroit as Pluto. As an experiment, they commuted in heavy traffic with local residents. Jim Ellis accompanied a young mother who took the family's secondhand car to work while her husband used the Jeep. On weekends, the couple used the Jeep for getaway trips. An electric car wouldn't replace their Jeep, but it would surely cost more than the second car they now drove. Who, Ellis wondered, would buy an Impact?

The next day the chiefs went on a scavenger hunt, driving from one end of L.A. to another to gather totemic items: sand from Venice; a classic rock album by the Doors; a signed business card from a salesman at Longo Toyota, the country's top dealership; a cutting of grass from the Coliseum. One obvious conclusion was that driving short distances in L.A. could take a long time. Another was that drivers trapped in that traffic wanted all the amenities they could buy. Alec Brooks and Alan Cocconi might disdain air-conditioning and a CD player, but they were a lonely minority.

A marketing survey was ordered up, and it helped, but not, Baker thought, very much. Based on their answers, participants were put in five groups, from the "early adopters" willing to pay any price to have the first electric cars on their blocks, to those unbudgingly committed to gas cars. Most participants fell in between. Curious about electrics, willing or even eager to do their bit for cleaner air, they tended to balk at the prospect of an electric two-door sports car, and to blanch when told an Impact might cost more than a comparable gas car. How much more, they wanted to know? When the hypothetical premium rose to more than $5,000, all but the richest "early adopters" fell away.

So uncertain was the market that Baker wondered if the car's goals might better be set by getting the chiefs to look within, rather than without. They had to reinvent a car on which every part would be perfectly integrated with every other part, expressing a common vision of mass, cost, and utility. To do that they should know what they stood for as engineers and human beings and what values they shared. Perhaps then they could instill a *culture* from which the car might issue up as a projection of their collective minds. What they needed, Baker decided, was that cure-all exercise of modern management, a rustic retreat.

One day in early October the chiefs drove an hour north to an estate called Copely Hill. Beyond the living room's big picture windows, deer grazed in a meadow by a pond. Within, flames crackled in the big stone fireplace. The chiefs convened around a big dining-room table. One member talked about a failed marriage, another about his troubled children. This was the so-called Johari Window: opening the window, taking a risk. It was all very un-GM, but then, so was the program.

"Mindscaping" came next. With an artist brought in to list their thoughts in different-colored inks on an easel-sized pad, the chiefs began a colloquy on values and goals, starting with their own and moving on to how those might define the program. Family got high marks, but so did winning. To a man, the chiefs had joined GM because they'd seen it as the acme of the automotive world. To a man, they were angry at the company it had become. The GM they worked for now deserved its sobriquet of Generally Mediocre. As it had declined through the seventies and eighties they had felt the worth of their careers decline with it. They had joined this program not just because Impact was electric, but because GM, for the first time they could remember, was taking the technological lead. It wasn't hard coming up with a cornerstone value for the program. They wanted to *win*.

The retreat produced walls of gaily colored charts and shared values, but amid the soul-baring, the volleyball, and the rounds of pool, a schism also appeared.

Ed Benson, the marketing chief, was the eldest of his peers, and the earthiest. After years of prodding program managers to take more account of customer desires before designing their cars, he'd cast off any pretense to corporate decorum and took a grim pleasure in saying exactly what he felt. *You can't make the dog eat the dog food*, he liked to say. *You have to give the dog the food he likes.*

Baker had said Impact would be different. And yes, it did break some new ground to put all the chiefs in this circle at the start, getting touchy-feely. But what in God's name did Baker think he was doing making a two-door sports car?

As the others listened in awkward silence, Benson reminded them that in recent memory GM had come out with three two-door sports cars: Allante, Fiero, and Reatta. All had failed. True, the Fiero had been plagued by a poorly designed engine that tended to cause fires, while the Reatta had been priced at well over $30,000—more than most European sports cars. Perhaps Impact could be made to sell for less, but it surely wouldn't compete with, say, the little Mazda Miata.

Look, Benson said, at GM's California market. Only four models accounted for more than 2 percent of the roughly 280,000 cars sold each year in the state. Three of them sold for under $20,000 each—far less than any first-time electric vehicle would cost. In fact, the only GM two-seater priced more than $20,000 was the Corvette, which in the last year had accounted for about 1 percent of the California market. Corvette had the recognition of a thirty-year-old classic. Also, like all gas cars, it drove a few hundred miles on a three-minute fill up. How could Baker hope to outsell Corvette with a limited-range electric sports car, let alone sell the 5,600 units it would have to put out in 1998 to meet the 2 percent mandate? Meanwhile, Benson pointed out, the big success story of the last decade was the minivan. Clearly, the market wanted an all-purpose family car. Shouldn't the chiefs at least consider making Impact a four-door sedan?

Tensely, Baker repeated the wisdom of Reuss and Runkle. The Impact production car had to carry through the achievements of the show car: brilliant acceleration, speed, and, as he put it, three-digit range. Stretching the Impact to accommodate a backseat would mean adding considerable mass to the car. It would cut the acceleration and speed; it might cut the range in half. The whole promise would be lost—and so would any hope of a market, whatever that market might be.

To Benson, this wasn't a marketing problem. It was a technology problem. The technology wasn't ready to meet the market's needs at a price the market would pay. Electrics were still in a gestation period. Fax machines, VCRs, computers—all had gone through that same period before maturing enough to meet their markets. Fax machines had been around in World War II. But for decades after that, they remained too expensive; and of course, a fax machine was only useful if the recipient of the fax had one, too. Finally, in the eighties, the cost had come down as the technology improved; the market barrier had been met and overcome, like a tide rising over a sea wall.

The electric vehicle, like the fax machine, required that sort of technology leap. It also required a vast infrastructure of charging stations—in homes, in office garages, on street corners. But as with the fax, none of that infrastructure would come to pass until the product met the needs of the market. Listen to the market, Benson urged, then design accordingly. And if the technology wasn't up to the job, wait until it was. Meanwhile, a two-door was doomed to fail.

"We're charged with the responsibility of bringing this car to market," Baker replied. "*Your* job is to teach the market it doesn't need a four-door car."

In one sense, Baker was right. Surveys had shown that Americans took nearly all their car trips alone, that the daily commute to and from work consumed most of their driving miles, that of the remaining miles driven, most were undertaken with one other passenger, and that their average daily range was under 50 miles. But marketing, as Benson knew, wasn't about reality. Most people *perceived* that a two-door, two-seat car was impractical, and if they could buy a four-door sedan for the same price—or less—they would.

On the third and final evening at Copely Hill, the chiefs were joined by their spouses for a dinner preceded by a summing-up session. When the wives had arranged themselves around the fire, each chief stood up in turn to explain his role on the platform and what he was committed to achieve. Like the exercises that had preceded it, this was, to say the least, untypical for GM. Maggie Williams, a one-time antiwar activist whose midlife marriage to John had not disabused her of a certain skepticism about corporate culture, found herself moved by the ceremony. Some of the chiefs, she sensed, lived still within such outdated marriage roles that they never spoke of work at home. The wives were delighted, if a bit taken aback, to be included, even if the underlying message was that they shouldn't expect to see their husbands home at regular hours for the next two or three years. It was clear, too, that the men *had* gotten to know each other better, and that they shared a quiet but palpable excitement about the program. No one had ever given them such an opportunity before. No one likely would again. For each chief, the right balance of luck and circumstance had brought him to this place: to be part of a team taking on the electric car for real.

After the vows, the chiefs asked their wives what *they* thought the car should include. When it came her turn, Maggie smiled brightly. "I really like it," she told the group. "But I think it should be a four-door."

Benson beamed. The other chiefs looked embarrassed. In a moment, the talk moved on.

By late fall, Baker and his chiefs had drawn a rough portrait of what they wanted the real Impact to be and do. The numbers and parameters that defined the portrait were called vehicle technical specifications, or VTSs. In the car business, as in the military, every term was made as terse and flat as possible—in part, perhaps, to make daunting challenges seem mundane. The engineers talked briskly of such VTSs as having Impact accelerate from 0–60 miles per hour in eight seconds; of having it carry no more than 1,000 pounds of batteries; of having the batteries provide no less than 100 miles of range, yet of adding all the comforts and durability of a real—much heavier—car. They also agreed the car should have one large motor instead of the two smaller ones that AeroVironment had devised. Smaller motors were easier to manage, but each required its own set of gears. More to the point, a motor on each front wheel was fine for a one-of-a-kind concept car, but what if one stalled on a production car? The car might spin out of control.

As yet, to be sure, the engineers had no idea yet how to *do* any of this. They just hoped by passing down the VTSs to teams of engineers, the VTSs might be made real. Wasn't that what systems engineering was about?

Over the succeeding months, the acronyms would proliferate like Michigan mushrooms, so that the acronym illiterate might well feel the engineers were speaking a foreign language. "What's your VTS on the IP?" an engineer might ask. "Does that include HFC, and the ICU? And does DE have that on the RASI?"

"It's the PCM that worries me," another might say. "The BPM is a snap. But of course, none of this is even CAD-cammed yet, much less DFA. So forget getting out of CI and into CA before next year, let alone FA. Maybe a BLT."

Translation: the first engineer was asking about vehicle technical specs on the instrument panel, and if they included human factors criteria, as well as the instrumentation control unit. Did Delco Electronics have that job on the overall Responsibility and Approval and Support Information chart?

The second engineer was worrying about the propulsion control module—the computer heart of the inverter—more than the battery pack module that worked as a computer to monitor the flow of current in and out of the batteries. But none of it was yet worked up to the computer-aided design stage, let alone run by the manufacturing engineers who would have their say before the part was design-ready for assembly. And until all the parts were DFA, the program would never graduate from concept initiation—the first of GM's many production stages in four-phase—into concept approval, let alone final approval. The second engineer was also suggesting he might have a bacon-lettuce-and-tomato sandwich for lunch.

Among the early arrivals drawing up their VTSs, two camps were forming: the product guys, restless to start on the work of designing parts, and the process guys, more deliberate, intent on defining not only the system but the sensibility, both of the car and of the program. Paul Huzzard, the chief body engineer, was the most outspoken of the product guys. That set him squarely against Jim Ellis.

Though his nearly four decades at GM might have steeped him in the worst of the old over-the-wall customs, Huzzard had no quarrel with the new approach of systems engineering. He just wanted to get to work *doing* that, and move on to hardware as soon as he could—hell, the car was supposed to be put into production in less than three years. But here was Ellis with his management mumbo-jumbo. Huzzard had a tendency, as he put it, to get *really pissed off.* And being slowed down by process talk got to him every time. "If you want to sit down and talk about the philosophy of building cars, or organizational structures," Huzzard would say evenly, "that probably has a tendency to bore me."

While Ellis held meetings to coax ideas from his growing band of engineers and inch toward consensus, Huzzard told his own teams to get to work. Of the three teams—one to do the outside of the car, one the passenger compartment, and one the skeleton, or structure—the last, incredibly, had nearly finished defining its goals. The notion of an aluminum frame might still be radical at GM, but to Tom Lobkovich, the matter was settled.

As early as 1972, GM had toyed with an aluminum-frame Corvette. In the mid-eighties it had turned out aluminum concept versions of each year's Fiero. But the weight saved was of little consequence with gasoline so plentiful, and besides, aluminum was tricky stuff. It yielded more than steel did when it took a rivet, and then bounced back; at its edges, it had a tendency to tear more easily than steel. If these traits could be predicted and accounted for with absolute exactness, an aluminum frame would be an enormous boon for an electric car; but the Impact's chiefs thought this might prove their greatest design challenge, more even than the propulsion system. Lobkovich had some ideas about that.

One was about the rivets. If they tended to corrupt the aluminum and add weight, Lobkovich thought, he would use fewer of them. Instead, he would use a new kind of adhesive invented by Alcan, so adhesive that it made Crazy Glue look like Elmer's. A car frame's parts held together by glue? *That* was radical.

So too were the extrusions. Steel car frames were made of parts created by stamping dies. You fed a piece of sheet metal into a die, or press, in the shape you wanted the part to be. The die came together, formed the part, you took it out, had it trimmed by another set of dies, then sent the parts to your assembly plant to be spot-welded together. With aluminum, you could make extrusions. You could heat a log-like chunk of the stuff, get it soft and pliable—more so than steel—then push it down a Play-Doh-like mold to make simple, light forms. A long hollow bar, say, or a flat, L-shaped hinge. There were limitations, to be sure. With a stamping die, you could make any shape you wished. Extrusions could only be formed in very basic shapes. But an extruded aluminum part was far lighter than its steel counterpart. It also came in at a fraction of the cost.

On a standard GM car program Lobkovich would have waited until all the other parts were designed, then struggled to stick a frame amid them: an exercise in accommodation. On the Impact, the reverse happened. Because the team had to see if aluminum would work, but also because Lobkovich knew exactly what he wanted and had an irksome way of being so briskly organized, so clear, and so adamant, like a perfectly drilled field commander, he pushed his structure straight through to full design on a 3–D scale plastic model while the process guys were still talking about *vision.*

That was in December. The next month, when the program started ramping up in earnest, the later arrivals would discover, to their shock, that they couldn't do as they wished and have structure catch up later on. They had to do the catching up, and fit their parts within Lobkovich's design. It was irritating, and yet also, in an odd way, something of a relief.

How much time the chiefs should spend sandboxing stirred endless debate in the corridors. As frustrated as the product guys were, it was hard to blame the process guys for wanting a map before plunging into unknown territory. Later, ironically, the most often heard criticism of Baker would be that he ramped up too soon: better to have had the chiefs design the whole car themselves, then bring on the hordes. But who could say for sure? It was all so new.

One process Baker had to face immediately was the drawing up of a business plan. With that, the program would get its first big chunk of money.

The fall of 1990 was not, as it happened, a propitious time to be asking the company for several hundred million dollars to make a new kind of car. American car sales had plummeted—the inevitable reaction to uncertain times, particularly ones involving Middle East oil and power-mad dictators with Scud missiles. Now the results of GM's decade of expansion under Roger Smith—more large-volume factories with too many union workers turning out mediocre cars that found too few buyers—began to pull the corporation down like so much lead weight.

Tragically, GM's new chairman acted as if the next boom was just around the corner, signing the most costly labor contract in the company's history, one that committed GM to a reserve fund of $3.35 billion to grant laid-off workers three years' pay. In return, the unions gave Stempel the freedom to close plants as needed, a modest concession if workers were to be paid anyway. In November, Stempel did announce that up to nine of GM's thirty-one North American assembly plants would close in response to the slackening market, and that GM would take a $2.1 billion charge against earnings to cover the losses. But this was not a game GM could play for long.

Against this somber backdrop, Baker tried to draw up a plan with Pat Campbell, his young finance chief. It was an exercise in the absurd. None of the car's parts was designed as yet. Many, if not most, would require new technology. How could he put a price on an inverter that had never been produced? And cost, after all, was a function of market. The bigger the market, the more cars that could be made, the better the economies of scale that could be achieved. But who knew how many people would buy this car? The potential customer of an Impact at one price might not be at another; at one level of range and charging time, but not at the one below. With every one of those fluctuations costs would fluctuate too. All Baker and Pat Campbell could do was arbitrarily draw worst-case and best-case scenarios, and fill in best-guess numbers accordingly.

By Christmas, the plan was set. Baker projected, boldly if blindly, that cars would start being produced on March 27, 1993—not coincidentally on his birthday. That was just over twenty-four months away, less than half the time allotted to a standard, far less complex GM car program. In the time leading up to production the program would need about $12 million a month, or nearly $150 million a year, to pay its engineers and their development costs: about $300 million out of pocket before the first car rolled off the line. That was the *investment*. But investment was only one part of the cost. Another was *piece cost:* how much the parts for each car cost. The plan called for 20,000 cars to be produced during each of four years, at a cost to the company of roughly $16,500 per car, which meant a piece cost of about $330 million. A small last chunk, perhaps $20 million, would be the one-time cost of making factory tools for production.

The budget was actually quite reasonable, considering that a mere restyling of an existing gas car model could cost $1 billion, and that Saturn had spent upwards of $3 billion just to produce its first all-new model. But

Baker was also asking GM to make a commitment of at least $1.5 billion over half a dozen years on a car as yet unproven, with no definable market.

Bill Pine, a somewhat saturnine member of Campbell's finance team, liked to refer to what he called the pelican curve. On a chart, the extent to which a program's costs sunk it in the red was represented by a line that curved sharply down and then—one hoped—curved slowly back up again in the shape of a pelican's bill. With Impact, the curve didn't come back up for more than ten years. In fact, the sweet spot of ROI—return on investment—was too far out along the forward horizon to be seen at all.

The only hope of *ever* making money on electric cars, Baker acknowledged in his business plan, was with follow-ons: second and third generations. When a market was established and an infrastructure was built. When batteries were better. When prices had come down.

When the cow had jumped over the moon.

The Ramp-Up

))))

Curious to see how other carmakers were coping with the headaches of EVs, Baker and Jim Ellis flew to Hong Kong for EV-10, the fifth biennial gathering of engineers, scientists, policymakers, and scattered eccentrics who met each time in a different city to give talks and trade papers about electric vehicles. From a tiny, club-like circle of true believers the EV biennials had swelled to include scores of engineers from major carmakers. After GM's announcement of Impact and the California mandate the exhilarated EVers felt like futurists whose time had come.

For Baker, EV-10 was a heady experience. He and Ellis spoke to large, enthusiastic crowds. In the halls they were thronged by questioners. In the morning, they found dozens of business cards from prospective suppliers shoved under their doors. For the first time but not the last, the stolid midwesterners felt like Hollywood stars. But a bit like frauds, too. Who knew if Impact could really be done at all?

To their relief, neither Ford nor Chrysler seemed yet to have reacted to the mandate. Each had had small R&D programs in EVs for years, but nothing new appeared to be in the offing. Of the Europeans, BMW and Volvo were working on concept cars and might be more of a threat. They didn't sell enough cars in California to be subject to the mandate in its first years, but they might seize the chance to bring out a few dozen handbuilt EVs before any of the larger carmakers and earn the press hype and image boost of being first to market. Europeans were fervent enough about the environment to have green political parties and to be banning gasoline cars from historic city centers whose stone-carved buildings and sculpture were worn smooth by smog. But European cars were the most expensive in the world; only the very rich owned more than one. Even for them, parking was a nightmare. Until EVs could replace gasoline cars, their appeal seemed limited.

The Japanese were the ones to watch. Dominant in electronics, still capable of getting cars to market faster and more cheaply than any of the Big Three, the Japanese also had the guiding hand of their government's Ministry of International Trade and Industry. MITI, as it was known, could fund and orchestrate an R&D consortium of the four big Japanese carmakers—Honda, Toyota, Nissan, and Mazda. Unhindered by U.S. laws of fair play, it could also pick a favorite. The best that Baker and Ellis could determine from casual talks with Japanese engineers was that none appeared to have anything close to the AeroVironment show car. But they would in short order. After all, GM had proudly described the show car's technology in pretty fair detail before choosing to go to production. Not only did the press hype serve as a how-to manual, it also showed the Japanese exactly where GM was headed. None of the Japanese companies, for their part, had revealed a thing.

Which position, Baker wondered, was the better one, GM's or Japan's?

With the approval of Baker's plan in January 1991, scores of new members began spilling onto the platform, though exactly how many was a matter of interpretation. The elite troops, directly under the chiefs, grew to about 200 in Engineering South. But other outposts of the kingdom were hiring too, not only Hughes, Delco Remy, and Delco Electronics, but Harrison Radiator, which would devise a heat pump for both heating and air-conditioning, as well as a radiator to cool the inverter and drive motor, and Inland Fisher Guide, which would make the car's seats. In all, some 400 people would work, sooner or later, one way or another, to make Impact happen. That was still a modest number; the Saturn program, GM's most recent start-up, had a payroll of 2,300.

The engineers had a show car to study, and they had their vehicle technical specifications—VTSs. But the show car was of almost no use, and the VTSs were like big squares of drawing paper on which a mere frame had been drawn. Within the frame, the engineers had to draw their parts, define what the parts would be made of, how they would be made, how they would fit with other parts. The chiefs were waiting to see their rough sketches to be able to make the critical decisions that would define the car in more detail. Not until they did would the program start moving to production. Yet Baker's start of real production date—his SORP, as the acronym wielders had it—was little more than two years away.

The engineers knew their parts had to be light yet inexpensive. Unfortunately, parts tended to be one or the other. So the engineers began the cumbersome process of seeing what the market had to offer, calling suppliers, testing different materials, doing the math to span the range from one extreme to the other of weight, of cost, of functionality. Their one given was Lobkovich's structure. For Tom Ruster, among others, that only made the job harder.

Ruster was one of the handful of veterans, the 10 percent who'd seen a car through to production. Veterans tended to bridle at their green compatriots, especially as the younger ones began making suggestions the veterans knew would be wrong. But Ruster was a friendly guy with an open, midwestern face and rust-colored hair who appreciated the neophytes' enthusiasm. He just didn't know how to work around Lobkovich's structure.

Ruster's job was to design the instrument panel, along with much of the rest of what a driver would see and touch when he got in the car. He had known that the show car lacked air bags, that its windows didn't roll down, that its displays were very much those of a concept vehicle. He could fix all that. But Lobkovich's structure had called for the batteries to be set in a bulky tunnel down the middle. The so-called I-pack bisected the passenger compartment like some huge arm rest, so wide that the seats on either side would be impossibly scrunched, so high that a passenger in one seat would be unable to reach over to lock the opposite door. With a veteran's disgust, Ruster told the young structures leader that there was no way he could cope with *that*.

Lobkovich explained why he'd housed the pack that way, and how he really had no choice. Reluctantly, Ruster began rethinking all he'd learned in designing passenger compartments for high-volume production. Instead of placing seats and safety supports on top of the underlying structure, he could *use* the structure as part of his design. The steering column and the battery pack tunnel could help brace the car in a crash. Instead of having the guy from Harrison Radiator put heating and air-conditioning ducts wherever he saw fit, Ruster could work with him to optimize the scant space they had by running ducts and wiring along the top of the tunnel. Wherever possible, a part or system could do double duty, a side of one used as the side of another, the strength of one used as another's support. Only in this way, Ruster began to see, would all the systems be fitted into the car's small space.

Getting engineers to share the use of their parts and systems was a more radical notion than it might seem. Ruster had been on GM programs where everyone stayed, as he put it, in his own backyard, working furiously to outshine his neighbors. The every-man-for-himself approach produced heroes, but only at the expense of everybody else: a car with bright spots was a car that robbed its other components of efficiency. Only when the car was absolutely uniform could it rise in quality. But uniformity required trust and mutual support. The Impact program, to Ruster's surprise, had that.

Near Ruster sat a young arrival whose job was among the least glamorous on the project yet among the most important. Ben Pusheck hadn't *wanted* to work on brakes when he graduated from the University of Wisconsin and came to GM. With brakes, you only got noticed if you made a mistake. Then you really got noticed. But brakes were what he was offered, and brakes were what he took. The previous summer, curious about regen braking on solar cars, he'd worked as an observer on the first U.S. Sunrayce, a spinoff of the Australia race sponsored by GM, helping the student drivers who competed with handbuilt cars. One thing had led to another, and here he was: positioned, as it happened, to be part of a team making the boldest decision about brakes in the modern history of cars.

Regen, as AeroVironment had shown, was not only feasible for electric cars but fundamental to them. It was an advantage unavailable to gas cars—recouped mechanical energy could not, after all, be turned into gasoline—and Pusheck figured it could extend Impact's range by almost 20 percent. But regen could never be an EV's only brakes. They slowed a car; they couldn't stop it on a dime. Also, when the batteries were fully charged, the motor/generator could pass them no more current, so the braking effect was nil.

Early on, Pusheck and a fellow engineer, Loran Brooks, decided to use the regen for the front wheels, with hydraulic brakes as a backup. In the rear, to avoid the heavy cables and cylinders that additional hydraulic brakes would require, they would try electric brakes, operated by computers that would send electronic signals to a motor, which in turn applied shoe assemblies to the brake drums. Then somehow—they didn't know how—these different systems would be *balanced,* so that when a driver stepped on the brake pedal, they sent an electronic signal that instantly communicated not only how much braking was needed but how much each system would provide—in ever-changing ratios of braking need and car speed.

Electric brakes seemed a wonderfully elegant solution. They even seemed possible. They'd just never been done.

For Pusheck and Brooks, the job was made somewhat easier by a team of half a hundred brake engineers down at Delco Chassis, in Dayton, Ohio. Ruster and many of the others worked more on their own, in-house, passing ideas or sketches to designers like editors giving assignments to a newsroom of daily reporters. Between engineers and designers, however, a caste system existed.

Engineers had graduate degrees and were salaried employees, even executives, driving company cars, hoping to rise from seventh or eighth level to unclassified and thus earn stock options and bonuses. Contract designers were freelancers who often had little or no college experience and drew an hourly wage. Engineers were company men; the designers' only loyalty was to the contract house that hired them out. Year to year, they moved like bedouins from one car company to another, as often for an extra dollar an hour in pay as for the end of one program and the start of another.

The contract designers were an odd, brooding bunch who often made the engineers uncomfortable, though the engineers wouldn't have said so. Some still worked at drafting tables. Most used computers. The tube men, as they were called, worked together in one large room kept dark to ease the strain on their eyes. It was a startling and rather eerie sight to walk past them for the first time, to see their rows of weathered faces lit by the cathode light of their screens, the darkened room silent but for the desultory clicking of keys. They seemed to work at a languid pace, and to take frequent breaks on which nearly all went outside to smoke. A bit irked by their lassitude, Joe Mercurio, a young engineer in charge of the trunk lid and roof, took a class in computer design to learn what they did. Peering at a car part on the screen, with its razor-thin lines and calibrated shapes, soon made his eyes ache and his head hurt. After that, he stopped begrudging the tube men their breaks.

For Baker, the ramp-up remained incomplete without a factory. Until he knew where the car would be produced, along with the configurations of that space and the labor that came with it, he couldn't start systems engineering; he couldn't integrate manufacturing with design as he'd promised to do, not only to Reuss and Runkle but to Randy Schwarz, his manufacturing chief. GM had no shortage of vacant factories to choose from—more, it seemed, every day—but these were vast, high-volume operations, with long assembly lines that made no sense for Impact. Fortunately, GM's latest attempt at a low-volume, sporty two-seater had failed. The space, as a landlord might say of a dying tenant's apartment, was available.

Lansing, 90 miles northwest of Warren, was the town where Ransom E. Olds had gone into the automotive business, actually throwing the switch on a small assembly line before Henry Ford's more ambitious version captivated the world. Of the six GM factories that employed most of Lansing's workforce, the Reatta Craft Centre, formerly known as Plant 2, was the smallest.

A long, beige hulk of a building, old Plant 2 stood within a fenced compound, unprepossessing but, to the members of Local 1618, imbued with a noble past. In World War II, the union's workers had built 75- and 105-millimeter artillery shells there, and landing gear for B-17 bombers. For three decades afterward, it had been the country's preeminent forging foundry, where second- and even third-generation workers turned molten steel into rear axles, pinions, and hubs for GM motors. Forging was hard, sweaty work, and other GM unions steered clear of it. Plant 2, as a result, remained the exclusive domain of 1618, which enabled it to avoid the turbulence that could arise when two or more local unions fractured the ranks. Even through the 1960s and 1970s, as forging became outmoded by new processes of casting and injection molding, and the factory's workforce of 1,200 was pared by two-thirds, the union never struck. As much in gratitude as because a small factory was needed, GM in 1985 gave the seasoned survivors the new Buick Reatta.

The Reatta was meant to compete with such luxury foreign cars as BMW. By the time it reached its market, runaway costs had pushed its sticker price above that of its established rivals. Each year, its volume was cut, and more workers laid off. No cut was enough: in the first three months of 1991, only 400 Reattas would be sold. For the workers of 1618, then, Baker's visit on March 4 brought nothing less than an eleventh-hour reprieve.

To an assembled crowd of anxious workers, a factory manager began by announcing Reatta's official demise. The good news, he declared, was that even before the last Reatta was finished in early May, work would begin to get the plant ready for GM's first electric car. Baker, gaunt as a scarecrow now from his relentless diet, told the crowd he was committed to making GM the leader in the international EV business.

From the back of the room came a loud cry.

"What?" Baker said, disconcerted.

"We'll back you one hundred percent."

Baker beamed. "That's what I need."

Publicly, production plans were not disclosed. Privately, Baker promised Stan Pewoski, the union's shop steward, that the expected run of 20,000 Impacts a year, beginning in March 1993, would provide work for two shifts— seven cars an hour off the line—so that all 652 remaining members of Local 1618 could come back to work.

Just after the speech, Baker was told he had a call from downtown. Bob Schultz was on the line. Had Baker given the speech yet? Yes, Baker told him, he had; everyone was really up, really excited.

Schultz had some tough news. The damned Gulf War was kicking hell out of auto sales, as Baker knew. It wasn't anyone's fault, but cash was suddenly very, very tight, and everyone had to sacrifice. Yes, Baker said, of course.

"So we've got to reschedule Impact's capital, and engineering budget, to get the portfolio in order."

Schultz said the $170 million earmarked for actually building the car in its first year would have to be cut to $150 million. The separate $150 million kitty for engineering, or R&D, would have to be cut to $120 million. "If it means a year's delay," Schultz said, "we're prepared to do that."

Baker's heart sank. "Look," he said, "let me get back to you about the schedule. I don't want to push it back by more than six months."

Delaying the program seemed a good way to inflate, not cut, the program's cost. Baker had just leased a factory for $20 million a year. At the Tech Center, he was spending $12 million a month; a year's delay would mean an extra $150 million to get to production. But at GM, the finance guys saw things differently. When you had a lot of capital, they said, capital was cheap. When you had none, its cost was infinite. And if money had to be squeezed from Impact, better that it be squeezed in the R&D stage; in production, with all meters running, the cost would be far higher.

That May, GM announced its third quarterly loss in a row for a staggering total of $4 billion. Detroit was accustomed to boom-and-bust cycles, but this was unprecedented. To GM executives downtown, to analysts on Wall Street, to shareholders, the realization dawned that this could not go on. Sooner or later, at this rate GM would go broke.

At this rate, too, the longer Baker delayed the Impact program, the less likely it was to be approved at all.

Filling in the Picture

))))

Architecture was a reassuring word for what Baker's engineers needed to do now, so they used it a lot. Here was each in his cubicle, defining his parts of the car, filling in his VTS, working up his first sketches. Soon, Baker and Ellis would have merely to assemble the sketches like building blocks and the whole car would be defined, its architecture complete. Then they could start making real parts.

In fact, if the sketches had been put together at that point, they would have resembled a Cubist painting more than a car. Jon Bereisa felt that to meet his VTS on range the car needed additional batteries and planned accordingly; Tom Lobkovich felt he couldn't accommodate more batteries without changing the car's structure, and strongly preferred not to do that. Arianna Kalian felt the car might have to be lengthened to make it crashworthy; a longer car would affect almost everyone else's design. Even the car's essential character was in dispute. Should it be as light and spare as possible for range? Or a muscle car for speed and style?

Ellis was the one who thought of sending a handful of engineers off as a skunkworks to settle the car's architecture on their own, though few of the others would know that. At this and every turning point, Ellis would throw out hints, so casually that others would end up taking them as their own. Ellis would stay in the background, a lanky, unassuming figure, self-contained, practicing the management philosophy he preached.

The one who got the hint on skunkworks was Latham Redding, the program's "vehicle architect" and one of its few blacks. No GM car program had ever had a vehicle architect, safeguarding the car's overall design; this too was Ellis's idea. Assertive, often argumentative, Redding, an ex-army helicopter pilot in Vietnam, saw himself as nothing less than the car speaking for its own survival. A skunkworks, he declared to Ellis soon after Ellis put the idea in his mind, was what the car needed; and Parts Fab, he felt, would be the perfect place.

Parts Fab, just outside the Tech Center across Twelve Mile Road, was a workshop filled with every imaginable tool, from giant milling machines to endless wrenches, where model makers fashioned prototype parts and concept cars. Later, the team would have cause to use those tools to build a prototype of their own. For now, Redding and his skunkworks group filed upstairs to a large room over the shop. There, on March 1, they split into four smaller groups, each taking a corner to pursue on paper a different vision of Impact in critical detail. One stressed functional simplicity, another went for luxury, a third imagined the most technically advanced car at the expense of all else. Lobkovich headed up the fourth group, shaping a vision that Ellis called Kaminari—Japanese for balance.

As they studied each system of the car, the skunkworks teams consulted the engineers in charge back at Engineering South. Still, for the two months they deliberated, the rest of the platform mostly waited, amid considerable frustration. Blocked from proceeding, the other engineers also felt left out. And every week lost, as they knew, put them one week closer to Baker's production date.

Finally, in early May, the skunkworks team announced its winner: Kaminari. The chiefs came over formally to *buy into* the Kaminari team's conclusions about each of the car's systems or to send the skunkworks back, literally, to the drawing board. No one expected them to do the latter; they didn't have the time.

One of the more fundamental revisions involved cooling the electronics. The AeroVironment show car used a 400-watt forced-air system that pulled outside air in. It was efficient, and light, but particles from dust to grasshoppers might be sucked in along with the air, short-circuiting the inverter. George Claypole, Impact's thermal expert, also found the system insufficient. Another 1,000 watts would be needed to do the job on a production car, he felt, and the resulting energy drain would cut into range. Better, Claypole argued, to go with liquid-filled hoses. The hoses would not only cool the electronics but pass the heat they absorbed to the passenger compartment; by the time the liquid circulated back to the electronics, it would be cool again. Liquid cooling was complex, heavier, and more expensive than air cooling, but it was more reliable, more compact, and it could be run, Claypole thought, on as little as 100 watts. The chiefs bought in.*

---

* The heat scavenged from the electronics would not be enough in itself to warm passengers on a brisk autumn night—not in a car that had neither the waste heat of a gas engine nor that of

Liquid cooling would require a radiator up front, and for that, observed Lobkovich, the car might have to be lengthened. Arianna Kalian, doing her first analysis of the car's crashworthiness, believed as much as 100 millimeters, or roughly 4 inches, would have to be added anyway. She needed longer support bars, so that when the car crashed into a wall at 30 miles per hour, the bars could fold like ribbon candy, absorbing the shock of the crash before the expensive and relatively uncrushable motor was affected.

Stretching the front end might have seemed easy enough at this early stage. But in fact, any change in length would affect virtually every aspect of the car, from its shape to its suspension. Most appalled was the GM design staff assigned to the car. They felt marginalized as it was, working out of another building at the Tech Center and taking on a car that had, in a sense, already been designed. But now to have to deal with *this*. With an almost childish stubbornness, the designers would insist on at least putting what they called a "halo" on the car: a little ring around the hood. Such were the depths to which design had fallen in the aerodynamic nineties from its all-powerful yearly style changes of the fifties.

As far as the chiefs were concerned, the real cost of the extra 100 millimeters was added mass, which would cut into range. But if the car wasn't crashworthy, range wouldn't matter; the car would never be sold. Reluctantly, they bought in, thinking that, at least, crashworthiness would haunt them no more.

Of all the architectural choices, the most hotly debated in skunkworks was one that might have seemed among the most routine: how many lead acid batteries to put on board. The car would need twenty-three 12-volt batteries to achieve a minimally acceptable range of roughly 90 miles. More than twenty-seven batteries, on the other hand, would add such mass that heavier tires would be needed, and suspension would be strained. The range gained by each next battery was offset, to some extent, by the mass it added, but not entirely, so the more batteries, the better. Net plus, as the engineers put it.[*] Except that the show car's tunnel could only accommodate twenty-three batteries; putting more on would mean going from an I-pack to a T-pack, with the crossbar balance somehow fitting horizontally behind the seats. The shape and size of the pack, in turn, would affect virtually everything in the car.

---

front and rear hydraulic brakes. The AeroVironment car had used a heat pump of the sort that employed a motor-driven compressor and refrigerant, so it could also be used for air-conditioning in summer. Kaminari adopted a variation of this, though the engineers knew it was only a short-term solution: no heat pump works effectively at below about 30 degrees Fahrenheit, so Impact's heating system would need to be reconfigured profoundly for a cold-weather state—a point that would later assume enormous political significance.

[*] Each additional battery, it was reckoned, would contribute an extra 3 miles of range after its offsetting mass was taken into account.

Lobkovich, whose structure would be dramatically affected if the car went to a T-pack, argued strongly for twenty-three batteries: less range, but also less mass and cost.

Baker nodded slowly. "Cost and mass hurt," he agreed, "but without the triple-digit range, I don't think you have a customer. I think twenty-seven's the way to go."

For most of the engineers, skunkworks seemed to clear the way. For Jon Bereisa, it only underscored how daunting a job he faced.

It was four jobs, really, or maybe five. The motor. The inverter. The batteries. The charger. And, of course, managing the quarrelsome princes assigned to turn his decisions into hardware. In a sense, batteries scared him the most. The inverter's electronics—and those of the charger for that matter—required dizzying innovation, drastic simplification, and cost reduction too dramatic even to worry about at this point. But miracles could be wrought with electronics; there was room to play, and improvise, and invent. Lead acid's advantage was its familiarity, but its apparent limitations were all too familiar as well.

Bereisa had Bob Bish's recombinant lead acid batteries, to be sure. Just because they'd worked in the show car, though, didn't mean they'd work in production. The real car would be heavier, sapping the batteries' already minimal range. How they performed would also depend on how deeply a driver discharged them. If he never let them lose more than half their juice before recharging, the pack might be good for 1,000 cycles, or tankfuls, in effect—about three years, though that was just a guess so far. If he tended to drain the batteries completely, or even nearly so, he might get only 200 cycles. But even 50 percent depth of discharge meant half of the 120-mile range—the warm sunny day range—advertised by AeroVironment. About all that Bereisa felt he could count on was that lead acid would be a *reliable* source of electric power. Soon, he would learn that even this assumption was wrong.

Impact's propulsion system was Bereisa's most impossible task yet, but only the latest challenge in a life of them. In this largely midwestern clan, whose roots reached deep into farm soil, Bereisa was an immigrant. His Lithuanian parents had arrived in America just after World War II with $11. Jonas, aged four, should not have been able to remember the family's three days in quarantine at Ellis Island. Years later, after it was opened to tourists but before its renovation, Bereisa took his wife Donna to see it. *Here's what that building will look like inside,* he told her as they approached. *The stairs will lead up to a floor with eight windows, and there will be a picture in the corner.* He remembered every detail.

Especially gifted in the sciences, but with no family money for tuition, Bereisa had won a full scholarship to the Missouri School of Mining in Rolla, a town so male-dominated—between the all-male university and a nearby army base—that one of the great accomplishments of his life was sidling up in his car to a car full of pretty girls and, after a spirited drag down Rolla's Main Street, meeting the one he would marry.

With his master's in electrical engineering, Bereisa worked first for Aerojet General on an AEC/NASA-sponsored project to develop a nuclear engine that could propel a "star ship" on year-long planetary journeys. The project later inspired the Star Trek *Enterprise.** In 1974 he joined GM to work on, of all things, electric cars. But the company's small program of that time soon died, and Bereisa found himself swept up by the microcontroller revolution, developing onboard computers. He joined the Electrovette program after Baker took it over, and the two became fast friends. In part because of that, in part because he knew how fast the technology was evolving, he'd hesitated not at all when Baker called him for Impact. The third time would be the charm.

All the chiefs worked hard, but Bereisa seemed to work obsessively. On the drive in from Bloomfield Hills, where he lived less than a mile from Baker, he punched in call after call on his cellular phone, gamely trying to keep up with a daily load of half a hundred voice-mail messages. Often when he reached the lot at Engineering South he remained in his car, still talking, for another twenty or thirty minutes. Upstairs, he went from meeting to meeting, declaiming with brilliance and a bullish charm that his subordinates sometimes found more bullish than charming; then he was gone, off to Indiana or California, to try, once again, to knock the princes into line.

Despite the killing pace, Bereisa liked living well and was, alone among the chiefs, a connoisseur. He bought foreign-made clothes, and often wore a Spanish-made jacket of the softest black leather. He knew something of music and literature and history. In the evenings, while the other chiefs took their wives to Charley's Crab, he and Donna went to the Lark, a small restaurant consistently rated among the best in the country, where he ordered his favorite dish, rack of lamb Genghis Khan, and paid, after much fine wine, $300 for dinner and tip.

The material pleasures never quite made up for the twelve-hour days, but for now, Bereisa felt, he could work as hard as needed. He was in his prime, after all, still on the right side of fifty; surely, in a year or two, he'd be promoted to another program. Wasn't that how GM rewarded its high-pot engineers?

A short period of giddy confidence followed skunkworks. Soon it was replaced by a collective hangover. The architecture made sense as far as it went. But while each change brought the car closer to one target, it pushed

---

* The project also marked the first use of controlled-slip AC induction motors, driven by the world's first power MOSFET transistors.

another farther away. The engineers now knew the car they wanted to build: what its parts and systems should be, how they fit together. They just had no idea how to make it meet the overall targets Baker had set for its mass and cost and range.

The extra batteries, for example, increased range but helped push the car's mass from 1,000 to 1,400 kilograms, or from 2,200 to 3,080 pounds, about 100 kilograms over the target. The clever proposals made to offset that increase were all alarmingly expensive. A magnesium steering wheel might weigh no more than a bird's nest, but had anyone stopped to consider the cost of magnesium? All told, the light composites pushed piece cost—the cost of parts for one actual car—up to $25,000. If you pushed one budget down, up went another. Somehow, mass *and* cost had to go down. Ingenuity was required, but also a dogged, daily persistence.

That was where Mike Liedtke came in. Liedtke was chief of the car's most amorphous realm: its progress as an integrated system. The other chiefs told him their goals, and Liedtke and his staff kept track of them. Behind their corporate decorum, one could sense in the other chiefs a certain impatience with one who had no deliverables—no hardware—yet made the others responsible for theirs. Liedtke seemed to sense it too and self-deprecatingly called himself the Data Keeper. The youngest of the chiefs, he was the most agreeable; some would say the most ambitious. Tall and lean, prematurely balding with a blond mustache, he radiated the gung ho spirit of a Boy Scout leader and maintained his charts accordingly.

In the wake of skunkworks, the Data Keeper assigned a trio of earnest adjutants to go from group to group tabulating trade-offs in mass and range and cost. Soon, the other engineers were all too well aware of one of them: Rich Marks, the young, bow-tied and beleaguered "mass czar." Unheard of in GM's history, Marks measured mass by the *gram*: every 1/454 of a pound, up or down, was duly and daily noted. Every 22 kilograms of mass was defined as a mile of range. So was every six counts of aerodynamic drag, and every 34 watts of power. Not content just to tabulate, Marks offered suggestions for improvement. Had an engineer heard about a new lightweight material Marks had just read about in a trade magazine? Had he considered changing his design? The adjutants became known, derisively, as the Clipboard Carriers, loathed on sight.

In fairness, the parts engineers, now split into nine groups called PDTs—product delivery teams—resisted even sensible suggestions from the Clipboard Carriers. Thanks to Ellis, they had a measure of power unprecedented for engineers at GM: to devise their own solutions to problems. They also had their own targets to meet, but quickly realized that early heroism might not be rewarded. If they said they could cut mass or cost by some measure, they were stuck with that commitment. And the more marbles one group sacrificed for the overall good, the more likely its neighbors might get to keep theirs. So the PDTs, in those weeks after skunkworks, tended to hoard their mass, and Marks had no real effect at all.

Again it was Ellis who decided the next move. The PDTs had to work more closely, share their problems, help each other find solutions if the targets were to be met. It was time, he suggested, for the PDTs to go to church.

On June 1, some 125 engineers reported to the Our Lady of Redemption Melkite Catholic Church on nearby Cole Street. In the auditorium of the adjoining church school, where bingo was played throughout the school year, they settled in at big round tables, one PDT to a table, and got to work. In the weeks to come, Baker would visit hardly at all, Ellis perhaps once a week. A manufacturing engineer was nominally in charge of the curious conclave, but really the PDTs were on their own.

In a program already removed from the GM culture of stern management control, the church summer was the most radical departure yet. It was also a gamble. Away from the rabbit warren of cubicles and meeting rooms in Engineering South, away from phones and senior staff, the PDTs might refine the architecture and reach their targets with a better-designed car. But that would also take time. An old-style, autocratic chief engineer would have made peremptory, perhaps less creative, decisions. Then again, the program would have moved that much faster to the making of prototype parts.

In classrooms off the auditorium, PDT teams of design engineers held all-day colloquies with their counterparts in manufacturing: systems engineering at work. "If you make it this way," a manufacturing engineer might tell his design counterpart, "I could make it with three stamping dies instead of four, and save twenty-five percent of the investment cost on it." Here, too, in each circle, were hourly union workers from the Lansing factory, twenty in all, who made the ninety-minute drive each way every day. Standoffish at first, they were soon offering candid suggestions on how to set up work-stations so that workers could reach for parts and attach them in ways that made sense.

Every morning, the first teams to arrive went on raiding parties for chairs and tables, for there were never quite enough to go around. Soon the blackboards would be covered with equations, and freelance artists would be sketching the engineers' rough ideas on easels. In each room, too, some member of each PDT team would be grimacing at a computer, trying to work up his BDI numbers.

BDI stood for a maddening software program devised by two professors named Booth-Royd and Dewhurst to help engineers make their designs manufacturable. The designer of a seat would enter all its technical specs, then the process of building it: first take the frame, then pick up a bolt, then a nut, put the cushion on, add the fabric, trim, or whatever. The software would compute how long it would take a worker to do those things. Then the engineer might try it a second time, using glue or rivets in his scenario, rather than nuts and bolts. Or cushions: what if he tried two instead of three? And again the computer would calculate assembly time.

The only order from Jim Ellis to the churchgoers was not to leave until they had their BDI "numbers," or specs. But the software wasn't designed for an electric car. For Arianna Kalian, among others, BDI became a huge frustration. Kalian had felt well on her way to defining the car's front end, with all its crush bars for crashworthiness—but now here was BDI, posing questions such as "Does this part rotate with respect to the other one?" "Rotate?" she'd mutter in disbelief. "None *better* rotate for us." In a hundred different ways, BDI slowed her down.

For the structure team, whose work was still in far better shape than other parts of the car, the church was a chance to make refinements on an already sound design. Other teams, still unsure of what they wanted to do, found this frustrating. They wanted to try different ideas, taking nothing for granted. Structure didn't want to entertain ideas that might force an undoing of what had been done. Structure was *set*. With no senior managers present to make them cooperate, the PDT teams remained islands, their members ever closer to each other, but marooned from other teams. One young engineer went so far as to term the church summer an utter disaster. For others, like Paul Huzzard, church seemed a waste of time. Few of the EV's body parts would be designed and manufactured in some new way just because the car was electric. So why was his team forced to sit around in little chairs, sucking their thumbs? This car had to be produced. It had dates to meet.

For everyone, the biggest frustration was the battery pack. Skunkworks had determined the number of batteries to be used, but Bob Bish and his Delco Remy team, working out of a secret, unmarked warehouse in Anderson, Indiana, were still wrestling with the batteries' design, and couldn't yet say what their dimensions would be. The batteries seemed to grow inexorably larger as they were refined, so that the tunnel that housed them grew out, threatening either to scrunch the seats or widen the car. As it did, every other system was forced to accommodate it.

Mike Liedtke, ever buoyant, felt by August that the church had paid off. For all its flaws, BDI was getting the car closer to production. As subsystems became more clearly defined, parts costs could be better gauged, along with the investment of tooling up for them. Until the church, many parts had existed only as blunt pencil drawings, and a supplier's estimate could only be as exact as the information he was given.

By summer's end, though, even Liedtke had to concede that the church goals remained unmet. Mass and cost were too high; until they came down, the BDIs would remain provisional at best. For many of the engineers, the church summer had shown that the mass and cost targets *couldn't* be met. But the chiefs would have to see that for themselves.

Had the PDTs remained in the church until the goals were met, as Ellis had decreed, they might never have left. As it was, on September 1, they had to decamp.

Bingo season had begun.

Baker made a point of staying away from the church—of being, as he put it, conveniently inconvenient. He sat in on the occasional mockup review, but otherwise stayed over in Engineering South. He was trying hard to let his chief engineer manage as he pleased. Besides, Baker had enough problems to occupy him. The most annoying—and, as far as he was concerned, the most unnecessary—was marketing.

Ever since the rustic retreat at Copely Hill, Baker and his marketing chief, Ed Benson, had seemed unable to agree on anything. Benson felt strongly that Impact had to be priced as low as, perhaps lower than, comparable gas cars. If power windows and doors and a tilt steering wheel and a fancy sound system could be put on board without raising the cost—great. But they couldn't. Besides, Benson argued, these were items that the "early adopters" —the real EV enthusiasts—would pay extra for. Why make them standard equipment?

Baker disagreed. The Impact was supposed to make a statement. It was supposed to be the technological frontier. How could it *not* have those perks as standard? Besides, in two or three years, when the car appeared, the perks would be "price of entry"—luxuries that had become so commonplace that no one would buy a car without them. For both reasons, Baker ruled that Impact would carry a radio with CD player, not cassette tape deck. It would also have power windows and mirrors and locks. For Benson that summer, the tilt wheel was the last straw, provoking strong words behind Baker's closed door and an abrupt departure. In a tersely worded memo, the team was told merely that he had moved on to another assignment. Baker told his chiefs he didn't want to discourage debate. But marketing was so *negative*. Rather than replace Benson, he decided, he would oversee the marketing staff himself.

In truth, it wasn't an easy time for Baker. The program was expanding, and he had the odd sensation of feeling his profile rise. Newspapers were doing stories on the program. Baker, who had never been interviewed before taking on the EV program, found himself on a first-name basis with reporters from *The New York Times* and *The Wall Street Journal*. Even his college magazine was doing a feature on him; he might need that tuxedo after all.

At the same time, Baker felt like the engineer on a runaway train: nice ride if he could only get the controls to work. In June, John Williams informed him, apologetically but firmly, that the program would have to fail itself at its first stage of four-phase development. Williams could not in good conscience tell upper management that the car should be moved out of Concept Initiation and into Concept Approval—the end, as GM jargon had it rather darkly, of Phase Zero, at which point Baker could start getting parts made. Finance hadn't hired the people it was supposed to hire; a detailed business case hadn't been made and, as far as Williams could see, no one yet knew how to make one that was positive enough to get top management's blessing. Reluctantly, Baker agreed to delay the program six months. Top management was happy to save its money from the coming year, but the investment would actually go up from $150 million to $200 million. So would the risk, as the corporation continued to lose money, that the program would not be approved at all.

Over in the church, the engineers fretted while Ellis counseled patience and talked of pyramids. In Indiana, and in California, simmering tensions among the princes threatened to erupt into all-out war. At home, Baker seemed to have the least control of all over a daughter who was exhibiting adolescent moodiness. His colleagues sympathized, but couldn't quite bring themselves to say what they felt. It wasn't just about his daughter's school and classmates, they saw, or adolescent angst. Baker, hard driven and competitive as he was, had pushed his daughter too hard, set expectations too high. He acted as if his love was conditional, a matter of how well she did. He'd brought the rules of his workplace home.

No easy answer came from Baker's soul searching, nor, really, did he expect one. A troubled family would take time to heal. Often now, though, he wondered if his other problems might not be solved by some small miracle of invention, one neat package that would make Impact a brilliant success. Give it a market. Make its business case. And usher in, at last, the era of the modern electric car.

From now until production, Baker knew, his engineers would spend long hours and lots of money and make everything on the car, from the tires to the electronics, incrementally better. What they'd still need was a better battery. A different *kind* of battery. A battery that could overnight double or triple the range of lead acid. A breakthrough eighty years after Edison, after the last fundamental, marketable advance in battery research.

A better battery would take a miracle indeed. But now, at least, Baker knew how to look for it. And the odds of finding it might have just dropped precipitously in his favor.

A Manhattan Project
for Batteries

))))

For a year now, Baker had held secret meetings with two men he'd never expected to meet, much less trust as partners in a Manhattan Project for advanced batteries. They were his rivals, his EV counterparts at Ford and Chrysler, and at first they had regarded him with the same mixture of curiosity, skepticism, and suspicion with which he had regarded them.

So ingrained was the competitiveness among them that none would ever have come up with the idea of a battery consortium on his own. Credit for that went to Michael Davis, who had decided to be more entrepreneurial as a new assistant secretary at the U.S. Department of Energy than anyone expected or perhaps even wanted a midlevel political appointee in the Bush administration to be.

Early into his brief tenure Davis had recognized that some $20 million was going out every year from his department of energy and renewable resources for advanced battery research. But the money was going in driblets, all over the country, to federal and university labs that either responded to market needs for better small, commercial batteries, or did wonderfully exotic work that produced nothing of use. Thanks to the California mandate, all three U.S. carmakers were now obligated to come up with marketable EVs, and batteries, clearly, were their greatest challenge. Davis had a simple, radical thought. Why not put those driblets into one pool, get the Big Three to add their own battery research funds to it, and get everyone working together on the most promising technologies so that an advanced EV battery might at last be made real?

As he pitched his idea up the ranks of DOE, Davis argued that a battery consortium would actually be free; the money was already being spent. Privately, he thought far more would be needed, but being a smart bureaucrat he knew to get the concept approved first and wrangle for funds later. To Don Runkle at GM, then to Runkle's counterparts at Ford and Chrysler, Davis observed that each of the Big Three would get, in effect, six dollars of R&D for every one spent. The Big Three could decide among themselves which battery developers should be given grants; they would not have to work with, let alone *for*, the federal government. The added beauty of a consortium for *advanced* batteries—beyond lead acid—was that the Big Three could collaborate without antitrust fears. Until new technology was commercialized, it didn't have a market, so antitrust laws allowed a greater degree of collaboration. If and when the big breakthrough came, the carmakers could share rights to it while competing vigorously on the development of vehicles into which the batteries would be put.

If they had believed in heavenly signs, Baker and his prospective partners might have abandoned the consortium at their initial meeting in September 1990. As the three shook hands for the first time in a conference room of the Tech Center, the sky blackened and a siren went off: a tornado was headed their way. The three joined the throng of executives heading deliberately, if a bit quickly, down to the basement. There they reconvened their meeting in a men's room.

It would have been hard to say of Baker's prospective partners that day who among them seemed the least corporate. John Wallace, of Ford, was a younger version of Ted Turner, the media entrepreneur. Same dark-blond hair and bristle-brush mustache, same deep streak of independence and disdain for bureaucracy, same love of betting on future technology, same brash confidence, blunt candor, and wit. If it were possible—and it was—Chrysler's Jean Mallebay-Vacqueur looked even less like a Big Three executive. Not only was he black with a strong French-African accent. With his dark shades, black leather jacket, French accent, and natural aplomb, he was *hip*.

Months of thorny issues lay ahead before the United States Advanced Battery Consortium—or USABC—could be approved by all involved. But in the second meeting, the partners hit their first snag on the simple matter of who would be chairman. Baker proposed that the title rotate annually from one partner to the next. But for the first year, he said, GM should have the honor. After all, the carmakers would be paying shares proportionate to their sizes, which meant GM would be paying the most. The real question, of course, was who would be in charge.

"Actually, I think *I* should be chairman," Wallace countered.

The two men bristled at each other, while Mallebay-Vacqueur looked on, bemused. Representing the smallest by far of the Big Three, he was also more laid back than his new partners. With some cajoling on his part the others finally agreed that Baker could be chairman the first year, but that Wallace would be in charge of all public relations; Mallebay-Vacqueur would be treasurer.

Wallace was playing a game. He knew that Ford's small EV program was far behind GM's, and that even now, Ford wouldn't make the commitment that crazy Roger Smith had. Yet with the mandate, he had to stay in the game. So his job, as he saw it, was to keep Baker off balance, slow GM as much as he could, and hope Ford could catch up in the meantime. Controlling the USABC's image seemed, for now at least, the most advantageous post of the three. "One of my strategic issues all this time," Wallace would freely admit later, "was to block Ken Baker."

Meeting every month or more, the three men began to share the grudging respect of enemies at a negotiating table. Like enemies, they knew that any one of them would demolish the others if he had the power—the battery—to do so. Yet for now, their greatest hope of an advanced battery lay in working together. Without the battery, their respective programs might be doomed to fail; without it, their own careers might sputter and stall. And so, not quite realizing it, the three began to play deep, fateful roles in each other's lives.

In his roundabout route to Ford's EV program, John Wallace had not been led, at any point, by a love of cars. His father was a chemist, his mother a science teacher, and John, growing up in Tulsa, Oklahoma, had leaned naturally toward math. At Rice University in Houston he studied electrical engineering, the most mathematical of the engineering sciences, and in his graduate years the new field of computer science. Silicon Valley was where the action was, so Wallace moved there to bounce from one start-up to another, until he had enough microprocessor experience to start up his own firm with a small band of fellow believers. By then, he had a full beard and hair down his back. Unfortunately, he and his partners launched their start-up in the teeth of the 1974 recession and barely scraped by. When the firm was sold, Wallace contracted to keep one customer to himself: Ford Motor Company, for which he'd helped design the first electronic engine control chips, just as Jon Bereisa was doing at Delco Electronics for GM. When Ford invited him to set up an integrated circuit subsidiary in Colorado Springs, Wallace was intrigued. It wasn't like going to work for Ford. It was another start-up.

By now he'd lost the beard and long hair, ended one marriage, and started another. He still owned only one suit, but that changed when his start-up was folded into Ford Aerospace and sold. Reluctantly, and with many new suits, Wallace came to Dearborn to head up Ford's electronics lab, overseeing more than a hundred Ph.D.'s.

One of the lab's smaller and less promising ventures, as it happened, was electric cars. Irked at the expense, Wallace almost shut the program down.

But then he reconsidered. Why not hedge his bets? Wallace had the EV team work up a proposal for DOE to fund the design of a powertrain that could be upsized or downsized for a van or sports car by changing just a few parts.

That was the program Ford was fiddling with in late 1989 when Wallace began to sense a groundswell. Partly it was the heat-wave summer of 1988, partly the grumbling in California, partly a sensitivity he'd honed working in Silicon Valley where new technology grew old in eighteen months. On his own, he began scratching for funds in odd nooks of the company, begging, as he put it, with his tin cup in hand. By Christmas, he had $8 million. Over holiday drinks with a friend he fretted it wasn't enough. "GM's up to something," he said. "I can feel it." The next week came Impact's unveiling at the L.A. auto show.

Impact was a blessing and a curse. It showed Wallace how far behind he was, but it made management sit up and listen. By March, he was assigned a planner—Ford's first show of commitment to a program. Still, the effort drifted, undefined, until CARB passed the mandate. And that, Wallace conceded, kicked the program into high gear.

By the time Wallace started meeting monthly with his new friends Baker and Mallebay-Vacqueur he had approval to produce a demo electric van, the Ecostar, as a conversion from Ford's European Escort van. Wallace was authorized to build 105 prototype vans, with eighty of them to be leased to utilities at about $100,000 each for thirty months—defraying at best 10 percent of the program's $80 million in development costs. The rest of the vans would be kept for testing. The program utterly lacked glamor—no one would write a book about the Ecostar van—but Wallace could live with that. From his years in Silicon Valley he knew the most expensive lessons to be learned with new technology came early on. Minimize those costs with prototypes and then, at the right time, blast off. Relative to GM's program, Ecostar would be a cheap way to get some understanding of the EV fleet market, establish a network of suppliers, and, of course, test the technology.

The program began as a skunkworks in January 1991, so during the first several USABC meetings Wallace said nothing of it. Some 200 engineers moved into three floors of a dreary office building in Dearborn called the Village Plaza, attached to a minimall. There were no signs on the doors, no flourish for the press. When it went modestly public in April, Baker congratulated him, but Wallace knew what he was thinking. A *van conversion?* How dinky could Ford get? Fine, Wallace thought, let him call it that. Aside from its metal body, he considered Ecostar a ground-up: low-rolling resistance tires, new suspension and chassis, regen braking, different climate control, different steering; all required when you chucked out the engine and its entrails and put in a battery pack.

For now, Ecostar would have lead acid batteries, with an inverter designed jointly by Ford and General Electric; GE would also make the van's one AC induction motor. Admittedly, a metal-body van with lead acid batteries would have unacceptable range, as little as 20 miles. But by the time those 105 Ecostars were finished in early 1993 Wallace intended them to have Ford's own advanced batteries, the hope of thirty years of research and a stack of Ford patents: sodium sulfur.

The lure of sodium sulfur* was as problematic as it was powerful. It held three times the energy of lead acid—100 watt hours per kilogram, versus lead acid's 35. It could also stand a deeper discharge and was less vulnerable to cold weather. Taking those advantages into account, sodium sulfur might have five times the range of lead acid—the real range of 60 miles, Wallace hastened to add, not the 120 miles inexplicably still hyped by Baker and his team. What was more, the cost was about the same as lead acid, given the prevalence of sodium and sulfur.

Unfortunately, a sodium sulfur pack was moody. When not discharging—as when a car was parked—its chemicals began to freeze, whatever the weather, and so had to be maintained at about 500 degrees Fahrenheit by a heating element plugged into a wall socket; the device heated a special oil that circulated through the pack. Left untethered for several days the pack's sodium would freeze, cracking its ceramic electrolyte and basically ruining the batteries. Yet the opposite occurred when the pack was discharging—as when a car was moving—so that the heating element had to be used in reverse, as a cooling agent, to keep the pack from overheating. These were problems, Wallace conceded, but Ford's two suppliers, Chloride Silent Power in England and the Swedish-Swiss conglomerate Asea Brown Boveri were working on them.

With any luck, Wallace thought, one of those two European suppliers would get sodium sulfur up to speed before any other advanced battery technology emerged. Then Ford would blow its rivals away. But participating in the consortium talks did no harm, he figured. If another winner emerged first, Ford would be able to use it, too. Meanwhile, he was learning a lot about his rivals' EV programs.

---

* Ford's sodium sulfur battery had 480 cells, each of which fostered its own chemical reaction. The cell was like a tiny lightbulb containing a small core like a lightbulb's filament casing. The ions of sodium within that core migrated through the ceramic that encased it and met the sulfur contained in the bulb; when it did, each sodium ion dislodged an electron from each sulfur atom, generating electricity. In a sense, as Wallace observed, it was the antithesis of a lead acid battery. A lead acid battery had solid plates that served as its electrodes, and liquid acid between them as the conductive electrolyte. In a sodium sulfur battery the properties were reversed. Sodium and sulfur were liquid electrodes while the conductive electrolyte between them was solid ceramic.

■ ■ ■

In Jean Mallebay-Vacqueur's modest office at the new Chrysler Technology Center in Auburn Hills was a sign that read: "Every morning in Africa a gazelle wakes up. It knows that it must run faster than the fastest lion or it will be killed. Every morning, a lion wakes up. It knows that it must outrun the slowest gazelle, or it will starve to death. It does not matter whether you are a lion or a gazelle. When the sun comes up, you had better be running."

At thirty-six, Mallebay-Vacqueur had done a lot of running, from one continent to another, ducking his share of bullets along the way. It had given him a somewhat different perspective on life than that of his two new partners. Chrysler might still be a barebones operation with too little money to do much playing around with EVs, but that didn't bother him a bit. "You know what luxury is?" he would say. "Luxury is walking in a place without having to crawl on the floor to avoid bullets! That's the reason I'm always laughing. I have no problem!"

His mother was a French civil servant, his father an African journalist in Paris where Jean was born. After growing up in Vietnam and Mali—both still somewhat French in sensibility though free of French claims—he returned to Paris to attend a technical college, earning his keep as a bartender in the scruffy ninth arrondissement. Graduating, he volunteered for military duty and spent two peaceful years in Mauritania, Mali's neighbor in western Africa. But then war broke out between the Mauritanians and Western Sahara, and Jean started ducking the bullets. Mauritania, he would say later, taught him that to survive one had to be strong but flexible. GM's approach to electric cars, he felt, was admirable, elegant even, but inflexible in its pursuit of the greatest possible efficiency. Perhaps, he would say, it was an elegant answer to a question no one had really asked; whereas Chrysler, under his direction, was a model of flexibility with all its options open.

Mallebay-Vacqueur had always loved cars, and after business school happily took a job at Renault. Eventually he was assigned to introduce robots into a French Renault factory, and met fierce union resistance. There were death threats, and small wooden coffins placed on his bed. In one year, Mallebay-Vacqueur had lost a quarter of his body weight and was smoking two packs of cigarettes a day. Worn down, he shocked his colleagues by leaving Renault to take a job as manager of special projects at Chrysler. The most special of these became the Viper, Chrysler's $60,000, limited-production muscle car. A good deal less special was Chrysler's EV program.

The program, begun in 1987 and funded in part by the coalition of utilities known as EPRI (Electric Power Research Institute), had looked at the latest battery technologies and made the inevitable conclusion that the costs of doing a ground-up were exorbitant. Conversions seemed far more sensible—more *flexible*—especially because Chrysler's wildly successful minivan was the perfect choice. Sturdy, with a wide flat bed, it could easily accommodate a heavy pack of either lead acid or nickel cadmium batteries, the latter a pairing that appealed to Chrysler because it had twice the energy, or range, of lead acid—if at twice the cost and weight. But the minivan could also take on any better battery that came along. Chrysler advanced a modest $5 million to learn just how that could be done, with matching funds from EPRI. It wasn't long after that that the mandate was passed and the USABC talks began.

Mallebay-Vacqueur was under no illusions as to why he was invited to join. Chrysler had no technology to offer; it would make by far the smallest financial contribution to the pool. But the federal government would be far less likely to go into business with *two* of the three carmakers. It needed all three to avoid any appearance of favoritism and to paint a vivid, dramatic picture of the American auto industry united against Japan in the quest for a better battery. That was fine, Mallebay-Vacqueur told his new partners. But before they started digging in their heels about one technology or another they should know just where Chrysler stood.

In the years since its brush with bankruptcy, Chrysler had fought back to profitability, but only by applying a brutal social Darwinism. Unlike its rivals, it did only what it needed to survive; anything else it deferred. It would join the USABC because six dollars leveraged for every one was good business, and unless the mandate was pushed aside, something would have to be done for 1998. But because Chrysler was so much smaller than its rivals, its 2 percent market share in California would only total a few hundred cars, not several thousand. It could meet the mandate by buying parts from suppliers and bolting them onto its minivans. The approach wasn't very sexy, but it certainly was flexible, and until costs came down Mallebay-Vacqueur could see no point in producing ground-up electric cars too expensive for its customers to buy.

Mallebay-Vacqueur wanted to be a good partner. He just had a modest vision of what partnership should involve.

Beginning in March 1991, the partners met at least once a month to work toward issuing RFPs—requests for proposals—to battery developers. At the outset, they faced a formidable stumbling block. How would the technology, and its profits, be shared?

Early on, Mike Davis made clear that the government, for its part, would allow the USABC to own patents, even though it was contributing half the pot. Davis simply recognized that the carmakers would never persuade themselves, let alone their shareholders, to take the government as a business partner and share profits with it. The government might, as a result, be said to lose out. But the point of spending taxpayer dollars on battery research was to produce results—not to make a profit. If the USABC produced results, the government's money was well spent.

Grant recipients could hardly be so conciliatory. Private battery developers, university labs, or even any of the country's national labs would not want to take grant money and spend their time on projects if they weren't allowed to keep patent rights to the intellectual property they produced. Yet the carmakers couldn't give up patent rights either. That would put them in the position of paying for work they didn't own; in fact, the patent holders could turn around and license the new technology to Japanese carmakers before the Big Three had time to commercialize it.

The answer was logical, but not reached without a lot of legal wrangling. Generally, battery makers would yield to the Big Three the rights for work done as it applied to EVs. Because the carmakers had managed to persuade EPRI to help defray their half of the pot, its utilities would keep the rights to work that was useful to them.* Other uses the battery developers could keep.

That fall, Congress, encouraged by the White House Office of Management and Budget to see the USABC as a money-saving measure, came through with the extra money DOE requested, so that Davis was able to put up $130 million, and have the Big Three, along with the utilities, match that sum: $260 million in all. Now that the USABC seemed such a shining example of how government and industry might work together to the betterment of both, the White House called for a Rose Garden ceremony to give it an official launch. On October 25, 1991, Baker, Wallace, and Mallebay-Vacqueur listened with various dignitaries as President Bush offered a short speech.

Parked off to the side to dramatize the occasion were handbuilt EVs from each of the Big Three: a converted Chrysler minivan, a Ford Ecostar van, and the original Impact show car. His speech concluded, President Bush hopped in behind the wheel of the Chrysler minivan, his choice predetermined by lot. Waving to photographers he turned the key and pressed the accelerator.

Nothing happened.

Panicked mechanics rushed over to check the van's electrical connections. After a long, anxious minute or two, Bush was able to drive the van a few hundred feet for the press.

Wallace, for one, was vastly relieved. He wasn't sure the Ecostar van would have worked at all.

---

* The carmakers would now contribute 23 percent of the pot; the utilities would pay 7 percent, and battery maker grant recipients would supply the remaining 20 percent.

Low, Lower, Lowest

))))

For all the good he felt the church summer had done, Jim Ellis, Impact's chief engineer, had to admit the car's mass and cost were still prohibitively high. Until the overall numbers dropped, every part on the car remained tentative, its design unrefined, its particular mass and cost subject to change.

Another chief engineer might, at this point, have lost patience with the dithering PDTs. He might have made his own decisions about where to cut. Made them over a weekend. Declared *this* was the car the program would produce. It would have been a car riddled with painful compromises, and feelings would be hurt, but the truth, as veterans knew, was that every new car, shiny and perfect as it looked, had its engineering trade-offs. There just wasn't time to keep refining its design. At some point it had to be *done*.

Many of Impact's engineers in those autumn months of 1991 wanted Ellis to do just that. They wanted him to take command, issue orders, to lead, so that at last this army might march in step and get somewhere: to concept approval and to the first handbuilt prototypes. Here were all these systems that had never been tried, from the electronics to the electric brakes; until they were transformed into real hardware, the engineers wouldn't know if they worked, much less if they could be produced.

But Ellis had shown already how committed he was to systems engineering: to having the car fully designed on paper by the engineers themselves, its mass and cost problems solved, its manufacturing process refined in hundreds of drawings that illustrated every step of assembly before a single part was made. There would be none of the old "over the wall" approach for Impact. That autumn, Ellis dug in further. For more than three months he forced the car's every system to be reconsidered, balanced, and weighed in a process suggested by a twenty-seven-year-old neophyte.

Like many of the program's young engineers, Dave DiPietro was a high-pot. Even among high-pots, though, there were standouts, young engineers or number crunchers so impressive they seemed likely to reach the corporation's uppermost tiers some day. DiPietro was one of these. He had majored in electronics at MIT, and hoped to jump right in as a designer of one of Impact's electrical systems. Instead he'd had to accept that even the highest of the high-pots at GM paid a few dues before getting what the engineers called release responsibility—designing parts that were "released" to suppliers and actually made for a car. Wisely, he'd maneuvered his way onto Mike Liedtke's team—the monitors of Impact as an evolving "vehicle system"—and began doing studies that gave him a better overall sense of the car than most of his peers. Eventually he became a Clipboard Carrier, managing to be more diplomatic at it than the dreaded Rich Marks. That was when he came to see how the program might benefit by a lesson from his father.

A highly regarded engineer at Kodak, DiPietro's father was long familiar with the tendency of his colleagues to solve their own problems at the expense of others. Listening to his son explain how balkanized the PDTs had become he offered a simple exercise. Line up your essential needs, he advised, in this case the car's lowest possible mass, investment, and piece cost. Then, he suggested, ask every PDT to come up with the best possible designs for each and have the chiefs judge which combination of "bests" produced the best car. DiPietro's father called the exercise "Low Low Low." Soon everyone on Impact did, too.

To the chiefs, Low Low Low was a revelation. For the first time, they could see all the trade-offs. One subsystem might be able to save 10 kilograms of mass for $50 by going to a lighter, more expensive part. Another might be able to save the same mass for $3. From where each PDT stood, any loss was a sacrifice. But the chiefs could see that some losses were greater than others.

The engineers, not surprisingly, abhorred Low Low Low. They resented being forced to reconsider their designs, especially at the behest of the Clipboard Carriers. *They* knew what was best. If the car was still too heavy, or too expensive, another PDT was to blame. Besides, they had a production schedule to meet. The longer they fiddled with hypothetical redesigns, the more actual design time they burned. And then who would be held up for blame?

Arianna Kalian, for one, had done a careful study with another engineer at the start of the program to determine how, on an electric car with no engine heat, the windshield should be heated. Her elegant solution was a thin, electrically conductive film between two layers of glass. Film-heated windshields weren't entirely new, but those on recent gas cars had been supplemented by air ducts. During Low Low Low, Kalian was forced to reexamine the possibility of air ducts that might use heat from the heat pump. A blower system, it was observed, might save mass because the two layers of windshield glass could be thinner.

Kalian did the exercise, but not happily. There wasn't room for a blower system now; the car's design was too far along. Also, a thinner windshield would let in more outside noise. It might break more easily and be less safe. It would be more difficult to produce and thus more expensive. Besides, even if the critics were right, the time lost redesigning the windshield would cost far more than the new approach gained. Low Low Low, she thought, was dumb dumb dumb. Finally, after much back and forth, stress, and uncertainty, Kalian won her battle: the windshield would stay as she'd designed it.

All that fall the chiefs met weekly to adjudicate. The biggest decisions were made in mid-December, in a grueling, marathon session of trade-offs hashed out in a basement "war room." One major battle was front suspension. Pat Campbell, the finance chief, felt strongly that Impact should adopt a McPherson strut system used by Saturn. The Impact team could get a break in price by going in with Saturn's larger order; the savings, overall, would be $600,000. But the Saturn system was mostly cast iron, designed for a relatively heavy gas engine.

Amiable but just as adamant, John Hepke, the chief in charge of chassis and suspension, argued for using a more sophisticated SLA design—short-long-arm—with two parallel pay arms rather than a strut. It was aluminum, so it would be lighter, and the two arms would help separate the vibration of the car's high-pressure tires on the road from the rest of the car. After considerable debate all the chiefs, including Baker, sided with Hepke. An SLA suspension might be more expensive, but it was right for the car.

The most dramatic result of the war room sessions was that the car's spare tire and jacking tools were removed. Doing without them would save 22 kilograms of mass and, as Mike Liedtke happily observed, add exactly one mile of range. Instead, the road tires would be equipped with a gum-like sealant under the tread. When the tread was punctured, the sealant would well up into the resulting leak and block it. As an ingenious backup system, the computer that monitored the ABS brakes would sense if one tire was turning faster than the others: a tire turned faster when its pressure was lower, and lower pressure indicated a leak. The computer's software algorithms could detect a change of as little as 5 pounds per square inch within five minutes, so the system also served as an early warning to the driver to inflate under-pressured tires—the main cause of blowouts and a drag on range. But the decision was bitterly contested by many engineers—not to mention the ever-despondent marketing staff—who worried that customers would balk at a car without a spare tire. For months afterward, the objections would reverberate.

When the weary engineers at last came back upstairs, they hadn't reached their goals. But they were close enough to hope that, over time, they would. On paper, Impact's mass was 1,450 kilograms; the goal was 1,320 kilograms. Its investment seemed to be holding at its upwardly revised budget of $200 million, but piece cost, as always, was the hardest target. It just didn't seem possible to lower mass further without driving up piece cost. Lightness came at a price.

Tom Lobkovich had a theory about that. "I like to think you've got three variables you can play with in doing just about anything," he liked to say. "How much is it going to cost. How long will it take. And how well will it perform. If you want it to perform really well and you want to do it really quickly, then just throw all sorts of money and people at it, and you can do it. If you don't really care how it performs, you can probably do it pretty quickly and cheaply. You can do anything you want with two of those variables, but you have to leave yourself one to play with." On Impact, the engineers were being asked to do all three at once.

It was just as Low Low Low ended that Baker got a second call about the program's budget. This time, the bad news came directly from Lloyd Reuss.

Stempel and Reuss had had a terrible 1991. GM had sold fewer cars even than in 1990, and would post $3 billion in losses for the year. With only $3.5 billion on hand—half the corporation's usual stockpile—Stempel had needed to use the $1 billion raised in an April stock offering just for basic operating expenses. The situation was so bad that Standard & Poor's had just put GM on a credit watch, which not only humiliated its management but meant the company would have far more trouble raising cash next time. At that rate, the company might well go bankrupt in a year. Alarmed, GM's board of directors at its December meeting had shaken off its torpor and demanded its chairman take action. On December 18, Stempel announced he would close six of GM's thirty-three assembly plants, as well as fifteen other factories, and thereby cut 74,000 jobs, both hourly and salaried. Unfortunately for GM, Stempel's prior agreement with the United Autoworkers Union meant that all those laid-off workers would continue drawing 85 percent pay.

Baker was doing a terrific job, Reuss said. But every program had to give. Impact's budget had been set to rise to $179 million for 1992—the year of tooling up for production. Now $40 million of that would have to be deferred until the following year. Of course, that meant delaying the launch, probably by a year this time, and thus spending tens of millions extra to maintain the program in the interim. It didn't make a lot of sense, but Reuss had no choice.

Baker had wondered, when the first call came, how safe the program was. Now he could feel its tenuousness, almost hear its fate being discussed in dolorous terms on the fourteenth floor. In a year, he would have the first pre-prototypes done: the first handbuilt Impacts that incorporated all the improvements the team was struggling to make. They would illustrate how profoundly the show car had been transformed and prove Impact could be produced. In a year, they might be too late.

Latham Redding, the vehicle architect, was the one who first suggested the fast-build, though he couldn't be sure, looking back on it, that Jim Ellis didn't have something to do with it. At Saturn, Redding had overseen a team that built a one-off—one car, by hand—early in the design process. It had given the engineers a model to work from. More important, it had made the car *real.*

Redding saw the fast-build simply as a way to help define the car's sensibility for its creators. The engineers could drive the AeroVironment show car and try to imagine what their improvements would do. They could draw their designs on paper, refine them on computer screens, and build elegant clay models. But until they went for a ride in the car they envisioned they wouldn't know how the doors opened and shut, how the seats felt, if there was really enough head room and elbow room, whether the sight lines were right, or how the car rolled and cornered. Also, Redding argued, if they did the fast-build quickly enough they could apply what they learned by midsummer of 1992 to the first batch of thirty Impacts to be constructed on the Tech Center's small, experimental assembly line in the cavernous building called Bumper to Bumper.

Baker and Ellis appreciated that. But the fast-build also had a more immediate, more important appeal. It would be a car that top management could see, touch, and drive. A car that might stir excitement. A car that might keep the program alive.

Redding did a feasibility study before Christmas of 1991 and concluded he could do the fast-build for $2 million. Baker couldn't see where the money would come from, but Ellis told him not to worry. As a chief engineer, he had a line of credit for discretionary expenses. The idea was that a program shouldn't grind to a halt while a chief engineer sought permission from corporate bean counters to order a few extra parts. The sums involved were in the four, occasionally five figures. Ellis tapped his line for the whole $2 million.

That put Ellis at risk. If he couldn't shave $2 million from the already truncated next year's budget it would be taken, with interest, from the year after that. He would also be seen as irresponsible, which might hurt his career. But Ellis didn't give a damn. For such a mild-mannered man, he spoke with surprising scorn about the whole ladder-climbing culture at GM.

He just wanted to build this car.

To an outsider, Baker's fears for the program's fate might have seemed almost irrational. In California, after all, the mandate was set, its timetable ticking inexorably toward 1998. But as an insurance policy for Impact its coverage was limited. *If* the mandate held—and few in Detroit thought it would when auto lobbyists like Sam Leonard swung into action—GM would have to meet it. But it could always kill its bold ground-up program and, like Chrysler, take the low road later on with a cheap EV conversion. Now mandate politics had taken an alarming turn that might help Baker's program, but might hurt it, too. Nine northeastern states, voting as a bloc, had chosen in October 1991 to adopt the California mandate for themselves.

At the heart of the matter was the amended 1990 Clean Air Act, which forced states with noncomplying air standards to begin reducing pollution by 3 percent annually in 1995, or risk losing hundreds of millions of dollars in federal highway funds. The thirty-one noncomplying states had a choice. They could either conform to federal EPA standards covering all states but California, or they could adopt California's more stringent plan, which zeroed in on auto emissions that accounted for two-thirds of their smog and moved the burden of compliance to Detroit.

With the northeast states' vote, Baker's market for Impact appeared to grow dramatically. Now enough EVs would have to be produced to comprise 2 percent of nearly a third of GM's U.S. fleet. A bigger market would bring economies of scale to EV production; it might make EVs commercially viable and help foster infrastructure. That should have made Baker happy. It didn't.

The problem was that in a northeast winter Impact's range, already minimal, would be drastically affected. The cold would rob lead acid batteries of energy; the heater to warm the passenger compartment would drain more. And as the engineers would discover later, other energy hits would come in the cold from unexpected sources.

Baker wasn't sure if he could build a saleable Impact for California. He *knew* he couldn't build one for the Northeast. But he was hardly about to walk away from the challenge of getting an electric car to market. Impact was his program. He had to prove it would work before politics and GM's deepening losses killed it off.

The $2 Million Gamble

))))

Impact would keep evolving, chrysalis-like, within Engineering South. But on January 20, 1992, Latham Redding emerged with a blueprint of its body and structure—frozen, as if from the wintry Michigan air—and brought it over to Parts Fab. The fast-build had begun.

Aside from the two that Redding had done for Saturn, no fast-builds had been ordered up at GM since the 1950s. Back then, Harley Earl, the legendary pioneer of annual style changes, had used them to see how his latest ideas looked. His Parts Fab craftsmen had been a breed apart, fiercely proud of being able to build concept cars under one roof, living by the 50-foot rule: everyone and everything needed to build a car within 50 feet.

By the time Redding had begun in Parts Fab as an apprentice in the early 1960s, those glory days were past. New GM models took longer and longer to get to market; the sense of urgency that gave rise to fast-builds was lost. But as he worked on more mundane mock-ups, Redding listened to the old men's stories, of fast-builds conjured from drawings on cocktail napkins, of concepts that looked more like rockets than cars that the old men had done for GM's touring "Motoramas." Years later, he persuaded his superiors at Saturn to let him test GM's newest line the Harley Earl way. The Saturn fast-build had taken four months. For Impact, Redding had promised a car in just 100 days.

Redding's band of helpers included Dave DiPietro, whose latest job was to keep thirty-five craftsmen to that ambitious schedule; a young engineer named Pat Bouchard, Redding's liaison with the program; and a big, full-bearded mechanic named Tiny Chickensky, with whom Redding had done his Saturn fast-builds. On that first day, the team started with a small clay model, as in Harley Earl's time. But then they turned to new technology. A laser gun fed the model's measurements to a computer, where it appeared, finely calibrated in 100-millimeter squares, on screen. Using those coordinates, a computer-operated milling machine cut a full-scale model from a big block of hard foam. Molds were taken—*taking a splash,* the model makers called it—from the foam car to form the fast-build's body panels. The skeletal structure evolved the same way.

These stages Redding could schedule with military precision. But for all the parts then added—from brakes to batteries to seats to wheels—he had to rely on Impact's engineers to give him their latest designs. As Redding soon realized, not all were available; or if they were, the designs conformed to earlier versions and might be crucial "mills"—millimeters—off. That got the vehicle architect mad. "You've had eight months to do a job that should take two months," he told more than one release engineer. "There's no way you can justify not having this right."

When the delays began holding back the build, Redding doubled his team of three designers without asking Liedtke or Ellis for permission. Irked, the chiefs came over to investigate.

"You don't have good drawings," Redding told them heatedly. "And you won't give me any more platform support. What else am I supposed to do?"

There wasn't the money to hire more designers, the chiefs said. The budget was so tight already that Ellis had decided not to spend $20,000 for a rolling-window assembly; the windows could stay fixed.

"Then let me have more time."

Ellis shook his head: the fast-build had to be shown to top management as soon as possible.

"You can't put so many constraints on me!" Redding exclaimed. "Something's got to give!"

"You either figure out how to finish the car for two million dollars," Ellis said evenly, "or don't bother doing it."

From then on, when a part wasn't ready, Redding didn't bother to wait. Instead, he used the Mona Lisa.

Next door to Parts Fab, the Mona Lisa was the world's greatest automotive showroom. GM bought and brought here two cars of every currently competing model. One was torn down to its component parts, one left untouched. A deck-lid engineer could observe in one stroll through the Mona Lisa what everyone else in the business was doing about deck lids, and come away with ideas to help create his own Mona Lisa masterpiece. Redding used the Mona Lisa as a chop shop, raiding it for parts to fill in his gaps.

The Mona Lisa, of course, was no help for those parts of Impact that were entirely new. The electric brakes, for example: fortunately, they were provided on time by Ben Pusheck and Loran Brooks, who had overseen the team that laboriously wrote 80,000 lines of software to balance the front- and rear-wheel systems, and saved, by avoiding rear hydraulic brakes, the mass of roughly 100 pieces. The drivetrain, too, was all new. For that, Redding had to depend on the princes. Had he known how bitter their feuding had become, he would have been awed to get anything at all.

At Hughes, Harry King and his team had moved from replicating Cocconi's inverter to a design of their own that had hundreds, rather than thousands, of parts—a reduction achieved largely because Cocconi's MOSFETs had been replaced by IGBTs. At Delco Remy, Bill Wylam and Bob Bish had upgraded their recombinant lead acid batteries to power the heavier car that Impact would be; the single motor needed refinement, but already it incorporated the differential in one compact package. At Delco Electronics, Al Laubenstein's team had provided a key piece of the inverter puzzle: a case heat resistant enough to contain an IGBT switching 320 volts of power 20,000 times a second, and passing along 100,000 watts of power.

Unfortunately, each of the princes was at the same time trying to put the others out of the EV business, which tended to impede communication among them.

The IGBTs had become one fierce point of contention. Hughes and Delco Electronics vied over which of the two would choose a supplier: whoever controlled the IGBTs would own the heart of the inverter. When Delco won that battle, Hughes retaliated by targeting the computer brain that controlled the IGBT switches—a job assigned to Delco Electronics. DE had merely refined Alan Cocconi's analog controller. Just before Christmas, 1991, Hughes came up with a digital version. It programmed the inverter so precisely that when hooked up to a motor it could direct the motor's hum to sound like the notes of a Christmas carol. When the EV chiefs bought in, DE's engineers angrily began working up an offboard charger better, it thought, than the one Hughes was trying to build. And so it went.

Meanwhile, Delco Remy's Bill Wylam was covertly trying to build his own inverter, as he'd vowed to do. He had the batteries and motor, after all; an inverter would give him a whole drivetrain with which he might compete head-on with Hughes—both for Impact and outside business. He was doing that even after Hughes sought, and received, a letter from GM's chairman confirming that Hughes would do the inverter for the production Impact.

This was war, as far as Hughes was concerned. Hughes's Pete Savagian began considering the smaller of Impact's two inverters, the one that Wylam had insisted Remy take on because it was, he said, like an alternator. Savagian thought Remy's rationale was specious: the little inverter was power electronics, stepping down the pack's 320 volts of DC to 12 volts for the headlights, radio, and so forth. If there was anything Hughes knew how to do, Savagian felt, it was *that*. One day in February 1992, Savagian sprung his own version on the Impact chiefs—the day after Remy had had to report its own progress on the inverter was stalled. Impressed, the chiefs took the job from Remy and gave it to Hughes.

Wylam never really got over the loss. It was humiliating and, he felt, undeserved. "I've learned a lot from Hughes," he would say. "They don't lose a sale. Promise anything to get the contract—and by God, you get the contract. Then you get the extensions, change the statement of work . . ."

Amid ten- and twelve-hour days at Parts Fab, as Redding coaxed and bullied his parts in one by one, the outside world seemed to fall away for the fast-build team. Immured as they were, however, they felt along with everyone else the corporate earthquake of April 6.

Since his December 1991 announcement that twenty-one factories and plants would be closed, GM's chairman had spent long hours studying how to proceed. This was time, he thought, that showed just how committed he was to bettering the bottom line. But as 1991's overall losses reached $4.45 billion, the largest in U.S. corporate history, the board of directors grew impatient. Discreetly, one director, John Smale, the former CEO of Procter & Gamble, was asked to conduct a fact-finding report. Smale concluded that Stempel's plan was too little, too late. When Stempel balked at the finding, the board, at its April meeting in New York, took action that made headlines around the world. Stempel was allowed to remain as chairman, but Smale replaced him as head of the board's executive committee. Though he declared he would not involve himself with day-to-day matters, Smale was widely assumed to be GM's new leader. Having an outside board member take charge like this had never happened at GM. It had happened at few other companies in the country.

Lloyd Reuss, Stempel's loyal number two, was also demoted, replaced as president and chief operating officer by Jack Smith, an unassuming, Massachusetts-born finance guy who had turned GM Europe around and then succeeded more broadly as head of all of GM's international operations. Hanging by a thread, Reuss was left with stewardship of Saturn—and Impact.

Feeling like soldiers in a bunker as the bombs flew overhead, Redding's team worked grimly on, checking their progress against a chart that listed goals for each of the fast-build's hundred days. By late April, Redding was able to tell Ellis that the team would not only meet its schedule but beat it by a day. Baker announced that the car would be exhibited at his regular weekly meeting on May 1. Everyone on the program was invited to come—nearly 200 engineers, designers, and secretaries, as well as the craftsmen from Parts Fab. Proudly, Baker asked Reuss to come, too.

Over at Parts Fab, Dave DiPietro did graveyard duty the last night. The fast-build appeared almost finished, its plastic body panels painted silver, its tires in place, its various systems bench tested and installed. Still, its odometer remained a row of zeroes; it hadn't yet come off the blocks. That night, DiPietro helped with the final trim and wiring. When Bouchard showed up at 8:00 A.M., in time for DiPietro to drive home and shower before the 10:00 meeting, the team was still awaiting the last parts needed to pop in the windshield.

At 10:00 A.M., Bouchard called over to the conference room to say the parts had just arrived. Twenty minutes later, the car came off the blocks. Bouchard got in the driver side, DiPietro the passenger side. Bouchard turned the power key to "on" and pushed the forward button. Silence. Then gently, he depressed the accelerator. Silence again, except for the roll of tires as the car eased out of the room, into the chilly spring day, across Twelve Mile Road, past the security booth, around Engineering South to an open garage door to finish its first quarter mile doing what no gasoline car could do: rolling right into the crowded conference room and idling amid the crowd without emitting any noxious fumes.

Amid the applause, Baker fought back a welling of emotion. This was not, after many tense months, a moment he'd known with any certainty he'd see. Lloyd Reuss, having arrived to awkward greetings, gazed at the car with strong feelings of his own. He had helped get it here, perhaps not at first but later, and now it was one of two last chances he had to salvage his career. Along with everyone else in the room, he signed the underside of the deck lid. Then he walked off, shoulders squared in a well-tailored suit, dark hair perfectly coiffed, salesman's smile in place. It would have been hard to say, of Baker and Reuss, who needed the other more.

Imperiled as it was by GM's worsening fortunes, Impact now existed not as a fiberglass show car but as a one-of-a-kind precursor, part for part, of the car Baker hoped to produce. That was more than Ford or Chrysler could claim.

Back in January, as the fast-build began, Ford had unveiled an EV concept car called the Connecta at the Detroit auto show. A small and lightweight sedan, the bubble-shaped Connecta had three rows of seats and was billed as a taxi. But it couldn't actually move, and Ford acknowledged there were no immediate plans to produce it. Privately, John Wallace admitted the Connecta, whipped up in nine months, was a smoke and mirrors move, undertaken, as he put it, just to flip out Baker.

Now, as word of the Impact fast-build reached him, Wallace was the one to feel nervous. Before the year was out, he expected his 105 Ecostar vans to be ready, but as yet, besides the Connecta, Ford had nothing to show. Wallace felt certain that GM's whole approach was wrong—the "muscle car" image was wrong for the market; the two-door decision was a fatal mistake—but his own strategy of spending as little money as possible until batteries improved was one that required patience, and Wallace was not a patient man.

Chrysler was so much smaller than Ford or GM, its mandate obligations so much more modest as a result, that Jean Mallebay-Vacqueur still saw no point in even considering a ground-up. He would have held off on conversions, too, but in April came the order from his immediate boss, François Castaing, to work up a demo fleet of TEVans, as Chrysler called its converted mini-vans, in time to compete with Ford's Ecostar vans for utility sales and public image. Mallebay-Vacqueur tried to explain this was impossible; he would have to have released parts back in January. It was explained to him, as he put it later, that he was not the boss. Somehow, the TEVans would be ready by year's end.

All this time, Wallace and Mallebay-Vacqueur—or as often from Chrysler, a dry midwesterner named Bob Davis—had continued meeting monthly with Baker to smooth the last wrinkles in the advanced battery consortium. Among the three EV chiefs, a certain partisanship was inevitable on the issue of who should get the largest grants: Ford thought sodium sulfur should be encouraged, Chrysler pushed nickel cadmium, while GM's own battery gurus at Delco Remy declared lithium polymer the best bet. To date, however, the best independent lab results had been achieved by a dark horse touting a different kind of battery altogether, and so to a dark horse, on May 19, 1992, went the spoils: $18.5 million to a tiny company in Troy, Michigan, founded and run by a voluble, septuagenarian inventor with white, Einstein-like curls named Stanford Ovshinsky, who accepted it with his wife and partner, Dr. Iris Miroy, a biochemist. In retrospect, the choice would seem remarkably fateful—and fortuitous.

To battery developers, Ovshinsky appeared to have come out of nowhere, with a pairing not of known elements, such as nickel and cadmium, sodium and sulfur, but alloys of his own creation. Among physicists he was better known as the pioneer of a controversial notion of amorphous semiconductors. On Wall Street, where his company, Energy Conversion Devices, was publicly traded, more than a few investors had come to feel they knew him all too well.

At a press conference held in his office at ECD to announce the grant, Ovshinsky announced that his prototype nickel metal hydride cells had just reached an energy density of 80 watt hours per kilogram, more than twice the 35 watt hours of lead acid, and nearly up to the USABC's mid-term goal of 100 watt hours per kilogram. "A vehicle with our battery could go two hundred to three hundred miles on a single charge," Ovshinsky declared. "There is no inherent reason that we cannot extend the range."

Whether Ovshinsky's battery could deliver on its promise remained, to his new corporate sponsors, a more ambiguous matter. "There's liars, damn liars, and battery developers," the engineers liked to say. Against the awesome chemical challenges that batteries presented—challenges that had stumped

Edison himself—battery developers tended, perhaps out of frustration, to make exaggerated claims. Even if they managed to pack a small prototype cell with more energy and power than ever before, who knew how long it would last, and how safe it was, and how it would scale up? And if it passed all these tests, how much would it cost? In the meantime, Baker had a business case to make for an Impact with lead acid batteries.

Certainly the fast-build helped. In the days after its unveiling, several top officers came to give it a spin and professed to be delighted by it. Stempel was among the most enthusiastic; his only caveat was that as he folded his six-foot-plus frame into the driver's seat, his head knocked against the door frame. Baker promptly ordered an extra inch of headroom.

Still, Baker told his team on May 12, the program wasn't ready to be presented to top management for graduation from Phase Zero to Phase One— from concept car to production status. Mass was 3 percent over target; investment and piece cost were high, too.

That month, the team was due to take a critical next step to production: building sixteen Impacts on a small three-rail line over at Bumper to Bumper, the mock-assembly plant within GM's Tech Center. The so-called proof-of-concept cars would be a first chance to test the manufacturing process by which the car would be made when full production began up at Lansing. The POCs would also incorporate all the subtle changes made by the engineers since the start of the fast-build six months before. Delaying them would probably mean delaying the start of production. But done before the car's design was truly ready, they would be a huge waste of money: about $450,000 each, or more than $7 million in all. Baker, for one, thought the POC build should be postponed until the targets of mass and investment and piece cost were met.

Meeting resistance, Baker took a vote. Every chief voted for not halting the POC build. Baker voted for stopping it.

This time, he told the others, he was pulling rank. For the next month the engineers would squeeze their designs a last time for mass and cost. Baker called it the thirty-day win period.

The chiefs thought the car was close enough to pass.

Baker insisted. He knew it wasn't.

Hollow Victory

))))

The thirty-day win meant thirty long days of trying to lose: a gram here, a dollar there. Rich Marks was a pervasive presence with his clipboard, making irksome suggestions. "How about titanium?" Marks would say. "Wouldn't it be lighter?" At 100 times the cost of steel, it would indeed. All the obvious, and perhaps all the feasible, cuts had been made already. Now when Marks came up with an idea, it was inevitably one the engineers knew their chiefs would rule out as impractical. So the engineers would nod, their midwestern courtesy strained, and wait for Marks to move on.

In the thirty-day win period, tensions sharpened and tempers snapped. The glow of camaraderie had given way, in many cases, to resentment and confusion. It wasn't unusual for one's immediate supervisor to look over one's shoulder and say do a fender this way, only to have *his* superior come by an hour later to say do it *that* way. More than one engineer committed to reductions he felt he couldn't deliver, just to get his boss off his back and move the process along.

Resolutely, Baker and his finance chief, Pat Campbell, did what they could to polish the numbers by considering different volumes of production. With the second budget cut, Baker had begun making incremental cuts in his projected annual production of 20,000 cars. Now he wondered: What if he went with only 10,000 units a year? How would that affect investment and piece cost? Was there a breaking point somewhere, below which he could use cheaper tooling, but just above which he didn't dare?

The best balance of costs, it turned out, dictated a volume of 9,000 cars a year. But even if GM sold every single car produced—at, say, $35,000, with piece costs accounting for half of that, and R&D costs the rest—the program would still be $500 million down the pelican curve before starting to curve back up. Getting into the black still required a larger follow-on car that could reach a larger market. But a larger car needed a better battery, or its range would be lower than Impact's.

Like a condemned man seizing at the slimmest reeds of hope, Baker considered any last-minute design changes that might make Impact more marketable. The trunk opening was too small, he felt; it ought to accommodate two bags of golf clubs. Wouldn't *that* make the car more appealing? John Dabels, the main marketing man after Ed Benson's stormy departure, thought not; Baker decided it would, and ordered the change. A small solar panel, put in the roof, might be rigged to run a fan that cooled the car on a hot day as it sat in a parking lot. Baker was all for it, until he learned that a panel large enough to make a real difference would cost $500. On this one, Dabels voted yea: even a small panel would send the right message. Baker, exasperated, said no. Dabels took the defeats with grace. The panel wouldn't make that much difference, he felt. None of the changes would. Not with a car that cost too much in the first place.

In Benson's wake, Dabels had become the program's unofficial ombudsman, and wasn't much liked for it. Tall and lean, with a sort of early Beatles cut of graying brown hair, he had come to marketing by way of finance. Neither route had instilled in him much empathy for engineers who buried their heads in their work, came up with an exciting new technological solution, and expected the world to buy it, regardless of what it cost and what need, if any, it filled.

Dabels had gone so far as to circulate a series of memos questioning the program's direction. One was called "They Shoot Horses, Don't They?" In it, he urged the team to get off the track to production, make ten or twenty Impacts by hand to ride the learning curve, and go on to a four-door sedan or van that fleets, at least, might actually want. The engineers were stung. "You aren't supporting the program," they said. "You don't understand."

Dabels felt he understood quite well: this was a program guaranteed to lose a billion dollars with a car no one wanted to buy at the price for which it would have to be sold. Baker just echoed the old view about jumping into a new market first to establish brand-name dominance. Impact, he would tell Dabels, could be the Kleenex, the Xerox, of electric vehicles. Why couldn't Baker see that that philosophy was rooted in a dying era?

Like Amory Lovins, the Colorado-based energy guru whose Rocky Mountain Institute had become a nexus for new ideas on the subject, Dabels saw the auto industry as perilously set in the ways of half a century of high-volume steel production; he believed that Impact, for all its innovations, was mired in the same process. GM was still committing huge capital to a design that would take three years or more to complete. It was still intending to produce the car in a traditional automotive factory. And so it would still require hundreds of thousands of units sold before it turned a profit. With EVs, Detroit had a chance to make cars differently, with less capital, lower volumes, more flexible production. Baker and the rest of GM were still blind to that, Dabels felt, because they couldn't grasp the essential, mind-blowing fact of the matter: that EVs were more like computers than cars.

Think of it, Dabels would say, warming to his favorite theme. EVs, like computers, were a lot of electronics in lightweight cases. No heavy steel; no need for Rust Belt factories. Their parts could be assembled anywhere in the country. Instead of a central production plant, there could be regional outposts, responding that much faster to local market fluctuations and putting into practice the "just in time" philosophy of manufacturing—parts arriving as needed, with no inventory pileup. Given how quickly electronics evolved, this approach would be more than convenient; it would be crucial to a producer's survival. Let Baker keep thinking Impact could be made the old way, Dabels said, and that a huge, steady market would appear because GM had made it; the future would come soon enough.

Baker did know, when the thirty-day win period ended, that Impact's business case remained unmade. But how close the team had come to its targets! On paper, at least, mass was actually under the original target at 1,319.8 kilograms, though the team had since agreed to try, prosaically, for 1,292 kilograms by 12/92. Investment was down to $150,450,000, just .5 percent over target. Piece cost, always the hardest to push down, had decreased, on paper at least, by almost $1,000, to $15,982.24, bringing it to within 3.7 percent of its target. Surely these triumphs would impress top management enough to let the program squeak through.

Before the team dispersed for GM's annual shutdown during the first two weeks of July, Baker held a birthday ceremony. The cake that was brought out had a single candle, representing the program's expected graduation from Phase Zero to Phase One. The Impact, Baker told his engineers, was not merely the best electric car in the world. It was, perhaps, the best car in GM's history. He was ready to make its case before the management committee, to ask for the program's lion's share of funding. In a year's time—on July 4, he vowed—he would be up at Lansing, watching the first Impact come off the assembly line.

The first Monday of every August, the GM board convened at the Milford test track, far enough west of the Tech Center to lie in real farm country. Here, along with monthly business, the directors reviewed the next year's models, all factory fresh and shrouded in secrecy. The Ride and Drive, they called it. Stempel and Reuss had told the outside directors about the fast-build. Intrigued, they asked to see it.

This was not, strictly speaking, the program's moment of truth. The directors, even after their April intervention, remained at arm's length from operating decisions. Which programs to start up or kill, plants to open or close, people to hire or fire—all these were still, ostensibly, the purview of the chairman and his management committee, who would, in fact, consider Impact's fate a week later. But most of the management committee members were on the board—a legacy from Roger Smith, who had made directors of his managers in order to solidify his power—so they were here for the Ride and Drive. What they saw and heard would be critical.

First, in a conference room, Baker did a show-and-tell of components. The technological challenge had been met, he said. GM now had a leadership position in the brand-new market of electric vehicles. Then, glumly, he reviewed the business case. What it came down to, he concluded, was something in short supply at the beleaguered company: faith.

Of the nineteen directors, the two who had the most faith, besides Stempel and Reuss, were the academics. Thomas E. Everhart, president of the California Institute of Technology, felt strongly, along with CIT's president emeritus, Marvin L. Goldberger, that Impact's achievement was extraordinary. Bleak as the short-term prospects were, this was just the sort of bold step GM needed to take to improve its corporate image. At the least, it would rub off in increased sales of gas cars. Wasn't that worth the cost of a program which, after all, would only account for a small measure of GM's red ink? But while Everhart and Goldberger had sympathizers, Baker knew they were the minority camp.

Impact's official day of judgment came on August 11, 1992, before the GM management committee: along with Stempel and Reuss, it consisted of Bob Schultz, F. Alan Smith, Robert O'Connell, Jack Smith, and Bill Hoglund. Baker gave a more detailed pitch about the program and its prospects. When he sat down, Hoglund, promoted in the April shake-up to be GM's new chief financial officer, was first to react. He was cordial, but direct.

"Do you want me to give up a freshening on the 'A' car* where I'm making money, to support a program that's got a negative cash flow for a long time?" Hoglund said. "Let's say it's four hundred million dollars. Do you want me to take it from a profitable program and put it here? The A car isn't as glamorous, but I know I can make money on it."

The meeting ended with an ultimatum. On October 12, Baker would appear again before the management committee. He should come prepared to present three or four options, from full speed ahead to full stop. The man-

---

* The family of A cars included the Buick Century, the Oldsmobile Cierra, and the Pontiac 6000, all built on the same chassis and structure, or *platform*. GM had seven car and truck divisions—Buick, Oldsmobile, Chevrolet, Pontiac, GMC, Cadillac, and Saturn. It had twelve platforms, each known by a letter of the alphabet.

agement committee would choose one of them. Whatever he could do to burnish the business case by then, of course, would be helpful.

Now, just when Baker needed him most, Pat Campbell, the finance chief, was gone. Back in March he'd been asked to recast GM's unwieldly domestic business structure—the various divisions lumped by Roger Smith into two sprawling camps—and replace it with the more streamlined North American Operations. Campbell had done double duty to prepare Baker for the management committee review, but finally left on August 1, taking enormous expertise about Impact's finances with him.

Campbell's replacement looked a lot like Rush Limbaugh. His politics echoed Limbaugh's, too. Smart but shy at first, Frank Schweibold, most recently from GM Truck and Bus, had known from perusing the books with Campbell how dire the financial picture was. Everywhere he looked he saw, as he put it, big red. As the program's projected volume had been scaled down, short-term losses, ironically, had grown. The program, for example, had leased more factory space than it now needed; even though Lansing was owned by GM, Impact was bound by its deal. Early on, the program had also committed to buy 100,000 battery packs from Delco Remy, rather than the 36,000 it would now require. Same story: a deal was a deal.

The more he looked at the numbers, the more Schweibold thought the program's best hope was to go into the EV components business. Impact's batteries, and inverter for that matter, were emerging as standard setters. Perhaps they could be sold to converters, here and abroad. Perhaps they could even be sold to Ford, Chrysler, and the Japanese. Rivals, of course, would then have GM's technology in hand to disassemble and knock off. But that was a risk with any new technology. If GM just kept ratcheting up its designs, not selling one until it had the next to use in its own EVs, the competition would always be one step behind. Resolutely, Baker told the princes to start soliciting clients—showing hardware to the enemy.

Told for more than two years to keep their programs top secret, the princes found the about-face puzzling, and more than a little disturbing. In theory, it opened exciting new markets, starting with California. But it also sent a clear signal of economic distress from the program. Already, schedules had started to slip, and the chiefs had grown oddly evasive when asked why. The chiefs kept *saying* the program was moving full speed to production. But the princes began to suspect the worst.

Of the three feuding drivetrain princes—Hughes, Delco Remy, and Delco Electronics—one, it was clear, would be far more affected by a shutdown than the others. For both of the Delcos, Impact was still a blip on the bottom line. It held promise, but virtually all the Delcos' revenue came from supplying components to gas cars. Not so for Hughes Power Control Systems, the small stand-alone business started up in Torrance, California, by Hughes expressly to do EV electronics. Impact accounted for four-fifths of its $30 million business. GM had actually ordered Hughes not to take on other EV business, to give its full attention to Impact because of the car's tight production schedule.

Ironically, the dark portents came just as Hughes seemed poised to succeed with a technological challenge as daunting as the inverter. Early on, Jon Bereisa had worried about charging the car using some scaled-up version of a standard conductive cord that had a plug with exposed prongs. The 110 volts that a household cord conducted was dangerous enough. The shock from a 220-volt cord was more so: dishwashers and other appliances that used 220 volts were not frequently disconnected and reconnected as an EV charger would be. As for a 440-volt conductor, which Bereisa hoped to use eventually for curbside chargers, it could be lethal.

The answer had come to Bereisa one day in the fall of 1991. He was in the backseat of a dusty Cadillac de Ville, being driven rather fast out of Anderson, Indiana, to the private airstrip from which the GM shuttle plane might or might not have left for Detroit. At the wheel was a Delco Remy engineer named Iftikhar Khan; in the backseat with Bereisa was a Delco Electronics engineer named Al Barrett. A blinking yellow dashboard light indicated the car was running on empty. Bereisa's greater concern was that Khan, steering with one hand, kept turning around to help Barrett demonstrate the bagel-like object in a box, nearly veering off the road every time he did.

Their Exhibit A was a chunk of ferrite, a ceramic form of metallic iron that conducted magnetism well and might be the basis of a better kind of charger than Hughes's. The ferrite was split down the middle, like a bagel's two halves, with copper coils on either side. Strapped together, the two halves could pass alternating current through the magnetic field created between them with the help of the copper coils, and thus become a transformer. The beauty of *inductive* coupling, as it was called, was that because the two coils never touched, there was no danger of electrical shock.

Barrett used a cardboard box to demonstrate the transformer, Khan driving onto the shoulder as he did.

"Now wait a minute," Bereisa said, suddenly very excited. The fact that Barrett kept dropping one of the core halves had just given him an idea. Maybe the halves didn't need to be kept so close together and used as one unit. "Why not use one core half at the end of the cable," he said, "and the other in the car? Isolate them. Then slip the primary coils in close enough to the secondaries in some kind of charge port, and presto — a magnetic field to pass your current directly."

The principle had found some industrial uses, and appeared in at least one household appliance: certain cordless toothbrushes, in which the plastic-encased end of the brush held one set of coils, the plugged-in base the other. Far more powerful current, however, would be needed to recharge a huge EV battery pack in the three hours the team had set as its goal, and neither Khan nor Barrett quite knew how to begin adapting inductive coupling to that task. Perhaps the ferrite core's halves could be at the end of a cable that led from a big transformer outside the car. The core could then be inserted into the car like a gas hose nozzle, where it could pass the current, somehow, to another transformer onboard.

In retrospect, that seemingly simple idea would mark a turning point in the program. It grew out of others—the established principles of inductive coupling; Barrett's and Khan's suggestions; the toothbrush—but then, what epiphany did not? That day, Bereisa took greater satisfaction in emerging from his ride—alive—to find the GM shuttle still on the tarmac. Soon, however, he was covering blackboards with equations. To the chagrin of Delco Remy's engineers, the blackboards were down at Hughes in Torrance, California. Remy had hoped to do the chargers itself; Bereisa had to tell Barrett and Khan that chargers remained part of Hughes's EV charter, and that Remy and DE would have to settle for honorable mention.

Appealing as Bereisa's notion seemed, it faced a number of obstacles, none of which might necessarily yield. The first involved stepping up the current that went from a wall socket to whatever sort of transformer Hughes would use, then on through the cable and into the car. Whatever its voltage, the current would still have the same frequency of 60 cycles, its electrons alternating back and forth sixty times per second. All electricity in the U.S., residential or industrial, had that same frequency; it was a standard, allowing current to travel easily anywhere on the national power grid, just as all railroad tracks were laid with same-width gauge to keep trains from derailing. The problem was that to pass along 100,000 watts of power at 60 cycles per second, a huge transformer would be needed. Early on, Bereisa found a company called Inductran making inductive chargers for factory use. Inductran's charger conducted large currents, all right, but with a 100-pound slab of iron as its transformer.

A Hughes engineer named Paul Carosa led the team that solved that problem, stepping up the frequency to several hundred thousand cycles per second so that the transformer remained modest in size: a square green post 3 feet high. The primary coils at the end of the cable—the first half of the bagel—were small, too. Set in concentric rings, they were sheathed within a protective, hard plastic case that looked not unlike a Ping-Pong paddle.

But that led to more problems. The paddle, when slipped into a makeshift charge port, had to be perfectly aligned with the port's secondary coils—the other half of the bagel—or current wouldn't flow. Moreover, when the transformer and paddle were stepped up to conduct even 5,000 watts, or 5 kilowatts, of power—nowhere near enough to charge the car in decent time— the small percentage of heat loss unavoidably generated by the current began to heat the whole contraption. The box had to remain sealed, as did the plastic paddle. But how then could the heat be dissipated?

Bereisa declared the whole thing would need to be reconfigured—a decision that led Carosa, the Hughes engineer, to quit in protest and, eventually, to join up with Alan Cocconi. Bereisa demanded there be no moving parts in the design, so the bagel halves could more easily be aligned. Carosa's replacement at Hughes, a whole team under Richard Bowman, worked with Inductran—and the Electric Power Research Institute, with a team from the University of Wisconsin also noodling around with inductive chargers—to build working models that conducted as much as 25 kilowatts of power. That, however, exacerbated the heat problem. To cool the charge port, the team ran a lead from the car's liquid cooling system. The outside box and paddle, though, seemed to present a wretched choice: limit the power, and thus the charging capacity; or swell the size of both components to let the heat escape. Bowman feared that doing the latter would produce a paddle the size of a tennis racket. But surely, *some* answer existed. "Nothing is impossible for the charger team, absolutely nothing," Bowman wrote hopefully in an interoffice memo. "It just takes a lot of time, work, ingenuity, and guts to eventually figure a way to cheat the laws of physics."

The answer remained elusive that summer of 1992. It would come to Bereisa some months later as he sat in an EV conference room, brainstorming with a GM propulsion engineer named Mark Kosowski. In a trade magazine, Bereisa had read that Intel, the computer chip company, had had a similar problem: its pentium chip generated too much heat when operated in laptops. There wasn't space to run tubes of liquid cooling around the chip, and to immerse the chip in liquid seemed folly: liquids tended to conduct electricity, as shown to drastic effect by throwing a plugged-in appliance into a bathtub of water. Now users of Intel chips began to employ what is called a florinert liquid—one that could absorb heat from the chip without conducting current. What would happen, Bereisa mused, if the team ran florinert liquid right up the cable into the paddle, cooling it and the transformer?

So equipped, the transformer and paddle would stay small, yet step up 60-cycle current to as high as 300,000 cycles for the largest of Hughes's emerging family of inductive chargers: a 440-volt curbside version that could take an Impact from 20 to 70 percent full in under ten minutes.* Two last problems remained, but they were easy ones. The AC, once transferred to the

---

* Current flowed fastest into the pack between these levels; the last 10 percent of charge would trickle in more slowly. Hughes's more modest home-garage version would fill the car at 220 volts in about three hours.

charge port in the car, had to be converted to DC for the battery pack; for that, the Hughes team designed a little rectifier. Somehow, too, the car had to "know" when it was being charged, and communicate to the charger how much current it needed. A radio transmitter was put in the paddle, another in the port; when the transmitters got within three-quarters of an inch of each other, they communicated on their own frequency. The battery pack's controller was directed to gauge the amount of remaining current in the car, pass the word on to the charge port transmitter, and have the transmitter convey it to the paddle, which then drew current from the charger as needed.

The charger was, in its way, as complex a challenge as the car itself, and Hughes's solutions as important a technological triumph as Alan Cocconi's inverter or Bob Bish's recombinant lead acid batteries. Yet here in this summer of 1992, with 25-kilowatt models already up and running, Hughes's charger seemed destined to be the latest example of technology invented in the U.S., licensed abroad, then sold back to Americans more cheaply by the Japanese.

If, that is, the dark portents up at GM's EV platform left Hughes's little start-up in business at all.

Desperate Days

))))

Baker and the chiefs kept the management committee's October ultimatum to themselves. To the rest of the team, they emphasized the committee's glowing reactions to the car itself. Vaguely, they alluded to business-case details that needed addressing before Impact could formally become a Phase-One program. Meanwhile, the team was told to proceed with the proof-of-concept cars.

The POCs, as they were called, would be an odd lot. Quite a few would be crash tested into walls; instead of being fitted out with expensive powertrains, these would be ballasted with comparable dead weight. Of the twelve driveable vehicles, most would be finished only to the degree needed. The POC for Lobkovich's structure team might have substandard braking, but that wouldn't matter, since the team would be sawing the car in half to see just how durable its structure was. All but one of the POCs would be built on the limited-assembly line at the Tech Center's Bumper to Bumper. POC #16 would be put together right on the third floor of Engineering South, in the mock-up room, and embody the evolving production design. On POC #16, unreleased parts would be represented by wood, plastic, and foam, like substitute puzzle pieces. When the last real part was slipped into place, the car's design would be done, fully refined, ready to be passed on to the factory at Lansing for full production. The engineers had a name for #16. They called it Metamorphosis.

Often now, Baker made the ninety-minute drive out to Lansing to meet with the manufacturing managers, or to see how Randy Schwarz's assembly line sketches looked in the space for which they were being drawn. The drive also gave him time to think—about the car, about the program, about himself.

In such fashion Baker set out one gray August dawn, driving his latest test-ride model, a new Corvette. As of August 11, Impact's prospects had grown abruptly dimmer. Still, he hadn't given up hope. Could the management committee really kill a program that had accomplished so much, one that had such promise? The team had solved so many technical problems. It had proved, with the fast-build, that the car *worked*. Surely the management committee could see that more than half of the river had been forded. How could it make sense to turn back?

Baker had begun to wonder, though, if he wasn't misleading the chiefs with his staunch optimism. Even now, he was exhorting them like a football coach whose team was a touchdown behind with two minutes to play. *You can do it. Don't give up. Go out and win it.* What would he tell them if they lost the game? That they'd won a moral victory? That they had helped develop technology that might, in someone else's hands—Japanese hands, perhaps—lead to EVs one day? At what point should he encourage them to make discreet job inquiries in a corporation that might not be able to accommodate them all at once? At what point should he start looking himself? If he did, what, after this second EV debacle, would he be likely to find?

Against a dark sky, the stolid buildings of the Lansing factory looked like an abandoned prison, their bare grounds surrounded by a high barbed-wire fence, the guard in its security booth the only sign of life. Baker drove through to Building 206 and parked around back amid two dozen cars all older and more humble than his company Corvette. The owners of those cars were waiting upstairs, on wooden folding chairs in a bare-walled, high-ceilinged room. They were union workers, there for their Friday readiness meeting. Most seemed older than Larry Zahner, the thirty-seven-year-old plant manager who, as if to compensate for his youth, emanated a brash confidence in greeting Baker, the meeting's honored guest. Baker was the suit from Detroit. Here in Building 206, Zahner was king.

From a podium up front, Baker told the gathering how much top management liked the car. Times were tough for GM, he allowed, and the program hadn't quite been pushed on to Phase One, but he still hoped to start up the prototype build—the first factory-made cars, perhaps fifty in all—in the spring, and move to full production by Independence Day, 1993.

The men knew the dates all too well. They spoke of the remaining time before the prototype build as days of readiness. As of that Friday morning, there were 128 days of readiness left. *Readiness 128*, they put it. Ever since the church last year, as many as twenty of the union locals had driven almost daily to Warren to help the manufacturing engineers draw up assembly plans. Others had come to these meetings and taken on assignments to check out a POC part or make suggestions for the line. The assignments were voluntary, as was attendance at the Friday meetings. The men were being paid no matter what they did. But they seemed to like coming. It made the car more real.

After the meeting, Baker met with Zahner and Stan Pewoski, the union shop steward, in upstairs offices. Then he walked across the factory floor, its three-rail assembly line motionless, its dark, cavernous spaces silent and empty, the floor itself marked with white masking tape to show where work-stations would go. In the middle he paused for a moment, listening to the echo of his footsteps. If the program was approved, 400 people, including the readiness volunteers, would have jobs on this floor, and the room would re-sound with the loud, industrial music of cars being made. If it didn't, the plant would remain silent and dark and the workers unemployed, bitter at being shut down again by the suits downtown.

To burnish the business case, Baker could make rosier sales projections of cars and components, and tote up the handsome revenues they would bring. No one on the management committee would be impressed in the least; everyone knew the market was unknowable. With Frank Schweibold, he pored over the budget, looking for cuts, and soon grew frustrated. Perhaps he could do with fewer engineers, but that would hardly dent the investment nut of $12 million a month. Nor could the car get to production any faster than planned. Already, it would reach the factory twice as quickly as a conven-tional GM car. Perhaps, when it did, manufacturing might be squeezed, but not by much: tooling costs were down to a spartan $21 million, far less, again, than for a conventional program, and Lansing had been cut already from two projected work shifts a day to one.

Desperate, Baker began reconsidering a strategy he'd scoffed at a year or more ago: going hat in hand to utilities and lawmakers for EV subsidies and incentives.

The idea still made him wince—a GM program manager didn't *do* that—but Baker had no pride left to lose. A state or federal tax break for EV pur-chasers might lower the sticker price enough to make the business case seem viable. Lower electric rates from California utilities for EV owners might help, too.

From the start, utilities had been willing and eager partners in the EV cam-paign. EVs, after all, could be a bonanza for them. If cars were charged at night, when demand on power grids was low, a whole new market might be accommodated without any capital investment. If EVs proliferated and day-time demand grew, the utilities could accommodate that too, at so much greater a profit. So lucrative might the new market be in the long run that in addition to helping underwrite the USABC, the utilities would be willing to buy prototype EVs at considerable cost and build infrastructure. But largesse had its limits, and for the utilities, those limits were set to a great extent by how much money they could raise through assessments of their ratepayers. For that, most needed was the blessing of an Oz-like character: the California Public Utilities Commissioner.*

One day in late August, a dozen or more executives of California utilities flew to Detroit at Baker's invitation, along with the commissioner, on a fact-finding mission. Baker had had to coordinate their trip with Ford and Chrysler, since any incentives would have to be given to all three carmakers. By the time the commissioner got to GM after touring the other EV programs he was glowering.

"I haven't learned or seen anything," Daniel Fessler told Baker, "other than people wanting my money." Before taking the job in early 1991, Fessler had been a college professor; he comported himself still with the peremptory manner of a skeptical academic. "Ford has a battery that costs $50,000. Chrysler has a van with no batteries in it. And even if GM has something better, I'm not going to commit a penny unless you commit to put jobs in California."

Jobs were a sore point. That very day, the last car had rolled off the line at GM's plant in Van Nuys, California, one of the twenty-one factories to be closed in GM's desperate plan to stanch its losses. Just as the state plunged into recession, Fessler said, 2,500 people were losing their jobs. Would GM commit to an EV plant in California in return for more incentives?

"If the market develops the way we think it will," Baker said carefully, "we would be well suited to put a plant in the state."

"Is that a guarantee?" Fessler asked.

Baker sighed. "No guarantees."

When the California delegation got its walk-through of Impact, Fessler seemed to calm down. He couldn't do anything without jobs as part of the deal, he warned. But the car was impressive. He would do what he could.

Within days, Baker secured an agreement in principle from the individual utility heads. By offering EV owners lower electric rates, the utilities could defray, theoretically at least, $2,000 of each car's purchase price. And when Impacts were commercially available, the utilities would agree to buy 5,000 of them over several years. But California had vocal watchdog groups that

---

* These were the state's "investor-owned" utilities, of which the largest were Southern California Edison, Pacific Gas and Electric, and San Diego Gas and Electric. They were profit-making enterprises, but operated under the jurisdiction of the California Public Utilities Commission (CPUC), a state government agency. The state also had municipal utilities, owned and operated by local governments. Among them were the Los Angeles Department of Water and the Sacramento Municipal Utility District. These were not governed by the CPUC and so could pursue their interest in EVs independently of it.

might campaign against the incentives as giveaways to an elite minority of ratepayers. In any event, hearings would have to be held, and the commissioner's verdict issued. Baker could take his pledges back to GM's management committee, but they were only worth so much.

From Washington, surprisingly, might come more definitive help. Congress was preparing to adjourn for its end of summer recess, and hoping to pass an omnibus National Energy Act before it did. Both the House and Senate versions contained EV incentives. A compromise before the House Science and Technology Committee proposed to grant a tax deduction of $2,000 on the purchase of an EV, a savings in real dollars of perhaps $700. The Senate's Ways and Means Committee was considering more: EV buyers would get a tax *credit* of 15 percent of the EV's retail price, meaning an EV buyer's tax bill could be downwardly adjusted by that much. Baker needed the credit. GM's lobbyists in Washington were pushing for it, but Baker felt he had to plead the case himself.

In one day Baker and the program's public affairs chief, Jean Crocker, roamed the halls of the Senate to visit the offices of six skeptical lawmakers whose votes on the bill's tax provisions were key. Appointments had been made, but few of the lawmakers were there. Baker was chagrined until Crocker explained that in Washington, educating legislators' staffs could be just as useful. By day's end, Baker had preached to curious, even enthusiastic staffers, as many as six in each lawmaker's office. One after another of the staffers, however, wanted to know how much an Impact would cost to produce, and what its sticker price would be. They were confused, they said, because the projected EV costs laid out by the American Automobile Manufacturers Association—the Big Three's lobbying group—were so high that a 15 percent tax break would seem too modest to make a dent. And why should their senators take a political risk in giving Detroit a perceived handout, when nothing of consequence might come of it?

When Baker started to answer, Crocker shot him a look. GM's own costs, she told him in the halls, were numbers he couldn't discuss, since the Big Three carmakers lobbied together and presented one set of representative costs to avoid having one undercut the others. Baker wanted nothing more than to lay out every number he had—he knew how much closer GM's business case was to reality than Ford's or Chrysler's—but every time he started to get specific, Crocker gently headed him off. The result was inevitable. When Baker told a staffer he couldn't answer the cost question, he could see the excitement curdle into wry skepticism.

In the last days before the October 12 management committee meeting, Baker and Reuss sat down together to craft the program's do-or-die pitch. One obvious point needed no discussion: along with the car, both their careers might be at stake. Soon enough, they lined up four options that seemed to span the gamut.

Plan A was the most aggressive of the four: to carry through with Impact as a two-door car, knowing it would lose money, but also commit to a follow-on, four-door EV that could sop up those losses as the market grew. Initially, Reuss was against it.

"Don't predicate your business case on the need for a follow-on," he told Baker. "From day one we haven't expected Impact to be profitable. What we wanted was to establish a preemptive place in the market." If management, in other words, could once again perceive Impact as an investment in the future, not as a business, then it could feel its money would be well spent and not spend more to try to get it back.

Baker couldn't agree. To ask funding for an acknowledged money loser with GM so beleaguered was like—well, it was like fiddling while Rome burned. Finally Reuss came around, and projections were drawn up for a two-car program that reached profitability by the year 2002. Before profitability, though, the hole got deep—more than a billion dollars deep.

For Plan A, Baker's incentive campaign would certainly help. Congress on October 8 had passed the energy bill with strong EV provisions, including a 10 percent tax credit on purchase, and President Bush would soon sign it; the California incentives remained tentative, but promising. Plan A's strongest appeal, though, had nothing to do with numbers. Did GM really want to give up its technological lead—to Europe or, worse, to Japan? Did it want to squander the chance to dominate a future market that might be huge? Reuss was cautiously optimistic. "I think I can sell them on it," he said.

Plan B was partial sacrifice. Delay production for two years, trim the platform to a small band of engineers who could turn out 50 to 100 handbuilt cars, and tool up to sell components. Baker and Reuss figured they could save $200 million of the $270 million the program was projected to spend over that time to go to production. Of course, the likelihood of cranking up to production after that would be slim—it had never happened before at GM, to either man's knowledge. But with Plan B, at least the company could keep riding the learning curve, and be in better shape if the mandate held. As a corollary, Baker would go against all his ingrained instincts of competition and pursue some sort of joint EV project with Ford and Chrysler: a way for all three carmakers to ride the curve together, saving money and responding to the inevitable progress Japan would be making if the mandate stayed in place. TeamUSA, Baker called it.

By Plan C, no cars would be built. Virtually the entire platform at Engineering South would be disbanded. Only Jon Bereisa's propulsion team would be kept on, to keep refining the drivetrain, so that GM might hope at least to sell EV components.

And then, inevitably, there was Plan D. Shut down the program altogether. Forget EVs. Do nothing unless and until forced to by the regulators. No one, Reuss assured Baker, would go for Plan D.

At 2:00 on Monday, October 12, the management committee met in a ninth-floor conference room of the GM building downtown to hear Baker's pitch and review his flimsies—the plastic sheets of charts and graphs that were a GM tradition, laid out on the illuminated glass box of an overhead projector. Jack Smith, GM's low-key new president and chief operating officer, sat at one end of the table. Along one side were Stempel, Hoglund, and Reuss. Along the other was a contingent of EV senior staffers.

Baker tried to be dispassionate in his pitch. The point was to let the committee choose the plan it thought best. He did make the case that the press hype about Impact had done more to improve GM's corporate image than any other program in years, and that as a result GM was perceived in California as the standard setter in EVs. The business case, admittedly, still showed short-term losses, but the incentives would mitigate them, and the follow-on car would eventually bring a return on GM's investment.

As Baker spoke, Smith sat with his hands folded, listening quietly, an unassuming, almost shy presence. Next to him, Stempel took copious notes, with an earnest energy that seemed belied by his appearance; not only did he look exhausted, but his complexion was oddly blotchy. Hoglund, the doubter from the first meeting two months before, sat back with an old-school casualness, his legs stretched out, his hands folded behind his head.

When Baker finished, Stempel spoke first. Like Reuss, he felt the program was too important to be stopped. The company couldn't expect it to make a profit in three years, but what program with all-new technology could? Forcing every project to account for itself would just bring short-term gain and long-term disaster. New technology would be obsolete almost as soon as it appeared, but GM had to keep developing it. Stempel thought the cost of Impact should be spread not just into one follow-on, but over the first three or four cars, while the learning curve was steep. By the fourth car GM would have a mature design and far lower costs. "What do you think, Jack?" Stempel concluded.

"Bob," Smith said, "you can't afford it." Then he stood up. "Please excuse me," he said. "I've got to get to another meeting."

An embarrassed silence fell over the room as he left.

The next day, at a luncheon meeting in Washington, Stempel felt suddenly ill. Within half an hour, he was in an ambulance, being rushed to a hospital for tests. The results seemed to indicate acute anxiety, though the chairman, back at work two days later, waved off the incident as nothing more than fatigue. A maelstrom of dark rumor swept the company as he remained, as if besieged, behind the closed door of his office. The outside directors were said to have made up their minds: if drastic action weren't taken to avert GM's deepening losses, the company would perish. Stempel and Reuss would have to go.

Amid the speculation, Baker got a call from Reuss, upbeat as always. The management committee was clearly troubled by Impact's business case, but hadn't yet reached a decision. Its members were to meet at the Milford proving grounds to talk out various matters; could Baker deliberate with them one more time about the program?

When Baker arrived he had to wait outside while the committee discussed how to develop better gasoline engines for improved emissions and fuel economy. The irony did not escape him: here he was, making his desperate pitch for a propulsion system that had those problems *solved*. Ushered in at last, he went through the options again with the committee, and with a sinking heart heard the members conclude Plan B was the best they could do under the circumstances. Production would be deferred indefinitely. The Lansing factory would be cut away. The platform's core staff would be drastically reduced. The limited production of fifty handbuilt cars was approved, however, and Baker should pursue his TeamUSA idea of some joint EV venture with Ford and Chrysler.

Determined to save money wherever it could, the committee seemed to have lost sight of the mandate, looming like a road sign ahead in the California desert. In fact, the members saw the mandate as one more reason for curtailing the program rather than pushing ahead to production. Everyone recognized that Impact, as a two-seat sports car, would not reach a wide enough market to satisfy CARB's escalating EV demands. If GM produced it, and the mandate stayed in place, the company would have no choice but to finance a four-door follow-on by the turn of the century, if not before. Better to pull back now, hope the mandate went away, and produce one EV later if it remained in force.

Ordinarily, the management committee's word on an operating matter was final. Impact, however, was no ordinary matter. Pained and frustrated by what they had to do, the committee members voted to have GM's board ratify their decision when it met in early November. As Baker left, Reuss pulled him aside. "Keep going, just as you have been," he said.

It was as if the management committee—or at least three of its members, Stempel, Reuss, and Schultz—secretly hoped the board would turn the program back on. Unfortunately, amid the rivers of red ink, they had lost the right to do it themselves.

The Downward Slide

))))

As Baker drove back alone from the Milford proving grounds, the verdict sank in, and for the first time he felt despair. He'd pressed every button he knew to press, but the committee members hadn't budged. They'd seemed unusually tense, barely looking at each other. Baker had the distinct feeling that Stempel and Reuss had demanded the Milford meeting, and that the others had gone along out of a cold sense of corporate decorum, their minds already made up.

Baker had been invited, at least, to outline the program's progress to date at the November board meeting in New York. Within a day or two, however, Jack Smith called to say, almost apologetically, that the agenda was getting rather full. Could Baker give Smith four or five slides and let Smith make the presentation himself? Earnestly, Baker suggested instead that the presentation be moved to December. He wanted to deliver it himself. He also knew that in December the board would meet at a GM-owned building outside Washington. By then, a few of the POC Impacts would be finished at Bumper to Bumper. Baker's private thought was that the directors could drive them around the parking lot; the cars were their own best advertisement. Smith agreed to the postponement, obviously distracted by other matters.

Despite the postponement, the presentation was all Baker could think about. On the afternoon of Thursday, October 22, he cleared out of the office and went home to start thinking it through. Perhaps, if he just worked hard enough, he might produce a speech so powerful, so persuasive, that the outside directors would resuscitate the program. So began a series of events that would seem, in retrospect, blackly humorous.

Baker set up a makeshift office on his basement pool table. He had a fax machine brought in. He spread out charts, speeches, and calendars. Outside his carpeted cell, *The New York Times, The Wall Street Journal,* and *The Washington Post* published front-page stories with unattributed quotes from highly placed GM sources that Stempel was about to go. The last straw, it was said, was his confused response to several factory strikes in recent months, which underscored management's tensions with the UAW while showing a too-great willingness to make concessions to it.

That same week in Southern California, the *Los Angeles Times* reported, some six dozen EV enthusiasts with makeshift vehicles gathered for a first International Electric Grand Prix, drawing press and crowds as they drove a three-day circuit from Long Beach to Santa Monica, northeast to Pasadena, and west to San Bernardino. Among the strongest entries was Alan Cocconi's converted Honda CRX, a sporty two-seater about the size of Impact, its inverter and motor designed and built by Cocconi in his Glendale home lab. The EV world was growing, and the car that Baker was trying so desperately to save had played the largest single role in galvanizing it.

Monday morning, Baker returned bleary eyed to the office to learn why Jack Smith had seemed so distracted. After more than a week of feverish press speculation, met by a deafening public silence from GM's board, Robert Stempel bitterly acknowledged reality by tendering his resignation. Quickly, the board went further, its directors sweeping away the rest of Stempel's management team and instituting its own. Stempel's dual titles were pulled apart, as John Smale became chairman and Jack Smith CEO; Smith would lead the company, but Smale would take an active role. Forced to resign were Lloyd Reuss, Robert J. Schultz, and F. Alan Smith — Stempel's gang and, as it happened, Impact's strongest supporters. As far as Baker could see, any chance that the Impact decision might be reversed had just been eclipsed.

The successors were notably younger, a new generation for a new kind of GM: Richard Wagoner, from GM of Brazil; Louis R. Hughes, who had taken Jack Smith's place as head of GM Europe; and Harry Pearce, GM's chief counsel. At fifty-eight, William Hoglund was the oldest of the group; before being brought on as chief financial officer in last April's shake-up, he had helped launch Saturn, and would now head North American Operations. In August, Hoglund had been the first senior manager to voice doubts about Impact's business case. Among other immediate tasks, he was assigned to be Baker's liaison for the rescheduled EV presentation in December.

Forty years before, GM's then president Charles ("Engine Charlie") Wilson had made a casual remark to a Senate committee that entered history as "What's good for General Motors is good for the country." GM's tumult now seemed a reflection of the nation's, as twelve years of Republican administration ended days later with George Bush's fall from the presidency. Though not much for politics, Baker was a Republican, and like most of his colleagues viewed the ascension of a Democrat to the White House as portending nothing good for the car business.

With speculation about the new regime's plans swirling through the company, Impact was said to be dead, its capital pulled. Baker got calls from other program managers asking if the rumors were true, and would some of his brightest engineers be available? In frustration, Baker called Hoglund. "Bill," he said, "if this is a foregone conclusion, we don't need to go through a bunch of calisthenics—let's make the decision and go on."

Hoglund agreed to see how Jack Smith felt, and called Baker back within a day. Smith did want the board to mull over Impact one last time, he said; the new CEO understood the risks of deferring the program, and felt torn, as did Hoglund. But the new team had a lot to consider at the meeting—a lot, though Hoglund was too polite to say so, more important than Impact's fate. For the December meeting, then, Hoglund made the same suggestion Smith had for November: Baker should give him an abbreviated pitch in advance, with four or five slides, and let Hoglund present it.

In the halls, Baker tried to remain cheerful, to be a buffer between the news from above and the doubts from below. The chiefs knew the score, but as far as anyone else on the program was concerned, management was still mulling over Impact's business case. Baker could feel all eyes on him as he went down the hall. He was the barometer. If he looked despondent, the engineers assumed the worst. If he radiated energy or mustered a smile, they took it as a ray of hope.

Baker understood that neither Smith nor Hoglund *wanted* to ax the program. Brutal choices had to be made, and Impact's deferral was just one of them. But he had put too much of his heart into the program to stand back from it now. He took it hard. He kept wondering what he could have done better, or sooner, or cheaper. He felt he had failed. All those who had trusted him to make the program work—he had failed them, too. Every working day for two years he'd come to the office fired up, surrounded by his inspirational sayings, and done his best. Still it hadn't been enough. What conclusion, he wondered, should he draw from *that*?

The weekend after Stempel's resignation, Baker drove alone north, 200 miles, to Lost Lake Woods, a hunt club near Alpena. He had his bow and arrows with him, to lend purpose to the trip, but he'd never cared less about bagging a deer. He wanted to sit in the crook of a tree, listening to the wilderness. Ordinarily Rosetta, his wife, was happy to stay home while he mucked around with his hunting buddies. Saturday morning, though, she called to say that Jeff, the Bakers' son, was staying with a neighbor, and offered to make the long drive up to join him. That afternoon, and the next morning, Baker and his wife took walks, and sat in the lodge, and reminded each other that there was, after all, more to life than Impact. In a union of twenty-five years that had had, like any long marriage, its gray patches, Rosetta's presence that weekend was an emotional reminder to Baker of what had first drawn him to her, and of what her company still meant.

At Engineering South, attitudes varied from denial to despair. Some, like Tom Lobkovich, the structure man, could not imagine the program getting canceled. It had come too far for that. To others, the December board meeting loomed, as Latham Redding put it, like approaching thunder. But if the platform did collapse, not everyone on it would be equally affected.

In a sense, the engineers could almost feel they'd finished what they set out to do. The first proof-of-concept cars were emerging from Bumper to Bumper, and proof-of-concept was just that: proof that the engineers' designs had worked. Seeing thousands of EVs produced, having them change the world—those would be greater satisfactions. But to know a fiberglass show car had been reconfigured into the first modern producible EV was no small beer. And the small, discrete triumphs of technical innovation would endure, perhaps in the engineers' next jobs, to which they might ascend with long-deferred raises in title and pay.

Jeff Dickenson, a tall, British-born chief in charge of finding and administering Impact's hundreds of suppliers, could take no such comfort. His two years of lining up parts for the production car would be wasted if the program was canceled. There would be nothing to show, nothing to bring to the next position. It would all just go up in smoke. Randy Schwarz, the manufacturing chief who had given up his job in Japan to work for Baker, would have nothing to show for his two years, either, except the hundreds of assembly drawings lining the four walls of a basement room in Engineering South. None would be used if the program was cut back to fifty handbuilt cars. As for John Dabels, the skeptical marketing chief, he would have nothing to market. But then, he'd never thought he would.

In these somber days, Baker tried to focus on the one encouraging sign he'd been given by the management committee: the go-ahead to do what he could with his notion of a "TeamUSA" Big Three EV consortium. If he could wring some resolution from Ford and Chrysler for the December board meeting he might yet produce an EV. The rivals might welcome the chance to share costs; since Impact was the only true EV among them, they might agree to produce it as a unified effort, a triumph for all three carmakers. An American triumph. A triumph, as well, over Japan's Big Four, who were showing, as it happened, new and disconcerting signs of EV activity.

None of Japan's major carmakers had announced EV production plans. But Toyota, largest of the four, had recently acknowledged it would soon have prototypes of a luxury four-door EV conversion. So had Nissan, Japan's number two. Mazda was said to be working on an EV sports car based on the Miata using nickel cadmium batteries. All were likely doing more than they let on. And so, Baker feared, was Honda.

Though not as wealthy and powerful as Toyota, Honda took more risks and used the element of surprise as a marketing tactic. Its only indication of any EV development to date was a concept EV displayed at a trade fair in Tokyo earlier in the year. But a telling development had just occurred: Honda had just withdrawn from Formula One racing. Though no indication was given of what its nearly 100 Formula One engineers would do next, the word in EV circles was that this pool of top talent would build a ground-up electric vehicle for California by 1998, if not before.

That rumor was linked to another. MITI, Japan's trade ministry, was said to have solicited bids from Japan's Big Four for major EV R&D funds, partly as a reaction to the forming of the USABC. Toyota, Nissan, and Mazda had lost the bidding, went the story; that was why they'd displayed their prototypes. Honda had won, and so showed nothing. No acknowledgment of this had been made either, but MITI had just declared that it wanted Japanese carmakers to produce as many as 200,000 EVs by the year 2000.

Whatever the truth behind the rumors, Japan was clearly serious about EV development—as the California mandate required it to be. And if EVs weren't exactly computers, they consisted of just the sort of high-tech electronics that Japan could excel in manufacturing. If the board did administer a coup de grâce to Impact, inviting Japan to take the technological lead in EVs, Baker wondered if the directors would appreciate the irony of the date on which they made their decision.

December 7.

Pearl Harbor Day.

If Baker needed more motivation to pull TeamUSA together in the short time he had, it came with the news that he would, in fact, be able to speak to the board in New York. Hoglund would still handle the formal consideration of Impact, but earlier in the day Baker would get to present TeamUSA to the public policy committee chaired by Marvin Goldberger, one of the board's two staunchest EV advocates. The public policy committee made broad recommendations to the rest of the board. Its endorsement of TeamUSA would be a valuable boost.

What Baker needed was the blessing of his EV counterparts at Ford and Chrysler. Somehow, he had to get it without seeming to need it. John Wallace and Jean Mallebay-Vacqueur might be genial USABC partners, but if they found out Impact was about to be emasculated they would hardly rush to provide a fig leaf. A little public humiliation, after all the bragging GM had done about Impact, would strike them as entirely appropriate.

With Thanksgiving just ahead, Baker would have to wait to schedule a meeting with them. Instead, he spent the holiday writing a new speech—a TeamUSA speech—for the board. On his family's long drive to Buffalo for Thanksgiving with his in-laws, he scribbled away in the passenger seat as his wife drove and the children observed an earnest silence in back. He worked on it all the way back, and much of the next week. He thought of canceling an annual deer hunt with old friends the next weekend in Maryland, but instead took his notebooks with him. He studied on the plane. He studied in the blind. He shot a nine-point buck, and a doe; flew back, and studied on the plane home. Then he set up a meeting with Wallace and Mallebay-Vacqueur for the earliest time both were free: late Friday afternoon before the Monday board meeting.

Saying nothing of his impending trip to New York, let alone the program's near-death condition, Baker told his counterparts that GM was ready to unite with Ford and Chrysler on EVs to share the R&D costs, speed the technology, and beat Japan to market. Perhaps the three would combine to finish developing one or more of their respective EVs. Perhaps not. That would be worked out later.

In principle, the partners agreed. Why not? For all the bluster about their own EV programs, both Wallace and Mallebay-Vacqueur realized GM was ahead. At worst, teaming up would give them a chance to study Impact in detail, and adopt the best of its new technology, before one or the other pulled out.

It would be nice, Baker went on, if the three could work up a letter of agreement. Nothing detailed. Just the general intention to try to make a TeamUSA consortium work. *That day.* Again, the partners agreed, though not without a few barbs from Wallace. This was *Baker,* after all, the same guy who'd scoffed at just such suggestions from his counterparts before. Later, Wallace would say he knew Impact was about to go down, that Baker needed TeamUSA as a public relations gimmick to offset the bad news, and that both he and Mallebay-Vacqueur went along as a friendly favor.

Saturday morning, at any rate, the letter was drawn up and signed by Baker and Wallace. Mallebay-Vacqueur couldn't sign for Chrysler; his boss, François Castaing, would have to do that. But the two men had spoken, and Castaing had said the agreement seemed fine to him. Presumably, he would sign it Monday.

By midday Sunday, when Baker flew to New York, Jack Smith and John Smale had learned of his progress on TeamUSA. Both wanted to hear more about it before Baker appeared before the board. A casual meeting was scheduled for that evening at Smale's suite at the Regency Hotel.

The Regency, on Park Avenue at 61st Street, was a short walk from the GM building on Fifth Avenue, and thus the hotel of choice for out-of-town GM directors. In his room, Baker laid out the little information packets he had assembled for the meeting. From a brand-new suitcase, he took out a new suit, new shirt, new shoes, and new tie. After a room service dinner he put on his new clothes, scooped up his packets, and, slightly early for the meeting, headed up to Smale's suite.

Baker was nervous, he had to admit. All he knew of the new chairman was what he'd read and heard. From the reports, Smale seemed a sort of corporate grim reaper, unlikely to appreciate any program that failed to contribute to GM's battered bottom line. As the leader of GM's historic board revolt, Smale was also the heavy who had pushed out men Baker liked and respected—Impact's biggest supporters, and his own highest patrons. Taking a deep breath, Baker knocked on the chairman's door. No answer. After a moment, he knocked again. No answer still.

Disconcerted, Baker went back down to his room and looked anxiously toward the phone. No messages. At precisely the appointed time, he went up to try again. No answer. Baker decided to stand outside Smale's door, awaiting his arrival. Fifteen minutes passed, then thirty, then forty-five. He drew his share of suspicious looks from guests getting on and off the elevator. Finally, after an hour, Smale stepped out of the elevator. He was genuinely apologetic; he seemed less imposing, more cordial, than Baker had expected.

Along with Smith, Smale had invited Tom Everhart and Marvin Goldberger, the board's two academics. They were in their rooms, awaiting Smale's call. When they arrived it quickly became clear that Everhart and Goldberger still felt Impact should be produced. They alone among the directors lived in California; they sensed how strong the EV market could be. They were also the board's only engineers and saw, more clearly than their colleagues, what a technological lead Impact had set. But their feelings were not unmixed.

Everhart, tall and balding, with a hawklike ruggedness about him, felt GM had wasted a year translating AeroVironment's elegant concept into a production design with all the perks of a GM luxury car. Far too many engineers had piled on too quickly, for the same reason they always did: the larger the program, the more important it was deemed to be, and the more powerful its managers. But Everhart did think a two-door was the right choice to start with. And he felt, strongly, that there were enough EV-obsessed Californians to give GM its 2 percent market share.

Physically, Goldberger was a striking contrast to his fellow Californian. Short and bulbous nosed, with fly-away white hair, he took wry satisfaction in being the only Jew in memory on GM's board. But he was a good deal less proud of his eleven-year tenure than other chapters of his career—working on the Manhattan Project and serving as president of Cal Tech before Everhart, among other things. Along with the other board members, he had let himself be gulled by GM's profit statements through the Roger Smith years, and had not asked the tough questions. Now, at last, he was speaking out, forcefully so, about Impact.

"Unfortunately, it's very simple," Smale said gently. "We can either do an electric vehicle or put several plants back to work and bring more short-term revenue to the company."

Then it was Baker's turn to talk about TeamUSA. He knew that in stumping for it he was, in a sense, arguing against his own program, drawing a line down the middle of the room that put the academics on one side and Baker on the other with GM's chairman and president. But he had to be pragmatic. The academics had nothing to lose by arguing that Impact go to production. They had nothing to win, either.

The two Johns—Smale and Smith—liked what they heard. TeamUSA, they said, seemed the right way to go.

For the first time in weeks, Baker felt things might just work out after all.

The next morning, Baker put on his new clothes, stood in front of the mirror, and said to his reflection, "You are *ready* for this meeting." Then he strode over to the GM building and rode up to the twenty-fifth floor.

For what seemed an eternity, Baker waited outside the closed boardroom. Finally, after a break, he was ushered in.

What he noticed first was the boardroom table. It seemed big as an aircraft carrier, all glossy, polished dark wood. On the walls hung life-sized portraits of every past GM president. Out the big picture windows he saw the castle-like towers of the Plaza Hotel and the russet hues of Central Park in winter. The directors and top managers sat in high-backed leather chairs, their names carved in small brass plaques on the back. Smale, as chairman, occupied a seat in the middle; Smith, as CEO, sat directly across from him. The directors and managers sat interspersed down either side, the new directors and less august managers farther from the center of power.

Baker nailed his fifteen-minute speech on TeamUSA almost to the second. Then came questions. Why, wondered more than one director, should GM share its technological lead with Ford and Chrysler? Baker suggested that the USABC might serve as a model for TeamUSA, with the government, as well as GM's rivals, sharing its costs. He noted that America's new vice president, in his bestseller on the environment, wrote of the need to have government work with the carmakers to get beyond the internal-combustion engine. TeamUSA could be the new administration's centerpiece for transportation, served up just as Bill Clinton and Al Gore took power. Besides, GM couldn't afford to go it alone.

Baker walked out of the meeting with the board's endorsement of TeamUSA, but also with its ratification of the decision to take Impact off production status. As he and Reuss had outlined in their Plan B, a pared-down platform would stay on to refine the design of a small limited-production fleet of fifty cars. Some of the LPFs, as they would be called, would be kept for testing, so that at least the team could keep learning about EVs. Perhaps thirty of them would be the basis for a two-year series of public test drives around the country. John Smale, the chairman and former Procter & Gamble man, was particularly keen on getting market response to the cars. GM had never done anything quite like this; for something so radically different as an EV, Smale felt, sustained market testing was critical.

Baker felt relieved, but hardly victorious. To the hundreds of people who had shared his dream of having GM seize the technological lead in EVs with a production Impact, a fifty-car build, talk of a test drive, and vague rhetoric about TeamUSA would seem a bitter defeat. He put his first call in to Frank Schweibold, the new finance chief, and heard, behind Schweibold's consoling words, the shock that it had come to this.

Schweibold had some bad news of his own. Chrysler's François Castaing had held off signing the TeamUSA proposal, and John Wallace at Ford was expressing new doubts. Their change of heart had come, no doubt, from a *Wall Street Journal* story that morning, speculating that GM's board would scale down the Impact program.

Baker's mouth went dry. He'd just sold the board on a plan he couldn't deliver.

Pearl Harbor Day indeed.

To John Wallace and Jean Mallebay-Vacqueur, Baker's motivation had seemed fairly transparent three days before. But the *Journal* story irked them nonetheless. They felt he could have leveled with them about the board's imminent decision; as USABC partners, the three had grown, supposedly, to trust each other. Given the timing, TeamUSA seemed a mere publicity stunt, and neither they, nor their superiors, felt inclined to sign on for that.

At the least, they agreed, higher executives had to get involved. Lawyers had to be convened. All this took time, which Baker didn't have. Thinking an agreement was in the bag, he'd assured the board that TeamUSA could be used to offset the embarrassing news about Impact. Now, until the agreement came through, he had to try to keep the Impact decision from leaking further to the press; he had to keep from announcing it to the program as well.

Three days after GM's board meeting in New York, lawyers at Chrysler and Ford were still redrafting the letter. Watering it down, to Baker's chagrin. Even insisting the term TeamUSA be scrapped in favor of the deliberately bland "electrical vehicle cooperative study effort." Meanwhile, reporters kept calling, seeking confirmation of the *Journal* story; on the program, engineers gathered in small somber groups to speculate on their fate.

The agreement reached on Thursday evening was, as Wallace observed, a modest one. In vague, gray language, it spoke of "exploring opportunities," and made no mention of Japan. The bland title was used, though as a concession Baker was told he could refer publicly to the consortium as TeamUSA. More important, he could end the suspense about Impact. Keeping the news from his program even one more day, though, would have been unbearable.

Before dawn on Friday morning, Baker set out for the Lansing plant with Randy Schwarz, the manufacturing chief. He wanted to break the news to the line workers first, so that they heard it from him rather than local television or radio later in the day. Notice of an all-employee meeting had only been posted at the close of the previous day, however, with no indication of its agenda. Because the plant remained largely unused, only the 100 or so union members working on a small job unrelated to Impact had seen it. A scattering of others had been alerted by calls from friends, but most of the union's 652 members remained at home, unaware of the meeting.

Larry Zahner, the plant manager, was there, with union shop steward Stan Pewoski, to greet the arriving guests. The glum contingent walked through the empty plant, its floor still marked up with masking tape to show how Impact's assembly line would be set up, into a lunchroom where their modest audience awaited them on bleachers. Baker announced the news, and said that this was a sad day for everyone. He said he had gone through the first stages of a grieving process himself—the denial, then the anger—and that the workers would, too. But as tough a blow as this was, he went on, he hoped from his heart that every worker, and every worker's family, would still enjoy a merry Christmas. At that, more than a few workers looked at Baker in disbelief.

For Zahner, the meeting marked the low point of his GM career. He felt he could see his workers crumble before him. When Baker and Schwarz departed, leaving him to carry on, he felt their hurt hardening into resentment. Zahner was salaried. He would be reassigned to some other factory; his career would keep on growing. For the workers, this time, there was nothing.

Back at the Tech Center, Baker presided over his second all-employee meeting, this one in the large auditorium next to Engineering North. At Lansing, he had spoken from the heart, but this was the home crowd. Looking out over a sea of familiar faces, the emotions of the last week welled up in him, and more than once he had to stop and swallow before going on.

Though most of the engineers by the end of this dark week had come to expect what they heard, they were jolted as Baker disclosed that the program of roughly 250 people in Warren would be winnowed to a core group of perhaps seventy to do the fifty handbuilt cars. This was not to say, Baker stressed, that any of those shifted to other programs should take the moves personally. There were no losers on this team. What the team had managed to accomplish as a whole was extraordinary. Electric vehicles would become commercially feasible years sooner than they might have; the innovations in management that the program had employed would be used on other programs, and surely help GM on its road to financial recovery. "The most important thing to remember," Baker added, his voice cracking, "is that programs come and go, but the friends we've made on this program we'll have for the rest of our lives."

Most of the engineers wandered back to their cubicles to spend the rest of the day working—a tribute, perhaps, to midwestern stolidness, or a collective exercise in denial. Arianna Kalian went home and cried. A few of the other unmarried engineers gathered for drinks across Twelve Mile Road at the Arriva, a local hangout. The married ones simply drove north on I-75 to their subdivisions, seeking solace on this cold Friday night. It was, all in all, a meager, dreary end to the most technically ambitious program in GM's history.

Over the next few days, Baker's efforts at spin control mitigated the press reaction, but not by much. The decision was still seen as the end of GM's electric car program, one further humiliation for a company that had suffered its worst year ever. GM's announcement that fifty prototype Impacts would be handbuilt and sent around the country for two years of consumer testing seemed a lame PR gambit. As for Baker's call to arms—TeamUSA versus Team Japan—it drew a sharp denial in print from the enemy. "If there is a Team Japan, Toyota doesn't know about it," said a U.S. spokesman for the company. A Mazda spokesman agreed; each of Japan's Big Four was going its own way. At the same time, each of the Big Three was actively engaged in lines of business with Asian carmakers. GM, for one, was exchanging information on electric vehicles with Isuzu, of which it owned 37 percent. Perhaps global economics had grown too complex and contradictory for such jingoism.

One consequence was clear as of Monday morning. The nearly 100 contract designers—the gypsies, with their cynicism and cigarettes—did not come to work that week in the darkened room on the third floor of Engineering South. On Monday morning, that room stood empty. The gypsies were in Dearborn, at the Village Plaza, working on Ford's Ecostar program.

Up in Lansing, the thirty hourlies who had commuted to the Tech Center arrived home Friday night to begin a long winter without work, but with the 85 percent pay their fellow union locals drew as part of the jobs bank deal that had helped doom Bob Stempel's chairmanship. The next week, about twenty workers chose to earn full pay by coming to the plant though they had no jobs. The union sent them to the cafeteria, where a shop steward, to occupy them, had them count, and recount, folded wooden tables.

As the 652 members of Local 1618 prepared for a bleak holiday, they received Christmas cards from the Impact program, with a drawing of the car on front. The cards were signed, with best holiday wishes, by Ken Baker. The cards enraged them. To address their fear and despair with a chirpy holiday blandishment was, at the least, insensitive. At worst, it seemed to underscore that back at the Tech Center, Baker and his white-collar engineers were still working on their pet program. Out in Lansing, a lot of laid-off hourlies had just had their chains pulled again. In protest, dozens of workers gave their cards to their shop steward.

"Here," Stan Pewoski said, passing the pile on to Larry Zahner. "Merry Christmas."

Picking Up the Pieces

))))

For nearly three years, Impact had set the pace. As it flew around the track toward production, the world's other carmakers, large and small, had eaten its dust, vainly trying to catch up with jerry-built conversions and concept cars. Now that it was pulled off into the pit, a colorful pack sped by. To judge by those on public display, the Europeans, not the Japanese, appeared in the lead.

One of the strongest prospects was BMW's E2, for which the German carmaker claimed a range of 267 miles using sodium sulfur batteries. Like Impact, the E2 had an aluminum structure and plastic body skin. Unlike Impact, it had a small backseat, the extra space available because of a smaller battery pack that weighed only 441 pounds, half that of Impact's lead acid pack. Of course, there were drawbacks. The sodium sulfur batteries cost at least $8,000 and, like Ford's, had to be kept at 600 degrees Fahrenheit. They also had a *practical* range of, at most, 86 miles. Only by poking along at 25 miles per hour could they achieve anything close to their vaunted range of 267 miles.

Still, this was progress, and others weren't far behind. Volvo's concept hybrid supplemented its nickel cadmium batteries with a gas turbine engine that could extend its range to 400 miles, but be disengaged for pollution-free urban driving. When a driver turned the key, the batteries took about thirty seconds to start the engine. "The car sounds like an earthbound jet fighter as the turbine whistles and whines into action," reported the London *Times*, "the most disconcerting piece of instrumentation on display being a rev counter for the turbine that registers up to 100,000 rpm." Without the turbine, the car started silently, but took nearly half a minute to reach 50 miles per hour. Another problem, admitted Volvo's British design director, Peter Horbury, was that the battery pack cost $20,000.

For the New York marathon of the previous November, Mercedes-Benz had provided an EV conversion as pace car. Engineer Jurgen Gaub reported a practical range of 78 miles for its sodium nickel chloride batteries, but allowed that the pack would have to be shrunk since it occupied the trunk and half the backseat; and like sodium sulfur, it had to be maintained at 600 degrees Fahrenheit. Gaub doubted Mercedes or any other carmaker would solve the battery problem with a breakthrough. "There is no magic," he said sadly.

Peugeot and Citroën had just shown not terribly surprising lead acid concept EVs at the Paris auto show. Renault, on the other hand, had the wackiest design. Its egg-shaped, two-passenger Zoom concept car, also shown at the Paris auto show, featured a folding rear that reduced its length from 73 to 49 inches to make parking easier on Paris's crowded streets. France's Big Two might seem a minor threat, but France was both politically and culturally poised to seize the lead in European EVs—perhaps even to steal a march on the American market. Its "green" party was influential; EVs were coming to seem a feasible alternative to four-dollar-per-gallon gas at the pump; and a single, nationalized utility served the whole country, enabling the government to plan strong EV incentive programs. EVs could also be smaller and lighter in Europe than in the U.S., where highway safety standards required greater mass for crashworthiness. Perhaps, for all these reasons, France might become the world's first EV-ready country.

To the dispirited engineers of Impact, however, the most unpredictable rival was a Swiss engineering legend named Nicholas Hayek, who had teamed up with Volkswagen. Hayek was Swatch Man, the savior of Switzerland's wristwatch market. In the early eighties, Switzerland's two largest watchmakers, SSIH and Asuag, had asked Hayek's consulting firm to help them fend off the Japanese, who had made devastating inroads in the global market. Hayek's Swatch watches triumphed because of what Hayek called the salt and pepper: a bit of cultural seasoning, sprinkled into the design, that a foreign competitor couldn't understand or appreciate. "If you know how to create a product that requires less labor in its final cost, and if you can add to it your personal culture and emotions," Hayek liked to say, "then you can beat them, because they have to learn your emotions."

A stocky, professorial pipe smoker with great bushy eyebrows and the energy of a man half his sixty-three years, Hayek told the interviewers who came daily from around the world that his Swatch car, in the R&D stage at his SMH watch company with $11.2 million from Volkswagen, would be a small car: a light, fun, in-town runabout, probably a hybrid, though one that might be made to run only on batteries in urban areas, qualifying it as a ZEV for

California's mandate. "Big enough for two people and two cases of beer," he said. One of Hayek's notions was to have body colors bright as a Swatch watch, and somehow have them be interchangeable, perhaps with body-sized decals. When interviewers asked if the difference in scale and manufacturing complexity between a watch and car wasn't daunting, he bristled. "Why does size impress you? Is an elephant more intelligent than a fox?"

Nothing could be further from the muscle power of Impact, or the workaday usefulness of Ford's and Chrysler's EV vans. But was it possible that Hayek had the salt and pepper for an EV market in Europe and Asia—perhaps even in the U.S.—that the Big Three, rooted in midwestern car culture, failed to understand?

In Warren, after the holidays, no one much cared. The race was over; GM had surrendered its lead. Bodies dispersed like so many electrons, beginning with many of the chiefs: Randy Schwarz, the manufacturing chief; Paul Huzzard, the body chief; John Dabels, the marketing chief; and Jeff Dickenson, the purchasing chief. John Williams, the process chief, left too, since the four-phase program he had monitored was moot; he would keep his hand in EVs, though, as the new chair of the USABC's Technical Advisory Committee. Among the other staffers, Dave DiPietro left for Harvard Business School, his tuition paid for by GM. Latham Redding went back to Parts Fab to do slow builds of conventional cars. Others, like Arianna Kalian, Tom Ruster, and George Claypole, stayed on, wondering if their departing colleagues were in fact the lucky ones, going off to start new jobs or lives while they themselves lingered on in a moribund R&D program.

Baker was not, in truth, much more excited than his engineers by the fifty-car build. But he had TeamUSA on which to hang a few hopes.

Early into the new year, the principals held their first meeting on neutral territory: rented offices across from the Dearborn Ritz Carlton. Rounding out the table were lawyers for all three carmakers, there to pounce at the first mention of costs and prices—the cardinal violation of antitrust law—or technical details that might compromise one or the other of the carmakers. The prospective partners had reached one understanding as a condition of signing on: none would say anything publicly, from now on, on the subject of electric cars unless all three agreed. GM's boasting had brought on the mandate and forced the others into this fix; enough was enough. Baker knew he was the one the new ground rule was meant most to silence. "They've got me muzzled!" Baker reported back to his staff.

A certain edginess remained between Baker and Wallace. Both were strong, proud, and sometimes arrogant men, accustomed to being in charge. When Wallace threw a barb Baker's way about keeping quiet at last, so that the partners could start cooperating away from the glare of the press, Baker bristled. "What about the one hundred designers Ford stole from GM the weekend after the announcement?" he asked. "Would you say that was in the spirit of cooperation?"

"We didn't call any of those designers," Wallace shot back. "They just answered an ad."

In that first meeting, the players filled sixteen pages of chart-pad paper with points of agreement. The first, they called the EV creed. *We believe that one day there will be a meaningful number of EVs in the world.* Another was that if the carmakers were going to accelerate the natural pace of EV technology in response to government's demand, government would have to help.

It was easy to agree on the problems, harder to agree on what the partnership should do. Should the carmakers choose one of their EV designs, and pool their resources to produce it? Or somehow combine the best ideas of all three, and use them to create an all-new design? Could one car be sold collectively? Or could a single platform be cloaked with different enough bodies to be badged by each carmaker as its own? Should they even work together on a car, or just on a drivetrain?

To Baker, the course was clear. The Impact was a ground-up, a real electric car, with POCs being finished even now. Ford and Chrysler didn't yet have prototype *conversions*. The three should produce Impact together.

Wallace and Mallebay-Vacqueur, not surprisingly, felt GM had a car but not a market, at least not at the prices GM would charge. Better to have the partners take the prudent course of doing Ford's Ecostars. Or Chrysler's TEVans. Each player thought his car was best. But none, at this stage in the game, would say why, in any technical detail.

"This'll get us nowhere," Baker said at last. "If we're going to be partners, we've got to see each other's cars—for real. Under the hood. Let's have a series of three garage shows, one for each car, and then see where we want to go."

Wallace and Mallebay-Vacqueur looked at each other. They looked at Baker.

"Sounds good to me," Wallace said.

On January 13, 1993, the unheard of occurred at General Motors. Ford and Chrysler came for a visit. A technical show and tell. Wallace and Mallebay-Vacqueur, each with a preapproved team of colleagues, strode into Engineering North, checked through security, and were led immediately downstairs, away from the wide main floor of confidential future car projects, into the Impact mock-up room. They saw a finished aluminum structure. On tables around it, the car's components were ranged, along with boards and charts to explain how the hardware worked. In the background stood the program's various team leaders, feeling very strange indeed.

Wallace, for one, was impressed by Impact's drivetrain, especially by the way the batteries and inverter were packaged. And the aluminum structure was awesome. "You couldn't get a magnet to stick to that vehicle," he muttered to one of his adjuncts. Baker, at the time, was amused to see Wallace feigning disinterest at Impact's rear electrical brakes and air-conditioning system, then lingering, as the others moved away, to take furious notes. Ford had neither rear electrical brakes nor a heat pump for air-conditioning. Not long after, Ford would hire away several GM brake engineers and approach Impact's heat pump supplier.

A week later, the party moved to Chrysler, where the one and only TEVan yet produced was brought out for inspection. The surprise was how much had been done with so little. Chrysler had assigned fewer than thirty people to the program, and still only committed some $8 million. Its secret was a strong reliance on outside suppliers: across the board, Chrysler purchased 80 percent of its parts from suppliers, whereas GM bought only 20 percent. With the TEVan, Mallebay-Vacqueur had made his suppliers R&D partners. It was economical, to be sure; whether or not it produced the best parts was a much-debated issue. The TEVan, at any rate, had a DC motor supplied by General Electric, and a GE controller to channel current to it from a nickel cadmium battery pack. The strength of nickel cadmium, as with all nickel batteries, was its energy, or the amount of current it stored: Chrysler estimated the pack would take its heavy TEVan 80 miles. Nickel's weakness was power—how much current it could generate in an instant—so its acceleration was poor. Cadmium's toxicity was an issue, too; recycling would be hard. Baker came away feeling that Chrysler had nothing new to show. Compared to Impact, he felt, the TEVan was a high school science project.

Ford's show came two days later. Wallace had arranged an elaborate showcase with rotating components. The GM team was impressed by Ecostar's motor transaxle design—the motor mounted on the axle's center line, so that it could do double duty as a differential and thereby save mass. Less impressive were Ford's sodium sulfur batteries. A pack still cost at least $50,000, and Ford hadn't solved the high-temperature problem. Sodium sulfur did have three times the energy of lead acid, but even so, the heavy metal van had a range of only 70 miles. With lead acid batteries, the van's range would drop to as little as 20 miles—in *mild* weather. It was better than high school, Baker thought as he rode in the just-completed first prototype van. But it wasn't a marketable vehicle yet, even to fleets.

So unrefined was Ecostar that Baker wondered if Wallace was using it as a decoy, keeping another, more sophisticated EV in the wings.

As it happened, he was.

TeamUSA—or EV3, as the others chose to call it, downplaying the nationalism Baker had hoped to stir—might lead to something quite exciting. But Baker found himself oddly nonplussed by the prospect. The collapse of Impact would have rocked any manager; to one whose emotions ran as deep as Baker's, it was devastating. He felt hurt; he felt angry, too, denied his big chance unfairly. Over the holidays, he'd thought hard about whether he wanted to stay at GM, and concluded he might not. Certainly his prospects at the company seemed bleak: how many managers of derailed programs became corporate vice presidents? Having presided over the fruitless expenditure of some $200 million, he might actually be asked to leave in this cold new era, or get shunted off to some corporate Siberia.

It was with some apprehension, then, that Baker accepted a lunch invitation from Arv Mueller and Mike Mutchler, two executive vice presidents who had urged Baker to take Impact on in the beginning. In a private executive dining room, Mueller and Mutchler asked Baker if he'd considered what he wanted to do next. Baker said he had, but had no answers. His lunchmates did: the vice president of GM's research and development labs was retiring. Baker, they thought, should lobby for the job.

Baker hesitated. A VP title was a VP title, but of all the nearly fifty vice and executive vice presidents, the VP of R&D was traditionally among the least consequential. The labs had a distinguished heritage, it was true, tracing to the barn in Dayton, Ohio, where Charles "Boss" Kettering invented the electric starter. And they had come to occupy nearly a dozen buildings at the north end of the Tech Center, housing some 750 scientists. But in the last two decades, the labs had lost their luster. The R&D Ph.D.'s fiddled with abstract notions while real change came from outside. So sleepy was R&D that its brochures, touting the labs' history and achievements, left off with the seventies; of Bob Frosch, a former NASA director who had held the job unhappily for five years, there was not a mention.

Baker tried to be diplomatic. "My initial reaction," he said, "is I really see myself as more than an engineer or scientist. I see myself as a general manager. And I'd really rather have an operating job." Operating meant leadership of a platform, from which real VPs sprung. And while a platform—for a basic, bread and butter, new model Buick or Oldsmobile—might lack the glamor and novelty of Impact, at least the company would want it. Baker was feeling pretty thin-skinned these days. No more risks, and if he could help it, not this R&D road to nowhere, either.

Baker's patrons could only encourage him, gently, to think about the R&D job. The board, which named all vice presidents, would likely want to fill it soon. Mueller and Mutchler could nominate him, but Baker had to want them to do it.

"Let me think about it," Baker said.

Too soon after to be by chance, Jack Smith called to invite Baker to join him for a day in California. Marv Goldberger and Tom Everhart had told Smith in December there was no way to gauge the eagerness for EVs in the state without experiencing it firsthand, and the new CEO had agreed to come meet true believers. The February board meeting was in Phoenix, Smith explained, so he had arranged to fly on from there to Southern California, where the twenty-four-hour show-and-tell would begin with a dinner at Cal Tech's Aetheneum Club, hosted by Everhart. Smith asked if Baker, as GM's EV expert, could come along to make informed responses to the lineup of ardent EV enthusiasts they would meet.

Baker's commercial flight to L.A. arrived late, so much so that by the time he burst into the library dining room of the Aetheneum Club, Smith and the others were just finishing their entrées, and Malcolm Currie, recently retired as Hughes's chairman and CEO, was making an impassioned speech. A corporate godfather to Sunraycer, Currie had gone on to become one of the state's most visible EV advocates. Now he'd formed his own California EV venture with two partners, and hit upon the novel approach of putting hundreds of small laptop computer batteries into converted Hyundais. Currie felt GM could do conversions for as little as $10,000 per car. And for factory space, he suggested, GM could use its shuttered Van Nuys plant. A big new market was out there just waiting. Would GM hold back out of fear, and let others jump in first?

Mike Armstrong, Currie's successor at Hughes, had scheduled Baker to lead the dinner discussion. With embarrassed apologies, Baker wolfed down his food as Currie finished, then tried, in a diplomatic way, to respond. "Mal," he said, "I know what it takes to do a conversion, and I know what you have. You've never done a car before; how are you going to produce it?"

Paul MacCready of AeroVironment, with somewhat greater credibility from the Impact show car, backed up Currie. "Not only do I think it's possible," he said, "I think a conversion can be done for *seventy-five hundred dollars.*"

"How much do you have in that estimate for warranty?" Baker shot back. "How much for dealer markup, and dealer service support? You need to look at this as a business, and when you do, there's no way to go in for less than five hundred million dollars."

California, Smith added, would have to ante up that much in subsidies and incentives if it wanted GM to bring EVs to the state; there was simply no money in the corporate coffers for any program whose ROI—return on investment—could not be charted with absolute certainty.

It was a frustrating evening until the end, when Smith invited Baker to ride with him back to the hotel. "Considering the audience you had," Smith said as they settled into the back of his limousine, "you did the best you could." Baker, alone with Smith for the first time as the car rolled through darkened streets, felt he'd passed a test.

The next day, Baker and Smith were challenged again, bluntly, by Daniel Fessler, the feisty California utilities commissioner, who didn't hesitate to speak his mind. After all that he and the utilities had done to try to comply with GM's SOS last fall, Impact's demise had left him feeling betrayed, and foolish. Meanwhile, the mandate wasn't budging, and the federal government was threatening to take away the state's highway funds if it didn't meet ever-higher air quality standards. "We're sitting here in California with a basket of lemons," he said. "We have no choice but to figure out a recipe for lemonade."

In the months since Fessler had demanded an EV factory in California, the state's recession had gone from bad to worse. A study done by the utilities showed that California within the last five years had lost 700 companies and as many as 224,000 jobs, many in aerospace. Fessler and others felt that aerospace could be replaced by a homegrown, California EV industry. Fessler was even willing to make low-interest loans to GM if GM would start a California EV plant. "On December 31, 1996, I'll walk out of this office a last time, turn off the lights, and go back to being a teacher," Fessler said. "By then, I hope to have created a manufacturing base for eighty thousand electric vehicles."

In Burbank, Smith and Baker visited a former Lockheed plant that Fessler and others hoped might be the start of that base. Here, in June 1992, economic desperation had bred a New Deal–like consortium of public and private interests called CALSTART, intended as a nonprofit R&D center to foster EV technology. Already it had won $20 million in federal and state funds, and built a showcase EV. From electric cars and buses, CALSTART was spreading out to hybrid vehicles, fuel cells, natural gas, and composites.

That same morning, Smith and Baker also met with Jananne Sharpless, CARB's chairwoman, and her fellow board members. The regulators, like Fessler, were furious with GM. For all the glowing press it had reaped from Impact as the EV innovator, GM had done its level best of late to thwart the EV mandate. And by this, the regulators did not just mean scrapping Impact's production plans.

On January 22, 1993, lawyers representing the Big Three had persuaded a federal district judge in New York that the northeast states could not adopt the California mandate as they had chosen to do the previous fall. For six reasons, the lawyers had argued, the Northeast, in demanding EVs, would be forcing Detroit to build a third variation of each car model—one for the country at large, one for California, and a third for the Northeast. The Clean Air Act forbade this to protect carmakers from unreasonable demands by different states.

The carmakers thought their most persuasive point was that the EVs planned for California would not have adequate heating for the Northeast. In fact, the judge had no sympathy with that claim. If the car companies felt better heaters were needed, that was a marketing decision, he ruled. It didn't define a "third car." But while dismissing five of the six issues, the judge sided with the carmakers on one. The Northeast wished to adopt California's emissions standards without the cleaner fuel that CARB had called for at the same time, principally because the fuel would be more expensive, and thus politically unpopular. It couldn't do that, the judge ruled. The Northeast had to adopt the mandate fully or not at all. Because of that, New York could not require EVs in 1998 as it wished to do.

The carmakers could do as they wished in the Northeast, Sharpless allowed. But if they thought they would wrest any significant compromises in California, they should reconsider. "If the mandate doesn't bring electric vehicles," she said firmly, "we'll do something more stringent that does."

After a morning of confrontations, Smith and Baker spent a more relaxed hour over at Disney's new corporate offices in Burbank, where they met with Disney chairman Michael Eisner and president Frank Wells. Wells, whose death the next year in a helicopter accident would throw the company into turmoil, was one of Hollywood's EV enthusiasts. He had had a converted Fiero; he had just bought a converted Toyota Corolla. It was great, he told his guests: went 45 miles per hour, with a 40-mile range, as long as he didn't go over too many hills.

"How much did it cost you?" Smith asked.

"Only forty-five thousand dollars!"

Everhart had arranged to have an Impact POC brought from the Tech Center down to the Disney parking lot for Eisner and Wells to drive. They went zipping around the neighborhood, delighted. "How much are *these* going to cost?" Eisner asked.

It was explained that as a handbuilt edition of fifty, they would cost about $500,000 each. "Great!" Eisner said. "I'll take a bunch. I'll write you a check; we'll put them in all of our theme parks."

If only every car buyer in California was an EV-obsessed multimillionaire, Baker and Smith agreed, GM would have it made.

That evening, Smith invited Baker to fly back with him to Detroit on the company plane. The R&D job, Smith said, broaching the subject at last, would be great for Baker; he hoped Baker would take it on. Swallowing hard, Baker reiterated the hope he'd expressed to Mueller and Mutchner of getting an operating job instead.

Smith had a reputation for succinctness. "So make R and D an operating unit," he said. "Make products we can sell. That's where I need your help."

"Give me your toughest operating job," Baker pleaded. "Give me five years to turn it around, and if I can't, I'll walk away."

"I think R and D is your toughest," Smith said.

Baker recognized a wall when he saw it. "R and D," he said slowly, and sighed. "Well, R and D it is, then."

Then the flight attendant brought dinner: lasagna. For three years, Baker hadn't looked at a plate of lasagna, not even his Italian wife's homemade, out-of-this-world lasagna. He hadn't dared.

"This is my favorite," Smith said. "You like lasagna?"

Baker hesitated, then grinned. "You bet."

Dead Cars,
Dying Hopes

))))

Impressive as GM's garage show had seemed, the Impacts on display that day had not been made to run without a lot of last-minute tinkering. So much tinkering, indeed, that the platform's chiefs had begun to wonder if even fifty limited-production cars could ever be made to work. Perhaps, they muttered privately to each other, the halt of production had been a blessing after all.

The problem was that the Hughes inverters were coming dead on arrival. When Jon Bereisa's engineers bench-tested them, the glitches they uncovered were inconsistent. To Jim Ellis, that meant Hughes had failed to follow through on its own process of systems engineering. Even after each inverter was fixed—usually a matter of finding the faulty connections amid the maze of circuitry—there was a larger issue. A *huge* one.

EMI.

Everyone had known that with an inverter that handled 100,000 watts of electricity, EMI—electromagnetic interference—would pose a problem. Not the low-frequency EMI, as from overhead power lines, that was unshielded and might be medically dangerous. *High*-frequency EMI. One hundred thousand watts was as much juice as that of two large radio stations combined. Two radio stations, packed in a small box, rolling down the street.

The point of a radio station, of course, was to *transmit* its high-frequency watts through an antenna. An inverter's job was to *transfer* its current to the motor, ostensibly in as contained a way as a microwave oven transferred its high-frequency emissions to the food it heated. But if emissions leaked out, or radiated as electronic noise, they could interrupt the car's AM and FM radio; they could interrupt other cars' radios and open electric garage doors as the car passed. Early on, an engineer at Milford had thrown a walkie-talkie into the show car when it was parked. The car had started to accelerate.

On Impact, EMI was compounded by about a dozen other sources, including the mini-inverter Delco Remy had lost to Hughes, the electrically heated windshield, and the charge port at the nose of the car. All could potentially interfere with the main inverter, with each other, with outside sources. Worse, the emissions varied as a function of speed. The whole orchestra of parts might be in concert when the car was at one speed, but at another, one of the violins, so to speak, might play off key. Other electric cars all had a lot more noise than music as far as Impact's chiefs could tell; no other carmaker seemed yet to have faced up to the problem. Ron Dork, the electrical chief, made a point at auto shows of going up to EV concept cars with a Walkman radio. They tended to knock out his Walkman immediately.

Dork, a small, shy engineer with more than thirty years at GM, was assigned ultimate responsibility for resolving what might be, as car guys put it, a showstopper. He was the sort who often went unnoticed, but then, so did his realm of the car.

Dork did all the electronics *except* the drivetrain, which might have seemed like doing everything but the important stuff. Yet without his network of computers regulating current like so many way stations pumping water from a central dam, the car would have been little more than a drivetrain on wheels. One of Dork's computers fed drivetrain information to the driver through the instrument panel. Another operated the CD and radio, a third the air bags, a fourth the rear electric brakes. There were electronics to make the steering wheel steer, the horn honk, the lights beam, and the HVAC blow hot and cold. Gas cars had electronics, too, but they could be run by the alternator hooked up to the starter battery, which was continuously fed by the engine. Dork's one battery had only the meager amount of current it contained, stepped down from 320 volts to 12 volts through the small, secondary inverter.

Early on, Dork and a rather wild-eyed young engineer, Joe LoGrasso, had tried to predict how much EMI the car's different sources would emit, and told Hughes and other suppliers to take measures accordingly. The inverter's EMI, for example, might be partly contained by shielding the electronics within an aluminum case. Unfortunately, cables protruding from the inverter could conduct EMI, too; their wires, if they remained parallel, could serve as antennae. Fortunately, the wires could be twisted so that the positive noise of one canceled out the negative noise of the other, and sheathed in insulating materials. Unfortunately, on the proof-of-concept inverters, these precautions seemed not to have been taken by the suppliers responsible—particularly at Hughes.

The chiefs were really irked by that. Hughes, they felt, had simply ignored the specs because EMI was seen as too arcane a problem to merit the investment of time and money. Now LoGrasso would have to start analyzing the contribution each component made to overall EMI; convince the various suppliers the problem was real, even if no EMI was generated by a part before it was put into the car and had a chance to clash with other parts; and help them find the filters or capacitors that might contain the emissions. Bereisa, for one, felt with EMI as if he'd fallen off a cliff and that there might be no way back up.

The ninety-nine engineers at Hughes Power Control Systems had a different story to tell. GM people never seemed to appreciate how hard and well the Hughes team was working to invent on schedule. All Hughes ever heard from Bereisa and Ellis was do it faster, better, and cheaper. In April 1992, Hughes's Harry King had grown so sick of the abuse that he'd taken early retirement. Vigorous when he'd started with Impact just two years before, he was burned out.

By then, much of the battling with GM had been taken on by King's successor, Rami Helmy. An Egyptian-born engineer, Helmy had fended off Bereisa's daily prodding and nearly finished refining the proof-of-concept inverters when Impact was taken off production status. In a stroke, most of the revenues Helmy had counted on were gone. Mercifully, that week a fast-growing EV conversion outfit in California called U.S. Electricar rushed to fill the breach by ordering more than a thousand inverters from Hughes— business that Hughes was now free to take—for EVs that state utilities and various agencies would buy to help the nascent EV industry. For the moment, Hughes Power Control Systems would survive. But the engineers were understandably rattled.

Days later in December came the second blow: a merging of Hughes and Delco Electronics. In a sense, the longstanding fear of Hughes's engineers that Delco Electronics would steal their inverter was made real by the news. In the reshuffling of corporate assets, Hughes Power Control Systems was to be folded under Delco Electronics so that all of GM's automotive electronics would be in one corporate box. Now Hughes would report to DE on Impact, rather than the other way around; whenever EVs did get produced, Delco Electronics would be in control. Ken Baker's handshake deal with Freeman Nelson had meant nothing after all.

Now it was early February 1993 and the bugs weren't out of Impact's inverters yet. And why, Helmy asked, should they be? GM was making proof-of-concept cars. These were proof-of-concept inverters. By definition, they weren't production ready.

Helmy knew the POC inverters still had problems when Bereisa demanded them for the GM garage show with Ford and Chrysler. He knew

EMI would be a problem as well. The previous fall, he had begun to plan how his engineers would test for it. When Impact was taken off production status the GM team had told Helmy to forget about EMI. "Why bother now?" he was told. Yet when the first inverters were sent to Warren and proved to have bad EMI, Helmy was the one hung out to dry.

Week after week, as the inverter recriminations flew back and forth among the engineers, the secret triumverate met, trying to define TeamUSA, better known now as EV3. The garage shows had established GM's technical superiority, Ford's claims notwithstanding. But that hardly made the course of action any clearer. Ford and GM felt that all three carmakers should pool their EV resources under one roof as a separate company, developing and building whole vehicles. Perhaps EV3 would make both Impact and Ecostar—the two complemented each other well—and join in the design of a follow-on four-door.

This begged a host of questions. When cars were built, which brand would they be? How would they be sold, and who would service them? The prospect of Impacts with an EV3 badge, in the showrooms of all three carmakers, was as hard to fathom as that of the same car wearing different badges. Even setting aside the challenge of meshing bitterly competitive cultures, the scenarios seemed absurd. *Would* have seemed, that is, were it not for the even more absurd scenario of each company spending $1 billion to ride the same R&D curve for a market that might not exist.

As far as Chrysler's Mallebay-Vacqueur was concerned, all this talk of doing Impact or Ecostar was beside the point. The point was that a suitable battery did not yet exist. "Look," he told his partners, "if you spend the money and the battery doesn't show up, you have spent the money for nothing! If you don't spend the money and the battery doesn't show up, you haven't wasted money in things which do not matter."

Mallebay-Vacqueur had a modest proposal. Instead of having Chrysler ante up even a small part of some very large pot, Ford and GM could help defray Chrysler's far smaller costs, share in the development of EV components by outside suppliers, and do the TEVan together. At that, Baker and Wallace rolled their eyes. What would they do with Impact and Ecostar—throw them away?

By early March, the talks had stalled. Sometimes Mallebay-Vacqueur seemed to yield a point to his more allied partners. By the next meeting, he slid right back to his previous position. Baker and Wallace were convinced that Mallebay-Vacqueur's boss, François Castaing, was acting as a puppetmaster. They began to think it made no sense to negotiate with Mallebay-Vacqueur because he had no power. What they didn't know was that week by week Chrysler's hand was being strengthened by secret road test reports on the TEVan. At the first EV3 meeting, Mallebay-Vacqueur hadn't known if the TEVan would actually work, so quickly had his team designed it. The reports he was getting now were that it did. They emboldened him—or perhaps Castaing—to consider having Chrysler go its own way.

The partners owed a report to their CEOs, who would meet on April 1 to discuss EV3.

"Right now," Mallebay-Vacqueur said, "I have to say no venture at the vehicle level."

John Wallace's boss at Ford, Dennis Wilkie, was sitting in for this session. Wilkie turned to Baker. "So where's GM?"

Baker smiled. "I'd like to hear from you, Dennis."

The two men locked eyes for a moment.

"All options still open," Wilkie said at last.

"That's GM's position, too."

"Even if it's only EV2?"

"Right."

An EV2 partnership—GM and Ford—might mean no government money. But even a fifty/fifty cost share between the two carmakers on EV R&D was preferable to going it alone. And the two together might be more than the sum of their parts. GM had the better car, but Impact was good for only a fraction of whatever EV market emerged, and the company was too poor now to produce it anyway. Ford's Ecostar seemed the more practical vehicle, but its sodium sulfur batteries remained unproven, and Ford had no more desire to spend $1 billion on EVs than GM did. Together the Big Two would not only halve their costs, but double their chances. Perhaps, too, Chrysler was bluffing. If they went ahead, Chrysler might feel it had to join in.

If a partnership had seemed closer at hand, Baker might have felt more conflicted about his own prospects. As it was, leaving the program loomed as a relief. In March, and again in April, the board postponed its official approval of his promotion—distracted by, among other things, the shocking departure of GM's purchasing chief, Ignacio Lopez, for rival Volkswagen. The nod came, at last, in early May, while Baker was in Arizona on business. The one to call him with the news was Lloyd Reuss, a frequent presence on the fourteenth floor despite his ouster, as if by lingering he could launder the past. His congratulations were warm and heartfelt, a graceful gesture from an ex-mentor whose protégé had just passed him by.

That was the morning, as it happened, that Impact's seventy-five survivors moved out of the Tech Center to occupy two floors of a bland office building in the neighboring city of Troy. Part of the remaining space was leased to Saturn, but the building wasn't owned by GM. Twenty minutes from the Tech Center, cut off further by the busy raised roadbed of I-75, the survivors unpacked boxes like castaways. For nearly five months they had tried to bring the same enthusiasm to the goal of building fifty cars as they had to that of building 50,000. It wasn't easy, especially without knowing if the program would continue when the fifty cars were done. And for all of Baker's talk of TeamUSA, the prospect of partnership seemed dubious at best; for many of the engineers, fired up so long by the idea of winning the race, it was actually offensive. The move to Troy only underscored the alienation they felt.

Baker broke his news to the platform by conference call, reaching everyone on the platform simultaneously. The best part, he said, was that Impact would still be under his aegis, reporting now to R&D. Of course, if a joint EV project went ahead, he would have to hand Impact over to a full-time program manager.

Putting Impact under R&D played directly to Jack Smith's new vision of what GM's labs should do. No longer would scientists be indulged to pursue projects that had little hope of application. Baker's mission, which he found himself explaining upon his return to nearly 1,000 researchers in a video teleconference, was to have R&D solve real-world problems and to develop ideas that led to products, not academic reports. His goal, he said, was to make R&D one of the most competitive assets in the new, leaner corporation GM was aiming to be. He gave his new troops, nearly all of whom had more education than he did, the mantras he'd imparted at Impact. *Life is not a dress rehearsal. We need a spirit of winning.* If his listeners found the pep talk disconcerting, Baker didn't hear about it.

Baker was a VP at last, and he had the office to show for it, in the R&D building overlooking the larger of the Tech Center's two lakes. John Williams came to visit and jokingly paced its dimensions. "Thirty by twenty!" he said. "It's as big as my first house!" One wall had sliding doors that opened to reveal an antechamber lined with bookshelves. His predecessor's books had filled them; now they were empty. "Where are all your books?" his new secretary asked Baker. Baker indicated two humble cardboard boxes. "Everything I need is in there," he said. "I'm going to count on the researchers to be competent; the last thing they need me to do is try to outlearn them."

A large office in Troy was set aside for Baker, too, but it remained empty. In his stead, Jim Ellis and Frank Schweibold became co-leaders of the program, Ellis overseeing the engineering side, Schweibold the financial; for the fifty-car build, that about covered it. They made a Mutt and Jeff–like team, Ellis so tall and lanky, Schweibold short and round, but they worked well together. If neither man had Baker's sense of command, neither did they have his ego. The boss was gone, and an unexpected sense of calm settled over the program.

But was it the calm before a historic EV partnership with Ford and Chrysler? Or the inexorable winding down of a program about to die?

The Partners
Square Off

))))

For the EV players in their top secret talks, the hard work came that April. Chrysler was still sitting in, despite doubts expressed by CEO Robert Eaton to his counterparts, to give the plan a last chance. Together, the three rivals ran numbers for every cost a freestanding EV business would incur, from engineering to manufacturing to marketing. As the exercise began, Ellis and Schweibold tried to use GM's four-phase plan. At that, Ford's John Wallace, at the sketch pad, rolled his eyes. "I don't care what your program says!" he said. "I don't care what Ford's program says, either. They all take too long! Let's just think logically how long it would take."

Since none of the carmakers wished to reveal too much about their own product-timing programs anyway, the partners put them aside and sketched a best-guess, thirty-four-month schedule. As they groped toward it, they realized how different their approaches were. Ford and GM did far more prototypes for a new car than Chrysler did, for example, and subjected them to more rigorous gamuts of testing. Chrysler, still strapped financially, simply made do with less, but also, as a result, moved faster. For the EV business plan, Ford and GM agreed to use fewer prototypes—twelve in all—and spend closer to what Chrysler spent on a new car program.

The numbers the partners used were vague, to avoid antitrust violations. Still, they provided yardsticks for comparison. A light conversion like Ford's Ecostar could be put through a first year of low-volume production—say 10,000 units—for about $100 million, they felt. A heavy conversion—like Chrysler's TEVan, with room for four or more passengers—would cost $145 million. A two-seater ground-up—like Impact—would cost the $275 million that had made GM's board gag the previous fall, while a four-passenger ground-up—say, a second-generation Impact—would cost $335 million.

The figures grew more daunting when stretched to fill seven-year scenarios. If the partnership did only conversions between 1993 and 2000, it would still spend between $375–500 million. If it did only ground-ups, the cost rose to $575–775 million. A limited program of conversions *and* ground-ups would cost between $725–925 million; a higher-volume, "maximum" variation of same would be as much as $950 million. The figures went down somewhat if all EVs were out by 1997, for CARB had decreed that early arrivals would get market credits to set against 1998. Still, none of the programs offered any real prospects for profitability.

The most depressing finding for Ford and GM was that Chrysler would be better off on its own than in joining even the most modest of the plans. Mallebay-Vacqueur had reached that conclusion even before the numbers were run: road tests had just conclusively shown that his TEVan prototypes worked. On April 12, the first five road-ready TEVans, rechristened Dodge Caravans, were delivered to eastern utilities. Technically, Chrysler had won the EV race to market, albeit at $120,000 for each handbuilt vehicle.

The TEVan's success provided yet another reason for Chrysler to shun EV3. For 1998, its EV conversion, should the mandate remain in force, would be based on its next minivan design. Chrysler's minivan was its great success story, defining a new market in the 1980s and remaining, with each restyling, far enough ahead of the competition to dominate it. Now that Chrysler had a working TEVan, why should it even consider sharing the secrets of its future minivan? "I just don't think we'll be able to make this work," Mallebay-Vacqueur told Baker one day.

"Well, then we're going to be tough competitors, aren't we?" Baker said evenly.

Mallebay-Vacqueur was startled. He'd come to think of both Baker and Wallace as friends, and the consequences of going it alone after all seemed not to have hit him until that moment.

If Chrysler confused the EV3 deliberations, so did a series of talks between the Big Three and members of the new Clinton administration. The talks raised the tantalizing possibility of federal research money being reallocated from national labs and other government programs to the development of a "clean car." The sum was never spelled out, though the press would report it as $1 billion.

But what *was* a clean car? Some participants saw it as pollution-free. Others imagined a high-volume gas car with up to 90 miles per gallon efficiency—clean but not emission-free, particularly as far as carbon dioxide was concerned. To the CEOs, the offer was compelling not only on its own terms but as a possible alternative to the California mandate. If they anted up their share and agreed to work hand-in-glove with the government, the mandate might be made to go away. A vaguely defined clean car with an even vaguer deadline and a billion-dollar budget sounded a *lot* better than EVs in 1998.

For the moment, the carmakers had to assume the mandate would stand, and to the CEOs of Ford and GM, "EV2"—assuming Chrysler bowed out— was still a cheaper course than each carmaker struggling alone. The two remaining partnership teams were told to keep meeting on their own, and to move their talks to a higher stage. They should define what the company EV2 would be and still aim for a fifty/fifty cost-share deal with the government. Most important, the EV partners had to show how they could reach profitability after 1998. The CEOs of GM and Ford wanted all this in thirty days so they could put the issue to their boards in July and choose whether or not to proceed.

The partners drew up a list of twenty issues to work through. With Chrysler gone, most points were agreed on without serious debate. The issue of background value, though, was volatile. The partners had agreed that each should have 50 percent equity in the new venture. But aside from prototype cars that had no commercial value, the equity they were bringing was knowledge learned in their respective programs. How much was each side's knowledge worth? Was worth a simple matter of money invested, or was one side's program more successful, and thus more valuable, than the other's? And if the partners allowed their programs to be judged, who would do the judging?

When the GM board met in New York on June 28, Baker reported that Ford's reluctance to submit to a background-value review had deepened his suspicions that its sodium sulfur batteries had serious problems, and that Ford's willingness to team up was tinged with a new sense of quiet desperation. At the same time, Baker was convinced Ford had plans for a ground-up EV that it hadn't revealed. That suggested a lack of candor that didn't bode well for the partnership.

No one on the board much *wanted* GM to team up with Ford. But with GM still mired in red ink, going it alone on EVs made no more sense than it had the previous December. Reluctantly, the board chose to have GM join Ford for the next step of working up a formal plan to approach the federal government for funding.

At the board meeting, Baker was asked if the EV was the ultimate clean car. He hesitated. "No," he said. "And the reason is that there almost certainly won't be a clean car solution as broad ranging as gasoline is today. In cities, an EV can contribute dramatically. But you're not going to see an electric-powered Suburban heading cross-country on a family vacation for a long time, if ever."

The Impact program had done amazing things, Baker added. It had made a vehicle 40 percent lighter than the average gas car, with 45 percent lower aerodynamic drag and far greater practical range than previous electrics. But barring a breakthrough in battery technology, electrics were simply too limited in range to be of wide use; and of course, the business case remained untenable. However, he suggested, Impact *could* be the critical link to hybrids and hydrogen fuel cells, the technologies increasingly seen as ideal solutions of a distant, but not unreachable, transportation future. Both solutions would use electricity—hybrids by generating it with an onboard generator, fuel cells by combining hydrogen with oxygen to generate direct-current electricity.

Not so long ago, Baker had bristled at the mention of hybrids. They had come to nothing in the early eighties for the same reason, he felt, they might in the nineties: they required two complex powertrains on a car, rather than one. They would be more expensive than EVs, heavier, and harder to engineer. EVs made more sense. As for hydrogen fuel cells—they were much too far from commercial reality to be worth considering.

To see EVs as a conduit to hybrids and fuel cells was a new, broader view for Baker. It was the VP's view. It was, in fact, wiser than the blindered view of a program manager whose only goal was to get his car to production. But in the coming months more than one Impact engineer would wonder if their leader had simply decided the program had no more political use for him and had coolly distanced himself from it.

Not by chance did Baker mention hybrids to the board. All three carmakers were suddenly fascinated by them.* No advanced EV battery had been commercialized as yet, and the business plan costs for EVs drawn up by the EV3 players had, as was said of scheduled hangings, concentrated the mind. Hybrids offered the allure of great range; besides, the Clinton administration liked them, and might back up its affection with some portion of a billion dollars.

No carmaker had yet managed to turn hybrid concepts into commercial reality, but almost every one was trying. In 1991, GM had unveiled a concept

---

* Hybrid drive, like fax machines, had been in limited use for decades. Many trains were powered by diesel-electric systems; so were many submarines. The engines varied, and so did the fuel, but all worked in one of two basic ways. In *series* hybrids, the two drivetrains operated in tandem: a small engine powered a generator that created electricity for the batteries that fed the electric motor that turned the wheels. *Parallel* hybrids were, as their name suggested, systems with two entirely separate drivetrains, each capable of directly running the car. Either way, hybrids could use their batteries for the peak power demands of starting up, or quick acceleration, so that the accompanying engine could be far smaller, and less polluting, than that of a gas car. The small engine, in turn, could extend a car's range to several hundred miles by kicking in for steady-speed highway driving. A hybrid would thus employ the strengths of each propulsion system—and none of the weaknesses.

hybrid minivan employing a small, three-cylinder gas engine and two AC motors to drive the front wheels. Since then, a GM team had worked on other hybrid designs in concert with AeroVironment. In February, both GM and Ford had submitted proposals for $150 million in hybrid R&D funds from a new Department of Energy hybrid-vehicle program put together by Mike Davis before he left Washington. By the end of the year, DOE would give out more than that: $138 million to GM, $122 million to Ford. Meanwhile, both Volkswagen and Volvo had introduced impressive concept hybrids. Amory Lovins, the energy guru and prognosticator, was not alone in thinking hybrids were the way of the future. "Electric cars may be cleaner, though probably not cheaper, than today's inefficient cars," he wrote that summer. "But they will almost certainly be costlier and dirtier than ultralight hybrids. . . . EVs look increasingly like a future technology whose time has passed."

Hybrids, though, had as many detractors as supporters. Baker had ticked off three of the drawbacks: weight, complexity, and cost. All, argued advocates like Lovins and Paul MacCready, would come down rapidly in time. The other problem was more intractable. Hybrids might be far cleaner than gas cars, but they were not emission free. To CARB, the carmakers began to argue that summer that emissions from a small hybrid engine—no more than 30 horsepower—would be far lower than from an internal-combustion engine, and that a driver could stick to electric power for in-town driving. But the regulators were unimpressed. One CARB member observed that only the U.S. carmakers were making the hybrid pitch. Foreign carmakers wanted the zero-emission clause kept in place to protect investments already made in EVs. Also, for all the frustrations carmakers still faced with battery-powered EVs, carmakers had done far more research on them than on hybrids. Changing the focus to hybrids now would push back the date that EVs of any kind could be produced.

No one denied that hybrids, at least the kinds designed so far, polluted. But how clean were EVs? As the carmakers pondered the magnitude of their predicament, they seized on a debate that had roiled the EV community for years. EVs were emission free, critics charged, but they used electricity. And where did electricity come from? Power plants, most of which were still operated by fossil fuels—in particular, high-polluting coal. There was, GM smog scientist Richard Klimisch liked to observe, no free lunch: EVs would simply generate their pollution from their fuel's source, rather than its end use.

The facts were complex enough to keep the debate humming, but in California, the issue was all but moot. Since smog had first become a threat in the 1960s, California had worked to make its network of power generators one of the world's cleanest. Most power in the state was generated by water, wind, nuclear, and geothermal plants. Fossil-fueled plants within urban areas used natural gas, not coal. Most had, or would soon have, new, very effective smokestack scrubbers and other emission trappers to curb even their limited emissions by a further 70 percent. A CARB study showed that after taking power plants into account, EVs in L.A. would still create 98 percent less hydrocarbon emissions per mile, 99 percent less carbon monoxide, 89 percent less oxides of nitrogen, and more than 50 percent less carbon dioxide greenhouse gas than gas cars.

The cleanliness of nuclear energy was, of course, a fierce debate in its own right. However efficient nuclear plants might be for the present, no safe way had yet been found to dispose of their spent fuel rods, which continued to pile up as some of the world's most toxic pollution. The issue made strange bedfellows of nuclear power advocates and those environmentalists in the pro-EV camp. But the environmentalists seemed to want to ignore nuclear's role in EVs, and most EV critics were nuclear advocates, so the nuclear debate was swept aside.

Instead, critics countered CARB's claims by declaring that California was an exception. What about Arizona, whose coal-fired plants supplied much of Southern California's energy? Wasn't California dirtying its neighbor's air to clean its own? And what about the Northeast, where energy was generated almost exclusively by older coal-burning plants that lacked adequate scrubbers?

But in Phoenix, Arizona, where 68 percent of the energy was supplied by coal plants, a study found that EVs would still reduce pollution dramatically. There, and certainly in the cold Northeast, too few EVs would reach the market over the next decade to have any significant effect on power plant production—to say otherwise would put carmakers in the position of arguing against their own pessimistic predictions of the EV market—so that even if coal remained the plant fuel of choice, EVs would make pollution no worse but only improve it by eliminating tailpipe emissions. Also, smokestack pollutants had been shown to cause far more damage to the smog-laden, mountain-confined air of Los Angeles than to air over the Arizona desert and other open landscapes. Besides, most electrical plants were able to release their emissions at night, avoiding the sunlight necessary for the formation of smog.

The carmakers were in a box, and neither hybrids, nor finger pointing at power plants, seemed likely to save them from the dreaded prospect of meeting the 2 percent EV mandate in 1998.

Ken Baker was right: Ford did have another EV in the works.

The Ecostar van, John Wallace acknowledged one midsummer day from his plainly furnished corner office in the Village Plaza building, had never been meant for production. It was a mule, as carmakers called a practice car, intended only to ride the learning curve. With a gusto for code that evoked the old TV show *Get Smart,* Ford had chosen to call the Ecostar the VZW108. The real McCoy, as Wallace put it, was the VZW109. The VZW109 would be based on a sport utility vehicle by Mitsubishi called the Expo LRV, and use a platform that could serve for various EVs. About 200 people were working on it. There were market studies and clays and interior bucks and package drawings. Ford hadn't shown any of this to GM yet, and might not at all.

The VZW109, like the Ecostar, would have sodium sulfur batteries. In late April, Ford's two suppliers, Silent Power of England and ABB AG of Germany, had announced delays in manufacturing batteries for the 105 Ecostars, and hadn't resumed production, but Wallace professed to be unperturbed. He had some three dozen sodium sulfur packs that worked; he had ten Ecostars on the road, the oldest of which had been running for five months.

Wallace was the first to admit that sodium sulfur was still too expensive, with too short a lifetime, to be commercially feasible. It also had a tendency to go up in flames, as the sulfur in its cells corroded the cells' seals and set off chain reactions. Of late, though, Ford had made dramatic progress with a "looping element" that closed a corrupted cell before its sulfur could spread to others. As soon as Wallace's suppliers fine tuned that looping element, Wallace would have a nifty battery. It would still cost tens of thousands of dollars, but economies of scale would bring that down sooner or later. The salient fact was that the battery would have three times the range of lead acid.

Wallace was ready to share this knowledge with his prospective partner, but only when GM stopped suggesting that Impact was more valuable than Ecostar, and that Ford, as a result, should pay GM millions of dollars for Impact's "background value" before an EV consortium could be established. That way, Wallace felt, lay chaos. How could anyone put a price tag on either side's intellectual property without testing it in the market? Each side would just attach inflated values to their own work and get nowhere. If the two companies really wanted to be partners, they had to trust each other, roll up their sleeves, and start working together. When they did, the GM team would find its new partner brought a *lot* to the party. "But we ain't telling them," he crowed, "until they sign the damn agreement."

Over dinner one night at Charley's Crab in Troy, Baker took issue with Wallace's view. "He's got battery technology they've been working on for years, it costs thirty thousand dollars per battery pack, and they still can't make it work," he exclaimed. "And the sodium sulfur batteries wouldn't fit on an Impact in any event." Wallace would try to bluster his way into a partnership that put aside the intellectual property issue, taking full advantage of GM's hard-earned knowledge while offering, in return, a failed technology. Baker wasn't about to let that happen. "Until we partner," Baker said of Wallace, "he's my competitor. As of today, I'm trying to put him out of business."

■ ■ ■

At an EVP meeting the day after that dinner, the partners finally confronted the intellectual property issue. Baker sat in to help Ellis and Schweibold deal with it. On the other side of the table, along with Ford's lawyers, was Wallace.

Baker declared bluntly that Impact had greater value than Ecostar, and Ford would have to pay for it. Angrily, Wallace disagreed. The partners should share and share alike, Wallace said; one partner trying to extract background value money from the other at the start of a joint venture was like a spouse demanding a prenuptial agreement. "Ken, I'm warning you, *drop* it," Wallace said.

Baker bristled. "You think we should just write off all our R&D on Impact and let you share it for free?"

"What about our R&D on Ecostar?"

"Well," said Baker, "what do you think the Ford program is worth?"

What, Wallace wanted to know, did Baker think Impact was worth?

The men glowered at each other.

"We'll figure it out," Baker said. "To the dollar."

"Fine," Wallace replied. "We'll do the same."

Gentlemen's Agreement

))))

The city of Troy, to which the Impact engineers commuted in the summer heat of 1993, was not to the casual eye distinct from the streets of Warren that surrounded the Tech Center. It, too, had broad boulevards lined with mini-malls and motor inns, Big Boys, Olive Gardens, Taco Bells, gas stations, and, on almost every long commercial block, a car wash. Troy's last open stretches had succumbed more recently, however, and to more affluent pioneers. Spanking-new office towers were set off by perfect lawns. The subdivisions were more easeful than Warren's, their mock-Tudor houses enclosing man-made ponds. As for the oatmeal-colored office building in which Impact's survivors worked, it had more modern contours than the Tech Center's bunkers, and inside, a sleekness of chrome and glass, with a central atrium from whose second and third floors the engineers could look down to greet waiting visitors below.

Every day in the halls, Jim Ellis, the program's de facto manager after Baker's ascendancy to VP-dom, was asked about the EV partnership talks. Every day, he had to say simply that the talks were continuing. He hated keeping secrets from his team. It violated the spirit of the inverted pyramid, and had a corrosive effect on morale. He could sense the engineers growing restless, wondering if the honor of being kept on after December 1992 was bad luck after all. He worried about that; for the restless to start leaving, he felt, would be a disaster. To a very real extent, the car existed in their minds. He had drawings, of course, and proof-of-concept cars. To coax the design through the fifty-car build, though, he needed the expertise of its creators.

On a raised platform in the mock-up room, the last of the proof-of-concept cars, the one called Metamorphosis, was days away from becoming the first of the limited-production fleet—the LPF—of fifty vehicles. Its wooden and foam surrogate parts were gone, replaced by bright blue body panels and Michelin tires; its passenger compartment fitted out with lightweight magnesium-frame seats and steering wheel; the instrument panel with its digital readouts and illuminated bar stacks for state of charge, range remaining, acceleration, and so forth; and a keypad for the driver to press in his code instead of turning an ignition key. But problems still bedeviled the car.

The inverter, for one. Most of the POCs were running, but the inverters would stall out every twenty hours or so. Software bugs, Ellis was convinced. They could be found, and fixed. The batteries, for another. Remy's fourth incarnation was more rugged and even provided a bit more range than the show car generation, but it had a tendency to heat and corrode under the brutal testing that Ellis's test engineers subjected it to up at Milford.

Ellis's nemesis was still EMI. He'd thought it solved after all the back-and-forth with Hughes earlier in the year, but when the finished POCs were tested for it in June, the EMI had grown worse. Joe LoGrasso, the wild-eyed EMI engineer, went back to testing each POC part by part in a special EMI-shielded room. It was a process known as *paradoizing*, after an engineer named Parado who had defined it, but at times it seemed more like an investigation conducted by Inspector Clouseau. When LoGrasso had identified the biggest EMI offenders, he put Band-Aids on them—adding filters or capacitors, twisting wires here and there—to avoid a complete redesign of the inverter. When he was done, the other POCs would have to be hauled back into the shop, taken apart, and outfitted with the new Band-Aids. At least, if GM ever did produce an EV, the team would know enough to stop EMI at the design stage. Ellis would see to that.

In a quiet way, Ellis had come into his own since Baker's departure. He moved more briskly, his shoulders squared, and spoke more candidly of his frustrations. Pinned to the bulletin board beside his desk was a proportionally greater number of iconoclastic declarations. One was a quote from Brooks Atkinson. "This nation was built by people dedicated to taking risks," the quote read, "pioneers who were not afraid of the wilderness, business people who were not afraid of failure, scientists who were not afraid of the truth, thinkers who were not afraid of progress, and visionaries who were not afraid of action."

Another was a list of ten EV "commandments":

1. Come to work each day willing to be fired.
2. Circumvent any orders aimed at stopping your dream.
3. Do any job needed to make your project work, regardless of job description.
4. Find people to help you.

5. Follow your intuition about the people you choose, and work only with the best.
6. Work underground as long as you can — publicity triggers the corporate immune system.
7. Never bet on a race unless you are running in it.
8. Remember it is easier to ask forgiveness than permission.
9. Be true to your goals, but be realistic about the ways to achieve them.
10. Honor your sponsors.

Questioning authority seemed an unlikely trait for one of GM's two dozen engineering directors, more so for a second-generation GMer whose father had worked in the personnel department, no doubt sifting for candidates who heartily eschewed those commandments. But Ellis had done so from the start of the program — had done so, indeed, from his arrival at GM in 1960 with a master's in engineering from Michigan State, because of the program into which he was put.

It was a program of short stints, beginning at the shipping dock, that taught Ellis to be what he called a change agent: coming in fresh, identifying problems quickly, pushing solutions through and moving on. Rather than graduate into one career groove or another, as he was meant to do, Ellis whisked through twenty-two jobs in his first twenty years. An engineer with top management ambitions would have lingered longer at various stations, but Ellis had none. "I don't respect people because of their titles," he would say. "I respect them based on their capability." He felt his job was to support his employees; he felt his boss's job was to support him.

Instead of angling up, Ellis had come to enjoy passing knowledge down. He had a tendency to look over one's shoulder and criticize, rather than encourage, as one young engineer observed; Baker was the one to offer praise and shore up spirits. But Ellis was the pure engineer, trying only to improve the design. Baker was the leader, better with people but not unaware of what their success could do for him.

Ellis was actually relieved that Impact hadn't gone to production as scheduled. GM had expected too much, too soon, from the program, he felt. Brand-new technology needed gestation time. It made far more sense to do the fifty-car build without a production schedule hanging overhead, to ride the learning curve before racing to market. He knew that many of his engineers felt the program had lost its momentum and expected it to sputter into a dead end. Ellis preferred getting the design right first, even if it never went further than fifty cars.

For Jon Bereisa, Ellis's right-hand man on engineering and, it still sometimes seemed, his rival for seniority, the greatest challenge now was chargers. For ninety years, cars had pulled up to pumps and hoses that were fundamentally the same. It would have made no sense for carmakers to compete by using different kinds of fuel, or different-sized filler necks so that customers would have to refuel at certain pumps but not at others. With EVs, none of this was settled. The Big Three had chosen not to compete on batteries—the fuel tanks of EVs, so to speak—by forming the USABC and agreeing to share whatever innovations came out of it. On chargers—the pumps and hoses of EVs—the carmakers might cooperate. But they also might compete.

For all the jingoism of the USABC and TeamUSA, the Big Three had met to discuss chargers twice already with Japanese carmakers. The goal was to agree on a charger standard so as not to divide the market between two technologies, causing a costly struggle that would bleed both sides. Amid their countries' continuing trade tensions, the Japanese were also eager to use the charger meetings as a show of cooperation with U.S. business. Toyota, after learning more about Hughes's inductive charger, had come to GM directly to propose a partnership. The two companies had made a success of NUMMI, their California factory consortium; working together on chargers might make a lot of sense. For the moment, Bereisa was politely noncommittal.

Chrysler, typically, was waiting for someone—anyone—else to come up with a charger it could use. Ford had shown initiative, but with a more conventional approach than GM's: a plug-and-socket charger, which was to say a conductive, rather than inductive, system. If it persuaded the other carmakers to go with conductive as a standard, Ford could render Hughes's paddle as obsolete as an eight-track tape deck.

Bereisa thought that threat remote. He believed Hughes's charger was not only more elegant and powerful than Ford's, but sturdy and utterly safe. Ford's charger, he suggested, had prongs that would bend or break upon repeated use. Even if they didn't, conductive charging of such high-voltage electricity seemed to him prohibitively dangerous.

Wallace, for his part, fumed at the notion of GM setting an industry standard with its own proprietary hardware—expensive hardware at that. And he felt reassured by tests that subjected Ford conductive chargers to salt and slush, making 10,000 connections without mishap. For Wallace, the issues were clear. "We don't give a damn if it's conductive, inductive, or seductive," he declared. "We want cheap and reliable!"

The standoff over chargers would not be resolved quickly or amicably. Nor, it began to seem, might the EV partnership talks, snagged as they were on the nettlesome issue of intellectual property.

At Baker's direction, Frank Schweibold and his young finance deputy, Pam Pudar, had done all they could to come up with a price tag on Impact. They couldn't just add up everything GM had spent on Impact so far and come up with a figure of, say, $300 million. A lot of money had gone into components that GM wanted to manufacture and market itself to other carmakers—including Ford. Among these, they counted the drivetrain's inverter, battery pack, and motor—and, of course, the charger. Out they came from the equation. The hardware that remained was in the proof-of-concept cars—everything from tires to steering wheel. The number crunchers had to decide how useful that hardware would be in the immediate future. If the partners chose to produce Impact, for example, how much money and time would they save by improving on what they had already, as opposed to starting from scratch? How much more would be saved by producing an EV that could come out in 1996 to take advantage of early bird credits from CARB?

Every way they ran the numbers, the crunchers came up with about the same figure: $100 million. That was what GM would bring to the venture. Ford, as far as Baker could tell from the January garage shows, had almost nothing to bring except a battery technology that might not work. So Ford would have to give GM a check for $50 million—half of what GM was bringing to the table—less any background value it could show, to be a fifty/fifty equity partner. To get Impact to production, the number crunchers noted, would cost another $125 million. Presumably, the partners would split that tab, too. All this was put in a memo of understanding and sent off to Ford.

The memo enraged Wallace. "Their attitude comes across as: Isn't the Impact wonderful? It was always the right way to go, we've got it done, therefore it's valuable and you ought to pay for it," he fumed one day not long after. "Yet it still needs one hundred twenty-five million dollars for engineering work. That ain't done to me! And every time we say what we're bringing to the party, they just sort of brush it aside. So we ain't going to pay for it. That's the bottom line."

Wallace responded by drawing up a list of what he perceived as Ford's intellectual property, with values attached. Sodium sulfur batteries. The Ecostar. Also, the VZW109, formally disclosed for the first time and described in vague terms. Not surprisingly, the numbers added up to $100 million. "We have more experience with advanced batteries than anyone else in the world by several orders of magnitude," Wallace declared. "We're putting out a fleet of cars with advanced electric batteries. Plus we have the design started for the real vehicle, the one that counts. We've got five hundred people working on EVs. So how someone can tell us *we* don't have any intellectual property—it's pissing us off!"

Wallace knew his $100 million total was somewhat facetious, but the point behind it was serious. If this was to be a true joint venture, the partners had to go in on an equal footing, not on a senior and junior partner basis. Along with his laundry list, he attached a memo that outlined his "rationales for nonpayment," as he put it. *Upfront payments create a winner and loser*, was one. *An impossible level of objectivity is required to judge the value of each party's contributions,* was another. *To keep equity costs low, each company would press hard to use its version of the technology at component or vehicle, which might be detrimental to the success of the joint venture.*

GM's Frank Schweibold received Wallace's memo with wry skepticism. "Gosh," he told Ford, "we think you're fine fellows, but we're in the car business! If we're going to attach value to this stuff, we'd like a design review—in detail." Meantime, Schweibold suggested, an independent investment banker could be brought in to assess the partners' equity, as occurred routinely in other lines of business when partnerships were forged. Indignantly, Wallace refused.

Wallace thought he could tough out the intellectual property issue, and based on what he knew, his stance made sense. What he didn't know was that at GM a new confidence was lifting executives' spirits, with potentially profound effects on the EV partnership.

To outsiders, GM was still a desperate company. Inside, the most dramatic turnaround of U.S. corporate history—in magnitude, far greater than Chrysler's—was well underway. Under Jack Smith's leadership, GM in eight months had changed money-losing policies entrenched for years. Smith, for example, had shrunk GM's twelve platforms to seven on the sensible assumption that different models could use the same structure, chassis, and underlying components. The sharp reduction in worldwide purchasing costs imposed by Ignacio Lopez—and continued after his stormy departure—was saving $4 billion from an annual budget of some $50 billion. As the national economy lifted and car sales generally improved, Smith was able to use GM's still-unequaled number of plants and dealerships to accomplish real economies of scale, reducing costs and filling customer orders more quickly than Ford or Chrysler. Incredibly, after its epic losses, GM would finish 1993 in the black by $2.5 billion. As the financial crisis eased, Smith and his adjutants wondered if partnering with Ford on electric vehicles was truly necessary after all.

In August, Jack Smith convened a meeting of his fourteen-man strategy board at the Tech Center specifically to consider the EV joint venture with Ford. Perhaps the company didn't want to squander its technological lead on EVs. And if Ford refused to ante up on intellectual property, perhaps that would be just as well. At the least, Ford would have to let GM in for a detailed technical review of its EV hardware, including the mysterious VZW109. That last sentiment was conveyed to Ford, where it was received with surprise and suspicion.

After considerable internal dissension, Ford agreed to let a GM contingent review its sodium sulfur battery; the VZW109 *might* be shown at a later date. To Baker's irritation, though, Wallace stuck by his insistence that Ford make no payment for intellectual property. Baker checked with Smith and the strategy board. Should he hold firm? Yes, came the word: hold firm. Baker called Wallace to tell him there was no point in meeting further.

Slowly, a compromise began to emerge. Both partners had felt the EV partnership should put out cars as soon as it could to take advantage of early credits. The only EVs that could reach the market that quickly were Impacts and Ecostars. But what if the partnership put both cars aside, and planned instead to create an all-new EV for 1998? The expertise acquired from Impact would still help in any new EV design, but with no actual hardware carried over GM could rationalize that intellectual property had ceased to be an issue, and no money need change hands.

As part of the peacekeeping process, Ford agreed to let GM review the VZW109. On October 19, Baker, Ellis, and Schweibold entered the Ford design dome where top secret new models were shown to Ford's executives. This was Ford's sanctum sanctorum. Privately, the GMers were amazed. To be in Ford's design dome was like entering the Kremlin.

The greater shock was the VZW109. Up in Troy, the GM EVers had been working on a 1998 design of their own. It, too, was a four-door microvan. It, too, was based on the Mitsubishi Expo LRV. That the rivals should have chosen the same model as a starting point was not, however, that unlikely; the Expo LRV's box-like body, unusually high from the ground, would accommodate a battery pack of any sort more easily than other vehicles. The GMers were more struck by the fact that the VZW109 was being developed, at considerable expense, to run on sodium sulfur batteries. If Ford was that confident of sodium sulfur, perhaps GM should be, too.

By the end of the month a new memo of understanding had been drawn up. Gone was its offending passage about intellectual property value. With Impact and Ecostar out of the picture, the partners now agreed on every point. So confident were the prospective members of EV2 of their impending union that they began looking together at real estate. They scheduled a press conference for November 9, 1993, to announce their agreement, and had a press release prepared. "Ford and GM today signed a memorandum of understanding," the release read, "outlining their intention to ground develop and build electric vehicles and electric vehicle components jointly for the late nineties."

At the last minute, the press conference was canceled.

The partnership had died aborning.

The Mandate Looms

))))

Reluctant partners from the start, Ford and GM had approached the altar of EV agreement as if for a shotgun marriage. Step by step, their resentment had grown: at each other, but more so at the mandate forcing them both down the aisle. By the autumn of 1993, as they prepared to exchange vows, their anger at the mandate got the better of them.

In part, that anger was stirred by the obvious: a better battery *wasn't* at hand. But electric vehicles, the carmakers were coming to realize, also augured a strange new world of fast-changing technology and flexible production. Perhaps—dread thought!—Detroit might no longer have the luxury of producing one kind of car for all customer needs, as it had for nearly 100 years. Perhaps, in the future, automotive transportation would fracture into several niche markets, each best served by a *different* kind of car. EVs, for starters, might not replace gas cars. They might instead provide a supplemental service, as fax machines had done for phones, as microwaves had done for ovens.

How in God's name were the carmakers to deal with that?

In September, Ford's chairman Red Poling made a trip to California to importune CARB's Jananne Sharpless and Governor Pete Wilson about the mandate. Later, it would appear the governor and the carmakers had come, at least, to an understanding. The carmakers would expect no action on the mandate until after Wilson's 1994 reelection campaign, since he could ill afford to be seen as anti-green while running for office. Assuming he won, he would then do what he could.

Chrysler made its own contribution to the nascent anti-mandate campaign in mid-September by publicly pronouncing its withdrawal from the EV part-

nership talks. "We have never had any plans to join in," Chairman Eaton proclaimed, despite the more than seventy hours of EV3 meetings the previous
spring. In speeches, he took to bashing the very notion of EVs. "There is absolutely no economic basis for electric vehicles in the world," he said in one.
"Not even in Italy, where gas is four times the cost of gas in California." In an
indication of what scant hope it had for EVs, Chrysler moved its TEVan team
under the broad aegis of its minivan division—rendering it just another minivan, the least loved of the lot—and reassigned Jean Mallebay-Vacqueur to
head up Chrysler's scientific laboratories. His new post, Mallebay-Vacqueur
admitted, was not a plum or even, necessarily, a promotion. "It is going to be
less fun," he said with a sigh. "But that is not something which affects me. In
life you have ups and downs."

In such a climate, the White House announcement on September 29, 1993,
of a "Dream Car" partnership between the federal government and Detroit
was seized on by the carmakers as another reason *not* to pursue the dream of
electric vehicles. President Clinton and Vice President Gore evoked the goal
of building, over the next decade, a five-passenger sedan capable of accelerating to 55 miles per hour in less than 12 seconds but achieving three times the
current average of 27.5 miles per gallon, possibly with something other than
petroleum. Government and industry would split all costs, as with the
USABC; the costs, as yet, were vague. Clearly, the ideas of both Paul Mac-
Cready and Amory Lovins had influenced the administration. The "Dream
Car" might use natural gas or hydrogen. It might be a hybrid. It would almost
certainly employ lightweight composite materials. But any suggestion of electric vehicles as the dream car of choice was studiously avoided; and to the Big
Three CEOs gathered for the White House ceremony, Clinton's comparison
of the partnership to Star Wars and the Apollo moonshot program was reason
to hope that the mandate, as a goal, might soon be supplanted.

The Dream Car deal—or, as it came to be drearily known, the Partnership
for a New Generation of Vehicles (PNGV)—might be Detroit's *only* hope in
combatting the querulous Northeast. In July, the same New York district
judge who in January had ruled for the carmakers had had second thoughts.
While not conceding that New York did have the right to adopt the California mandate without the cleaner fuels that went along with it, he declared the
issue debatable enough to be tried in court. In the meantime, the state could
pursue the program it wished.

The Big Three's lawyers thought they might still win against New York—
and Massachusetts, where a similar case was about to be decided in a Boston
federal court—and thereby intimidate the rest of the Northeast. But instead
of arguing the issues in one state court battle after another, GM's Mr. Emissions, Sam Leonard, began privately crafting a compromise. By 2001, he calculated, gas cars might be made so nearly pollution-free that the Northeast

could use them to meet its clean air standards without adopting the California mandate. The beauty of the plan was that these cars, if Detroit chose to make them, could be sold in forty-nine states—California's mandate required increasing percentages of them before 2001 as it was—so that the Northeast would not have its freeways trafficked by less-clean cars from other states. In return, of course, there would be no more talk of mandating EVs. Leonard even had a CARB-like acronym for his plan: FED LEV, for Federal Low-Emission Vehicle.

One day in September, CARB's Jananne Sharpless came to Detroit for a tour of the Big Three's EV programs, then got a personal run-through on FED LEV from Leonard. By now, she was all too familiar with Leonard, the corpulent emissions man. *A heart attack waiting to happen* was the first thought that always came to mind when she saw him. Leonard hadn't yet gone public with FED LEV; he hadn't approached Ford and Chrysler on it either, for which he would incur some sharp rebukes. He wanted to know what Sharpless thought first. The CARB chairwoman might even like FED LEV enough to consider substituting it for the mandate in California; it would mean no wrangling with Detroit for *years*. And if California adopted FED LEV, the northeast states would be stopped cold: they could do what California did, but no more.

Sharpless listened to Leonard with a sinking heart. The Northeast's call for a mandate, she realized, was having a perverse effect. Without the northeast threat, the Big Three might be trying even now to work with her, pushing to meet the mandate while squeezing reasonable incentives from CARB and the California legislature. Now, if they did that, it would send exactly the wrong signal to the northeast states, strengthening their resolve to adopt the mandate, too. As a result, the carmakers had to fight the mandate as fiercely as they could—on both fronts.

The Impact team could hear the rumblings. They knew the delays in the EV2 talks could not bode well. But no one had told them not to finish fifty handbuilt Impacts, nor to refrain from publicizing what they'd done, nor to abort the PrEView test-drive program. So to the discomfiture, no doubt, of a few top GM executives—say, those in Industry Government Relations, command center for the anti-mandate fight—the engineers pressed on.

On a warm, drizzly day in September, Gary Witzenburg, the program's manager of vehicle testing and development, welcomed a first group of auto magazine journalists to Milford's top-secret proving grounds. Witzenburg explained they would be driving proof-of-concept cars, and shouldn't judge them as they would production cars. One had been optimized for ride-and-handling, one for acoustics, a third to look as spiffy as possible for the photographers on hand.

The POCs looked so much like the show car that the journalists might be forgiven for thinking little had changed. One obvious improvement was the single motor that instantaneously delivered 137 horsepower to the wheels when the pedal was floored. Another was the heat pump—the first such mobile heat pump used in an automobile. A cannister-like device that resided, for lack of any other available space, in front of the left front tire, the pump worked as long as the outside air was warmer than its refrigerant.* For temperatures below 20 degrees Fahrenheit, something else would have to serve and no one, as yet, knew what that might be.

The journalists took the cars outside the grounds for a drive of 19 miles. The temperature was fairly warm, so the cars would likely go 70 miles without a charge, but Witzenburg was taking no chances: during a ninety-minute lunch break at a local restaurant, the cars were recharged across the street by Hughes chargers brought for the occasion, so that the journalists could drive them back fully charged. By day's end, the journalists seemed pleased. But like theater critics, they left without divulging their opinions. Witzenburg, and the rest of the engineers, would have to wait until the verdicts appeared in print three or four months later.

Meanwhile, Impact's other public test, the so-called PrEView drive, was being organized back in Troy by a young marketing man named Sean McNamara, the lone survivor of his department after John Dabels's departure.

A certain bemusement had greeted GM's announcement, the previous December, that they would send thirty Impact prototypes around the country for consumers to drive. Linked as it was to the news that Impact was being pulled out of production, it had seemed a mere face-saving ploy. McNamara's job was to help make the plan happen. Given that GM had never done anything of the kind before, nearly everything about it was seat-of-the-pants.

McNamara had begun by sending a survey to residents in nine of the EPA's twenty-two "non-attainment" areas where air quality failed to meet federal standards. From this he had worked up a base of about 30,000 respondents, and defined five groups, starting with the "early adopters" ready to buy an electric car at any price. The most intriguing group were the "apprehensives," interested in EVs but not willing to pay much of a premium for them.

That fall, McNamara arranged to have flyers slipped into the bills of utility customers in the first of twelve cities, inviting them to call an 800 number to apply to be one of nearly 1,000 Impact test drivers beginning in the spring of 1994. Thirty of the fifty LPFs would be consigned to PrEView and sent as a

---

* Current from the batteries powered a motor that drove a compressor that compressed ozone-friendly R134A refrigerant. When the compressed refrigerant passed through an evaporator, it was drawn out into the hotter ambient air, and ambient air, in return, was drawn back into the pump and pushed into the passenger compartment as heat. In reverse, the heat pump also generated cooled air for air-conditioning.

fleet from one city to the next; the balance would be kept by the platform for in-house tests. The PrEView cars would be equipped with electronic data keepers, and drivers would be asked to keep daily logs over two- and four-week trials. McNamara had no idea what to expect. He guessed he might get a couple of thousand calls from each city, and from that pool fish out as many "apprehensives" as he could. But even if the drivers did respond, would they take it all seriously? Would they fill out the daily logs? What would happen if the cars broke down—or crashed?

The PrEView drive was announced by Baker at a press conference on October 13, 1993. By then the rumors of a Big Three offensive against the mandate were in the air, and the automotive journalists were openly skeptical of PrEView. "What if the feedback isn't positive?" asked one. "Would EVs go by the wayside? And if so, what's the alternative for dealing with the mandate?"

Either way, Baker said, the company would gain valuable information.

"Is that part of the tactic to fight the mandate?" asked another journalist. "To have proof that the customers wouldn't be happy with the car at this stage?"

Baker bristled. "Absolutely not."

In early October, two of the fifty limited-production-fleet Impacts began to roll out each week from Bumper to Bumper. The cars were handbuilt, but final assembly was done on a three-rail conveyor belt to simulate low-volume production. In parts and labor alone, each car cost $340,000. The cars and the PrEView drive together would cost, by GM's estimate, $32 million. If GM's secret agenda with PrEView was to discredit EVs, it certainly had chosen an expensive ploy.

Smoothly as they appeared to run, the LPFs soon provided a nasty surprise. The first day that temperatures dropped to 40 degrees Fahrenheit, the cars' range fell off precipitously. Not long afterward, Andrew Farah, a young propulsion engineer, drove an LPF home, 8 miles away, and let it sit outside all night in zero-degree weather. When he got to work the next day, the range gauge was down by nearly 70 percent. Other engineers soon confirmed that after roughly twenty hours of cold weather exposure, range seemed to diminish even more.

The problems, as it turned out, were manifold, with batteries only the most obvious of them. One contributor was the air itself. The colder the air got, the denser it became; on a car where every mile of range counted, the losses in aerodynamic drag as the car pushed through denser air were significant.* Another culprit was the oil used to lubricate the motor. In a gas car, oil was kept hot and viscous by the heat of the engine. An EV had no such heat; the mod-

---

* Gas cars lose range in colder weather, too, but given how cheap and plentiful gas is, and how great its range to begin with, the losses go unnoticed.

est amount generated by its electronic drivetrain was mostly offset by liquid cooling. Cold weather diminished that heat further. So did the heat pump used to warm the passenger compartment, as it discharged cold air through the front-end fan. Like maple syrup put in a refrigerator, the oil grew thicker, which affected the motor's efficiency and, ultimately, the car's range. The only answer was to concoct a better lubricant. Eventually, with some help from GM R&D, one would be found.

To the surprise of the test engineers at Milford, tires were shown to be the real range robber. To give them 25 percent less rolling resistance than ordinary tires, Michelin had used an unusually tough rubber compound, with a lot of silicone, to produce a springier tread. The tires worked perfectly on a sunny California day. Unfortunately, when the temperature dropped even to 50 degrees Fahrenheit, the tires began to experience an effect known as glass transition. The rubber compound's molecular structure began to change into a crystalline state, inhibiting the tires' springiness. Worse, as the temperature continued to drop, the glass transition effect proved exponential. For a cold-weather state like Michigan, Michelin would have to reinvent the wheel. Ellis, for one, was confident they could. Tire makers could play endlessly with the variables: the cord, the angles, the rubber, the composition, the tread design. They were really magicians, he felt.

Yet even as the team addressed these concerns and trumpeted PrEView, its own top management was making public pronouncements against the mandate, and seeming, to some of the engineers, to wish EVs might just go away. At a board meeting of the Association of Automobile Manufacturers of America on October 19, Detroit's CEOs agreed to lobby together against the mandate and to push FED LEV. On November 1, Ford's anti-mandate stance grew tougher as a new chairman, Alex Trotman, took command. Trotman's predecessor, Red Poling, at least had endorsed the Ecostar program, and had hopes for the EV talks. Trotman, the Scottish-born son of a carpet layer and upholsterer, prided himself on a tough, working-class pragmatism honed in British pub brawls. Even before he took office, his vice chairman, Lou Ross, announced that Ford's EV program might be one of the first casualties of a new campaign to trim R&D costs.

Barely had the carmakers fired that volley when a federal judge in Boston fired back. Massachusetts had been even more aggressive than New York in taking up the mandate: its legislature had actually passed a law in 1990 requiring emissions standards that escalated to 2 percent zero-emission vehicles by 1999. The carmakers had sought an injunction against the state, but on November 2, 1993, a U.S. district judge refused their plea. Both the Massachusetts case, and its counterpart in New York, would still go to trial. But the federal judge in Boston told the plaintiffs he was persuaded the northeast states *could* adopt the mandate without its accompanying fuel standards which had, he felt, a negligible effect on overall emissions levels. Unless a state appeals court struck down his judgment, the case would be tried in his courtroom, all but dooming the carmakers' chances.

Two weeks later, the field of battle appeared to shift. On November 18, Jananne Sharpless was out, her resignation from CARB forced by Governor Wilson. In January, she would step into a lower-visibility role as a member of the California Energy Commission. In her place, Wilson named a former assistant secretary of the navy from the Bush administration, Jacqueline E. Schafer. Detroit's lobbyists speculated that the governor now might be willing to trade the mandate as a "high card" in exchange for new or reopened automotive factories in his recession-plagued state. Actually, Sharpless more likely had been the loser in a turf battle within the state's environmental ranks, and her departure was less portentous than it appeared.

Exhilarated by Sharpless's fall nonetheless, Ford and GM twice postponed the news conference at which they were to announce their EV partnership, then canceled it altogether.

The Impact engineers had mixed feelings about the partnership's demise. Some were relieved not to have to share Impact. Yet without a partnership, the program seemed certain to die.

Some new incentive was needed: that much was clear. And so, secretly that autumn a small group of frustrated engineers began planning how to provide it. For justification, they had to look no further than Jim Ellis's second commandment: "Circumvent any orders aimed at stopping your dream." For help, they turned to an incongruous pair of counselors: Stan Ovshinsky, the white-haired battery inventor whose innovative approach had won him the first USABC grant—and GM's ex-chairman, Robert Stempel.

A Covert Operation

))))

On August 9, 1993, a small crowd of engineers gathered by a low-lying box of a building in a small industrial park in Troy, Michigan. They were less than a mile from Impact's offices, but none worked for GM—or for Ford, or for Chrysler. They watched as a trim septuagenarian with white curly hair operated the hoist that lowered a battery-powered minivan to the ground. Spryly, he slid in behind the wheel, turned the key, and pressed his foot on the accelerator.

The minivan stood still.

A pained look crossed the man's face. "What's wrong?" he exclaimed. A mechanic looked in. "The emergency brake!" he said with relief. "Ah!" The white-haired man released the brake. As the minivan rolled silently away on its maiden voyage, its driver turned back to the crowd, his face as gleeful as a small boy's. Off he went, around the corner and gone. The crowd waited five minutes, then ten. After twenty minutes, they were restless; after thirty, concerned. Finally the minivan rolled silently back: the white-haired man had not been able to resist riding the freeway with it, speeding along in the passing lane.

In its own way, the drive was as dramatic as the first flight at Kitty Hawk. A little more than ten years after a lab experiment with nickel and metal hydride, Stanford Ovshinsky had used his $18.5-million USABC grant to produce a prototype pack of what he called Ovonic batteries that had twice the energy, or range, of lead acid, yet most of lead acid's considerable power. A pack that *worked*. The pack in the minivan weighed 1,500 pounds—no small amount of baggage—but its 35 kilowatts of energy would propel the heavy, steel-bodied vehicle 85 miles. A smaller Ovonic pack, put in an Impact, would surely take the lighter car at least twice as far on a single charge. The first of the USABC grant recipients and, so far, the only one to show such progress, Ovshinsky alighted from his drive assuming the battle was won. The Big Three would rush to produce his batteries, put them in all their EVs, meet the mandate in a burst of glory, and triumph over Japan. He would learn, once again, that the world had a way of lagging behind his vision for it.

In the more than thirty years since Ovshinsky and his wife Iris had rented a first modest bunker of offices in Troy, their R&D start-up, Energy Conversion Devices, had grown to occupy other local buildings. The original site, though, remained. Here on the walls of nearly every office hung a colorful poster of the periodic table of elements. The table was Ovshinsky's sacred tablet. From it he had developed not only a battery, but a new field of physics.

Most battery developers were like miners, Ovshinsky liked to say, excavating to find the perfect pair of existing elements that might store more electricity when put together. Ovshinsky and his team had turned, as he put it, not to the mines, but to the mind. Using the inventor's landmark theories of amorphous materials, they had created new metallic alloys. *Engineered* them. No one else had done that. The battery that had emerged from their alchemy was, as a result, not merely new but unique. Whether or not it could be manufactured, produced at a reasonable price, perform consistently well, and last as long as Ovshinsky thought it could were questions for others to ask. As far as Ovshinsky was concerned, the drive had answered them.

Ovshinsky's wood-paneled lair indicated an enjoyment of creature comforts very different from, say, Alan Cocconi. Iris, a biologist by training, worked in a smaller adjoining office. At lunch, the two usually drove over in Ovshinsky's late-model Cadillac—its license plate read OVONICS—to a fine Lebanese restaurant whose mustachioed owner served up plate after plate of home-cooked specialties to them in their special corner booth as they detailed their progress to USABC members like GM's John Williams or Ford's John Wallace. At night, they repaired to their ten-acre estate, replete with landscaped gardens, a man-made pond, and a basement swimming pool. With license fees from some 300 patents in the U.S., and more than 1,500 abroad, the Ovshinskys were a rarity in the world of physics: wealthy inventors. Energetic, curious, passionately committed to their work and to each other, they were also, more rare still, happy. But not satisfied. For all they had achieved in those years, they had failed as yet to transform one of their energy inventions into a manufactured, mass-marketed product that might help wean the world from its dependence on oil.

The Ovonic battery might, at last, be that product.

Quite literally, the battery had its origins in Ovshinsky's own, as the middle child of a Lithuanian immigrant who sold scrap metal in Akron, Ohio: the metals his father collected Ovshinsky would collect, too, though with more ambitious intent. For all his obvious intelligence and love of reading, Ovshinsky was too poor to go to college, so he joined a machine shop. Soon he had a shop of his own, and was tinkering in his off hours with a design for a high-speed, automated lathe. The design, which Ovshinsky patented while still in his twenties, incorporated an early use of robotics, and set an international standard. It instilled in him a fascination with electricity: how it was formed, how it traveled, and how it could be harnessed.

The most mysterious passage of electricity was in the human brain, from one neuron to another. Neurologists had come to agree that neurons communicated electricity from one nerve cell to another, in seemingly random order, with the help of a cell membrane composed of amorphous materials. Ovshinsky, delving into biology on his own, thought the same principles of amorphousness might be found in physical elements, and that those elements might be used to channel electricity in machinery. In physics, this was the equivalent of ignoring jewels and studying, instead, the rough rock from which they were extricated.

The jewels were crystalline materials, silicon prominent among them, that had neatly arranged molecular structures like snowflakes. For some time, physicists had known that when certain impurities were added to them, their electrons were jostled free, conducting electricity. Silicon and certain other solid materials could be made more or less conductive depending on the impurities added; so they were called, logically enough, semiconductors. That, physicists realized in the late 1940s, might be very useful indeed. Pure silicon, heated, cooled, and sliced into wafer-like chips, could be used to make transistors that served as little toll gates, or switches, of electricity. Whether or not the transistors let current through depended on how they had been doped by impurities. Controlling the flow of electricity was the essential tool of modern electronics.

By comparison, amorphous materials seemed useless. Their elements were arranged in no particular order, and while they might conduct electricity, they did so in a random way that defied mathematical analysis and seemed, as a result, uncontrollable. Most liquids were amorphous, as were the solids they hardened to become—glass, for example. But so were many common metals, like titanium and vanadium. Ovshinsky thought amorphous materials bore further scrutiny, if only because they were so inexpensive and so easy to manipulate. Silicon had to be grown and cut with great care and at great expense to avoid tainting it with the wrong impurities—including oxygen. Amorphous metal elements could simply be melted in a crucible to form new alloys. The ways in which their atoms bonded might seem random but had an overall consistency if the same elements were used in the same proportions each time. And certain alloys might conduct current better than the skeptics imagined.

On his own, Ovshinsky began building simple electric switches of amorphous materials using the chalcogenide elements: sulfur, solenium, telurium, and others in column six of the periodic table. What these elements shared was a tendency to bond easily with their neighbors—two atoms of each bonding with two atoms of the next—so that they formed chemical daisy chains that looked, to the naked eye, like liquids congealing into gooey messes, then hardening into solids. The glass-like mix that resulted could be used, like silicon, as a toll gate for electricity. Ovshinsky thought he'd hit on something big, but as a lone inventor, unallied with some major R&D laboratory, he didn't know quite what to do about it.

By the mid-fifties Ovshinsky had come to Detroit and landed a research job at Wayne State University despite his lack of a college degree. There he met Iris Miroy, an attractive biology Ph.D. candidate who shared his fascination with the brain and saw the potential of his amorphous switches. Ovshinsky was married; Miroy was married and pregnant. Powerfully attracted, they divorced their respective spouses and in 1959 began a life together. A year later, they started Energy Conversion Labs with $50,000 in savings. The plan was to turn Ovshinsky's amorphous silicon materials into commercial products.

With a growing number of patents, but no profits, the Ovshinskys went public, as Energy Conversion Devices, in 1964. They took in license fees from large electronics companies in Japan—Matsushita, Sony, Hitachi, Canon, Sharpe—where Ovshinsky came to be viewed as a modern-day Edison, and where his patents were used to produce solar cells, magnets, optical memories, and flat-panel displays. On Wall Street, the inventor was viewed with less reverence, as ECD failed to move to manufacturing and the company posted losses year after year.

As for the academic community, it was outraged, in 1968, by a short paper submitted to the prestigious Physical Review Letters in which Ovshinsky argued that his amorphous switches were semiconductors no less effective than crystalline materials. The physicists felt that this unschooled rube had merely witnessed the chemical change that occurred in any element when enough voltage was applied. When lightning hit a tree it caused a chemical transformation due to the voltage and heat of the lightning. But that was a one-time switch. Ovshinsky, they said, was doing this on a more subtle level; the proof, they suggested, was that heat would soon wear out his switch. The inventor knew they were wrong because his switch had already worked far too long for its effect to be thermal. It had to be *electronic*, its electrons moving coolly back and forth without any degradation. As it continued to work—more than twenty-five years later, the original switch, still working, occupied a prominent place in the inventor's office—Ovshinsky's theories were grudgingly accepted.

In that time Ovshinsky had graduated to using the same principles of amorphous materials to make solar cells, then applied them to inventing batteries that might bank energy from his solar panels. Batteries were, in a sense, an arcane departure from switches, but both were about controlling the flow of electricity, after all. And who was to say batteries might not also be made from amorphous materials?

On February 9, 1982, Ovshinsky called his senior engineers into a conference room to show them a black box sitting on a round table. A wire led from the box to a little fan. Ovshinsky flipped a switch on the box, and the fan began to run. The engineers opened the box, expecting to see a battery inside. They saw only a beaker with some electrolyte, a thin-film negative electrode, and a positive nickel electrode taken from a Kmart nickel cadmium battery. "This is going to be the basis of a new industry," Ovshinsky told his staff. "This battery is not only going to be in every battery-driven consumer product someday, but it will *drive your car.*"

There seemed about as much need for EVs in 1982 as for cars made of Swiss cheese: Ken Baker's Electrovette program had just been canceled, and other carmakers had given up on theirs, the latest OPEC oil shortage having eased. Ovshinsky was undeterred. Soon his engineers scaled up his lab experiment to a C-sized cell—the standard flashlight battery size—protecting the process with some thirty patents. Again, Japanese manufacturers responded first. Ovshinsky's C-sized battery could power laptop computers, cellular phones, and more as cheaply and efficiently as nickel cadmium, but without cadmium's toxicity. Ovshinsky produced the batteries' essence—metal hydride powder—and shipped it off to licensees like Hitachi-Maxwell, Gold Peak, and Matsushita, where the batteries were produced. Meanwhile, he kept his chemists working on larger cells that might one day power a car.

Most of the metals used in Ovshinsky's battery were recycled from scrap, like that collected in his father's street wagon. The titanium might come from an old airplane fuselage. Vanadium was a major additive to steel, and so might come from tool steel. Zirconium was heavily used in the chemical industry and reactor industry. Cobalt, manganese, aluminum, or iron, all commonly available, might also be used. Eight or nine in all were melted in a crucible and made into an ash used as the negative electrode. For his positive electrode, Ovshinsky used nickel, just as Edison had done with his nickel iron batteries. Critics were fond of declaring that the amount of nickel needed for an EV pack would prohibit the use of any nickel-based batteries for powering cars. But instead of using solid nickel plate Ovshinsky used a new nickel foam whose porosity enabled him to make do with less—much less. As his electrolyte, the inventor used a liquid mix of water and potassium hydroxide. The battery's amorphous materials made it new and different. But not complicated. Indeed, the beauty of nickel metal hydride was that its elements were simpler, and seemed to act more predictably, than the old standbys of lead and acid.

Ovshinsky won his USABC grant with bench-test results that outperformed any other advanced battery. His nickel metal hydride cell had strong energy *and* power—hardly any battery had both. It also took a faster recharge than lead acid because its electrolyte remained chemically unchanged as the battery was discharged and was thus more receptive to incoming electrons. Ovshinsky claimed his batteries could be charged 1,000 times; if each charge lasted 100 miles, that meant one pack would last the 100,000-mile lifetime of the vehicle. When it wore down, both the nickel and metal hydride were completely recyclable. And the cost? No more than $5,000 per pack, Ovshinsky predicted, as soon as the packs could be manufactured. This wasn't merely a better battery, he felt. This was the breakthrough.

In the fifteen months since ECD had received its first part of the USABC grant of $18.5 million, Ovshinsky's engineers had produced enough cells to make an EV-sized pack. In making cells work together, failures were as common as they were mysterious, but the engineers had prevailed. The next step, clearly, was to put the pack into a car. Each of the USABC grant recipients worked in concert with one of the Big Three as its program manager; Ovonic's manager was Chrysler. Ovshinsky persuaded Bob Davis, who had taken over from Jean Mallebay-Vacqueur, to lend him a Chrysler TEVan but not to tell anyone else on the consortium about the plans for his solitary drive. Ovshinsky knew he faced his share of skeptics. The best way to combat them, he felt, was to let the battery prove itself in action.

Surely, Ovshinsky thought as he posed obligingly in the minivan for a newspaper reporter that August day in 1993, the skeptics would come around now. Didn't they always, in the end?

John Williams, the former four-phase planner for Impact who had taken over the technical affairs of the USABC, heard first about Ovshinsky's little drive from the local newspaper that covered it. Williams was furious. The story, with its picture of Ovshinsky's beaming face, made a mockery of the consortium's right to control its own programs. It broadcast Ovshinsky's progress to the Japanese. Worst, he thought, it would raise too-high expectations in the U.S., especially at CARB. This was vintage Ovshinsky, Williams felt: give the press the rosiest results, get everyone excited, but fail to mention that the miracle wasn't being manufactured, perhaps never would be, and that even if it could the costs might be astronomical.

Coldly, Williams admonished the inventor to say no more about his findings. The USABC had funded his latest effort, Williams reminded him, and it was up to the consortium to say when findings should be made public. The first step was to have one of the national labs review the battery. A report would be sent up the corporate chains of command, eventually reaching the CEOs of each of the Big Three. When they gave their blessing, and not before, results would be announced. To be sure the message was clear, the USABC's attorney detailed it as such, in cold legalese, in a letter to the Ovshinskys' attorney.

When the Ovshinskys got the letter, they were stunned. It was all so . . . *Orwellian*. The consortium's stance, they believed, violated the spirit with which it was founded: to show the world that TeamUSA, as Baker put it, could win the battery race against Japan. But it also violated the rights of American taxpayers. Hadn't they contributed half the $260 million that the consortium had dispensed? Shouldn't they know what their money had bought? And what about his rights as an inventor? How could the consortium tell him what to do with a technology he'd invented a decade ago? The more the Ovshinskys thought about it, the more it seemed to them that the consortium had an ulterior agenda: to prove to California, and to other states as well, that EV batteries wouldn't work, and that EVs, as a result, were hopelessly impractical.

In the weeks after Ovshinsky's TEVan drive, as angry letters flew back and forth between his lawyers and the consortium's, Ovshinsky came to a private decision. He would refrain from announcing his battery results, as his lawyer advised. But at this critical juncture, with the Big Three embarking on their campaign against the mandate, he would not sit silent as the carmakers declared no battery breakthrough to be in sight. He would start by making them see it, whether they wanted to or not, by getting an Ovonic pack into an Impact.

What Ovshinsky needed was a powerful ally at GM who shared his sense of mission about EVs. An ally who appreciated the need to prove the battery quickly. An ally capable of getting him past Williams, who still occupied an office at GMEV in Troy and might hear of any backchannel plans. Ovshinsky found one, soon enough, in the ex-chairman of General Motors.

A year after resigning as chairman, Robert Stempel seemed fully recovered from his ordeal. He had undergone a heart valve operation and regained his physical health. Emotionally, he had had several tough months, anguishing over his record. He told ex-colleagues that without the Gulf War, he would have prevailed; he pointed to pieces of his recovery plan that Jack Smith had chosen to keep. Slowly, though, he had seemed to accept the past. With the strong urging of his wife, he had also decided what he wanted to do with his future. He wanted to do electric vehicles.

The new regime had made Stempel a consultant and installed him in outlying Southfield on a high floor of an office tower bordered on every side by heavily trafficked highways. It was an oddly appropriate exile for the former head of a car company—as if a king had been shut up in a stone watchtower and guarded by his former serfs—but no such symbolism was intended. Unlike Roger Smith, forced off the board the previous May with good riddance, Stempel was viewed by nearly all with affection and sorrow: the right man in the wrong job at the wrong time. Early into the new year, he had begun counseling his successors, for whom he seemed to feel no bitterness, on what to do about EVs and the mandate. "Don't get the technology confused with the politics," he advised the president's council. "The mandate is bad, but that shouldn't mean we abandon EVs, especially when GM has so many patents for them. Fight the mandate, but push ahead with the cars."

With Jack Smith's blessing, Stempel had visited fledgling companies doing EV conversions of gas cars. In July, he had helped orchestrate the latest Sunrayce, a now annual U.S. version of the Australian Solar Challenge he had established as a way of spurring interest in EVs among university students. That summer, he also met Stan Ovshinsky, and drove the souped-up Chrysler TEVan.

Fascinated by the inventor and his claims, Stempel pored over the science of Ovonic batteries and studied the patents. Other battery suppliers always had a secret elixir, as Stempel put it, some magic box whose contents they couldn't reveal and that wasn't quite perfected. Ovshinsky's battery was understandable. There was no alchemy in nickel metal hydride. And the patents were solid—gold plated, as Stempel put it. Stempel was impressed enough to tell Ovshinsky he'd do all he could to help him. The Ovonic battery, he felt, was the breakthrough a new industry needed. It wasn't the ultimate battery, or even one that in ten years' time would still be in use; technology was moving too fast for that. But it could be the bridge between gas cars and EVs. And Stempel thought he had just the car to go with it.

For months, the ex-chairman had rued privately that GM would even consider handing over its technological lead on electric vehicles to Ford instead of daring to be first to market. As he put it later, "it frosted my ass." Urged on by his new comrade-in-arms, Stempel began lining up suppliers in the fall of 1993 to do Impact himself. Not on his own, exactly; John DeLorean had shown the folly of that. Stempel envisioned Impact more as a GM satellite, financed in part, perhaps, by outside investors, if GM was still skittish about the costs, then pushed through the GM pipeline of distributors, marketing, and service. Stempel would use Ovonic batteries; Ovshinsky had assured him they could be scaled up in eighteen months. Jack Smith heard out his plan, and asked Stempel to wait, at least until the president's council resolved the issue of partnership with Ford.

By then, Ovshinsky was on to Impact himself.

One day in mid-August, Ovshinsky drove his souped-up TEVan over to the GMEV building in Troy. Bereisa and a young battery engineer, Robin Vidas, put it to a good many of what Bereisa called his Nifty Fifty parking lot tests, and came away impressed. They urged Ovshinsky to get the USABC to sanction putting a pack in one of the first Impact prototypes—the limited production fleet of fifty. Ovshinsky tried. Soon he returned to say the consortium was stonewalling him. He would have to do all the tests first, go from battery cell to module to pack systematically, then get the Impact-sized packs tested at a national lab in Idaho. Months might pass before permission was granted. Meanwhile, the mandate might be pushed aside. For Ovshinsky—and all other hopeful EV suppliers—that would be ruinous. The mandate meant a new market overnight, with seven reluctant carmakers as potential customers. Ovshinsky had to show what his batteries could do in a lightweight Impact—now.

"I'll tell you what," Ovshinsky told Bereisa. "Forget going through the USABC. I'll just make you a pack for Impact. You pay me whatever you can."

Bereisa was intrigued. Like most of his GM brethren, he disapproved of the mandate. But he could see where Impact was headed. The fifty-car build was under way; the program had no further goal. By February, if the partnership with Ford fizzled, it would surely be dismantled, the engineers redeployed, the drawings filed away. For three years, Bereisa had lived every day with the dream of this car in his head, working late into the evenings, working weekends, growing chronically exhausted. Bereisa didn't want to see that time go up in smoke. He didn't want to let the program die.

"I can't buy a battery pack," he told Ovshinsky. "It'll show up as a purchase order, and sooner or later, I'll be told I can't do it. What I can do is buy a service."

Bereisa agreed, on October 1, to lend Ovshinsky an Impact battery-pack tray, harnessing, safety circuits, and the battery-pack computer module that monitored the pack. Ovshinsky promised that by November 24—his birthday—Bereisa would get back an Impact-tailored Ovonic battery pack. That seemed too little time in which to make a pack to new technical specifications, but if it was to do the program any good, it had to be ready by then. Over ninety days, Bereisa and a small team would test it in an Impact, hoping to show that an Ovonic pack would double the car's range, which might in turn persuade top management to keep the program alive.* If the pack worked as promised, and if it went 10,000 miles without appreciable losses, then Bereisa would pay Ovshinsky a fee for services. Either way, the two men would return their parts to each other.

Bereisa laid down one other condition. Ovshinsky would have to keep the plan secret. If Bereisa got good results, he would float them up the appropriate channels at GM and let higher forces than he determine what to do about

---

* The pack would have to produce 70 watt hours per kilogram of *energy* to achieve that range, while matching lead acid's impressive 100 kilowatts of *power* for fast acceleration.

them. But Ovshinsky could say nothing about the tests, or the results, unless Bereisa let him. "No press release from you," Bereisa warned him, "not a public whisper of this."

For the seventy-five-year-old inventor, Bereisa's offer was both an opportunity and a risk. Ovshinsky felt utterly confident in the science of nickel metal hydride. Still, if his Ovonic pack failed because it was done too quickly, he would lose all credibility. As a younger man, he might have hesitated. But his time had suddenly come to seem precious: a faulty heart valve, his doctor had told him, would have to be operated on soon. Reluctantly, he agreed, though not without securing Bereisa's promise that *some* public acknowledgment be made by GM of the results—if they were favorable—within a month of the test's conclusion.

Even within GM, the secret remained closely held. Baker had to be told; he merely advised Bereisa that with the company so politically roiled by the mandate, the burly engineer should "run silent, run deep." Some of the chiefs were told, and a team of three, led by Robin Vidas, was recruited to help order parts and carry out the tests. But no one else on the platform was let in—including John Williams, the former GM chief who now chaired the management committee of the USABC from an office at the EV platform.

The pack that Ovshinsky had put in a Chrysler TEVan was one of five he'd committed to build by hand for an additional $1.4 million from the USABC, and as the autumn weeks passed with no evidence that the remaining four packs were being finished, Williams grew suspicious. Sheepishly, Bereisa acknowledged the plan. Williams was furious. He was convinced Ovshinsky had postponed the USABC packs to build the secret Impact batteries. And surely, there would be political consequences; Ovshinsky would put out one of his over-promising press releases, make the California regulators think the perfect battery was ready to go, and thus derail GM's campaign against the mandate.

Not least, the secret plan put Williams himself in an awkward position. As the USABC chief, he had an obligation to report battery progress to GM's corporate partners, Ford and Chrysler. But this, Bereisa stressed, was a GM *application* of the consortium technology. The consortium had been set up to commercialize new battery technology; that was its whole point. The partners would have equal access to any technology that did get to market; that was in the contracts. But GM had every right to deal with Ovshinsky privately now.

Williams could rationalize keeping the project secret—barely. But he wasn't happy about it.

Out in Troy over the next eight weeks, an Ovonic team spent late nights on the Impact battery pack—working, Ovshinsky later averred, after-hours so as not to shortchange its USABC commitment. Scaling up a cell to a battery to a pack was tricky work. Making one kind of battery pack fit the tunnel allowed for another was harder yet.

By chance, the width and length of the Ovonic battery—its footprint—almost perfectly matched that of Impact's lead acid counterpart. But the voltage was different. Each of Impact's 12-volt batteries contained six cells of 2 volts each; the twenty-six batteries supplying torque to the wheels thus provided 312 volts.* A nickel metal hydride cell contained 1.2 volts, which had to do with the physical property of nickel—how many electrons it held, how it worked as a battery. Because the Ovonic cell produced less voltage, each Ovonic battery needed more of them to be a 12-volt module. Fortunately, nickel metal hydride took up less space. In fact, the requisite ten cells for each Ovonic 12-volt battery fit in less space than that allotted for Impact's six lead acid cells; and thirty nickel metal hydride batteries filled the same space as Impact's twenty-six.† Yet because they contained twice the energy of lead acid, they would theoretically take the car more than twice as far.

There was more to it, however, than putting thirty batteries, like giant Pez, in the same tunnel that had held Impact's twenty-six. Set in series, battery modules became competitive creatures. If one discharged faster than its fellows, it might reverse the polarity of current to the others, and knock them out. To avoid that, the batteries had to be filled up evenly, just as an ice tray had to be filled evenly with water so that each cube equaled its neighbors. But with batteries, as with ice trays, that was hard to do.

Technically, the Ovonic team completed its GM battery pack by Ovshinsky's birthday. It took three more weeks of debugging before the batteries were delivered, and another week for the pack to be bolted into an Impact. Then, with the car ready at last, the holidays intervened. Not until January 20, 1994, was the car loaded onto a flatbed truck and hauled south to GM's desert proving grounds in Mesa, Arizona.

On the wide, flat maze of tracks, shielded by high bushes to keep snoops from photographing GM's newest models, Robin Vidas and three test engineers unloaded their souped-up Impact from the truck and began four days of testing. They drove the car at various speeds. They did coast-down testing to judge its aerodynamics. They took a trip outside the proving grounds to "Space Mountain," the one hill in the area, to see how well the battery recouped energy on the way down with regenerative braking. Finally, they ran the range test.

* The 312 total was simply 12 (the number of volts in each cell) multiplied by 26 (the number of propulsion batteries). Another battery, the twenty-seventh, provided power to the secondary inverter that Hughes had wrested from Remy—the "alternator" that sent 12-volt current to headlights, radio, and so forth.

† The Ovonic pack actually held thirty-two batteries, with the extra two substituting for the lead acid pack's twenty-seventh battery.

On a big round track, the car rode mile after mile at a steady, 55-miles-per-hour speed. At 150 miles, Vidas let himself feel pleased. At 175 miles, he started getting excited. When the car finally rolled to a stop after 201 miles, the entire team was delirious.

Vidas called Bereisa, who called Ovshinsky, who called Stempel. The ex-chairman was so delighted that he chose that day to make a dramatic public announcement. Without any reference to the secret range test, the ex-chairman of GM declared that he was back in the car business. The EV car business. He hoped, he said, to form an independent EV venture in the near future, and added that Stan Ovshinsky would be part of it. In fact, he had just joined the boards of both Ovonic and its parent company, Energy Conversion Devices. More details, he promised, would come soon.

For Ovshinsky, the magic number of 201 was sweet vindication after months of what he viewed as a campaign of disinformation waged against him by the USABC—in the person, principally, of John Williams. Asked by CARB to submit its latest findings in preparation for a May 1994 formal review of the mandate, the USABC had filed results for the Ovonic battery that differed dramatically from Ovshinsky's own. Without elaborating, the consortium reported that the Ovonic battery failed to meet mid-term goals, and could not be considered commercially viable, at least in the near future. Of the battery's success in the Chrysler TEVan, there was no mention.

Bob Stempel, Ovshinsky's new partner, sympathized, and admitted privately that the consortium was making too-conservative judgments. But he saw logic on both sides. The USABC had to assess all batteries in terms of their commercial feasibility. It had to subject them to four-season testing. It had to know they were safe, long lasting, and reasonably priced. The Ovonic battery was well on its way, but it wasn't market-ready yet.

Within a week of the Mesa range test, Ovshinsky checked into a local hospital for his heart valve operation. John Williams and the rest of the USABC, he felt, would do their best to discredit his battery at CARB's upcoming biennial review; the consortium's whole agenda now, he believed, was to push the mandate aside. Wasn't that the carmakers' avowed intent? And weren't the carmakers the USABC's dominant partners?

Ovshinsky wasn't about to let his benefactors get away with that, however. Not if he still had breath to fight back.

Up from the Ashes

))))

Perhaps the USABC had lost none of its commitment to the search for advanced EV batteries. Perhaps Ovshinsky was paranoid. Still, for at least two of
the consortium's three automotive partners, a breakthrough battery in February 1994 would present problems, to say the least. Both Ford and Chrysler
knew how far behind GM they were on the rest of EV development; until
they caught up, a better battery would only help GM corner a new market.
And how real might that market be? As news of the range test reached GM's
highest officers, that question acquired new currency. Intriguingly, Sean Mc-
Namara had some new answers to it.

Impact's sole remaining marketing man had spent his fall coordinating the
campaign to recruit Impact test drivers in twelve cities. Since the utilities
were willing allies, McNamara's sensible plan had been to have them slip flyers about the PrEView drive in with their ratepayers' monthly bills. Los Angeles was his first drop. McNamara thought he would be lucky to get eighty
responses in all, let alone enough to choose a representative pool of eighty
candidates.

The calls kept coming.

From mid-October 1993 until the turn of the year, when he cut off the
lines two weeks ahead of schedule, McNamara logged 10,000 calls. Ten
thousand people—just in L.A.—who wanted to drive an Impact for one or
two weeks and keep a daily record of every distance driven, problem encoun-
tered, impression remembered.

On November 1, McNamara opened the lines in metropolitan New York.
He had to shut those down a month ahead of time: 14,000 calls. Of course,
people were being asked if they wanted to drive a cool new car for free, not to

pay for it. Still, McNamara had to wonder: what did this eagerness mean? Was there more of a demand for EVs than anyone yet understood?

In January 1994, the first few outsiders who had driven Impacts—the automotive journalists—had published their reports. The car buff magazines had always ridiculed electric cars as glorified golf carts, and derided concerns of automotive pollution as the muttering of environmental fascists out to curb their freedom. Though perhaps no more ecology minded than before, the journalists weighed in with raves. One *Motor Trend* writer marveled at the "unparalleled breakthroughs" Impact had made "in its drive to the electric highway of the future." Another declared: "The Impact is precisely one of those occasions where GM proves beyond any doubt that it knows how to build fantastic automobiles. This is the world's only electric vehicle that drives like a real car." *Automobile* magazine called the car's ride and handling "amazing" and declared that the "most eye-opening aspect of the Impact's performance is its smooth delivery of power." Gary Witzenburg, the Milford development manager, had invited writers from *Popular Science* and *Popular Mechanics* as well, and their reviews were no less glowing. "Electric cars may have had their share of jokes," declared *Popular Mechanics*, "but no one is laughing at GM's Impact—the first real-world, practical electric-powered passenger car for the twenty-first century." The journalists' only caveat was range. "If the Impact had but a 200-mile range," opined one, "by God, she'd be a car."

The hoopla produced a sort of Dr. Strangelove reaction at GM: one hand shooting up, the other reaching over to pull it back down. Sensing the ambivalence, a *New York Times* reporter in a front-page story suggested that despite the great interest expressed in its PrEView test drive, GM expected the program to fail as drivers came to resent the range limitation and cost of the car; indeed, the test might now serve as GM's best means of persuading CARB to push the mandate aside. Sean McNamara was furious when he read that; he felt his integrity as a market researcher had been impugned. Jim Ellis was angry, too. "You've got to be kidding!" he said one day with uncharacteristic heat. "Thirty-two million dollars sunk into this test-drive program, and all we're trying to do is prove these things don't work?"

Unfortunately, it was all too easy to believe, given the carmakers' loud protests against the mandate. In announcing the delivery of Ford's first Ecostar prototypes to utilities, for example, Dennis Wilkie scornfully noted that the vans' $100,000 unit price did not begin to recoup their costs. One utility, the Sacramento Municipal Utility District known as SMUD, was so irked by Ford's attitude that it reneged on its offer to buy three of the vans. Meanwhile in the California state assembly, anti-mandate bills bubbled up. The carmakers claimed not to be pushing them behind the scenes, but they certainly did nothing to discourage them. Now, too, they appeared to be working in concert with an even more powerful ally: the at-last awakened giant of Big Oil.

By the winter of 1993–94, the Oilies, as they were known, had finally begun to see in electric vehicles a small but growing threat to their hegemony as automotive fuel providers. Bashing EVs directly, of course, would look bad. Instead, they focused on the utilities, their energy nemeses. The state's four investor-owned ones presented a fat target, having just announced their hope of raising $630 million for EV infrastructure and incentives by levying a six-cents-a-month surcharge on all ratepayers.* To the Oilies, that seemed a boondoggle of a subsidy, especially since they themselves were even now spending billions of dollars in California to upgrade their refineries for reformulated gasoline. The utilities opined that cleaner air was in everybody's interest. EVs, the Oilies countered, were also in the utilities' financial interest.

That winter, the oil companies' California lobbying arm, the Western States Petroleum Association—WSPA—hired a public relations firm, Woodward and McDowell, to galvanize California voters with a "grassroots" campaign against the utilities' plan. The firm sent letters to 200,000 ratepayers, reminding them that California's electric rates were already among the highest in the country, and warning of sharp, unjustified rate increases if the mandate passed. Postcards of protest were enclosed, to be sent to local lawmakers. The letters failed to mention that the lobbying effort was sponsored by the oil industry; instead they employed a front, "Californians Against Utility Company Abuse," or CAUCA. Woodward and McDowell's flacks took to the phones for a follow-up campaign, identifying themselves as members of CAUCA and asking if the ratepayers wished to talk directly to their lawmakers. If the ratepayers agreed, the lobbyists would transfer the calls. The campaign was as maladroit as it was cynical: when lawmakers discovered their lines were jammed by callers who weren't even sure why they were calling, they were furious.

So were the utilities. The rhetoric, they pointed out, ignored the reality that a state mandate for EVs was in place, requiring thousands of EVs to be on the road beginning in 1998, and that utilities were traditionally obligated to upgrade their power grids—the wiring on their side of the meter, as the catchphrase had it—to meet ratepayers' ever-growing needs. True, the upgrades for EVs would be amortized by all ratepayers, but so would those required by a new subdivision, say, or an industrial park. And true, the utility plans called for incentives to be granted EV owners, such as extra-low nighttime rates to encourage overnight charging, but steering EVs away from the "spike" of peak daytime demand helped everybody, too, by postponing the need for new power plants that all ratepayers *would* subsidize. EV owners, to be sure, would pay for the charging equipment and wiring put in their

* These were the utilities that would need the blessing of the California Public Utilities Commission (CPUC) in order to do so.

garages—the hardware on the "customer side of the meter." At heart, of course, this was a fight about money: the money the utilities thought they could make from EVs; the money the oil companies and carmakers thought they would lose if EVs came to pass.

For GM, the Oilies' entry into the issue marked the start of an odd, increasingly awkward alliance. The Oilies had always had far more presence in California than the Big Three, and spent ten times as much money in lobbying to preserve the clout that came with it. By fighting the utilities now, they might help dislodge the mandate as they tarred it with the same broad brush. But the Oilies' real intent was to quash EVs, while GM's was to make a business of them—unmandated, at whatever speed technology and consumer demand allowed. Letting them lead was like fording a river on the back of a grizzly bear. The bear might get you to the other side—only to kill you when he did.

Yet even as these notes were sounded, Jacqueline Schafer, the new chairwoman of CARB who had replaced Jan Sharpless, startled carmakers at the L.A. auto show in January 1994 by declaring she saw no need to dicker with the mandate. "There is no Plan B," she said. And if the Big Three couldn't meet Plan A, other fledgling companies could.

As the L.A. auto show and others made clear, carmakers large and small, in Europe and Asia as well as the states, were rising to meet the EV challenge. None had a car to match Impact yet, but none was acting as sullen and defeatist as the Big Three, either. In Tokyo, Honda and Toyota had shown promising prototypes, while BMW showed an improved El hybrid. France's PSA/Peugeot-Citroën Group planned to bring two EV subcompacts to market by summer—and price them only $3,000 higher than comparable gas cars. "I do not understand the politics of the American manufacturers," declared Jean-Yves Helmer, director of PSA's automobile division, about the Big Three's EV stance. "Their cost estimates seem to be highly inflated."

One of the most ambitious American efforts was under way in the riot-torn DMZ of south central Los Angeles. In the last year, U.S. Electricar had been reorganized and expanded under a new CEO, Ted Morgan, an ex-marketing man from Xerox who had gone on to create a $3 billion chain of warehouse supply stores for home offices called Office Club. Thanks to Impact's retreat from production, Morgan had Hughes inverters, along with lead acid batteries, to pop into his gutted gas cars. The company was poised to start other production sites around the country, cost-sharing with local utilities and manufacturing perhaps 600 EVs a year, mostly vans and pickups, exclusively for fleets.

Further from production, but more dramatic, were the displays at the L.A. auto show of flywheel batteries. Flywheels were like high-tech potter's wheels. Instead of storing current chemically, as lead acid and other battery types did, they stored it mechanically.* One of the technology's most promising advocates, American Flywheel Systems of Bellevue, Washington, had designed a prototype flywheel powertrain in partnership with Honeywell, which had built flywheels for the aerospace and defense industries for years. At the L.A. auto show, a pack of twenty flywheel batteries was hooked up to a state-of-the-art inverter and 136-horsepower motor designed, as it happened, by the restless rebel of Impact's formative stages, Alan Cocconi.

In the three years since he'd walked away from AeroVironment, Cocconi had spent a little time biking, and then a lot of time building. At first he had worked in his home lab, designing a next generation of inverter. Not only did he have to outdo his own work, he also had to avoid duplicating parts that Hughes and GM had patented. Meanwhile, he worked with a company called Optima to design a lead acid battery with more power and energy than those in Impact. To round out his own drivetrain, Cocconi also needed a tailor-made motor. His first thought was to get in touch with GM. Perhaps, he suggested to Jon Bereisa, GM would help him develop a motor in return for licensing his new inverter. Bereisa was interested, but only if GM could have the hardware exclusively. At that point, as Cocconi put it dramatically, all dialogue with GM ceased.

Instead, Cocconi designed and built his own motor with help from Wally Rippel, the motor consultant on the AeroVironment show car. When he was finished, in the fall of 1991, he bought a Honda CRX—the first new car of his life—ripped its guts out, and installed his drivetrain. The CARB regulators, eager to test any new technology that might make EVs seem more feasible, took Cocconi's CRX for a ride and declared its performance better than Impact's: at an average speed of 51.5 miles per hour on level freeways, it had a range of 131 miles and accelerated from 0–60 in eight seconds. These were results unrivaled by any other EV in the world. They helped Cocconi sell his first drivetrain to Honda for a prototype premium of $40,000. They also emboldened him to commit savings of $250,000 to start his own company, AC Propulsion. When skeptics spoke of EV technology as immature, and won-

---

* To charge up the flywheel, current was passed through a motor that made the wheel spin up to 100,000 rpm. The wheel itself was made of hard composite materials, and spun in a vacuum between two magnetized bearings. Without any friction to retard it, it would spin indefinitely. To make the car move, mechanical energy would be siphoned back from the flywheel through the motor, which now acted in reverse, as a generator; that generator, in turn, would supply electrical current to the larger motor that turned the wheels. As electrical energy was drained off by the motor, the wheel would gradually slow down, until it stopped—the equivalent of a discharged battery. Serious issues remained to be solved, however. If a flywheel flew apart at such high speed, it might become, in effect, shrapnel. Also, like a gyroscope, it might resist being turned at an angle—as, for example, if a car went up or down a hill. Much expensive R&D would need to be done before flywheels approached commercial reality.

dered if a breakthrough battery would ever arrive, Cocconi bridled. The technology, he declared vehemently, was at hand, the batteries quickly improving. All EVs needed was time for the market to grow.

Of course, the quirky entrepreneurs and EV converters, even the smaller established carmakers of the world like Peugeot and BMW, could *wait* for the market to grow.

They had no mandate to meet in 1998.

For months, the carmakers had nursed private hopes that the vague Partnership for a New Generation of Vehicle might extricate them from the mandate. Somehow, Clinton and Gore would nudge California into a compromise so that the Big Three could work earnestly on their PNGV fuel-efficient gas cars into the hazy, non-mandated future. On February 1, 1994, those hopes were battered.

That day, the Ozone Transport Commission, representing the northeast states and the District of Columbia, held a formal vote on whether or not to petition the EPA to let them adopt the California mandate. Due in part to a last-minute campaign by the American Lung Association that recruited nearly 100 organizations to lobby for the measure, the petition passed by a vote of 9–4.

This was not to say that EVs were now required by the Northeast—nothing so simple as that. Months of horsetrading lay ahead among the states, the EPA, and the automakers before the EPA's deadline of November 15 when it would vote to accept or deny the petition. While FED LEV seemed dead, some similar compromise might be crafted by the automakers and found acceptable by the states. Some states might insist on electric vehicles; others might feel they could meet their air-quality standards without them. The EPA wanted clean air, but if the Big Three proved their claim that EVs could not be made feasible in the Northeast's winter climate, it would have to acknowledge reality.

Even if EPA did side with the carmakers, however, and chose not to accept the petition, New York and Massachusetts would not be denied: within two weeks of the vote, federal judges in both states ruled that both could require electric vehicles after all.

To GM's president's council, the northeast vote was bad news indeed. But it was offset, most intriguingly, by the 201-mile range test at Mesa, which Baker had reported. That week, Jack Smith asked Baker to brief the president's council in detail on the range test—and to make a case for restarting an EV program. He wanted to rethink the whole thing.

On February 7, 1994, the council met at the R&D building, trooping downstairs at the end of the day to an old storage room that Baker and his new staff had turned into a war room. On the walls were 3×5 cards and display boards suggesting long-range ideas. The room was redolent of freshly popped popcorn. "Have a soda," Baker told his guests, "grab some popcorn, sit back and relax. This is a voyage to the future."

The voyage began with the Mesa results. Not only had the Ovonic pack repeatedly achieved its 201-mile range at 55 miles per hour, it had shown a city range of 135 miles, nearly twice the 70 miles of Delco Remy's recombinant lead acid batteries. Of course, this was a prototype battery. It had worked fine—for about two weeks. Still, it was incredibly promising.

Baker then explained just how Impact might lead to hybrids and fuel cells.

In five years, GM might be able to produce a hybrid that used nickel metal hydride or some other advanced battery for its "surge" power source, as Paul MacCready put it: for starting up, or accelerating, when maximum power was needed. Or, instead of chemical batteries, it might use a flywheel, or a so-called ultracapacitor. For long-range highway driving, it might use a small turbine engine, fueled by relatively clean natural gas, perhaps even by propane. In fact, Baker declared, he could see only one reason why a hybrid in ten years would not equal or even surpass the range of a gas car: by then, fuel cells might be available.

Of the several kinds of fuel cells being developed, Baker explained, the most intriguing was the so-called proton-exchange membrane cell, or PEM, that used solid polymers and platinum, in wafer-like stacks, to produce electricity from hydrogen and oxygen. The hydrogen might come from an onboard tank; or, because hydrogen could be explosive, a tank of some fuel like methanol might be *reformed* into hydrogen as it entered the cell. The platinum membrane, in any case, acted as a catalyst, splitting the hydrogen on one side, splitting incoming oxygen on the other. The hydrogen molecule's negatively charged electrons were siphoned off to combine with the oxygen's positive charge, forming electricity. The hydrogen's positively charged ions, or protons, migrated through the membrane—hence the name proton-exchange membrane—combining with the oxygen's negative charge to form non-polluting wastewater.

A battery could generate no more current than could be stored within it. A fuel cell was like a switching station, producing electricity as long as oxygen and hydrogen were fed into it. Enough hydrogen or methanol could be packed aboard a fuel-cell car, Baker suggested, to give it the range of a gas car. Like a gas car, it could be refueled in minutes.

If the hydrogen for a fuel cell came from natural gas or methane, a small amount of carbon dioxide would be produced. One day, though, that hydrogen might be produced onboard by *solar* power, the sun electrolyzing water into hydrogen and oxygen, the fuel cell reforming the water even as it created electricity, the whole an elegant closed loop of forming and reforming energy with no toxic emissions at all. That would be the free lunch, the ultimate clean car.

That would be the dream come true.

By going beyond batteries, ironically, hydrogen-fuel-cell cars would obviate the need for electric recharging. The Oilies and the utilities would find their roles reversed. The utilities would be trying to *impede* change, since fuel cells would take them out of the car business. The Oilies could provide the methanol, and so would be urging innovation on. Whatever sides America's energy powers found themselves on, however, future cars would produce electrical current that powered electric motors. The age of the electric vehicle had dawned—again.

If the mandate held, Baker observed, GM would have to do EVs anyway. Why not seize the technological lead by producing Impact, and then *keep* ahead, along a continuum of car development that stretched not five or even ten years into the future, but half a century?

A new ally, to Baker's delight, was Harry Pearce, the GM attorney who had become an executive vice president in charge of most of GM's non-automotive business, including GM Hughes Electronics. Pearce had just returned from California, where he had taken soundings from regulators and politicians. He had a blunt report to make. The carmakers' campaign against the mandate was going badly, he said. There were simply too many political forces aligned behind the mandate for common sense and lobbying clout to thwart it. Rather than keep fighting it, GM should begin quietly planning how to meet it. It could lead, or it could follow: those were the only choices.

One last time, the council considered the merits and risks of an EV partnership with Ford. For the moment, Ford seemed averse to the most basic alliance on EV R&D. But under the best of circumstances, partnerships were bound to be tricky, observed Louis Hughes. Look, he said, to what had happened with Nicholas Hayek, the Swatch Watch entrepreneur. A year ago, Volkswagen had pulled out of its EV joint venture with Hayek after investing some $10 million. In his search for a new partner, Hayek had met with Jack Smith at his Tech Center office only the previous week. He had driven an Impact and pronounced it the best electric vehicle he had seen. Days later, the GM executives had been stunned to read that Hayek had thrown his lot in with Mercedes.

As due diligence, Frank Schweibold, Impact's rotund business chief, outlined all the possible routes by which GM might meet the mandate on its own. Perhaps the most sensible was to cobble together a conversion program, as Ford and Chrysler were doing. A GM pickup truck or minivan might be loaded with lead acid batteries; the work might even be done by an outside contractor like U.S. Electricar. It wasn't a glamorous or exciting prospect, but compared to Impact, it was cheap—as little as $20 million—and would enable GM at least to pitch the fleet market.

By now, however, the council had made up its mind: if GM *could* still take the initiative with EVs, it would. The most appealing course was to get Impact out by 1996, take advantage of the credits that CARB would bestow to early arrivals—fewer EVs required in 1998—and do a conversion vehicle at the same time. With the credits, and with a lot of luck, the company might keep from losing money and establish a market lead that paid off later. At the same time, GM might want to consider doing some sort of side deal with Ovonic, in the hope of producing Ovonic batteries by 1996. The meeting ended with Smith's promise to make a formal decision soon.

By chance, both Ellis and Schweibold had scheduled skiing vacations with their families for the middle week of February in Colorado. They returned the same day to calls from Baker. *We've got a program,* Baker said. *We're going to do Impact, we're going to do conversions, we're going to do a battery deal with Ovonic, we're going to work with Bob Stempel.*

This time, Baker went on, the program would go black, just as John Williams and Don Runkle and Bob Stempel and others had suggested it go four years ago. For the next year, everyone in the industry would be assuming that GM's agenda was to do the PrEView test-drive program grudgingly; hope the mandate went away; and do conversions for 1998 if it didn't.

The PrEView now could serve as a cover, a Trojan horse while the team in Troy raced to prepare a production Impact after all. Suppliers might wonder why they were being asked to give quotes for quantities of 2,000 rather than 50, but carmakers routinely asked for a range of quotes. The engineers in Troy would simply say replacement parts were needed for PrEView cars and that they were bench marking to learn more about the market. Suspicions might be raised, but no one would believe that an abandoned program was being revived. That didn't happen in the car business. In fact, it had never happened. How long GM could keep this a secret was anybody's guess. But every month that it did was a month GM would be ahead of the competition. With luck, it might still be first to market.

By the end of February, Baker added, Schweibold and Ellis had better be ready with a full, fleshed-out program plan for how to make all this happen.

Schweibold was stunned. To date, the Impact program had cost some $300 million. Taking the car to production might cost nearly that much again. This was serious money. Of course the president's council would want to do the program for far less. Schweibold would have to do some fancy juggling. For Ellis, the engineering challenge was more than daunting. It was downright scary. The fifty prototype cars might seem finished, but he knew better than anyone how jury-rigged they were.

The first several times Schweibold ran his numbers, they came to $300 million—over and above the $300 million already spent—to produce Impact as a low-volume car. He kept running the numbers. By the time he presented them at the president's council meeting on February 24, he had them down to $235 million. The council balked. Somehow, the budget would have to be pushed a good deal lower.

Two weeks later, on March 7, GM's board voted in New York to give the plan its tentative approval.

Pending a pared-down budget, barring the unforeseen, Impact was back.

On March 8, the whole Impact platform was convened for a special meeting in Troy. The engineers knew something big was up: the previous week, a short, balding, heavyset stranger had appeared in Ken Baker's unoccupied office and presided from behind the desk at closed-door meetings with Ellis and Schweibold, conducting himself with a brisk, off-putting air of authority that led more than one observer to call him Napoleonic. As the engineers filed into the conference room they saw him again, sitting up front beside Ken Baker under a twenty-foot banner that read "Making Automotive History Together—It's Electric."

Baker spoke first. Impact was alive again, he told the crowd. The long hours that everyone had put in for three and a half years would lead to a real car after all. Impact could still be the first production EV to market. It could beat Ford and Chrysler, and it could beat Japan; it could reassert GM's technological leadership and lead the way into a new century of automotive innovation. It could do all this, Baker said, but only if everyone in the room kept the news an inviolable secret.

Historically, secrets had been short-lived in Detroit. Engineers talked; corporate spies listened. This would have to be different, Baker stressed. Not only would the news produce a race to market, it would also kill any chance GM had of getting the mandate pushed aside at CARB's biennial review in May, as the regulators would doubtless assume that an up-and-running program meant all problems were solved. The program would have to "run silent, run deep," as Baker put it.

As Baker spoke, he looked from one familiar face to another in the crowd, taking in the expressions of stunned delight, and did his best to show the same excitement. That was what a leader did when the news was good, when his team might triumph after all. Inside, he felt hollow. The program into which he had poured such passion—*his* program—was restarting without him. He had made his decision to leave, or it had been made for him—the line between personal choice and corporate will was always blurred—and he'd been given what he wanted, or thought he wanted. He was a vice president. But now the man sitting beside him would be finishing the job he had begun.

Baker couldn't help wondering, too, if he should feel passed over. Clearly, if the president's council had felt he was the best choice to lead the revived program, he would have been chosen. Someone else could have taken over

R&D; the awkwardness of a vice president serving as program manager could have been dealt with; too much was on the line for such proprieties to interfere. In fact, his suspicion was well founded. He wasn't the best choice: not now, not at this stage.

Impact was an invention, and like any invention—any successful invention—its evolution was proving to have three stages. First had come the ideas that made it work, from mavericks outside the corporate constraints within which most engineers labored. For Impact, the mavericks were Alan Cocconi, Alec Brooks, and the rest of the AeroVironment team. The second stage was implementation: bringing the invention in from outside, making it work within a corporate system, making it manufacturable. That stage needed creative minds, too, but not mavericks: corporate engineers with inordinate vision and passion. That was Baker's stage, the stage for which he had been the best choice. By restarting the program, Jack Smith was pushing Impact into the third stage: making a business of the invention; making it work in the market; making it sell at a price that yielded a profit. He'd made his choice of program manager accordingly.

For nearly four years, Baker told the packed room, he had been proud to lead this program. But from R&D, he could hardly do the team justice as the program ramped back up. Impact needed a full-time manager again, and now it had one, he said, turning to the Napoleonic figure beside him, in one of Jack Smith's closest, most trusted advisors: Bob Purcell.

The man who stepped forward to address the team was clearly a different kind of leader from Baker. Aside from the obvious physical incongruities, Purcell seemed to lack Baker's public ease and political savvy. He appeared nervous but determined, very serious, and very tough. Though he spoke of a lifelong love of cars, he said he had spent his career at GM on the finance side. In fact, he'd been at the board meeting in New York the day before, presenting other business, when the board ratified the president's council decision to start up Impact again.

The program was on again in *theory*, he emphasized to the group. "We're on a sixty- to ninety-day window to get back to the board of directors with a world class business case," Purcell told his audience. "And by that I mean we have to demonstrate that *no one in the world can do this car better than we can.*" Not until the board approved that business case would Impact get its first chunk of production money—and it might not be, if the case wasn't good enough. But Purcell was determined it would be. "I'm going into this assuming up front we're going to be successful," he said. "Therefore, we are going to start moving today as if this program is in implementation mode.

"I do not want anyone sitting back waiting for approval," Purcell added. "We are going to ramp this program up now with engineering, with manufacturing, with facilities, whatever we need to get a car to market. *We are going to make this happen.*"

The engineers shifted in their chairs and exchanged worried glances. Purcell sounded less like a program manager than a boot camp drill sergeant.

This was their new boss?

Aiming High

))))

He seemed the epitome of old-style, downtown GM—a brusque, bottom-line-minded finance guy. Bob Purcell, one of the chiefs muttered, was just the sort of corporate white blood cell that would have attacked the Impact program early on, if he could have, to protect the status quo.

In fact, Purcell was more complex than that. And as the chiefs began to discover, he wasn't typical at all.

Unlike most of his corporate colleagues, for example, Purcell had not joined GM until he was thirty. Nor, like most, did he possess an engineering degree. The entry job he'd landed at Pontiac, and from which he'd risen in thirteen years—faster than most of his peers despite his late start—involved repositioning the division to have a sportier image. He got the job in large part because of his years as a race car mechanic.

A carpenter's son, with six brothers and sisters, Purcell had grown up working class—not poor, as he would point out with pride—in Rockville, Maryland, just outside Washington, DC. By fifteen, he was drawn to a gasoline alley of auto garages on Dupont Avenue in nearby Kensington widely known for their work on European race cars. He began as an apprentice mechanic on weekends; by nineteen, he was a service manager. Yet he went on to college, and by majoring in the philosophy of science, seemed to go out of his way to challenge the stereotype of the grease monkey as illiterate. Not by chance would he come to regard *Zen and the Art of Motorcycle Maintenance* as one of his favorite books.

In his college reading Purcell was hugely impressed by the ancient educational traditions of the Oriental nobility. The nobles began with philosophy to acquire logical minds. They went on to the arts to learn creative thinking, then business to enter government, or the martial arts to join the military. After studying philosophy, Purcell spent two years at a studio art school in Boston, earning a Bachelor of Fine Arts degree, then an M.B.A., while continuing to work in automotive service. By now he was married and realized that to move up in his field he would have to start his own dealership or garage. With no capital to speak of, joining one of the Big Three seemed a more feasible next step.

At Pontiac, and later at GM Powertrain, Purcell worked in a succession of "forward programs," doing the numbers for big new-car programs. His Oriental balance of disciplines helped distinguish him; and clearly he was driven, a self-professed Type A personality with a military sense of duty. He moved forward so fast himself that in the spring of 1992, the week before Jack Smith was named president, he was appointed director of business planning for North American Operations, assigned to rethink the clumsy business structure that Roger Smith had imposed eight years before. When his role expanded a year later to plotting long-range strategy for the entire corporation, Purcell was among those who made the case that GM should seize intellectual leadership of new technology, to take the dare of being first to market. After decades of driving down the middle of the road, that was, for GM, an almost radical notion.

Though he struck his new team as rather dour, Purcell was thrilled by the Impact assignment. He saw the car as the first step in GM's new course; for himself, it was the operating job he'd longed for after too many years of finance and planning. He tried to make clear to the chiefs that he wasn't the number cruncher they assumed him to be. "Everything I did until the age of thirty was hands-on," he told them, "and I've got the scars to prove it." He pointed to a black line below his left eye. "See that? That's a tailpipe on a Volvo that I was cutting off with an air chisel, and it broke off the mount and swung off and hit me below the eye and knocked me out, imbedded a little piece of the pipe in my face."

Before his first day was out, Purcell convened the chiefs to pose the essential question: how soon could the car be done? A new gas car, brought as far along as Impact, would take at least thirty months to produce, he knew. But by then, if the mandate held, Toyota and Honda, among others, might get their own EVs to market. To all the directors, but especially to John Smale, being first to market remained of critical importance. The board had told Purcell he should try to do the car in twenty-seven months—or sooner. Purcell put the question to Jim Ellis. How *much* sooner?

Ellis knew better than anyone how steep a challenge the team faced in restarting the program. The limited-production fleet had myriad "Band-Aid" solutions, starting with those for EMI, because formal design changes for fifty handbuilt cars would have wasted money and time. Mass and piece cost had increased prohibitively: not problems for a fifty-car fleet, but big problems for production. Even the car's body design was incomplete; with the program's diminution in December 1992, the engineers had stopped refining it and based the fifty-car fleet on what they had at hand. Many of the engineers who'd done those designs were gone, taking valuable knowledge with them. Outside suppliers might be unable or unwilling to oblige a low-volume program that was, as far as they knew, dead. Almost every design detail, every part, every step of assembly, had to be reconsidered.

At the same time, Ellis relished the prospect of showing how fast a car *could* be done at GM. What an example it would set, to help wrench GM back into the sort of company he had once admired. "We're doing the limited-production fleet already," he told Purcell. "So really, we could do without prototypes."

"And if we did that?"

"Eighteen months."

"Eighteen months." Purcell nodded slowly. It was March 9, 1994. "Let's go with that."

Others on the team, when the word went out, rolled their eyes in disbelief. The LPFs were no substitute for prototypes, the engineers muttered to each other; management was being deceived, as one put it, by a car that looked production-ready but was in some ways less so than the earlier proof-of-concept cars. And how could a factory be tooled up, even for low volume, in just a year?

A two-day technical review not long after revealed a slight misunderstanding about timing, but not one the engineers might have predicted. One by one the engineering groups presented their parts of the car and spoke of refinements they hoped to make. As Arianna Kalian finished speaking about plans for the car's front end, she said she saw no problem about doing what needed to be done in the eighteen-month time frame Purcell had decreed. Something about the way she put that gave Purcell pause.

"When does the eighteen months start?" he asked.

Kalian looked surprised. "When the program ramps-up again," she said. "When we hire more people."

Purcell shook his head. "Eighteen months started the day the board turned on the program again," he said: March 7, 1994.

Jim Ellis blanched. "Bob, we don't have the people we need, we don't have the resources and suppliers. The program starts when we get those people in. A month from now, maybe two."

"We'll talk about this later," Purcell said, all eyes on him in the silent room. "But for anyone who's concerned, the program started March seventh."

Behind closed doors, a small compromise was reached. Purcell hadn't signed his first paperwork on the program as its manager until April 1. In the eyes of corporate accounting, that was when his new job had begun. Fine, he agreed: that was when the clock had started, too.

Purcell wasn't sure the eighteen-month schedule could be met either, but why aim any less high? If the team ran up against a showstopper, they'd deal with it when it came. Usually, programs drifted as engineers kept dithering with their designs; that, at least, he could stop. There would be strict "freeze dates" for all designs, Purcell declared. To keep from freezing innovation in the process, a first batch of Impacts would be followed by a later one to which improvements could be applied. The first would be called 5.0's because they would be, in a sense, Impact's fifth generation, after the AeroVironment show car, the fast-build, the proof-of-concept cars, and the fifty-car limited production fleet.

Amid the warrens of open cubicles, dispirited veterans tried to put the best spin on their new boss and his impossible schedule. After the first day, they observed, he stopped wearing a tie; by the third day he doffed his jacket; surely he was loosening up. To some of the chiefs, he talked of brewing his own beer, fifty gallons of bitter a year; a home brewer couldn't be all bad. The program would clearly benefit, too, from Purcell's connections to Jack Smith's inner circle, especially when GM-owned suppliers were pressed for low bids on low-volume EV parts. But in more than one meeting Purcell publicly chewed out one of the chiefs; and in the tech reviews he nixed certain accessories while calling for new ones, thus violating Jim Ellis's cardinal tenet of letting the engineering teams come up with solutions themselves. Over in R&D, Baker's voice mail began to fill with angry reports. Finally, Baker called Purcell to suggest, testily, that there were two ways to lead, and that the team would respond far better to one way than the other.

Purcell was taken aback. The way he saw it, the engineers had to be snapped awake. Consigned to build a few show cars, they had lost the discipline of a production program—the hot breath of the marketplace on their necks. They had to be pumped up now, Purcell felt. They had to be as driven as he himself felt coming in fresh, and not be wounded by criticism meant to toughen them for the challenge. But he was sorry, he admitted, if he'd come across as a drill sergeant. Late one afternoon, he looked out the windows of his corner office to the rush-hour traffic on elevated I-75 and said softly, "What I want is for everyone on this platform to feel that this is their destiny. That this is not their job, this is their destiny. They are here for a reason, to do this. It transcends going to work.

"What did Vonnegut call it?" Impact's new program manager searched his memory. "In *Cat's Cradle*. A *karass*. We're all in the same karass."

Bob Stempel had wished to do Impact himself, but he was, in a sense, happier to know GM would do it for him. He didn't need to produce a *Stempel*.

Still poignantly loyal to the corporation, he was thrilled to think GM might be first to market after all. Besides, he remained in the game with the next best thing to the car itself: its future battery.

In his meetings with members of the president's council, Stempel had argued that whatever GM did with Impact, it should draw up its own development deal with Stan Ovshinsky—apart from the USABC grants co-funded by Ford and Chrysler—to get his battery into production. GM had a golden chance to scale up the battery and use it in Impact. Stempel was speaking as a GM consultant, but now also as a board member of Energy Conversion Devices, Ovonic battery's parent company, with Ovshinsky urging him on.

If GM needed a better battery soon, ECD needed GM sooner. "We can't wait, Bob," the inventor had confided to Stempel. "We're deep in the red." ECD had just declared its fifth consecutive year of losses, a long dry spell between infusions of R&D cash from corporate titans. NASDAQ had dropped ECD from its stock listings, declaring its assets insufficient, and Ovshinsky had acknowledged in his latest annual report to shareholders that unless some corporate patron was found, he would be forced to slash ECD's operations. If that was not trouble enough, the SEC, in June 1993, had opened an informal inquiry into the propriety of stock options the company had given its employees. ECD needed more than cash; it needed corporate respectability.

If Stempel's two roles created a conflict of interest, no one seemed to care. He was aboveboard about his commitments; he was also the only person who, as talk of a deal developed, could bring the sides together, batting down the disparaging rumors about Ovshinsky that swirled through GM's executive corridors while soothing Ovshinsky's fears that GM, so set on thwarting the mandate, might secretly want to buy his battery in order to bury it. It wasn't a conflict of interest, Stempel would say later, somewhat affronted. If anything, it was a *congruence* of interests.

The obvious course was for mighty GM to buy tiny ECD, but neither party wanted that to happen. Ovshinsky had managed to avoid selling out for nearly thirty-five years, and he was far too proud and independent to think of doing it now. GM had reservations of its own. As its lawyers went through ECD's history of shareholder lawsuits they came to feel buying ECD might mean acquiring future liabilities, each with the potential to cost GM and besmirch its reputation. Still, the wily old goat did have that battery—the battery that might solve the whole EV quandary. Perhaps the answer, despite the comical disparity in the companies' sizes, was a joint venture.

To GM's management, Stempel confirmed that Ovshinsky's patents on nickel metal hydride were solid. A wariness on GM's part was understandable: not long before, the USABC had granted $34 million to Saft America, a Georgia-based company, for research in nickel metal hydride EV batteries. Saft claimed the chemistry it was using was too generic to be covered by

Ovonic's patents; Ovshinsky, and now Stempel as his ally, accused Saft of theft. GM, however, could go into business with ECD and still stay out of that fray.

On ECD's behalf, Stempel pushed for a major commitment of funds from GM. This shouldn't be a pilot process, he argued, with half an assembly line set up somewhere, and a wait-and-see approach. It had to be large enough that economies of scale could drive the batteries' cost down. Nor should GM make hardball claims to any intellectual property that a joint venture might produce. Stan had the goods; his rights to the goods should be protected.

At 10:00 on the morning of March 4, 1994, a curious group filed into Bob Stempel's office in Southfield. Stan Ovshinsky, looking frail a month after his open-heart surgery, was there with Iris, his wife, and Ovonic's president, Subhash Dhar. Representing GM was Ken Baker. But there, too, were Harry Pearce, as a GM executive vice president, and Leon Krain, corporate vice president of finance. Ranged behind the circle was a gathering of lawyers, like watchful crows.

Stempel, as host, brought the meeting to order, but quickly deferred to Harry Pearce. "We are here representing Jack Smith and John Smale," Pearce said. "We have the direction, and the authorization, to negotiate a joint venture—and to sign, if we can come to terms."

Pearce laid out the logical parameters of a deal: a stand-alone company funded mostly by GM, with a board comprised of three members from GM, two from Ovonic, and some division of profits to be determined. Krain suggested a system of royalties. At that, Ovshinsky bridled. "You don't understand," he declared. "I'm in this relationship for success, not to make a quick buck. I want both of us to be successful. I want to be part of a team that's going to create a new industry. A joint industry; no royalties. We'll share equal participation, and share in the profits."

Krain and Pearce adjourned with their lawyers to an anteroom and returned in a matter of minutes. "If we understand you correctly," Pearce said, "this is what you're offering," and repeated the terms laid out by Ovshinsky. GM and Ovonic would be sixty/forty partners down the line. Because Ovonic had no capital to spare, GM would supply the start-up investment of roughly $25 million. Ovonic would provide the technology, but also owe GM 40 percent of the seed money. If the venture lost money, GM would absorb the losses. Assuming it made money, Ovonic would start receiving a 40 percent share—after its debt was made up. Ovshinsky nodded, and Pearce declared, "We have a deal."

As lawyers worked out the details, Baker couldn't help noticing Iris Ovshinsky reach over, more than once, to squeeze her husband's hand. At one point she went out to get Stan a cup of coffee, and when she put it in front of him, she leaned over and gave him a kiss on top of the head. Baker, whose own marriage had weathered some rocky months as he adjusted to R&D, found himself envying the affection these two shared, a love strong enough to distract Stan even as he negotiated the crowning deal of his career.

For Ovshinsky, the memo of understanding meant a long-sought dream come true. At last, he would be taking one of his inventions to market. *Manufacturing*, not merely inventing and patenting, then having to battle licensees who failed to pay up, and rivals that tried to break his patents. For GM, the deal was a $25 million gamble on the field's most promising midterm battery. To Ford and Chrysler, when they heard about it, the deal was dirty pool.

To both carmakers, GM appeared to be cornering the market on a battery developed with their money, as fellow partners in the USABC. Angry calls flew back and forth; a USABC meeting was canceled in protest. Stempel was astounded. "Go back and read the USABC contract," he told Ford's John Wallace. "The whole point of USABC is to commercialize the best findings." Ford and Chrysler, as USABC partners, would be able to buy batteries from GM-Ovonic at the same price GM paid, yet not have to contribute a dime of the start-up money. The only reason GM was taking the initiative, Stempel observed, was that neither Ford nor Chrysler had shown the slightest interest in commercializing the battery themselves. Of course, no one at GM explained why the joint venture decision had been reached with such haste.

Frank Schweibold presided over a peace meeting with Ford and Chrysler to confirm the terms—equal access to batteries, at equal price, to all—and tempers began to cool. "GM still should have told us," Wallace said later. "That's all. When we asked them why they didn't, they said, 'Well, it's a small company, there were confidentiality issues.' I don't buy those excuses." But having seen Ovshinsky in action—the Great Promoter—Wallace left the peace meeting laughing up his sleeve. To invest $25 million in a battery based on bench tests and a ride around the track in a handbuilt Impact was not only precipitous, it was bizarre. That battery wasn't alive yet! *Let* GM throw away its money.

And what was that about *Stempel*, doing the deal with a foot in both camps? Very un-Fordlike, Wallace muttered. Very un-Fordlike, indeed.

A Horror of
High Expectations

))))

If the Mesa range test had not in itself inspired GM to restart Impact, certainly it had tipped the balance. Without that new hope—201 miles!—the president's council might have put its money into EV conversions and pared Impact to a skeleton crew of propulsion engineers.

None of the engineers who'd helped stage the range test had expected such dramatic results. To buttress their hopes, another group had actually run a second very quiet operation over these last months. If an Impact could be made to go not only farther but *faster* than any EV the world had seen, that might help their case. And so, as the program's fate hung suspended, they'd reduced an Impact's already low drag by removing the side mirrors, covering the wheels with smooth discs, lowering the car closer to the ground, and adding a tail cone. They'd kept the same motor but upped the gear ratio and removed the current limit. For batteries, they'd stuck with lead acid—lead acid's great strength was its power, for acceleration, as opposed to its energy, for range—but replaced the passenger seat with a "six-pack" of additional batteries. As GM's board met to weigh Impact's future in New York, an Impact raced secretly down a remote test track in Fort Stockton, Texas.

The team had a surprisingly high mark to hit: in 1974, a one-of-a-kind EV called the Battery Box had been clocked at 173 miles per hour at Bonneville. But on March 11, GM test engineer Clive Roberts drove the souped-up Impact past the timing lights at 183.822 miles per hour over a kilometer length, 183.075 over the mile. By then, the board had voted and Purcell had given his speech. Still, a world land-speed record for EVs was no small feat.*

---

* In May 1995, a Batmobile-like race car called the Z.E.R. Bertone (Z.E.R. for zero emission

Thrilled, the chiefs talked of breaking the news at the so-called Phoenix 500, a fast-growing EV counterpart to the Indianapolis race, which would begin March 18. But on the president's council, reactions were mixed: good news about Impact was bad news for the anti-mandate campaign. After much debate, the race car was displayed in GM's tent at the Phoenix 500, but no efforts were made to publicize it. Aside from a few short mentions months later in the automotive press, the record was all but ignored.

GM's new partner in batteries, however, was not so easily muzzled at the race.

The Phoenix 500 in its fourth year had begun to draw real crowds, with the EV drivers sponsored by major battery makers: Trojan, Eagle Pitcher, Champion, and GM's own Delco Remy. Most of the race cars—as low-slung and sporty as those at Indy—used lead acid batteries, but here and there a zinc bromine or nickel iron pack could be found. This time, one car was powered by nickel metal hydride, its pack provided by Ovonic to a laconic, twenty-five-year-old EV entrepreneur named James Worden.

Back in 1987, Worden's entry in the Australian Solar Challenge had failed to complete the race that Sunraycer won. Worden hadn't had many false starts since then. Graduating from MIT, he and a fellow alum, Anita V. Rajan, had started their own EV company in Wilmington, Massachusetts. Solectria might never challenge the Big Three, but it had grown impressively, selling converted Geo Metros with lead acid packs to utilities and municipal fleets and building an EV components business that pushed its gross sales to $2 million a year.

Like the young Henry Ford, to whom he was often compared in the press, Worden raced his own cars, entering every EV race on a growing circuit; like Henry Ford, he usually won, which helped promote the cars. Bob Stempel admired the young man's intensity and pluck. *He doesn't know what he can't do,* Stempel marveled, and so he just might do it. Worden reminded him of Cocconi, in a sense—both so young, both with such a grasp of the subject, both so determined to advance the field. And so it had seemed natural for Ovshinsky, encouraged by Stempel, to lend Worden an Ovonic pack. A victory in the race would help promote both Solectria and Ovonic batteries; a victory, as usual, was what Worden delivered.

Among GM executives, newly jangled by Impact's land-speed record, this did not sit well.

As far as they could see, Stan Ovshinsky, whose trustworthiness as a prospective business partner had stirred sharp debate, was already double-crossing GM, and more broadly the USABC, with the ink barely dry on his

record) was clocked at 188.9 miles per hour on a circular track in Italy using lead acid batteries. On a one-way course its time would be unofficial, so that GM's record stands.

GM-Ovonic memo of understanding. To GM, he had promised to say nothing of the 201-mile range test at Mesa. Yet in newspaper stories about the Phoenix 500, he declared his battery could go 250 miles on a charge. Before long, he promised, it would go twice that far.

Ford and Chrysler, as members of the USABC, were furious with Ovshinsky as well. The inventor had still failed to deliver two of the five battery packs for which he'd received $1.4 million from the consortium. Yet here was Worden using one in the race—using, it appeared, a USABC battery paid for by the Big Three, making EV batteries seem feasible even as the carmakers tried to persuade CARB to put the mandate aside because the technology was premature. Stempel, a vigorous presence at the race, flatly denied the accusation, proving just how awkward his new position would be. The pack was not a USABC pack, he and Ovshinsky declared. As for Worden, he was a long-time Ovonic customer, and Ovonic had every right to give him a pack if it chose.

If Ovshinsky had indeed slipped Worden a USABC pack, the irony of his gift must have amused him. *Speak truth to power*, he liked to say. Having endured months of acrimony with the USABC about how his batteries would be represented to the California regulators, he had to feel that having Worden win a race with an Ovonic pack was a fitting retort to the consortium that kept claiming his batteries weren't ready to go.

Somehow, not long after, an Ovonic pack found its way to the CARB regulators so they could bench test it before their biennial review of the mandate in May. And somehow, one of Worden's Ovonic-equipped Geo Metros was placed in the CARB building garage so that each of the regulators could drive it. The car, a four-seater, went 174 miles before running out of juice. The regulators were thrilled. The USABC was furious.

"They tried to stop us from going to California," Ovshinsky railed later about the USABC. "They threatened us! I said to them, 'Look, the Communist Party no longer runs the world. A party line cannot be imposed upon people who don't believe in it. The consortium is set up to make sure the American public has an electric car. It was not set up to fight the mandate. We are a battery company, and we're not going to lie to the public!' "

John Williams, the churchgoing GM head of the USABC's management committee, deeply resented Ovshinsky's implication that the USABC had deceived anyone, and that he, Williams, was slanting the facts. Williams was, indeed, a deeply moral man; Ovshinsky, true as he might be to his own gods, was a promoter of his own work, as inventors had to be. In the process of invention, each was an archetype, Williams the skeptic, Ovshinsky the optimist. At each step of the process, Williams's facts would be more solid, more truthful, even, than Ovshinsky's. Yet it was the optimist who climbed each next stair and forced the skeptic up to the stair below him, there to declare that *that* stair might be solid, but clearly the next one up was air.

As far as Williams was concerned, the facts were clear. By the mid-term goals that the USABC had set and Ovshinsky committed to meet, batteries were to cost no more than $150 per kilowatt hour. That was still expensive: a pack of thirty batteries would cost $4,500. But for the prototype batteries he was making for the consortium, Ovshinsky was charging $6,000 per kilowatt hour!

Now, those were prototypes; by the same standard, a prototype Impact with a lead acid pack had cost close to $500,000. But by the inventor's own optimistic estimates, three years would be needed to bring the battery to production. The first ones off the line would cost at least $400 *per kilowatt hour*. That meant a still unacceptable pack cost—figuring thirty batteries to a pack—of $12,000.

Ovonic's people claimed they could get 10,000 cycles per battery: 10,000 fill-ups, in effect, before the battery died. They didn't say that their data was based on tests of an A-size flashlight battery. Scaled up for EVs, the battery performed rather less well. "At the cell level," Williams declared, "we're getting perhaps five hundred cycles. The mid-term goal is six hundred; we're approaching that. At the module level—cells put together to form one battery—we're getting a couple of hundred cycles. But at the pack level— well, you put these cells together, all in series, cycling up and down consistently as a *pack*, we're getting fifty to one hundred cycles—period."

Despite Williams's arguments, there seemed little doubt that CARB's regulators would uphold the mandate at their biennial hearing in May 1994. Ovshinsky's rosy forecasts were irresistible, at least for a body of regulators who wanted so much to believe. All the carmakers could do, as the hearing loomed, was try to sway the court of public opinion.

For this, their greatest asset was Tom Austin, a former CARB executive officer who had become an apostate of sorts. Austin now ran Sierra Research, a consulting firm in Sacramento that took on environmental issues, usually from industry's side. Though paid well enough for his labors to maintain sleek offices and drive a late-model Porsche, Austin also worked with a real sense of mission. He felt strongly that auto emissions could best be improved by making gas cars ever cleaner, and by instituting centralized inspection and maintenance stations to catch high-polluting "clunkers." To be sure, Los Angeles and other coastal California cities remained smog-shrouded for all the tailpipe improvements of the previous twenty-five years, and centralized I&M stations, as they were called, were proving a political failure. But Austin was undeterred. EVs, he argued, would accomplish far less. With their still-limited range, they would be bought as third-car novelties by a few wealthy Californians, replacing no gas cars and thus helping the air not at all. Moreover, they would be so expensive that carmakers would have to raise the prices of gas cars to subsidize them; higher prices would mean fewer sales, as owners hung on to their old cars longer, which would actually make the air *less* clean. And so, when the auto and oil industries came calling to solicit studies that would prove the mandate misbegotten, Austin was delighted to oblige.

From the carmakers, Austin borrowed confidential data to average the prospective costs of upgrading cars to meet CARB's tightening emissions standards. It would cost carmakers only $323, Austin concluded, to make the average gas car meet the first tier. For the highest tier—zero-emission vehicles, which was to say EVs—the numbers were alarmingly higher. Even allowing for a 5 percent drop in costs each year as manufacturers improved production, Austin concluded, EVs would add about $21,000 to the cost of a gas car. "CARB wants GM to build Impacts at forty thousand dollars apiece," he told a Detroit reporter, "then have you suckers in the Midwest subsidize them by paying ten thousand dollars more for every conventional car."

Over the winter, Mobil had begun a series of paid op-ed ads castigating the mandate and giving short shrift to existing EVs; the ads were based on Austin's Sierra Research findings. Lobbyists for the Big Three used the findings, too. Reg Maudlin, Chrysler's Environmental Affairs manager, declared on television, not untypically: "On that window sticker for your—in Chrysler's product line, maybe a Dodge Neon . . . will be a line item that'll say twenty-seven hundred dollars extra charge, thank you for your contribution to your neighbor's electric car."

Much of the Austin-fueled rhetoric was directed at the northeast states, where the February 1, 1994, vote to adopt California's rules had been followed by confusion. The vote had not pledged the states to zero-emission cars, as many news stories reported; ZEVs were optional. As it happened, only the two states that had called for ZEVs before the vote—New York and Massachusetts—demanded them after it, and both might be open to persuasion.

As Austin's findings kept turning up, like a computer virus, in the arguments of lobbyists and editorialists, oil company ads and auto executives' speeches, Bob Stempel shook his head in disgust. "Advocacy research," he said of Sierra. "From guys who are in this business . . . They've got to look in the mirror in the morning when they're shaving and know full well we've never cost-accounted anything that way."

Sierra, Stempel observed, made the most conservative assumptions possible: that the market would be small, that costs would stay high. And it showed short-term losses, rather than amortizing losses over a span of years and assuming the market would grow. Viewed Sierra's way, any innovation of the last two decades—from catalytic converters to computer controls—would have cost too much and forced carmakers to charge premiums. But that wasn't the way Detroit worked. "In our business," Stempel said, "you look at the car over its life and you decide the selling price, and lo and behold as you work it down you get a profit."

In view of its importance, CARB's mandate hearing of May 12–13, 1994, was held at a municipal building in downtown L.A., within sight of MacArthur Park. Protesters milled outside, wearing gas masks and holding signs that urged the regulators not to kill the mandate. The Oilies, with their public campaign of sneering rhetoric and salted facts, may have won some hearts and minds, but had also provoked an angry, and growing, grassroots opposition — one that seemed not to depend on "astroturf" tactics to get out the bodies.

Inside, high-profile advocates made passionate pitches. Bernie Richter, a state assemblyman whose anti-mandate bills had stalled in committee, reiterated his calls for deregulation. Tom Hayden, the sixties radical turned state senator from Santa Monica, spoke as his ideological opposite. Hayden felt he'd done much to keep Governor Pete Wilson from waffling on the mandate: every day, when the governor stepped out of his limousine in the underground garage of the Sacramento Capitol building, there was Hayden's EV Ford Escort, plugged into the wall. Upstairs, there was Hayden himself, ready to pounce on any gubernatorial utterance that hinted he might be bending to the auto and oil lobbyists' pressure.

Sam Leonard, speaking for GM, struck a moderate tone. "It may surprise some of you to hear me say this," he suggested, "but General Motors wants electric vehicles to be a marketplace success." He ticked off GM's impressive investments in EVs to date, but went on somberly to declare that no mid-term battery would be ready by 1998, and then recited the litany of Sierra Research statistics that made EVs seem so unfeasible.

In the end, none of it seemed to matter. The regulators' minds were made up, mostly by what they'd seen of the Ovonic battery. In a crisp statement, they recommended no fundamental change to the mandate's tiered schedule. In reference to the highest of those tiers, they stated that nickel metal hydride batteries would be commercially available by 1998, and that other battery technologies, such as Ford's sodium sulfur, seemed not far behind. "Tremendous technological progress has been made over the last few years," the regulators wrote, "and the staff believes that the ZEV mandate is the reason that much of this development has taken place. Changing the mandate would remove the main incentive for continued technological progress, potentially penalizing those companies which have already invested heavily in the development of future technologies as a result of this mandate. The gradual phase-in of zero-emission technology is the mechanism needed to help California progress toward a clean transportation future."

■ ■ ■

The same day the CARB hearing convened, Bob Purcell appeared before the GM North American strategy board to offer his first report on Impact. More than two months after its revival, the Impact program remained a secret to most of the corporation, and nearly all outside it, which meant that Bob Purcell, its manager, remained largely an invisible man.

Impact's budget, Purcell reported, was still above target, but not perilously so. If the team could get the car done in eighteen months, he thought the target could be met. The 5.0's piece cost—the parts for one car—was still high, too, but might be reduced with further work. The car would yield no profit, but if it could be sold at cost, the return on investment might come with a follow-on car. Technically, Purcell felt, the primary challenge was scaling Ovonic batteries up to production and troubleshooting a worrisome tendency they had to heat up and dissipate charge. The bottom line was, he could do this car.

Money was still tight at GM, but Smith's turnaround was in full swing: in its first quarter of 1994, profits had jumped 66.5 percent over the quarter of the year before. With Smith's blessing, the program was given a next installment of $25 million. Purcell was told to work toward late June for formal approval of the rest of his budget.

Now all Purcell had to do was shave a miserly budget by 15 percent, deliver a car on it in less time than any car had ever been done at GM, make its new technology work, and keep the whole program secret.

Regrowing Pains

)))

In his best military manner, Bob Purcell had given the GM strategy board an account of the program and its prospects so stirringly upbeat that drums and bugles might have accompanied it. The facts were true, the forecast plausible, but if pressed, Purcell might have admitted he had a less than complete idea of *how* the program would reach its goals. His chiefs would have said the same.

Purcell had a hundred problems awaiting solutions, but all began, in a sense, with the chiefs. Until they believed in the program again, the enterprise would drift. Purcell could feel their skepticism, like a low hum, under their corporate deference. Eventually, one asked the questions point blank. How committed *was* the corporation to restarting the program? Why hadn't it given Purcell his full budget? Why did the chiefs have to keep the restart a secret even from their suppliers? Wasn't it because publicizing the program would hinder GM's political agenda of pushing the mandate aside? And if the mandate did go, wouldn't the program go with it?

Purcell answered as best he could. Yes, the restart was real. Withholding the budget was fiscal prudence, part of the new GM. Keeping the secret was just good business; publicizing Impact had been the mistake. He himself was curious about whether the program hinged on the mandate, so he asked the president's council. He came back with an unequivocal response. Assuming the program made its targets, it would go to production, regardless of what happened to the mandate. The chiefs were mollified but not, Purcell thought, convinced.

Restarting a program, Purcell had come to see, was actually harder than starting one from scratch. Not only did the team have to be reinspired: the car itself had to be dusted off and reconfigured, like a child's half-finished model left too long on the shelf. Scores of makeshift fixes done for the fifty handbuilt LPFs had to be undone, and true solutions found, each reconceived and re-designed for production. The aluminum mounts that held the car's electron-ics to the motor, to name just one, had been found early on to be too light. The mounts were resonating; their bolts were loosening. For the fifty-car fleet, there had been no cause or budget to retool the design in aluminum, so heavier steel mounts from a gas car were used instead. Indeed, weight was such a negligible issue after December 1992 that the team had abandoned its radical practice of measuring by the gram. The car's mass, as a result, had swelled considerably above its old production target of 1,320 kilograms.

Batteries accounted for nearly a third of the excess. There weren't more of them. The same batteries had simply expanded, like loaves of bread, as a re-sult of a campaign on Jon Bereisa's part to establish a standard EV battery size among the world's major carmakers. Having a standard made sense—it would broaden the market for all battery makers—but to gain a consensus, Bereisa had had to acquiesce to the Japanese carmakers' insistence on a larger battery size. That meant every one of the twenty-seven batteries on an Impact would weigh more.

The extra weight strained the car's tires and suspension; it hurt the car's range, almost negating the larger batteries' extra energy. The team could throw away two batteries; the car would have the same energy with twenty-five fatter batteries as it had with twenty-seven smaller ones. But when the Japanese got to market with cars designed to accommodate twenty-seven larger modules, their cars would have more energy—and range. The choice was for the team to go on a mass diet, as Bereisa put it: back to trimming a kilogram here, a kilogram there, to allow for the extra battery weight. But that would be a tortuous process.

The propulsion system had the most makeshift fixes. Over the winter and spring, Hughes's inverters for the fifty-car fleet had arrived one by one as if de-liberately packaged to drive the GM engineers mad. It was déjà vu all over again: back and forth they went, from California to Michigan, afflicted by endless glitches—connectors incorrectly soldered, wires attached to the wrong capacitors—as well as recurring electromagnetic interference. The problems frayed tempers and delayed the planned April 1994 start of the PrEView program.

As if all this weren't enough, the surface of the car had to be refined— "sweetened" and "trued," as the vernacular had it. The process had just begun when Impact was taken out of production, and rather than follow it through at great cost, the chiefs had made the sensible decision to use the ex-isting rough draft design of the proof-of-concept cars for the fifty-car fleet. To tiny but critical degrees, the sweetening would force changes throughout the car's body. And then, unlike any other car in GM's recent history, Impact would go directly to production without time to refine the designs.

Along with a new infusion of engineers to help solve these problems, Purcell had to ramp-up long-flattened departments and have them take on crucial issues. Purchasing, for one. (How would the program get bids from suppliers when it had to remain invisible to them?) Manufacturing, for another. (Where would the car get made?) Marketing and service. (Who would badge and distribute it?) He'd need his own band of gypsies, too: the freelance designers in their cathode-lit room. And how would designers, or salarieds for that matter, be persuaded to keep the program a secret?

Another program far enough along to be turning out handbuilt cars might, at least, have had its major suppliers lined up and working together. Not Impact. The quarrelsome princes of the propulsion system had abandoned, in the eighteen months since December 1992, any pretense of harmony. Set loose at the start of GM's new Darwinian age of profit or perish, Hughes and Delco Remy in particular had become sworn rivals. Each had worked up whole drivetrains and gone out to drum up new business, bad-mouthing each other as they did. Now they were to work together on Impact, integrating their parts into one drivetrain, again? Purcell might as easily have dealt with Croats and Serbs. At Jack Smith's suggestion, he began planning a "virtual" entity that would put the princes under one roof and be managed by GM executives with no ties to any of the warring factions. But the princes would remain physically where they were, which made the plan seem tenuous at best.

The other GM-owned suppliers involved with the car—Inland Fisher Guide for body components, Harrison for heating and air-conditioning, and Saginaw for steering—had clearly defined roles and thus no need to quarrel among themselves. Their beef was with Purcell. Grimly, Purcell was demanding that the ACGs—the Automotive Components Group—sell him parts at or near cost to help push down Impact's piece cost. When they protested, Purcell, the insider's insider, fixed them with a level gaze. They were free not to participate, he told them. Though how would they feel when he was forced to "source" outside because GM's own divisions had chosen not to help on the electric car? Top management was eager to see the car succeed, after all; and though he denied it, Purcell's closeness to Jack Smith and others made his requests hard to refuse.

Purcell had no such leverage, of course, over outside suppliers, and here the program's secrecy hindered it. When engineers asked suppliers to bid, they could only suggest GM *might* produce Impact in some hazy future, and ask for price quotes at several different volumes—bench marking, as the term had it—to disguise their true planned volume. Many suppliers came back with "no-quotes," declining to bid because they saw no profits to be made from bench marking for a dead program which, even if it were revived, would sputter along at volumes laughably low for the car business. Purcell's new purchasing chief, Gary Wahl, used the "rolling billboard" pitch—that the car, whenever it did appear, would be a free advertisement for its suppliers as the world's press lavished attention on it. But Impact had had more than its share of hype already. Wahl invoked the virtues of getting into a new business at the ground level. But then the suppliers opened their newspapers to read how far corporate GM felt it had to go to make EVs a commercial success.

Every day, it seemed to his engineers, Purcell would recite the succinct advice Jack Smith had given him at the March 7 board meeting that turned the program back on. "Make a business out of it." *Make a business out of it,* he would echo, as if, like a mantra, its repetition might shake more profound truths from it. He could keep the platform lean, getting by with perhaps 200 full-timers, half the number of the original program. On future vehicles he could try to drive down costs, particularly of the propulsion system, which accounted for half the piece cost of the car. For the next several years, however, Impact would remain an expensive item.

One way to mitigate costs, as the president's council had suggested when it turned on the program in February, was to produce, in addition to Impact, some EV conversion of a GM truck or minivan. Introduced by 1997, it would also earn more early-bird credits from CARB against the 1998 2 percent quota. To look into the issue, Purcell assigned Dave DiPietro, the young high-pot who had just returned to the platform after graduating from Harvard Business School.

DiPietro's obvious starting point was U.S. Electricar. The L.A. converter claimed to be making a profit by purchasing fully equipped GM S-10 Chevrolet pickup trucks and Geo Prizms, converting them to EVs, and selling them at a premium to utilities that wanted to prime the EV market. Both GM and Electricar could profit more, argued Electricar's CEO Ted Morgan, if GM supplied "gliders"—factory-delivered shells unburdened by the engine, transmission, muffler, and the other appurtenances of gas cars he had to purchase and discard now. He could put in EV drivetrains; the carmakers could sell the cars as their own. There was a touch of comedy, if not pathos, in the prospect of mighty GM sending its gliders to a small shop in L.A. to have them outfitted as EVs, and doubtless paying, in the process, a premium for inverters made by its own subsidiary. But in the strange new world of mandated EVs, the niche marketers might be king.

So confident was Morgan that over the last year he had made a string of acquisitions and could now claim to be both the largest and fastest-growing producer of EVs in the country. *Carpe diem,* Morgan felt. EVs were coming, and by moving so aggressively, U.S. Electricar was poised to become the IBM of the nineties. But after meeting Morgan and getting a tour of Electricar's L.A. plant in June, DiPietro came away unimpressed. Electricar, he felt, was overpromising and underdelivering. He didn't want to sit in the same room again with Morgan and his staff, much less do business with them.

DiPietro also went to Wilmington, Massachusetts, to study James Worden's Solectria, the nascent industry's other most active converter. Fellow MIT graduates, close in age and coolly confident, DiPietro and Worden recognized each other as kindred spirits. DiPietro came away persuaded that Worden and his small team of mostly MIT grads were as different from U.S. Electricar as Massachusetts from California. They developed their own hardware, they didn't oversell it, and they shunned growth through debt-fueled acquisition. Still, quality and safety issues would be difficult for them, too. Worden might be a modern-day Henry Ford, but for better or worse, the modern world, with its wilderness of regulations, established carmakers, and litigious customers, was a hard place in which to be an automotive entrepreneur.

DiPietro felt sure now, too, that the oft-repeated metaphor was wrong. EVs might be stuffed with electronics, but they weren't the computers of the nineties. It was very simple, actually. A bug in a computer meant you were annoyed. A bug in the brake system of an EV could mean you were dead.

Unlikely a business as Impact remained, Purcell went to the crucial president's council meeting of June 13, 1994, with real confidence. He had vowed to bludgeon his budget down to target, and bludgeoned it was. Quickly the debate moved from whether the program should be formally approved to where the car should be made and under which division it should be badged.

Initially, Purcell had ruled out Lansing as a plant site. For an ultra-low-volume program, he needed only a fraction of its space; better to sublease some corner of an up-and-running plant. But after sitting dark for months, Lansing had just acquired two relatively low-volume jobs, the 1995 Chevrolet Cavalier and Pontiac Sunbird convertibles. They would take up only half the plant's space; Impact could use the rest.

Badging the car—deciding which of GM's car lines it should belong to—was a trickier issue. Like finding adoptive parents for an orphan, the match had to work on both sides. Some divisions were leery of Impact; if it failed, other models might be tarred. Oldsmobile, on the other hand, had lobbied hard to get it. Struggling with a reputation as GM's fustiest and least successful line—humdrum cars for aging buyers—its managers saw Impact as a means to lure younger, more affluent buyers into its showrooms. But what would Oldsmobile bring Impact? Not as much, they felt, as Saturn.

Everything Saturn represented made sense for Impact. It was GM's fresh, clean start, begun as a stand-alone experiment in 1983 to change the way GM built cars; Impact was that, too. Saturn was the start-up that redefined GM's relationship with its buyers, so service driven that it held huge barbecues for grateful owners long after they'd bought their cars—and the owners *came,* like happy members of some automotive fraternity. Caring service would help reassure customers that buying an Impact carried no risk. Also, though its sticker price was modest, Saturn sold to a surprisingly high-income market, often as an affluent buyer's second car. That was the same niche Impact hoped to fill.

For now, the council agreed, the choices of Lansing and Saturn would be confided on a strict need-to-know basis. Most of Impact's engineers would know soon enough, but even among themselves they would refer, for months afterward, to the "unnamed manufacturing site" and the "unnamed marketing division."

The program's last hurdle to a formal, fully funded go-ahead was the board of directors, due to meet June 27 in New York. Their approval could almost be taken for granted—it seemed inconceivable that the directors would reverse a Jack Smith decision, with the turnaround going so well—but when John Smale, GM's chairman, asked to borrow an Impact for the preceding week, the chiefs could hardly help worrying. And when Purcell received a memo of appraisal from Smale the Friday before the Monday board meeting, his hands shook as he opened it.

Smale reported putting 250 miles on his Impact. He and his wife had found the car quite comfortable. The acceleration had dazzled them. The range of the car's lead acid batteries had been better than expected: on one day, Smale had driven 95 miles before pulling in, with the charger still showing 5 percent. He felt the brakes needed refining. But the regen seemed important. "I think people will react positively to the idea of regenerating energy using that feature," he wrote. "Why not put it on a vertical display using green rather than red?"

The chairman went on to make other suggestions that showed keen interest. "It would be helpful if there was a release on the driver's seatback so it would be easier to store a briefcase on the back shelf," Smale wrote. "Currently you have to lift the briefcase around the back of the seat or put it in the trunk. I wonder whether an ignition key would not be easier than the special code you have to use to turn on the machine. Maybe there's a special reason for that, but since drivers are accustomed to using keys, I think a key feature would make it simpler and easier. Since there's relatively little space behind the front seat, a trunk release button would help. . . ."

Smale's conclusions might have surprised GM's lobbyists, ostensibly soldiering on his behalf. "I ruminated a little with Jack and Harry yesterday," Smale wrote, "about the dilemma we face in trying to manage on one hand expressing the pride and confidence we feel in this revolutionary product as it begins to be exposed to consumers, while on the other hand we try and persuade authorities to not go off the deep end in mandating the California legislation in other states. . . . I could be dead wrong, but it seems to me as you

214 ■ THE CAR THAT COULD

begin to get the Impact exposed to the marketplace in California and other cities around the country, we're going to generate a lot more excitement than you anticipate. If that is the case, I think we will have no choice but to accept the praise gratefully. Said another way, I don't think we would want to be in a position of stating the car is experimental and is not something which might find broad scale use in the future.

"I realize the risk of getting the car to the market might preclude California changing their regulations, but I also think we'll get a lot of credit if we do this well, for trying to do the right thing. . . . Again, it's pure speculation, but my instincts are that we could sell a lot more of these cars than we might think. Certainly it's a niche market and will remain so for a long time. But I think if we can get there first, the niche may be big enough to allow us to get profitable with an electric vehicle."

By a unanimous vote, the board endorsed Impact's progress and gave the program its next big check. Targets still needed to be met before the final go-ahead to production, but Purcell allowed himself to feel, privately at least, a cautious confidence that the team would succeed.

That day, the board also took up the more troublesome matter of GM's joint venture with Stanford Ovshinsky and Ovonic.

Ever since the March memo of understanding that outlined GM-Ovonic, Stan Ovshinsky seemed to have gone out of his way to irk his new partner, promoting his battery with no regard for GM's delicate position. Whether his zeal was heartfelt, or the calculated pitch of a master salesman, mattered little to GM's top executives. To John Williams, the USABC chief, it mattered not at all.

The last of Williams's patience ran out with the news that Ovshinsky had let James Worden race with an Ovonic pack *again*, this time in the American Tour de Sol. An overland race of several days' measured distances conducted over a different northeast route every spring, the Tour de Sol, like the Phoenix 500, now drew much local and national press. Along the latest course, from the World Financial Center in Manhattan to the Franklin Institute of Science in Philadelphia, Worden grabbed the headlines by driving 214.2 miles at roughly 60 miles per hour on a single charge. Ovshinsky knew how misleading the record was, Williams felt—how far from proven the Ovonic battery was as a producible, commercially viable EV power source. So, he felt, did Stempel. When GM's top management turned to Williams for his opinion of the GM-Ovonic deal on the eve of deciding whether to ratify it, Williams felt bound to respond with blunt candor.

In a memo, Williams ticked off the recent improprieties: the battery packs given to Worden and CARB while the USABC's order went unfilled; the overstating of the battery's capabilities; the refusal of Ovonic to seek the

USABC's permission for public statements about its EV batteries as required by its USABC contract. Overall, Williams wrote, Ovonic had acted in a "manipulative and duplicitous" manner.

Stempel, Williams felt, could not be excused from blame. The ex-chairman, according to Williams, had been too bullish in describing the battery technology to the press. If GM went ahead with GM-Ovonic, it could expect more overpromising and underdelivering, unless strict, enforceable guidelines were imposed.

At the same time, Williams admitted, Ovonic *did* have the best chance of achieving the USABC's mid-term goals. Investing in it was, he felt, a one-in-five gamble of $25 million. But with every other gamble, the odds were longer still.

At the June 27, 1994, board meeting, GM-Ovonic was ratified. The shareholders' agreement, however, made clear that GM wanted control of how the batteries were produced, it wanted its 60 percent of the profits—and it wanted control of progress announcements.

Purcell had a car program. He had a battery program. But he was a long way, further than he knew, from either a car or battery.

A Company
of Two Minds

))))

If a psychiatrist had treated GM as a patient in the summer of 1994, the di-
agnosis would have been of a full-blown split personality.

Overall, a disparity was widening between Jack Smith's bold advances
toward fiscal recovery, buoyed by the biggest upturn in U.S. car sales in years,
and the old ways of automotive production that were proving more resistant
to change than anyone had imagined. New models had to be produced more
quickly, but GM's already-slow schedules—fifty months versus thirty-seven
for Chrysler—tended to slip, the result of inflexible factories and managers
letting problems fester. When they appeared, the new cars of GM's seven divisions still competed with each other as much as with outside rivals. Once,
GM had owned 60 percent of the U.S. market and there had been room for
all; with its share down to 32 percent, the divisions were choking each other.
But axing a division, even for GM's CEO, was a fierce political challenge.
Soon, the old ways would cost GM its first quarterly loss in a year and speculation that the turnaround had stalled.

In its handling of Impact, GM's symptoms were, if anything, more pro-
nounced. Now that the fifty limited-production cars were debugged and
ready to be sent on their two-year odyssey of test drives around the country,
the so-called PrEView program became an almost comical exercise of two-
mindedness in action.

Purcell remained invisible, so Baker was elected to front the official Los
Angeles launch of PrEView on June 23, 1994. Sean McNamara, GM's PrE-
View market researcher, had tried to insure that his first eighty prospects were
neither gasheads nor environmental extremists; closed minds from either side
would be no help. The PrEView drivers had to have off-street parking and be

able to accommodate 220-volt Hughes inductive chargers. They had to be willing to keep daily logs for their two- or four-week drive periods, and participate in follow-up focus groups. Clean driving records helped, too: each of the handbuilt Impacts, after all, had cost $350,000.

Baker met the press flanked by the heads of the Los Angeles Department of Water & Power and Southern California Edison. The utilities would rewire drivers' garages to accommodate chargers; they would help troubleshoot problems; already, they had begun building prototype charging stands and stations for the Los Angeles area. But even as GM reached out for their help in making PrEView a success, its lobbying money was being spent to thwart the mandate that the utilities saw as their guarantee of an EV market.

For Southern California Edison and the other investor-owned utilities, GM's greater sin was in doing nothing to distance itself from the Oilies' frontal attack on their bid to raise $630 million for EV infrastructure. Already, the Oilies had cowed the utilities into trimming their request to $425 million in a campaign of misleading print ads, op-ed pieces, and the like that seemed to sway public opinion. At an upcoming hearing before the Public Utilities Commission, the Oilies hoped to reduce that figure to zero. The carmakers had nothing to do with that campaign, they protested, and piously lamented the Oilies' tendency to trash EV technology along with social policy. But as Richard Klimisch of the AAMA acknowledged, the interests of the Big Three and the Oilies were parallel. And as John White, a seasoned environmental lobbyist in Sacramento observed, it was hard enough fighting either the Oilies *or* the Big Three. Together, they were almost insuperable.

In one interview that week, Baker was asked if GM had any plan as yet to market the Impact, or any plan to build it. "No, there isn't," he said. Strictly speaking, he was right. There *was* no marketing plan for Impact yet, nor any manufacturing plan, and his interview preceded the board's conditional approval of Impact by three days. As for PrEView, Baker said, it was a long-term test; so far, it only suggested that people wanted to try an exotic new car for free.

Despite the campaign to lower expectations, PrEView soon demonstrated dramatically that EVs worked. Aside from a spilled root beer on the instrument panel of one car that shorted a switch on the dash and proved the need for sealing the attaching screws, there wasn't one stall-out during the entire L.A. PrEView. The drivers loved the car; they also quickly became comfortable with its range limitation, taking care to plug in at night. At the follow-up focus groups, they spent hours rehashing the Impact's performance, asking astute questions about battery life and ground clearance for speed bumps and the relative contribution of power plant emissions to EVs. If the campaign against the mandate was failing—and so far, despite the headway against the utilities, it seemed to be—perhaps the cause was an assumption among its lobbyists and media consultants that voters were as dumb as cattle, and as easily led. They might have benefited from a day behind the one-way mirror of one of the PrEView focus groups.

Purcell and most of the chiefs flew to California to attend one of the first sessions, held in a consulting office in Marina del Rey. They sat behind the one-way mirror, sipping sodas and munching popcorn as if at a private movie screening. The half dozen PrEView drivers on the other side of the mirror knew they were being watched and listened in on, but not by whom. First they ticked off their likes: among the men, torque and performance ranked high; the women appreciated the car's environmental benefits, and liked not having to go to gas stations. All were delighted by another perk that no gas car could offer: Impact's thermal system could be set like an alarm clock to start heating or cooling the car before its driver came out of the house in the chill of early morning or the heat of midday.

The dislikes were modest. One driver wished the car had a remote trunk release. ("That's coming!" the chiefs exclaimed, unheard through the glass.) A woman complained that the noise of the charger was louder than a refrigerator. ("We're working on it!") Another woman explained at 5'2", she'd found the seat too low, and with no vertical seat adjuster had had to sit on a pillow. ("Good point!") The car met most of their needs, the drivers agreed, and for most, that was enough, though one driver, a retired engineer, declared he'd never buy a car that met only 80 percent of his needs. ("Typical engineer," the chiefs muttered.)

How would the drivers feel, they were asked, if a better battery was available, one that would double the car's range but cost $6,000 a pack rather than $2,000? Three of the six said they'd pay for the difference. Two expressed doubts. The retired engineer said he'd wait until the cost came down and not buy an EV until then.

Behind the mirror, the chiefs groaned.

By midsummer Purcell was starting to feel the cadence, as he put it, of a program in gear. The team had met his freeze date of August 12 to sign off on parts for the first production Impacts, the 5.0s; the ramp-up was proceeding, if still fitfully; Bereisa's propulsion team was having problems with the Ovonic battery's tendency to overheat, but said it could be dealt with. Purcell was conscious of the emotional distance that lingered between him and his team, and he worried about that. But perhaps Excel would help.

Saturn had given the upbeat name to a series of outdoor team-building exercises partly military in nature, partly New Age. One August morning, the chiefs and other senior staffers followed Purcell up to Saturn's Excel course near the Lake Orion plant, a short drive north. Herded into a building that looked out across an open field, they were told to take note of a pole, some 300 feet away, to which a white flag was affixed. Then they were blindfolded. Not until everyone in the group reached the pole could the blindfolds be removed.

Quickly enough, the engineers realized they would do better as a group than on their own. They formed a line, holding hands, elected a front person and a rear person, and made their way downstairs. Outside, they ran into a Portosan, and snaked their way around it. Guessing their course from the gravel road underfoot, they stumbled forward and reached the pole in just ten minutes.

The next exercise required real stamina. At the base of a spiked phone pole some 22 feet tall, the chiefs attached themselves, one by one, to safety harnesses, then climbed up. The harnesses were hooked to high cross-wires, making the chiefs feel like laundry on a line, but that precaution did little to mitigate the challenge of standing on a small wooden dish that revolved, unnervingly, on *top* of the pole, then jumping off, the harnesses still attached to the guide wire, to ride at a gentle angle down to the ground. For Frank Schweibold, the heavyset finance chief, for Purcell, and for the new manufacturing chief, a big bear of a man named Bob Thompson, it was a tense and arduous challenge. But with the group below calling out encouragement, everyone reached the top.

By the time the chiefs had rappeled a 50-foot wall, strapped together in groups of three, they were exhausted—but also, as Purcell had hoped, exhilarated. Each had risked embarrassment and failure among his peers yet made the grade, helped along by the others. For Purcell, the stakes had been especially high. What if a leader lacked the courage to stand on top of a 22-foot telephone pole? How would he look his troops in the eye after that? But Purcell, given to such military terms, came away from the day with a more relaxed sense of leadership. He didn't have to do more than anyone else, he felt; he only had to do his best, and encourage his troops to do their best, too.

Bob Thompson, the bear-like manufacturing chief who'd come along for Excel, was the new arrival on whose broad shoulders much of the responsibility rested for turning finished designs into cars. Though he projected a folksy optimism, his job was now perhaps the hardest on the platform, its outcome the least certain.

Thompson's problems began with the disconcerting fact that Impact would be by far the lowest-volume production car in GM's history—much too small to justify an army of expensive robots or, for that matter, many human beings. Thompson would have to try two new, largely unproven manufacturing tricks, with no assurance either would work.

In most factories, workers had job cycles of perhaps sixty seconds. Every minute, they started the same job again, screwing in a panel or bolting a door, minute after minute, day after day. The jobs were simple enough, went the logic, that workers wouldn't mess them up; simple enough, too, that a worker out sick for the day could be easily replaced, and not hold up the line. Because Thompson would have so few workers, each would have a job cycle of more than forty-five minutes. Each would have to master and repeat a long series of tasks, with far more room for error. An intelligent worker might welcome the change; certainly a forty-five-minute cycle was more challenging. In a sense, too, the work was more important: if the worker took sick, he would be irreplaceable unless other workers were trained to perform his whole work cycle. It was a risk, no doubt about it. But with Thompson's budget constraints, he had no choice.

The other trick was tooling made from the hard plastic called epoxy. A high-volume stamping operation used steel tools, or dies,* that cost millions of dollars but lasted forever and could, over the life of a car line, be amortized. On an ultra-low-volume program, using steel dies would be like using gold plates for a picnic, then throwing them away. For years, the industry had used epoxy tools as a cheap alternative for prototypes, but scoffed at using them for production since, like plastic plates, they tended to break with repeated use.

Epoxy, though, might be perfect for low volume. Epoxy tools could be replaced again and again, and still cost far less for a short production run than their steel counterparts. GM, moreover, had designed and patented an improved kind of epoxy that might enable the lightweight tools to last not just for thirty or forty pressings, but 30,000 or 40,000. Besides, as the energy guru Amory Lovins had pointed out, the short life span of epoxy tools might be a keen advantage in a world of ever more fickle consumer tastes. Instead of being locked into a run of 250,000 units because of a model's huge sunk cost in steel tooling, a carmaker could make changes as quickly as the market demanded them.

As Thompson was the first to admit, there was a risk. No one had used epoxy tooling on a production car before. "Now if it doesn't work, what's the alternative?" Thompson asked rhetorically. "Here's a secret: we don't have an alternative! So that sonofabitch *has* to work." But Thompson liked a challenge: a big-game hunter, his idea of fun was getting dropped in the Alaskan wilderness for two weeks with one week's provisions, a partner, and three or four guns for grizzlies and moose.

By September 12, 1994, when the engineers convened for a two-day review of where they stood, many of the designs for Thompson's epoxy tooling had

---

* Dies are molds made in the shape of car body parts. Molten metal is poured into a "female" mold; a "male" mold then sandwiches the metal. When the metal cools and hardens, the molds are pulled apart, yielding a production-ready part.

been finished, approved, and sent out to be produced by an outside supplier. Fewer than a dozen parts of the car itself had gotten that far. Purcell had proclaimed the designs frozen, but endless small adjustments were needed to make them fit together: to sweeten, or refine, their overall design. Inevitably, a few last-minute ideas were shoehorned in, too. The trunk would have a remote control release, despite Purcell's misgivings about the cost; the so-called charge port, into which the inductive charger paddle was slipped at the front of the car, would be cooled not by a fan, which had proved noisy to the first PrEView drivers, but by a liquid cooling element attached to the system that cooled the electronics.

As for the targets—of cost and mass and range—they remained just out of reach. The team was below its engineering budget by about 2 percent, but as much as 10 percent above its goal for the piece costs of each car itself, so that the overall budget had bulged slightly. Mass was still 20 kilograms over the new target of 1,330 kilograms, so that Purcell couldn't sanction further tipping the scales by putting the twenty-sixth and twenty-seventh new-sized batteries on board, which might, in turn, nudge the car up to triple-digit range. As the chiefs pored over thick three-ring binders of design-release specs— each page of each book stamped with the appropriate chief's name, to help deter industrial espionage—the battery debate dominated the review.

Whatever their number, the batteries would be marketed, along with the rest of the propulsion system, from under the single roof that the GM president's council had envisioned. The new entity was called Delco Propulsion Systems, and announced on September 21, 1994; Impact was not mentioned, but GM did say it considered EV components a future business of consequence. Unclear was whether the new roof had any walls and foundation under it: DPS would merely package and sell the princes' EV components from a building on the highway outskirts of Indianapolis, Indiana.

For John Williams, named the new company's engineering director, DPS was at least a way out of USABC politics. On October 1, he began his new weekday life, renting a small apartment near the DPS building, flying home for weekends, and spending his office hours in pursuit of the future, a future which in his new incarnation as a prospective EV parts supplier ironically put him in Stan Ovshinsky's camp, taking the most bullish view possible of the market, and hoping the mandate would stay in force to augment it. He had a staff of salesmen, but they belonged on the road, trying to forge client relationships for sales when that market appeared. So Williams sat virtually alone in a building at the end of an industrial park cul-de-sac, condemned, like the hotel caretaker in Stephen King's *The Shining*, to wander the empty halls, waiting for people to come.

▪ ▪ ▪

For all its growing pains, Impact was a real program, speeding along with extraordinary promise. That was a lot more than could be said of EVs at either Ford or Chrysler. That summer, both maintained a public silence on the PrEView launch, perhaps on the general theory that one tried to refrain from adding to a rival's hype, more likely because both were more interested, at the moment, in killing the mandate than in making electric cars.

Chrysler, from its chairman Bob Eaton on down, had become by far the most vocally bitter of the Big Three on the mandate. "Who'll buy 'em?" Eaton scoffed of EVs. Chrysler's vice president of engineering, François Castaing, said grudgingly that Chrysler would meet the mandate if it held—by waiting until the last possible moment to see what batteries others developed, and putting the best prospects in its new minivans. While touting as proof of its interest in cleaner vehicles a one-of-a-kind hybrid race car called the Patriot that so far remained an unmovable display, Chrysler was devoting far more corporate time to mobilizing its northeast dealers to scare consumers with the promise of a $2,700 premium on all gas cars if EVs were forced into the market.

Ford, at least, still had an active EV program. The previous spring, however, Wallace's worst fear had come true: sodium sulfur batteries in Ford's Ecostar vans had caught fire. A first incident had occurred May 2, 1994, at the Electric Power Research Institute in Palo Alto, California, where one of the $100,000 prototypes was being evaluated. The second came later that month as a van was recharging overnight at CARB's El Monte offices. Reluctantly, Ford recalled its fleet of thirty-four vans and began reexamining the looping element that had seemed the solution to just this sort of problem.*

Wallace's engineers found that they could design software to shut off the battery when the fires began, but they couldn't keep the fires from occurring unless they redesigned the battery from scratch. "From a program manager's point of view," Wallace admitted with uncharacteristic somberness, "it's a disaster." Ford was out more than a battery now. Its VZW109 prototype—the secret EV design based on a sport utility vehicle for 1998; the *real* EV intended to replace the too-primitive Ecostar van—had been designed for sodium sulfur. It was all but useless. Wallace had nothing. Resolutely, he swallowed his pride and went calling at U.S. Electricar.

---

* The element, it turned out, did keep a shorted-out cell from setting off a chain reaction; if a string of 100 cells was diminished by one, the element, as designed, knocked out a cell in the next string, so that a balance of current was maintained. But within the pack's high-temperature casing, the looping elements themselves were firing—as semiconductors, they were more subject to the heat than Ford had hoped, and sometimes failed to close after taking a cell out of the system. They, in turn, cracked the ceramic tubes of the batteries' sodium electrolyte, releasing molten sodium that quickly led to a runaway heat reaction, explosion, and fire.

By mid-November an agreement had been reached in principle. Ford would send "gliders" of unnamed models to the California converter, after establishing strict safety guidelines for the process. Assuming Electricar could meet the guidelines, the EVs it turned out would likely wear, as Wallace put it, the Ford oval. As a longer-range measure, Ford entered into a five-year research project with seven smaller U.S. partners to explore all manner of hybrids, and to pursue, among other technologies, flywheels and fuel cells; the $122 million cost of the project would be half-funded by the U.S. Department of Energy. Meanwhile, Wallace would do what he could to hold GM back.

For some time Ford and GM had carried on their edgy debate to set a standard for EV chargers. After three years and $10 million, GM had refined its inductive system enough to mount Hughes-made, 220-volt chargers on the walls of its PrEView drivers' garages; aside from the complaints about the noisy fan that whirred during recharging, the chargers had worked perfectly. Ford had stayed with a basic prong-and-socket conductive charger. In March 1994, Ford had pushed the major carmakers to a vote between the two systems but failed to gain a majority for conductive. That was when Bereisa had suggested, as he put it, a Betty Crocker bake-off.

In principle, Wallace had agreed. But when Virginia Power offered to host the showdown at a September 1994 trade show in Richmond, Ford boycotted the gathering at the last minute, claiming the utility was too closely allied with GM. Instead, it announced publicly that six carmakers had agreed to a conductive charging standard, which wasn't the case. At the bake-off, GM demonstrated the safety and power of a Hughes inductive charger by putting its plastic-sheathed heating elements in a horse trough with water and passing 120 kilowatts of current through them—100 times the power of a household wall plug. In about a minute they made the water boil.

Grimly, the two rivals readied for a marketplace war to match Beta vs. VHS. Except that with chargers, more than entertainment would be at stake.

On the larger issue of the mandate the rivals remained allied, and so for all, the election results of November 1994 buoyed hopes that CARB's draconian edict at last might be thwarted. Across the country, Republicans unseated Democratic governors and made such huge gains in both houses of Congress that new Speaker of the House Newt Gingrich seemed to have a clear shot at enacting most, if not all, of the tenets of his ballyhooed "Contract with America." Among other consequences, a quarter century of environmental statutes might now be gutted, including the 1990 amendments to the Clean Air Act on which all debate about emissions standards in California and the Northeast was based.

For the carmakers, the most immediate benefit seemed the reelection of Pete Wilson in California over his Democratic rival for governor, Kathleen

Brown. Wilson's private plea to Detroit to mute opposition to the mandate until he won his second term suggested compromise might be in the air. In New York, the upset victory of Republican George Pataki over three-term governor Mario Cuomo also augured well. Pataki seemed a willing tool of Republican New York senator Alphonse d'Amato and would surely help big business reverse the state's regulatory call for EVs. Indeed, with new Republican governors in Connecticut and Pennsylvania as well, the Northeast's political landscape seemed transformed.

As GM stepped up its lobbying battle, some high executive in GM's corporate ranks hit upon the notion of placing a GM lobbyist directly on the Impact platform, with an office amid the engineers and carte blanche to audit meetings. The better the lobbyists understood the technical challenges that remained, went the logic, the more effective they might be in lobbying against the mandate. To more than a few of the engineers, Bill Way's arrival was an unsettling development, like having a double agent in their midst.

Brooding and intense, Way brought the zeal of a born-again to his work. A visitor to his cubicle could hardly help noticing the two knitted JESUS signs, the size of small bumper stickers, that his wife had made for him. In lunchroom conversations, he inveighed against the mandate with jesuitical fervor. "Where outside Russia have you ever seen that attempted?" he would demand. "I don't think that anywhere in the free world a mandate like this has been tried." Having Way around reminded more than a few of the engineers that despite GM's enlightened new leadership, countervailing forces within the company remained strong.

Until the Republican sweep, plans had proceeded for a formal announcement of Impact's production schedule at the January auto shows in Los Angeles and Detroit. One day in late November, however, Purcell came to a strategy board meeting with details in hand to learn the plans had been scrapped. If GM had a better shot now at influencing CARB to put the mandate aside, why announce the car and give the impression that all EV issues were solved?

A new strategy was emerging: one that might cure GM's case of split personality with a single-minded clarity. If GM helped push the mandate aside now, Ford and Chrysler would fall back with relief and kill their clunky conversion programs. So, for that matter, might most if not all of Japan's Big Four carmakers. Because, incredible as it seemed, none yet seemed to know that Impact was turned back on: for nearly nine months, the secret had held.

That was when the Impact of Troy, Michigan, might, like a Trojan horse, enable GM to conquer the market while its rivals slept.

The Threshold

))))

Ken Baker looked out from a podium over the crowd gathered in Anaheim, California, for the latest biennial EV symposium, and marveled at how far this industry had come since the one he and Jim Ellis had attended in Hong Kong just four years before. Then, the participants had seemed a lightweight bunch: techno-nerds, tree-huggers, conversion-kit types, with a smattering of small, would-be suppliers to a market that didn't exist. On this day in December 1994, every significant carmaker in the world had reached the EV prototype stage and was represented here. Just in the past year, it seemed, a threshold had been crossed. Whether or not the mandate held, EVs were coming. "The time for debate is over," Baker told the gathering at the Disneyland Hotel. "The time for action is now."

This was a curiously upbeat declaration, given GM's stance on the mandate, but Baker managed to please the partisan crowd while explaining that "action" meant a lot more government help, without which EVs might still fail in the market. John Wallace, as chairman of the symposium, stressed in his own remarks that EV technology had a long way to go, and that Ford was still ambivalent about it. "Why should we rush about and produce a car that no one wants?" he told one interviewer later. "And what happens if, after a couple years, we develop the *battery?* What happens to all those people who bought the lead acid battery cars early on? You can't just drop the new battery in. There's a real obsolescence problem." But asked if he was trying to discourage the industry, Wallace bridled. "I've already spent five years of my life on this," he said. "Why would I want to spend another 'X' years just to drive this thing over a cliff?"

To show just how wary it was, Ford chose to unveil what it called an EVent concept car—emphasis on concept—without benefit of a press conference, and announced that its 1998 EV would merely be a converted Ranger pickup truck. Chrysler's one grudging bit of news was that it had chosen, for its planned conversion of a 1997 minivan, advanced lead acid batteries from an Austin, Texas, supplier called Electrosource, whose Horizon battery featured a patented lead mesh lighter than standard lead plates and appeared to have twice the life of conventional lead acid batteries.* With GM taking the public stance that it would meet the mandate with lead acid conversions, too, the Big Three were, for all of Baker's rhetoric, the gathering's glummest guests.

Toyota and Honda joined the Big Three in issuing statements that EVs would not be commercially feasible by 1998. But all four of Japan's major carmakers were making progress. Toyota showed a sport utility EV conversion with a range of 70 miles and said it planned to deliver a first fleet to U.S. utilities in the next several months. Honda had just sent three EV conversions, based on its Civic hatchback, to Southern California Edison, and was said to be designing a new chassis for its 1998 version; since November 1993, when a handbuilt Honda solar car had easily beaten Sunraycer's record at the third World Solar Challenge in Australia, the threat of Honda as an EV rival had only grown. For that matter, even Mazda had a sporty EV Miata to show. Because the Japanese remained far more secretive than their European or U.S. counterparts, no one assumed that the concept cars on display were their only programs. Gunnar Lindstrom, chief engineer of Honda's EV team, admitted as much. "It's a chess game," he said. "If you show people exactly what you're going to do, the other companies will react."

The Europeans were more open about their EV projects, more creative, more exuberant than either the Americans or Japanese—in large part, of course, because their modest sales volumes in California exempted them from the mandate in its first years, allowing them to ease into the market. But in the last four years, EVs had also captured the European imagination. The Swatchmobile approach was especially compelling in Europe, where an egg-shaped mini-runabout seemed adorable, rather than diminutive, as it might in the U.S. The Swatch Man, Nicholas Hayek, suggested his Mercedes-funded EV might be exhibited at the 1996 Olympics in Atlanta, Georgia, and ready for sale soon after. BMW had moved from its E1 prototypes to parallel hybrids, one kind designed for urban driving, another for the autobahn, and

---

* In the fall of 1995, the Horizon battery would be tested at Argonne National Lab and found to have 44.2 watt hours per kilogram of specific energy, which theoretically would give it a third more range than the lead acid batteries to be put in the first Impacts. But the battery also appeared to have internal design problems that might affect its cycle life.

seemed likely to reach California by 1998, too. Meanwhile in Gothenberg, Sweden, Volvo continued to refine the hybrid based on its 850 sedan, and to hope, as well, to reach the U.S. market by or before 1998.

The Germans and Japanese might yet be beaten to market by one of France's Big Two. Both Renault and Peugeot-Citroën spoke of reaching the European market in the next year with four-passenger EVs powered by nickel cadmium batteries; Peugeot might introduce a tiny, Swatch-like city car of its own, tentatively called the Ion. Already, in the Atlantic seaside town of La Rochelle, Peugeot-Citroën had leased fifty of its ZX and 105 model prototypes, with residents *paying* for the privilege of being test drivers, and the municipal government, backed by the nationalized Electricité de France, paying for EV infrastructure—all without a hue and cry from "AstroTurf" taxpayer groups. Neither carmaker currently sold to the U.S., however, and none of the prototypes was a ground-up EV, so the news was of limited interest to the largely American crowd at EVS-12.

Put off, even angered, by the Big Three's pessimism, the crowd found an obvious favorite in the symposium's one homegrown, American-designed, ground-up EV: the Solectria Sunrise. A four-passenger car that looked like a Honda Accord, the Sunrise came equipped with a Hughes inductive charging system. It would be put out for sale by 1997 at $20,000 per car, declared James Worden, if Solectria could get 20,000 orders. Along with price, its greatest selling point was range: the Sunrise would travel more than 100 miles between charges because its batteries would be nickel metal hydride, supplied by Worden's patrons at GM-Ovonic, Ovshinsky and Stempel.

Worden's scenario assumed, of course, that GM-Ovonic batteries would be in production by 1997, too. Baker, in his speech, suggested they would not; Chrysler's François Castaing declared they wouldn't be ready until at least 2001. Yet John W. Adams, the GM executive put in charge of the joint venture, took the occasion to declare that Ovonic batteries would be produced within a *year*.

First Stempel, now Adams—it was as if the stolid GMers partook of some intoxicating potion over at Ovonic that led them to doff their pinstripes and make the most wildly optimistic claims. In part it was the battery, in part Stan Ovshinsky's infectious enthusiasm. But also, to move from the car side to the battery side was to acquire a profoundly different point of view. Carmakers had a market to serve already, and begrudged the mandate for forcing them into another one too soon; EV battery makers had none, and cheered the mandate for bringing them one, while issuing the rosiest scenarios possible to help keep it from going away.

It was at Anaheim that Mary Nichols of the EPA officially conceded the northeast states would be allowed to adopt California's mandate, that they could do without its clean fuel provision, and that each state could decide whether or not to require EVs as part of its package.

This meant more than it might have to a stranger wandering in to hear her speech.

After voting the previous February to adopt the mandate, the northeast states had had to "petition" the EPA for permission to move ahead, as dictated by the Clean Air Act. Normally, the EPA would have been quick to endorse any state's desire to embrace California standards. But these were not normal times. Nichols feared that the northeast states might mire themselves in car-maker lawsuits for years, while the air worsened overhead. She also felt that the forty-nine-state FED LEV plan first proposed by GM's Sam Leonard was a pretty fair compromise. But after months of trying to broker a deal behind the scenes—and missing her own deadline for a decision in the process, bringing legal threats from environmentalists and carmakers alike—she had given up. She did, however, urge New York and Massachusetts to reach a FED LEV–like accord with the carmakers on their own, one that would take the legal and lobbying heat off the whole Northeast. For with EVs seemingly far from ready for any percentage of a cold-weather market, the carmakers would still do anything they could to avoid being forced to sell them.

As far as they could see, they had no choice.

Quietly back in Lansing, preparations that would have startled the Anaheim crowd were being made: union agreements worked out with no press leaks from Local 1618, floor space mapped and assembly drawings made, and a new plant manager, chosen by Bob Thompson, just arriving. Thompson's pick was not the first female assembly plant manager in GM's history, but she certainly was one of a select few. The gender line Maureen Midgley was crossing put her in charge of some fifty members of Local 1618, all of whom were men, most of whom had never expected to report to a woman plant manager and weren't entirely sure how they felt about that.

Midgley called herself a plant rat—and she was, in a way. The daughter of a GM factory worker, she loved the sounds and rhythms of a plant, the blunt honesty of men on the line. She could be blunt herself, enough to shock the white-collar engineers after a day of tedious meetings in Troy by declaring, "You know, I've been kissing so many butts my lips are sore."

But Midgley was also tall and beautiful, with the high cheekbones of a New York model. A serious runner, she tried to compete in at least one triathlon a year. An environmentalist, she did volunteer work wherever she lived, along with composting and cultivating an organic garden. When Bill Way, the zeal-ous lobbyist, arrived on the platform, she wound up in more than one tense debate with him; and when GM sent its employees letters urging them to sup-port the anti-mandate campaign, she balled them up and threw them away.

By early January 1995, the factory arrangements were set, so Midgley moved with her husband—a Saturn engineer—and two small children to Lansing. She was thrilled to get her own plant, less so to learn that almost every aspect of production would come with a problem attached.

The problems began with the fact that Impact was to be put together in the smallest assembly space ever allotted for a GM car program. The car's epoxy tooling was being made expressly for it, but Midgley needed other equipment, too. When she tried to place orders through GM's purchasing system, she got nowhere: the system was set up for high-volume factories, with minimum orders far greater than she needed. She could try to share purchase orders with the plant's other operations, but meetings were needed to debate every purchase, and Midgley found that someone was always left out. Finally, she began summoning every conceivable party to every meeting. "Why am I here?" some puzzled person would ask. "I don't know," Midgley would say. "I just figured you had a part in it."

Midgley's partner at the plant was Bill Szkodzinski. As engineering director of manufacturing, he spent his time setting up the body shop, where Impact's skeleton and panels would be assembled, and the larger assembly area, where the finished body acquired everything else it needed to become a car. Though much remained to be done, the body shop already had big aluminum weld guns that hung like oversize dentist's drills. In a normal plant, the weld guns would be automated, but automation was too expensive for a low-volume car. Instead, the guns would be handled manually. Each conducted twice the force and three times the current of steel-weld guns—aluminum's properties necessitated that—so two men were needed to operate it. Yet Midgley's body shop foreman was another woman, and a petite one at that: Arianna Kalian, the cello-playing Impact engineer.

For Kalian, who had yearned for manufacturing experience, getting into the plant was a dream assignment. She had arrived, soon after the program restarted, to find the space still empty, and begun working with Szkodzinski to get the weld guns in, along with the adhesive guns that would help keep Impact's aluminum structure parts sealed using the glue that Tom Lobkovich, the structure czar, had helped devise, and the more conventional rivet guns, which played a part, too.

Of the fifty-plus union workers who would put the car together—the lowest number of any car program in GM's history—Kalian came to oversee twenty. At first, it was all the burly locals of 1618 could do to hide their skepticism of her. Soon they realized she could answer all their technical questions in brisk detail; she was, unlike traditional foremen, an engineer. Soon they were calling her "mom," with both affection and respect.

Already, the fledgling plant team was working fiercely toward its first deadline: to get one production-ready car done by March 7, a year to the day after the board had tentatively revived the program. As the pace picked up, Kalian, who had kept her apartment in Troy, was forced to wake up every morning at 3:30 A.M. in order to make the 70-mile commute to Lansing by 5:45 A.M. Many days that summer lasted twelve hours, many work weeks lasted six days; by the time Kalian got back to her empty apartment at 7:30 P.M. she had just enough energy to heat up one of the dinners she'd prepared the previous weekend before falling into bed. Her mother worried about her: twenty-eight years old, and no man in her life. Kalian might have liked one; she got lonely sometimes. But a romantic relationship was out of the question. She simply had no time.

It was Purcell who had set the goal of having the first prototype car go through the line at Lansing by March 7, 1995. By the start of that month, a small first generation of parts had been manufactured and shipped to Lansing. From the hundreds of boxes, an Impact emerged. A video of it, being driven away from the line, was shown the next week to the GM board, and elicited great applause.

That was the good news.

The bad news was a series of unexpected setbacks, each of which threatened to become a showstopper.

Six months before, a few new engineers had warned that the car might not meet one or more crashworthiness requirements. Early on, the team had crash tested front ends on "sleds." It had crashed proof-of-concept cars, and later sacrificed several of the fifty limited-production cars to the cause. All the tests had shown that while Impact's front end was tightly packed with heavy components, the car would have a soft enough "pulse" to meet crashworthiness requirements. Which was to say that upon hitting a wall at 30 miles per hour—the speed at which such tests were done—the car would crumple enough to absorb a critical number of G's and not push the front end into the driver. But from LPF to production design, a worrisome change had occurred.

Before, the motor had been held in place with a welded structure. As the POCs and LPFs accumulated miles, the structure's parts began to loosen. The engineers replaced them with a single cast piece, or "cradle," made of aluminum. The cradle was solid, but new engineers, brought on to refine the car's restraint system for production, warned that the change could make the car stiffer, giving it a harder pulse, robbing it of the critical milliseconds needed for the driver's air bag and belts to be fully effective.

After several barrier tests, the worst fears were confirmed. The pulse was indeed harder, enough so that Impact might fail one of the federal safety tests. A conventional car would have had space to spare in the front end. Impact's front end was so efficiently designed, however, so up-integrated and tightly packed, that it afforded the engineers no leeway. Perversely, the car's overall design, so beautifully streamlined, only made the job harder. For the best aerodynamics, it was low to the ground, with low-slung seats, so that the driver's legs extended almost straight in front of him—right into the densely packed front end of heavy, noncompressible parts. Fixing the problem fell to Tom Ruster, the engineer who had designed the passenger compartment. For help, he had Dave DiPietro.

In December 1994, DiPietro had finished the study of EV conversions that had led him to visit U.S. Electricar and Solectria, and made the sensible recommendation that GM not go with any outside supplier; rather, it should do conversions through its own North American Truck Group. A prototype S-10 truck had been chosen, a business case drawn up, and DiPietro had nursed hopes of being named manager of the new program. Instead, the job had gone to a more experienced engineering manager, with DiPietro offered the job of liaison between the Impact platform and the Truck Group.

With some bitterness, DiPietro had turned down the offer, and reconsidered his career. For young high-pots, he knew, GM's fast track began in the New York treasurer's office. But working in finance had always seemed like watching the game from the grandstand. Even after Harvard Business School, DiPietro had made a point of returning to the EV platform because it was part of the core—part of the business that made the product. He felt, too, that the next generation of GM managers should go, like soldiers, where the problems were. GM's most entrenched problems were in engineering and manufacturing—the slow production schedules that kept slipping. Those were the areas that needed leadership. But if there was a fast track in either engineering or manufacturing, DiPietro was unaware of it. Being denied the conversion program made clear, on the contrary, that to rise in the engineering ranks, one had to move from station to station as predictably as the seasons. Which was why, reluctantly, he found himself working on crashworthiness, helping redesign the underside of the instrument panel so that a driver's knees, when brought up against it in a crash, would meet a device of collapsing steel brackets that could provide enough give for the car to meet its crashworthiness requirements.

As Ruster and DiPietro started in, Purcell asked them how long they thought the work might take. Anywhere from three to nine months, they replied. Three months then, Purcell agreed. And so officially, for the first time, the program slid, from eighteen to twenty-one months. The fix would add perhaps $50 in piece cost, 2 kilograms of mass, with a modest investment of about $200,000. But the delay would also cost $3 million a month in overhead, and give rivals that much more of a chance to beat GM to market.

The second potential showstopper occurred one day in February. It was the oddest thing: one of the twenty limited-production cars the team had kept for testing simply shut down as it was being driven. Switched back on, the car worked fine. Then the glitch occurred in another of the cars. Days of tedious testing uncovered the culprit, a computer chip in the inverter's propulsion control module. But if the chip was flawed, as it seemed to be, redesigning its silicon would take months. Delco Electronics took on the problem, and the chiefs tried to hope for the best.

They had enough to worry about, in any event, with a third potential show-stopper. The Ovonic battery—the great EV hope that had given courage to GM's management to restart the program, and courage to CARB to uphold the mandate—might be fundamentally flawed.

Setbacks on Every Side

))))

Through much of the previous year, Stan Ovshinsky had been on a roll. Saved from financial peril by GM's $25 million commitment and the formation of GM-Ovonic, he had shaken another $5.5 million from the USABC in August 1994 to help scale up his batteries. In September, the International Trade Commission had voted unanimously to pursue his complaint against three Japanese companies infringing upon his nickel metal hydride patents. Within weeks, the companies had capitulated and become grudging new licensees—a major victory for Ovshinsky in a country where patent battles were notoriously hard to win, and one that would likely deter other Japanese producers from challenging him.

That fall, too, a steady procession of GM engineers had inspected the Ovonic battery, beginning with its new president, John Adams, and come away impressed. As Ovonic's president Subhash Dhar put it, they'd assumed he was fiddling around with beakers; yet here he was, overseeing the hand-built assembly of EV-ready battery packs. As soon as machinery could be put in place to relieve the workers who painstakingly trimmed the wafer-like electrolyte with scissors and backed it into battery casings by hand, Adams was sure that the cost curve would start to come down. "It will be tough, our schedule is extremely aggressive," he allowed. "But it's achievable. There are no showstoppers."

By then, not many of Impact's engineers would have agreed with him. The battery, quite simply, had a tendency to heat up. It heated while it was charging; on a hot day, it heated while it was *discharging*. When its temperature reached 45 degrees centigrade, a self-heating effect began to occur, rapidly eroding the battery's charge; at 65 degrees centigrade, the heat also began to affect the pack's cycle life.

As much as Bereisa and his team knew about batteries, they had overlooked an obvious consideration: the first Ovonic packs had been tested in *cool weather*. The Mesa range test had occurred in January, when Arizona was temperate. Other packs had been tested on laboratory benches, cooled by indoor air-conditioning. On such evidence, the GM-Ovonic deal had been inked. Over the summer, as the packs had started to overheat, Bereisa's engineers were so startled that for two or three months they worked in a state of denial. Perhaps some other equipment had been left on while the batteries were charging. Perhaps a faulty connector was to blame.

The problem grew unavoidable in early 1995, when Ovonic delivered its next generation of prototype packs to the USABC, which distributed them to the Big Three. Those put in Impacts overheated now even in the Michigan cold because Ovonic had scaled the batteries up to 80 kilowatt hours, which caused the thermal effect to occur sooner. Equally troubling, packs left to sit, as they would be in a parked car, dissipated their charge in a few days. This was a showstopper, all right. Angrily, GM's propulsion team declared that Ovonic had a bum battery. Ovonic said GM had a badly designed car. Stempel, caught in the middle, did what he could to calm tempers on either side. But the partnership seemed to have an overheating effect of its own.

On balance, Ovonic had slightly more cause for indignation than GM. To be sure, Ovshinsky had underplayed the challenges of scaling up his packs to greater levels of energy and power. It wasn't just a matter of putting more magic powder in; the current among all cells had to rise and fall evenly, and there was delicate, not entirely predictable, chemistry in that. But packs put in other kinds of cars had experienced far less overheating; and let sit, they lost, in a week's time, just 20 percent of their charge, better even than GM's own target for the packs of 20 percent loss in forty-eight hours. The difference was that in those vehicles, the packs lay exposed to ambient air, or were cooled by fans, and what heat they did create was easily dissipated. In Impact, batteries lay immured in their T-shaped aluminum tunnel, insulated, padded, with no air circulating at all. "So do you have a cell discharge problem with the battery?" Dhar asked rhetorically. "No. Do you have a cell discharge problem with the Impact? Yes."

It was a standoff until, to the private delight of the Ovonic team, the propulsion team discovered one day in February 1995 that lead acid needed air management, too. One of the fifty limited-production cars at the Milford proving grounds incurred a combustion of hydrogen gas. A small amount of hydrogen, it turned out, had escaped from the batteries instead of being recombined within them to form acid. In the airtight case, the hydrogen had become volatile. The thirty LPFs in the PrEView program were promptly recalled, and holes put in the backs of their battery casings to prevent more hydrogen buildups.

At first, the team resisted Stempel's advice to add a cooling system at the same time. Numbers were run; it would cost $100 per car, which displeased Purcell. After some back and forth, Stempel helped persuade the engineers that the hundred dollars could be squeezed out somehow from the rest of the car. Reluctantly, the propulsion team set about designing a solid-state blower—no brushes, and no sparks, could be risked, now that traces of hydrogen might migrate out from the batteries—that actually pulled air in from the back of the car, up around the tunnel, and out the front. At the front end, the air had to exit in places where the pressure of onrushing air from outside didn't reverse the flow; and flappers had to be devised to keep the hoses from taking in water if the car went through a major puddle. So byzantine was the system that the team gave its parts nicknames; where the front duct forked became Gumby's Drawers.

The hoses might prevent overheating when the car was engaged, but they could do nothing to keep the battery's charge from depleting so quickly when the car was parked. For that, Dhar and his team went back to their chart of the elements and began trying to concoct a new recipe of disordered materials that might provide a better magic powder. Before the battery scare, Purcell had hoped to put nickel metal hydride in the first preproduction Impacts off the line at Lansing in the spring of 1995. Now, he felt, he would be lucky to get Ovonic packs into a token few of the first cars for sale a year later.

Even if a new, more effective alloy could be found, and production began as hoped for by the spring of 1996, the other unresolved issue about Stan Ovshinsky's battery was cost. John Williams, from where he sat now in his empty DPS building, saw no way for Ovonic to produce its first batteries for less than $500 per kilowatt hour—not even close to the $150 per kilowatt hour that the USABC had set as its mid-term goal. With 30 kilowatt hours onboard, that would bring the cost of a single pack to $15,000. Jon Bereisa felt slightly more optimistic. He'd seen numbers to suggest that the battery might get as low as $230 per kilowatt hour. That, he felt, was a charitable figure, since it only included the battery's materials. For its labor, and the machinery to produce it, let alone the sunk investment, the figure allowed zero. And labor couldn't be dismissed so easily, not when an Ovonic pack included perhaps 1,000 fasteners, endless nuts and bolts and screws, all manually attached as yet, seemingly defying mass production, and certainly raising the spectre of reliability issues down the line.

To Stempel and Ovshinsky, that was just the sort of skepticism that had dogged the battery at its every stage; and at every stage, the skeptics had been disproved. Already, Stempel observed, GM had helped Ovonic reduce the number of parts in a module from forty to six. Batteries did have to be hooked to each other, but that could be done on a line by riveting, not screwing. And if the battery that cost $200 per kilowatt hour lasted the life of a car, that meant its real cost, relative to lead acid, would be $5,000. "And that," he said triumphantly, "is the cost of gasoline at a dollar a gallon times twenty miles per gallon over one hundred thousand miles."

Ovonic's growing pains remained a private issue within GM's corporate walls, as did the other potential showstoppers. But the skeptics outside—Ford and Chrysler, the Oilies, journalists and analysts—had all the statistics they needed to sustain their attacks on EVs. The most damning came from Sierra Research. That winter, other studies supplied more. All claimed to be objective, the better to influence the debate; none was entirely so.

The first, and in some ways most persuasive, came in December 1994 from the U.S. Government Accounting Office, which warned that EVs would be too costly in the near term to be a marketplace success, with too-limited range and infrastructure. Worse, the report concluded, EVs would increase emissions of sulfur oxides by as much as 760 percent because of the extent to which power plants were still fueled by coal. But the U.S. Department of Energy was dismayed enough by it to attach an objection, observing that the 1990 amendments to the Clean Air Act forbade utilities from increasing emissions of sulfur oxides, so that the GAO's warning was meaningless: utilities would either be able to service EVs without an increase in sulfur oxides, or not be allowed to service them at all. Cars, in any event, contributed only about 1 percent of the sulfur oxides in the air, a fact the GAO must have known. And if EVs were supplied with electricity from clean-source power plants, they would add no sulfur oxides at all.

In early May, three researchers from Pittsburgh's Carnegie-Mellon University published in Science the more alarming results of a study done on the potential hazards associated with mining, smelting, and recycling the lead that a large fleet of lead acid–powered EVs would need. Before publication, the study found its way to The New York Times, which reported it in a front page story on May 9, 1995. "This could be the kiss of death for electric vehicles," declared one environmental economist quoted in the piece. "Lead particles can move long distances," observed a toxicologist. "This is potentially a global problem."

Using the Impact as their example of "available technology," the researchers concluded that if just 5 percent of the 200 million vehicles in the U.S. were displaced by lead acid EVs, as much as 21,000 tons of lead would be released into the atmosphere each year from the mining needed to unearth the extra lead, the smelting needed to manufacture batteries from it, and the further emissions arising from recycling it. That would be twice as much lead as was currently released each year, after decades in which lead levels had been steadily reduced with cleaner gasoline, lead-free paint, and other precautions. "Getting rid of lead in gasoline was one of the great public health triumphs of our generation," declared Lester Lave, one of the study's three authors. "It would be a tragedy if we reversed the benefits in the name of environmentalism."

A first indication of serious confusion in the study lay in the chart that accompanied the *Times* story. The battery weight of an "available technology" EV, identified as an Impact, was said to be 1,389 kilograms, or 3,062 pounds. But that was more than the weight of the entire car! The batteries, as any news article on Impact would confirm, weighed roughly 1,100 pounds. The same chart suggested that Impact batteries had an energy density of 18 watt hours per kilogram, when their density was twice that level. Later, Lave would say his figures for battery weight and energy density were *not* intended to reflect any specific car, but rather a composite of possible EVs.

The study's innocuous-seeming assumption that EVs might comprise 5 percent of the U.S. fleet was also a gross distortion: 10 million EVs would be at least twenty times the number required to be on U.S. roads by 2003 if all three of the states mandating EVs—California, Massachusetts, and New York—were able to follow through on their plans. In fact, the batteries needed to power the 127,000 EVs required in those states between 1998 and 2000 would total less than 2 percent of all the lead batteries already in the country's 188 million gas cars, trucks, and buses.

The study's conclusions about the migratory dangers of lead in smelting and recycling were also hugely distorted.* New smelting methods contained lead extremely well. Besides, whether a plant processed 2 tons or 100,000 tons of batteries per year, the lead allowed in the air could not exceed strictly monitored federal standards. Once in use, the lead in car batteries could be completely recycled, and usually was. Certainly some car owners failed to recycle their batteries; but how likely would even the most derelict owners be to dump a whole EV battery pack?

---

* To estimate how much lead was lost during mining and smelting, the authors used U.S. Bureau of Mines statistics for a forty-nine-year period ending in 1988, and concluded that 1 percent of lead was lost as emissions during manufacturing. But the statistics meant nothing, since most of the period they covered predated relevant environmental regulations. Under Clean Air Act standards, current losses came to $\frac{1}{200}$ of that level. In fact, while battery production in the U.S. had nearly doubled in the last fifteen years, the average lead concentrations in Americans' blood had fallen by 78 percent. The study suggested that residents living near a lead plant might be more vulnerable to lead emissions. But measurements taken of lead in water near the Electrosource plant in Austin, Texas, revealed no more than one-tenth the level allowed by federal standards, with most measurements far lower than that. And while toxicologists were right to warn against lead particles in the air, almost no lead escaped into the air during manufacturing; the few emissions still associated with the process were mostly solid slag, which did not migrate, and was easily recycled.

Could the Carnegie-Mellon study be based on innocent mistakes? From the authors' defensive tone amid a barrage of outraged reactions from battery makers and EV advocates, one could hope so. But as the report's credibility went up in smoke, suspicions lingered. The study had been supported largely by the National Science Foundation, with help from IBM and AT&T, all presumably neutral parties. But buried within the authors' National Science Foundation grant summary was the admission that "the Ford Motor Company will work with us in transferring the research results." And like many university research centers, Carnegie-Mellon's listed a number of industry supporters whose interests, in this case, certainly presented potential conflicts. Among them were British Petroleum America, Exxon Research and Engineer, General Motors Delco Chassis, General Motors Packard Electric, Mobil R&D, and Shell Development. Industry sponsors, in return for contributions, were invited to suggest subjects for research, and might offer counsel as studies unfolded.

GM's Mr. Emissions, Sam Leonard, sat in his office some weeks after the *Times* story and smiled when asked what he thought of the Carnegie-Mellon results. While the author was "qualitatively right," Leonard suggested, "he's probably off by an order of magnitude of at least two. But I'm not going to get up there and rebut his statements. He's serving my purpose! There's no reason in the world I want to be out there screaming how bad that study is."

Leonard paused, wishing he had a cigarette; he wasn't allowed to smoke in his office anymore. "You have not seen me out there supporting it either," he said in a softer tone. "Because I won't support bad science."

The Carnegie-Mellon study could still be put to good use with lawmakers not up to speed on the issue. With California's Pete Wilson, who knew the issue all too well and more than any politician in America had the power to affect it, a new opening appeared by May: his own presidential ambition.

So far, the reelected governor had failed to live up to what the Oilies felt was his side of a bargain: their support in exchange for his action on the mandate. True, November had brought some hope in the decision by California's legislature not to confirm CARB's chairwoman, Jacqueline Schafer, after her one-year trial period following Jan Sharpless's resignation. Though a Bush Republican, Schafer had shown as much reluctance to change the mandate as her feisty predecessor, and the carmakers were pleased to see her go. But Schafer's Wilson-picked replacement, thirty-seven-year-old John Dunlap III, was a veteran of the South Coast Air Quality Management District, an agency known for its aggressive and informed measures to clean California air. And while preaching "flexibility," Dunlap had already asserted his hope that the mandate would stick.

Over the winter, Wilson's silence on the mandate had put him increasingly at odds with his fellow Republicans' all-out attack on government regulation and subsidy in every form. In their free-market philosophy, the Republicans went so far as to suggest that government environmental standards be made secondary to business needs—that the Clean Air Act and Clean Water Act be effectively junked. In such a climate, Wilson had stood firm on the mandate, if only because a majority of his constituents seemed to want it. Now, though, he needed a national base. In the Rust Belt, support had its price.

On May 1, 1995, Michigan's Republican governor John Engler sent Wilson a letter putting the price in no uncertain terms. Kill the mandate, urged Engler, backed by his fellow Republican governors of Ohio, Illinois, and Wisconsin, or write off the whole Midwest.

California Blinks

))))

From the outside looking in, GM in the summer of 1995 seemed torn by dissension on EVs, its forces of light, as one environmental lobbyist put it, vying with its forces of darkness. Within, the course was now clear: it was simply a matter of going in two directions at once. Neither outcome could yet be assured — the Impact program could be killed, despite all the assurances Purcell had been given, until the day it was announced; the mandate, for all the lobbying against it, might stay in force — but *something* would happen. Something decisive, something soon. On the platform, in the corporate corridors, an air of nervous expectation prevailed.

Within the oatmeal-colored GM Electric Vehicles building in Troy that looked out on I-75, engineers hurried from meeting to meeting, or paused in the halls in earnest groups of three or four. The cubicles were filled, the conference rooms in high demand. All day, suppliers passed through, carrying sample parts, making chirpy small talk in midwestern tones. The suppliers wore ill-fitting suits and ties, and sported choppy haircuts. The engineers, whom the suppliers had to please, wore open shirts in stripes or patterns, chinos, and sneakers.

Had a stranger wandered into one of the larger meeting rooms, he might have found the platform's various teams tensely engaged in their weekly PPRs — product problem reports. One by one, the team leaders put flimsies on the projector and showed mea culpa lists on the screen. "We've got a primary seal bulb kinked in the top rear corner of the header on both sides," a leader might announce. "We never should have designed it with such a small radius for the B&R flange. We rushed it through POC."

Early on, Ellis had drummed home the point that blame was exactly what the PPR meetings weren't about; the more PPRs the leaders found, the fewer there would be later on. "I've got thirty-seven PPRs closed," a leader announced typically one morning. "Twenty-eight were related to the charge port, which had the highest number on the car." The cable on the charge port had proved too short for PrEView drivers, for example; lengthening it meant this PPR could be resolved and then, after time to prove the solution, closed.

In another room, a long table of engineers reported on progress made to cut costs and mass. "I think we're going to take out two kilograms when we redesign the instrument panel for crashworthiness," Dave DiPietro announced in one. Mike Liedtke, the chief in residence, beamed. "That might get us down to thirteen fifty," he said. "Because the battery pack guys are going to take out two point one, and we get one point one from the mid-rail guys."

The same morning every week, the engineers met to announce parts actually released. "We've got forty-four parts being released," announced Tom Lobkovich in one. "Fasteners on the pack, structural nuts and studs, clamps, forks, extrusions from castings."

"We're releasing the water deflectors," another engineer declared. "Emblems, fenders, deck lid, front facia."

"PDT Five?" Liedtke asked.

"The steering wheel and driver side inflator system," DiPietro said, now team five's leader. "Driver seat belt, passenger seat belt, the passenger knee beam."

DiPietro's report that day was important progress: after six months of anxiety, crashworthiness was almost resolved. The engineers had changed the seat belts, stiffened the steering wheel, put in a more powerful air bag. To a driver, the cockpit would look no different than before. The difference was that when the car was next subjected to crashworthiness tests, it would pass.

That month, two other of the car's potential showstoppers were resolved. The inverter chip that kept causing PrEView cars to stall out did not, as Jim Ellis had feared in February, need a redesign of its silicon. Merely switching two bytes in its software—a zero, and a one—prevented the chip from getting a message to shut down when current passed through it at a certain speed. By that tiny change, as Ellis put it with visible relief, the team had escaped the executioner.

There was more good news: Ovonic had come up with a new magic powder—alloy 139, replacing alloy 62—that even in Impact's airtight battery case would decay less than 20 percent in three days, rather than discharge completely. The Ovonic pack would still need to be air-cooled by the propulsion team's jerry-built system of hoses and ducts, and for the future, some better design would be needed. But the crisis of alloy 62, at least, was over.

Showstoppers took priority, especially those related to performance and safety. Inevitably, as a result, the lower priority of "pleasability" still got short shrift. Marty Freedman, the test engineer assigned to acoustics and range problems—major pleasability issues—understood that. But in the five years since he'd driven the AeroVironment show car around the Milford track, he had come to feel a bit like Sisyphus.

Acoustics, for one, had come to seem an almost insurmountable pleasability issue. With each next generation of car—from the fast-build to the proof-of-concepts to the limited-production fleet—new hardware had brought new sounds. In all that time, Freedman had had only one enduring victory: the motor that drove the hydraulic pump in the car's power steering column. Now, when the car sat idle, the motor subsided to an almost inaudible hum.* But to the test engineer whose ears were attuned to hear them, there were still clicking noises from the brakes, gnashing noises from the gear teeth, airborne noises, and noises that moved as vibrations along the car's aluminum structure. Some, at least, would diminish with production.

Perhaps Freedman was just doomed to frustration: in the cold-weather testing so critical to his other main mission, there was little good to report, either. The only way to keep lead acid batteries from losing range in the cold was to keep them warm, which would take some doing—next time around. Jim Ellis had thought the rolling-resistance losses could be solved by the tire guys, the magicians of rubber. But more than a new mix of rubber and glass would be needed. Complex trade-offs would have to be negotiated, between the tires and the chassis, the chassis and the shock absorbers, the shock absorbers and the bushings. All would have to be redesigned together. Meanwhile, Impact would remain a warm-weather car, no matter how much the Northeast wished it not to be.

Outside the cocoon, EV politics continued to roil both the northeast states and California. New York and Massachusetts remained troublingly stubborn in their demands for an EV mandate, despite all the cold-weather problems. In California, however, CARB's new chairman, John Dunlap III, had signaled an eleventh-hour willingness to open the 1998 ZEV mandate to debate—a sign either of common sense or cravenness, depending on whom one asked. A series of workshops would be convened, Dunlap declared, to review all aspects of EV feasibility, from infrastructure to battery progress. For one on marketability, held on June 28, 1995, Bob Purcell decided to make his first public appearance, hoping to convey, by his presence, how serious GM was

---

* By starting up only when needed, the motor also used just 20 percent of the power it would normally consume to operate the hydraulics.

about EVs even as he decried how far they were from reaching a 2 percent market share.*

Outside CARB's El Monte building, Purcell met a gauntlet of pro-mandate protesters, with sixties-style placards on sticks. DON'T SELL OUT EVS read one. WE WANT CLEAN AIR. One in particular he found wryly amusing: WHO KILLED THE FORTUNE AD? Earlier in the month, Stan Ovshinsky and Bob Stempel had submitted a full page ad to *Fortune* for Ovonic batteries; in the ad, the two of them were pictured beside an Ovonic pack for Impact, above claims that an advanced EV battery was now a reality. The ad would have appeared two days before the El Monte workshop—putting Purcell in an awkward position—but was pulled by Ovshinsky after heated words from Bereisa and Ellis, among others. To the protesters, apparently tipped off by Ovshinsky, the yanked ad suggested GM was so set on killing the mandate that it was suppressing its own technology. In truth, Ovonic batteries were at best much farther from production than the ad suggested. The picture also revealed in close detail the system of ducts and hoses—Gumby's Drawers—that Bereisa's team had just designed to keep the pack from overheating. Competitors, particularly the Japanese, would have known exactly what problem the team had faced, and how it had been solved.

Nearby was a large if somewhat less vocal contingent of anti-mandate protesters. They were under a misunderstanding of a different sort. Most were senior citizens who had begun the day by responding to flyers that urged them to attend a "taxpayer alert." The flyer instructed them to gather behind Ruby's Diner in nearby Fullerton, where they would board a "free luxury bus" for "free breakfast, lunch, and refreshments." The flyer failed to mention that they were being bussed to El Monte to be political shills, or that the arrangements were being paid for by the Western States Petroleum Association.

Inside, Purcell's message to the regulators was terse and clear. All of GM's surveys suggested that the total EV market for California in 1998 would be about 3,500 cars, not the 20,000 that the mandate called upon seven carmakers to provide. His speech, however, was soon obscured by the tumult of more extreme views. Most dramatic was the entrance of actor Ed Begley, Jr., and singer Jackson Browne, who strode to the front to make impassioned pleas for CARB to maintain the mandate, without which, they declared, the carmakers would walk away from EVs altogether.

To the protesters, Purcell knew he must seem the embodiment of corporate GM at its most conservative, a short, balding, bottom-line guy whose real

---

* Technically, Purcell's cover had been blown in a *Business Week* story of January 23, 1995, which drew on unnamed sources to paint a fairly accurate picture of the program's plans, and named Purcell as Impact's manager. But no other publication had picked up on the speculation, in part because GM denied it, perhaps also because other carmakers found it too hard to believe. So by default, Impact's production plans remained secret.

mission was to kill EVs and buy Detroit more time to pollute the air. He could tell them that Impact was the most reviewed program in GM's history, that everyone from the chairman on down called him regularly to check on its progress and cheer him on—they would have none of it, for the environmentalists were as close-minded as Big Oil. Until GM produced the car, it would remain the enemy. And when the announcement came, Purcell mused, the protesters would no doubt take credit for forcing GM to market.

Yet the suspicions were not entirely unfounded. Purcell's testimony was honest, but it wasn't the whole truth. Aside from failing to mention that his was a program hurtling toward production, Purcell described Impact as a $350,000 car in search of a market. The cost of a handbuilt prototype, however, bore little relation to the numbers he presented, two weeks later, to the GM president's council. Impact's piece cost, Purcell suggested—the cost of parts and labor to make one car—was within a couple of hundred dollars of its target.

To the president's council, and later to GM's board in New York, Purcell also went over his plan to lease, rather than sell, the first generation of Impacts. If the cars were put out for sale, customers might balk at assuming responsibility for future problems. They would resent having to replace their lead acid battery packs after 25,000–30,000 miles. They would wonder what the car's resale value would be. Better that GM lease the cars with a full-service warranty, replacing battery packs at no cost. Assuming the life of a car to be 100,000 miles, GM would have to count on replacing the packs three times. Clearly, the first Impacts would be heavily subsidized.

Within a few years, Purcell observed, one nickel metal hydride pack might last the life of the car. True, he didn't yet know how the cost could drop below $230 per kilowatt hour. But three years before, he pointed out, who would have thought that laptops could sell for less than $2,000, when the first ones had appeared at five times that cost? "Or that you'd see fax machines for three hundred dollars, and modems for seventy-five dollars. . . ."

Sounding very much like a California EV advocate, Purcell added, "We don't know what we don't know yet. And until we get started, we don't know how low we can go." With luck, he told the various boards, he felt he could cut costs on all fronts—lead acid and advanced batteries, chargers, especially the electronics of the propulsion system—dramatically in just two years.

In their CARB testimony or comments to the press, Purcell and other Big Three executives were coached by company lobbyists. All other statements were issued through the group the carmakers funded together, the American Automobile Manufacturers Association. Over the past two years, as their alarm over the mandate had risen, the three had increased the AAMA's annual budget from $20 million to $34 million, and moved it from Detroit to a suite of offices one block from the White House. In charge was a smooth, baby-faced former U.S. transportation secretary, Andrew Card, Jr., paid $500,000 a year. Card had clout that other lobbies envied. But on the California mandate, he appeared to be having no tangible effect as of June 1995. In the Northeast, to their anger and humiliation, the carmakers had actually lost ground.

The slippage had begun with an October 1994 ruling by the New York district court judge who had chosen, after initially finding for the carmakers, to let the state implement a California-style mandate, including EVs, without accompanying cleaner fuels, while letting a trial on the issue proceed. In court, the carmakers had argued that the Northeast's coarser fuel would force them to redesign catalytic converters made expressly for California's cleaner fuels, thus triggering the "third car" clause of the Clean Air Act. The judge observed, in dismissing the issue, that cars designed for California's cleaner fuels would surely be driven out of state and gassed up when they were; why hadn't this bothered the carmakers? An appeal had been filed in May 1995, but the legal prospects looked dim.*

The carmakers *should* have had easy political recourse. Both New York and Massachusetts had Republican governors now, presiding over mandate initiatives undertaken by Democratic predecessors—presiding, too, in a national climate of churning conservatism in which mandates were viewed as government manipulation of free markets. The way Card and his fellow lobbyists saw it, New York's George Pataki, still learning his way around the Albany state capitol building after his victory over Mario Cuomo, would take his cue on the mandate from Massachusetts's William Weld, whose staff had been dealing with the issue since 1991, when Weld took office. Weld had shown surprising reluctance to abandon the mandate, but that would change now that he was finance chairman for Pete Wilson's presidential campaign— because Wilson, in turn, would have to change the mandate if he wanted Rust Belt support.

To the carmakers' mystification, however, neither Pataki nor Weld was going along with the script.

Sam Leonard, GM's Mr. Emissions, thought he knew why. In Massachusetts, the problem was Trudy Coxe, Weld's secretary of environmental affairs. Coxe was inflexible, a zealot; she was keeping Weld's feet to the fire. As for Pataki, he had an unexpected green streak: some notion of establishing an identity separate from that of his patron, Senator Alphonse d'Amato, by becoming a Teddy Roosevelt Republican. Underestimating the complexity of both situations, Leonard and his counterparts assumed they could push the

---

* In fact, a second-circuit federal judge would dismiss the carmakers' appeal on January 9, 1996.

governors to capitulate without ceding any ground of their own. They were wrong.

In both states, the groundswell of support for EVs was surprisingly deep. In both, it was as much economic as environmental. James Worden's Solectria, supported now by seven-figure state and federal grants to build its first 20,000 cars, seemed to augur a nascent EV industry. On Boston's outlying Route 128, hundreds of high-tech companies saw a big future market in EV electronics. Pataki's staff, after studying the issue, concluded that EVs were feasible, later if not sooner, and why should New York not be among the first to jockey for EV assembly plants? In both states, too, not insignificantly, utilities had at least as much political power as either carmakers or the Oilies.

The carmakers' appeal to both states was a blunt reiteration of the FED LEV deal. If the governors abandoned the ZEV aspect of their mandates, the carmakers would agree to produce gas cars in 1997 that would be cleaner than required for that year by federal standards. By putting such cars in the forty-nine states other than California, the Northeast would get the same clean air benefits as with ZEVs, since out-of-state cars migrating into the Northeast would be that much cleaner, too.

In early March, Weld offered a compromise. Massachusetts would delay by two years the demand for ZEVs—if Detroit started building its forty-nine-state gas car immediately. Angrily, the carmakers refused. They would make a quid pro quo deal or no deal at all, Card reported. What was more, the states had to decide whether or not to accept it by July 31, when 1997 tooling decisions would have to be made. The ultimatum, observed Trudy Coxe, among others, merely revealed the carmakers' callousness. If they *could* make a cleaner gas car sooner than the law required, why didn't they do so for the general good, rather than playing it as a chip in the game to knock out EVs?

When further talks with Massachusetts led nowhere, Card and his team in mid-July brought their terms—unchanged—to Albany. At the local Omni hotel, they met with state officials, who tentatively agreed to a *six*-year delay on ZEVs. Yet the carmakers, angry and arrogant, refused even this deal. The ZEV mandate had to go.

Like some feckless troupe of traveling salesmen, Card and his cohorts packed their bags and moved on again, this time to California. CARB's workshops were proving a welcome chance for industry views to be aired. Most promising was an imminent one on battery technology. The lobbyists sensed it could be their big break.

This time, they were right.

Through this period of hapless lobbying and legal setbacks, GM at least had a car in the wings. For Ford and Chrysler, with so little to show, the failure to make any headway against the mandate was becoming a nightmare.

Of the two, Chrysler had far less cause for grievance. It had set its sights so low with EVs, spent so little money, and nurtured so little innovation, that it could hardly complain at having accomplished nothing. Ford had tried, albeit grudgingly; it had had a plan. But on EVs, it seemed, Ford was jinxed.

With the demise of sodium sulfur, John Wallace had thought he could count, at least, on having U.S. Electricar do pickup truck conversions. The little California start-up was booming. Over the previous year, it had established joint ventures in Hawaii, Malaysia, and Thailand. It had taken lots of its new partners' money; its payroll had expanded from thirty-five employees to more than 300. But it had grown too fast. To fill its orders—mostly from utilities—it had shipped out hurried, shoddy conversions that proved unreliable at best. As word spread, orders dropped. In March 1995, the company announced huge quarterly losses and acknowledged it might soon go out of business. The greater shock, for Electricar's joint venture partners, was learning that CEO Ted Morgan and two senior officers, while issuing bullish growth predictions, had begun quietly selling their stock in November after the Republican election victories cast what Morgan admitted was "a significant chilling effect" on efforts to raise capital.

Trying to save face, Wallace blustered about readying a "qualified vehicle modifier program" that any of several converters might join. In April, he announced that tiny Troy Design & Manufacturing Co., a van converter based in Redford, Michigan, would convert Ford's Ranger pickup for 1998. But the Ranger, he admitted glumly, would have a range of just 35 miles with lead acid batteries. "The Ranger at least allows us to put all componentry into production," he said. "That's consistent with Ford's strategy. It minimizes investment in the vehicle. Because there's no market."

With the Ranger announcement, Ford mentioned that the pickup would retail for $30,000, a whopping premium over the $11,000 price of the Ranger's gas-fueled version. Somehow, an internal Ford memo outlining the truck's specifications found its way to environmental advocates on either coast. The memo, with jottings from a strategy meeting, seemed genuine; the "target" price it set for the Ranger, the price Ford thought it could achieve by the first quarter of 1998, was $21,000.

Over the summer of 1995, Ford wielded its $30,000 estimate like a club over the California commissioners. At that price, Ford lobbyists told them, no one would buy the truck. In private talks, the rhetoric took on a menacing edge. Though the lobbyists were careful not to be overt, the commissioners got the message: Ford would sabotage its own EV program, if necessary, to *make* the mandate fail.

The long summer and fall of workshops exposed the commissioners not only to more lobbyists backstage but more speakers and vocal audiences at hearings. Both were manipulated, on occasion, by the Oilies. One day, a flock of firemen came forward to raise concerns about EV safety. How crashworthy were EVs? Might their batteries in a crash release explosive hydrogen gas? In water, might drivers be electrocuted? The firemen's concerns were legitimate, if easily addressed,* but the Oilies, seeing an opportunity to scare the public, had co-opted the group, paying to send them around the state to local talk shows and prodding them to testify before CARB.

In the past, the commissioners had been protected by their chairperson—first Jananne Sharpless, then Jackie Schafer—who took the hard line for them. John Dunlap III was, all sides agreed, a smart and sensible fellow. But in his seeming desire to please every constituency, he could appear, as one environmental lobbyist put it, the Bill Clinton of California regulators. The commissioners sometimes felt, as a result, confused about where he stood. Certainly they knew Governor Pete Wilson wished CARB's emission standards might somehow be maintained without a mandate, and Wilson had appointed Dunlap.

To some degree, the pressure on Wilson lightened at the end of September. Less than six months after declaring himself a presidential candidate, the humbled governor bowed out, having failed to generate the slightest stirring of national support. Whether or not his withdrawal affected the mandate was harder to tell. With the Republican "revolution" of 1994, California had acquired a markedly more conservative state legislature, where dark mutterings about the mandate could be heard. Outside, the Oilies continued to mold public opinion, as Woodward & McDowell, their L.A. public relations firm, burned through its $1 million budget by blitzing the state's print, television, and radio journalists with "news" bulletins that summer on an almost daily basis.

Perhaps, feeling the heat, Wilson did help nudge his new CARB chairman into convening the blue-ribbon battery panel that fall. Just as likely, Dunlap did it himself. Certainly he was shrewd enough to know that forming a panel was the oldest trick in the book for defusing volatile issues.

This was the panel that Andrew Card and the carmakers began to regard, in September, as their great last hope. It was the panel to which environmentalists looked with hope as well, since the four panel members, led by

---

* The shortest answer to the safety issue was that no major carmaker would be allowed, much less want, to produce EVs whose electrical components were not approved by Underwriters Laboratory, the independent group that tests the safety of all electrical devices sold in America. In Impact's case, any failure in the electrical system, as in a crash, would shut down the system; so would any spillage of acid or release of hydrogen gas. The battery pack and wiring were also completely insulated; as a dramatic test, the batteries had been charged underwater. Because the pack and inverter transferred high-frequency watts, they were even safety certified and licensed by the FCC, as if they constituted a radio or television station.

Dr. Fritz Kalhammer of EPRI and Carl Moyer, chief scientist of a West Coast environmental consulting firm called Acurex, were academics with battery expertise. More than ever, batteries were the heart of the matter. Though Dunlap never said it, the implications were clear: the panel's findings would decide the game.

That September, the panel members visited every serious prospective EV battery supplier in the United States, Europe, and Japan. They studied hot batteries and cold batteries, near-term and long-term prospects. Inevitably, they focused on nickel metal hydride, still the most promising successor to lead acid. GM-Ovonic, they quickly confirmed, was closest to producing an NMH battery. To their surprise, however, the partners of the joint venture had sharply conflicting claims to make about their own product.

Subhash Dhar, Ovonic's president, told the experts when they came to visit that the battery was ready to be produced. The new alloy—MF139—had solved its high-temperature problems; the battery in EV packs was up to 80 watt hours per kilogram. It had been put through 600 cycles, 200 miles' range per cycle. Why, that meant a pack would take a car 120,000 miles!

At what cost? the experts asked dubiously. They had heard the battery was still as much as $1,800 per kilowatt hour—more than $50,000 a pack.

"Sure, when you order only seven hundred packs," Dhar said. "You give me an order for twenty thousand packs, and I'll give you packs for two hundred fifty dollars a kilowatt hour, with the promise that in two years, they'll go down to one hundred eighty dollars." The USABC's mid-term goal on cost was still $150 per kilowatt hour, but perhaps that had always been unrealistic. At $180 per kilowatt hour, a pack of thirty batteries would cost $5,400. If the pack did have 200-mile range and last the life of the car, $180 was within striking range of rendering gas engines obsolete.

"Are the costs high?" Dhar added rhetorically. "Sure. I'd like to sell these batteries for one hundred dollars a kilowatt hour. But the first cellular phone I bought for my car, I paid two thousand eight hundred fifty dollars for in 1984. It was so big that I had to be creative just to mount it in my car. Today, you can get a phone which has more features, at one-tenth the size, and the phone company will beg you to take it for free. How many people in 1984 would have predicted that?"

The only barrier to production, Dhar declared, was GM's own confounding slowness. Bereisa and the others kept talking about a process of validation that would take years, and acting as if theirs was the only right way to bring a product to market. "It's like in India when a bureaucrat tells you how much time something will take," Dhar exclaimed, "and you say no, it can be done faster. And he says: not in India. But that doesn't mean it *can't* be done faster."

On a Sunday night in early October, Impact's finance chief, Frank Schweibold, flew out to San Francisco with Jon Bereisa to give the panel a different view of Ovonic batteries. They checked into an airport hotel at midnight. At six o'clock the next morning, the panel experts filed into a downstairs conference room to find the two portly chiefs ready with easels and artists' pads, flip charts and memos. For nearly six hours, as John Adams, the GM-appointed president of GM-Ovonic, participated by speaker phone, the chiefs rattled off confidential numbers about the Ovonic battery and GM-Ovonic's seven-year business plan.

"The batteries *are* great," Bereisa explained. "But we can't just go from handbuilt prototypes to twenty thousand packs. We've got to validate these things on a pilot production line, produce a few more, validate those." Ovshinsky and Dhar simply didn't understand the need for that process when a commercial product was involved—to iron out all the variability; to make sure the 20,000th battery worked just as well and lasted just as long as the first. And of course, Ovshinsky had an agenda of his own, the chiefs observed. His first business, ECD, was never far from the red. It needed the revenues GM-Ovonic could bring.

"Look, we're in a unique position here," Schweibold said. "We're the only carmaker making batteries too. We want the batteries to succeed—it's in our interest to do so—but there are some technical deliverables that haven't been proven yet. The first batteries off the line probably will *not* be eighty watt hours per kilogram. They'll be seventy. We'll be lucky to get the initial cost down to five hundred dollars per kilowatt hour, which means fifteen thousand dollars per pack—not including the wiring and vent harness, the computer that monitors charge, and the case itself, all of which add another five thousand dollars. As for cycle life, the chemistry hasn't settled down enough to put a number on it. We *think* it has the potential to double lead acid range and go one hundred thousand miles. But we won't really know until we test the battery more."

Adams, who had startled his colleagues the previous December at the EV symposium in Anaheim by declaring Ovonic batteries would be ready in a year, seemed to have recovered from his bout of euphoria. The business plan he conveyed by speaker phone was positive, but pragmatic. With luck, he concluded, the batteries would be out by the year 2000. No way by 1998.

As the meeting proceeded, Bereisa taped page after artist's pad page of confidential numbers, in gaily colored magic markers, to the walls. At the end, he pulled down the pages, folded them up—then, dramatically, handed them to the startled experts. The gesture was as much about symbolism as substance. The chiefs had, as they liked to put it, opened their kimonos. Now it was up to experts to take them at their word.

The panel's initial findings, submitted at an open CARB hearing on October 11, 1995, were optimistic overall. Advanced batteries *would* soon be commercially available, and every effort should be made to help them along. At the same time, the experts agreed, only lead acid would be available for EVs in 1998. And despite improvements in its technology, lead acid would still have limited range and performance, short battery life, and high cost. Lead acid EVs simply wouldn't appeal to 2 percent of the California market without substantial public subsidies. As for advanced batteries, the first would likely not reach the market before the year 2000 or 2001—exactly the timetable Schweibold and Bereisa had outlined. "More realistically, one should add a year or two to that timetable," observed Kalhammer.

The carmakers were ecstatic. The report, declared Schweibold, would help silence the "braggarts" from small manufacturers who claimed advanced batteries were market-ready, a pointed reference to the Ovonic team, among others. Clearly, it suggested that CARB at last would abandon the 2-percent-in-'98 quota. For the Oilies, it was actually just the first of two gratifying developments.

The second came on November 21, with the decision by the California Public Utilities Commission to ratify a CPUC judge's July ruling on how much the state's investor-owned utilities could assess their ratepayers for EV infrastructure. The judge had slashed the utilities' already-reduced original request of $630 million to less than $160 million. Southern California Edison, largest of the bunch, had applied for the largest amount; its original request of $425 million, already trimmed to $103 million, was cut by the judge to less than $72 million. The oil-backed taxpayer groups that had spent the previous year inciting fears about the issue with willful distortions were delighted. The utilities would still be allowed to build up EV infrastructure on the "utility side" of the meter, however, as they had for any new electrical need. "If the oil companies think they won a victory here," declared Charles Imbrecht, chairman of the California Energy Commission, "they'll find it was a Pyrrhic one."

By then, amid much hand-wringing from environmentalists, CARB's chairman had officially asked the carmakers to propose alternatives to an EV sales quota in 1998. They should understand, he stressed, that all seven major carmakers—in the U.S. and Japan—would still be obligated to meet the mandate's high bar of 10 percent EVs by the end of 2003. Dunlap declared that the plans should not sacrifice "even a pound" of CARB's planned emissions cuts for that same period.

In effect, if not in deed, the California mandate's most radical page was set aside on December 14, 1995. During a CARB hearing at which angry environmentalists berated the commissioners for selling out, three alternative proposals to 2-percent-in-'98 were put forth. The Oilies, allied for respectability with the Chamber of Commerce, blithely suggested that EV compliance be entirely voluntary during the years leading up to 2004. Carmakers should be allowed not only to substitute cleaner gas cars for EVs, but trade emissions credits with stationary polluters—factories and the like. This would allow carmakers to make no improvements in gas cars at all if they chose to buy that freedom. A proposal from environmentalists, at the other extreme, called for relaxation of some but not all ZEV sales quotas in 1998, with escalating quotas after that.

By comparison, the carmakers' proposal seemed centrist: voluntary compliance until 2003, with a voluntary goal for the seven major carmakers of 3,750 EVs by the year 2000. "Production capacity is not something to be taken lightly," Leonard had observed to the *Los Angeles Times*. "That means we certify a vehicle, we enter into contracts for the parts, we have the assembly line ready to go. It's a very, very big investment." But 3,750 was a far, far cry from the 60,000 EVs the mandate would have required carmakers to produce in that period.

The carmakers' plan, which CARB approved unanimously, would be worked out in detail over the next months and ratified on March 28, 1996. In broad strokes, it required the seven major manufacturers to submit confidential EV plans and disclose capital expenditures over the next critical years. It subjected them to a formal review by CARB in the year 2000. To compensate for producing fewer EVs, the carmakers also agreed that all gas cars sold nationwide beginning in 2001 would meet the low-emission standards of FED LEV—the same standards the U.S. EPA had not planned to require until 2004 in the forty-nine states outside California.

Tucked in amid the terms was a commitment to fund the next stage of the United States Advanced Battery Consortium—an issue that had taken on special importance in light of an August 1995 progress report on the USABC by the federal General Accounting Office. Less than half the $260 million budgeted for the consortium's first four years had been spent, the GAO observed, due largely to legal wrangling over intellectual property rights early on. More than $70 million had been disbursed in mid-term battery contracts, yet no battery had reached production, and the two most promising grant recipients, Ovonic (at $25.4 million) and Saft America (at $20.7 million) were now in court over their patent dispute. Though the Department of Energy remained proud of its commitment to the consortium, the GAO reported that Congress had not yet agreed to fund its Phase II through 1997—and might not, given the tenor of the times. Now, with the mandate pushed aside, the carmakers' commitment was crucial to keeping the consortium, and its advanced-battery grantees, alive.

EV battery developers were among those most threatened by the loss of a mandated market. But so were the growing numbers of other EV entrepreneurs. For four years, CALSTART, the Burbank-based network of private companies pitching for public funds, had invoked the prospect of an EV industry to replace declining aerospace. Some 175 companies had come under its big hangar roof at the Burbank airport, purportedly working on $80 million of EV- and other alternative-fuel-related projects. Some 40 percent of that pie came from public co-funding, but 60 percent was from private sources, CALSTART's managers declared. Had the compromise come two years before, CALSTART's seedlings would surely have died. Now, at least, the market might grow on its own. But the mood under the hangar roof on December 14 was grim.

More uncertain was the fate of the northeast states. Entitled to copy California's standards but not exceed them, they seemed, in a stroke, to have lost their right to enforce EV mandates, too. A delighted Sam Leonard of GM thought the states had "not a legal leg to stand on" in demanding ZEVs now. The northeast governors weren't so sure. Perhaps, their lawyers began to theorize, the California standard was simply an emissions level. Perhaps different states could pursue that standard as they chose.

Of course, if New York and Massachusetts demanded ZEVs now, the carmakers would say that that violated the infamous "third car" clause. But did it? The carmakers, after all, were agreeing to make ZEVs for California, even acknowledging they had the capacity to make more than they would introduce voluntarily at first. If two or more of the northeast states asked for some of those cars, for which the carmakers already had assembly lines and capacity, why would those be *third* cars?

From the start, the carmakers' real fear about the Northeast had been the effects of cold weather on EVs. Cold would cut the range of lead acid batteries so severely as to make EVs unsaleable, they felt; and no heater yet existed that could keep the passenger compartment of an EV warm below 20 degrees Fahrenheit. But at least one recent study had suggested that range need not be so diminished by cold weather;* and the heater issue, if real to the carmakers, had been stopped cold in court.

Perhaps recognizing that the Northeast might have a legal leg after all, the carmakers in January 1996 offered a compromise. Rather than take the hardest line—that the states had no right to a ZEV mandate ever—the carmakers would grant them California's terms: no mandate until the end of 2003, but 10 percent ZEVs after that. In the governors' offices of both New York and Massachusetts, resentment toward Andrew Card and his AAMA cohorts still burned. But the logjam, as Card casually put it, might soon be over at last.

---

* In October 1994, a study conducted by Arthur D. Little Inc. had concluded that the lead acid packs of Solectria cars had 75-mile range in daytime, 30 degree Fahrenheit cold, using commercially available heat pumps that kept the cars' passengers warm. At 0 degrees Fahrenheit, the range was cut to 60 miles, a far more modest loss than the Big Three had reported. The carmakers were quick to observe, however, that the study was commissioned by an EV advocacy group, the Northeast Alternative Vehicle Consortium.

■ ■ ■

Among carmakers, a lot of crowing went on that Christmas season. CARB, they said, had finally come to its senses. Invention on schedule never worked—why, with EVs, it had *slowed* the pace of progress, gummed it up. Now that it was gone, the carmakers declared, EVs would come to market just as fast as invention and demand impelled them. That was what free markets were all about.

If the carmakers really believed that, they were deluding themselves. Impact, to be sure, had reached the show car stage without a mandate. And in March 1994, GM had gone the high road by reviving it, rather than cobble together a simple conversion. Whether GM would have plunged back into EVs so soon *without* a mandate, however, seemed highly dubious. Certainly without the mandate, no other carmakers, large or small, domestic or foreign, would have instigated serious EV programs at all. Without the mandate, the USABC would not have been formed, and the advanced batteries nurtured by it—Ovonic's among them—would not have been scaled up.

If the mandate's demise underscored the continuing technical challenges of battery development, the innovation it had inspired remained real. In 1989, two patents in the United States had been granted for EV-related technology. In 1995, 200 patents were granted. What the mandate had done, in short, was to leverage the only force that could induce an industry as powerful and entrenched as the auto industry to challenge itself, to take technological risks, to change.

Now the company that had risen best to that challenge—that had, arguably, provoked the challenge with its own daring—was about to unveil what it had done.

The Dream Comes True

))))

Early the morning of January 4, 1996, a black limousine drew up to GM's private terminal at the Detroit Metro Airport. Out popped Jack Smith. An icy wind tousled his cowlicked dark hair and brought an invigorating tinge of red to his round face as he hurried inside. As the executives waiting for him were pleased to note, the boss was in a very good mood.

He had very good reason to be. For the fourth quarter of 1995, GM had just earned a record profit of $1.87 billion. Profits for the whole year totaled $6.88 billion. That was a record, too, more than making up for the wobble of mid-1994, and scotching any talk that GM's recovery had stalled. In gratitude, John Smale had passed Smith the chairmanship, restoring the tradition by which GM's chief executive officer assumed both titles. Smale would keep an oar in as chairman of GM's executive committee, which had lain dormant since the boardroom revolt of 1992, but Smith's test period, such as it was, had ended officially as of January 1, 1996. Which meant that his first public act as chairman would be today's trip to the Los Angeles auto show to announce, after nearly two years of extraordinary secrecy, that GM was about to produce its electric vehicle.

In fact, *The Wall Street Journal* had run with a leaked story the previous day, and the *Los Angeles Times* had followed that morning. "Were you the one who leaked to the *Journal?*" Smith teased Bob Purcell as the plane took off. "I thought it was you, Jack," Purcell said. "Bullshit!" Smith declared to happy laughter from his listeners, Jim Ellis and Bob Thompson among them. At this point, the leaks only helped. Based on them, and hints from GM that Smith's announcement would be even bigger than the stories implied, CNN had chosen to cover Smith's news conference live. Over the next several days, as CNN and other stations replayed excerpts of the broadcast, the news would reach more than 95 million people—12 million more than watched the previous year's superbowl.

Smith and his contingent reached the L.A. convention hall at 10:00 A.M., an hour before the conference was to begin. In the vast, high-vaulted space, the day's first visitors were milling around the latest concept cars. The GMers made their way to the Saturn banner unfurled beside a low, round stage. Hidden within a car-sized container at the back of the stage was #31: the thirty-first pre-production Impact, assembled just weeks before at Lansing.

Mercifully, the car had been rechristened EV1, after much debate at Saturn. The "numeric," as company speak had it, had "clinicked" well. EV1 sounded clean and clear. It jibed with Saturn's similarly named gas car models. It also signaled just how novel the car was, and how central it had come to seem to GM's future. To underscore that—and, admittedly, to allay lingering jitters among the Saturn tribe that this huge gambit might somehow mar Saturn's hard-earned image—the EV1 would be badged, quite simply, as a GM car: a first in the company's eighty-eight-year history.

To keep reporters from gathering too early, the GM executives scattered. Smith stood backstage, in effect, behind a wall-sized Saturn display. As the moment approached, he could hear a crowd gathering. Still, he was startled by the size of it when he appeared—well over 500 reporters—and by the intensity of the television camera lights. Shy by nature, he dreaded public speaking. This morning, though, felt different. This morning felt good.

"This coming fall," Smith declared with an upwelling of pride, "General Motors will be the first major automaker in modern times to market specifically designed electric cars to the public. We have the assembly plant tooled. We have the distribution system ready. We have the markets identified. And we have the automobile."

At that, the door to the container swung open, and #31 rolled silently onto the round stage. At the wheel was Maureen Midgley—plant rat, triathlete, Lansing plant manager. Late the previous night she had taken care to rehearse this maneuver and thanked her lucky stars she had. Usually when new cars were introduced here, they were put on stage at the start of the day and a pretty female model posed beside them, making the stage revolve by pressing an unobtrusive foot pedal. As the EV1 rolled out on its midnight test run, one of its front wheels hit the pedal. The stage began to revolve. Had the stage started to revolve during the press conference, Midgley realized to her horror, the car might even have flipped over. In an instant, the work of almost six years would have been wiped out by one ghastly image, broadcast around the world.

With the button disengaged, #31 rolled smoothly onto the stage. Midgley and her passenger, Tim Driver of Local 1618, were introduced by Smith.

"This is not a concept car," the chairman said, turning back to the crowd. "This is not a conversion." Proudly, he ticked off EV1's state-of-the-art attributes. "It is a car," he added, "for people *who never want to go to the gas station again.*"

In PrEView focus groups for well over a year now, that last appeal had proven consistently strong, especially among women. This morning, to Smith's palpable surprise, it stirred the most applause. Among the press corps, the Oilies' campaign had left a bitter aftertaste that would not soon be forgotten. On the periphery of the crowd, a loose pack of oil lobbyists exchanged worried looks and did their best to seem invisible.

Smith went on to explain that the car would be sold initially by Saturn dealers in Los Angeles, San Diego, Phoenix, and Tucson, beginning sometime in the fall. At about $35,000, it wouldn't be a car for everyone, he stressed, but neither was the Corvette. GM did think its market, if limited, was real, and would grow. Its importance could not be overstressed. "This EV1 is important not just because it's the first car built from the ground up as an electric car," Smith said. "It is even more important as the first product in a portfolio of high-technology products that we will be bringing to market in the years ahead. These are products that will define the GM of the future."

There it was, the key idea debated for weeks in high-level meetings. Until mid-November, GM had planned to announce EV1 as a product unto itself: a low-volume, limited-market experiment under Saturn's aegis. At an NAO strategy board meeting, Smith, Rick Wagoner, and Harry Pearce had begun wondering aloud if more shouldn't be made of it. Wasn't EV1 as much a statement about GM regaining technological leadership as about an individual car? Didn't it signal the start of the journey to hybrids and fuel-cell cars? If so, why not say as much?

The risk, as Saturn's top executives observed, was all too obvious. If the car failed, what would that do to Saturn's credibility—and GM's?

The other consideration, of course, was CARB.

In retrospect, CARB's abandonment of the mandate and GM's splashy introduction of EV1 three weeks later would seem linked, a quid pro quo deal. GM would deny this, and the record in a sense would support that denial: by the time CARB blinked, EV1 was hurtling toward production after an investment of nearly half a billion dollars, with the first of the pre-production cars already off the line at Lansing. Yet just as clearly, neither CARB nor GM had acted in a vacuum. And when GM decided, just before Christmas, that Smith would introduce EV1 himself, speaking of a *portfolio* of future cars and taking Saturn's whole time slot to do it, it sent, at the least, a strong signal of approbation to CARB for CARB's own December decision. A lesson. Forget mandates, Smith's appearance underscored; GM would do the right thing without being forced. To a generation raised on Ralph Nader, such trust would have to be earned. But Smith's announcement was a bold step in the right direction.

At the news conference, Smith also announced that by 1997, an electric conversion of GM's S-10 Chevrolet pickup truck would be available. For months, the truck had served as a wonderful decoy, as GM solicited bids for its parts, not very secretively, from suppliers. Ford and Chrysler, among others, had assumed the truck had become GM's sole response to the mandate—one as conservative and grudging as their own. Instead, it would complement EV1, appealing to the fleet market that no two-door sports car could hope to reach. By the end of January, GM would log nearly 1,000 orders for S-10s at roughly $22,000 each after government incentives, most from delighted utility chiefs.

The broad coverage of Smith's announcement made clear just how important his news was perceived to be. Yet a strain of skepticism informed the press questions that followed, and some, though not all, of the television commentary. The EV1's range of 70–90 miles still seemed meager, for all the assurances that 97 percent of Californians drove no farther than that each day; more than one commentator made the old crack about needing a long extension cord. The range seemed that much poorer given the EV1's projected price, which might have seemed less dear if mention had been made of the federal tax credit for 10 percent of an EV's retail cost that was still on the books from 1992, or of Saturn's plan, still being worked out, to lease, rather than sell, EV1. But if misperceptions provoked some of the doubts, so did the speed of GM's about-face, from mandate basher and market skeptic in one month to bullish EV booster the next. Only time would soften the seeming incongruity.

Ironically, the scale of GM's accomplishment was mitigated, too, by how closely the EV1 resembled the Impact show car. John Williams did car duty that weekend in L.A., standing by the EV1 to answer questions, and felt flashes of déjà vu. Six years ago to the day, there he'd stood, answering all the same questions about what seemed the same car. But within its familiar teardrop-shaped body, everything had changed. Every system, every part—except, as Jon Bereisa wryly observed, the thin laminated metal discs that helped make up the motor—was new. Only two parts were even borrowed from other GM cars: the door handles and the radio. Every other part was reconfigured to make the EV1 the most energy-efficient car in the world, to squeeze the greatest possible range from its batteries—batteries that possessed, in fact, twice the energy of the Impact show car's, though that, too, was easy to overlook.*

Perhaps more clearly than any other of the chiefs from the original Impact program, Williams saw both sides: the goals achieved, the goals still out of

---

* See the Appendix for EV1's technical specifications.

reach. By far the lightest car ever built by GM, EV1 had come in under the team's incredibly stringent mass target: about 1,330 kilograms, *including* the two extra standardized batteries that Bereisa had hoped to use. Investment and piece cost had met Purcell's targets set nearly two years before; both, however, had swelled far above Ken Baker's original estimates. That was what tended to happen, of course, to original estimates, especially with new and untested technology. But until Purcell cut costs as dramatically as he hoped, the car would make no economic sense in the market. As for Baker's target of triple-digit range, that, too, remained unreached. If the Ovonic battery fulfilled even GM's conservative expectations, EV1 would have a 150-mile range, perhaps more, by the turn of the century. If Purcell and his team failed to meet either target—of piece cost and range—the car's promise would surely fizzle and die.

Even skeptics, however, had to acknowledge the ways in which EV1's innovations were affecting the rest of GM. One by one, other divisions were learning about low-rolling-resistance tires and electric brakes. Saturn had adopted EV1 suspension components; the J cars now used its duoflex lightweight magnesium-frame seats, 60 percent lighter than those of a conventional car; plastic body panels, though not used first on EV1, had gained wider acceptability as a result of the program. The adhesive that kept chassis parts together was lighter, cheaper, and less labor intensive than using rivets; new lubricants lowered drag on wheel bearings; the one-piece instrument panel made assembly easier; epoxy tooling, the radical shortcut for assembly, would help GM become a more agile, lower-volume manufacturer of gas cars, too. In all, the car bore the results of twenty-three new patents, most of which could be used by other GM cars.

Whether or not GM had learned a larger lesson of EV1 remained unclear. Purcell still bridled at the team's sense of itself as a rogue cell hidden from the corporate immune system, but Ellis and Bereisa, among others, were adamant that much of EV1's success was due to just that. Set apart, given the budget and freedom to grow as an almost independent business, EV1 had also developed its own culture. Kept lean—flat, as Ellis put it, with few layers of management—the team had accomplished more, in less time, to create a car with entirely new technology, than a far larger, more stratified team at GM did in far more time, and at far greater expense, to restyle an established model.

Perhaps, with a new, younger management in charge at GM, and a bolder board of directors, that lesson might be taken to heart. As of that January, the EV program was given a new, broader name to reflect the corporation's hopes for it—the Advanced Technology Vehicles Platform—and new quarters at a nearby address in Troy that seemed nothing if not auspicious: 1996 Technology Drive. The new building's dimensions—a flat roof, one story, mostly open space, as wide and long as two football fields set end to end—perfectly expressed Jim Ellis's management philosophy of horizontal organizations. In the center, at Ellis's suggestion, were the design engineers. Around them—supporting them—were their chiefs.

One other indication boded well. On a cold clear winter day the entire team had been assembled outside around an EV1 for a wide-angle portrait. The portrait, Jack Smith declared, would be the cover of GM's annual report for 1995.

The rogue cell, the cover implied, was a rogue cell no more.

It was the essence of the new GM.

John Williams was not the only one at the L.A. auto show who experienced déjà vu. For Ford's John Wallace, the show brought back an all-too-familiar taste of defeat: here he was, caught off guard again by GM's EV news.

Three weeks before, Wallace had felt better as he stood on a stage at an Atlanta convention on EV infrastructure, and co-introduced, with Chrysler's Bob Davis, the conductive charging system he hoped would become an industry standard. Unfortunately, the next day, Toyota announced a major licensing deal with GM for inductive chargers. Ford and Chrysler might have a cheaper charger; it might be just as safe as GM's inductive paddle. But with inductive chargers already in production, Wallace had his work cut out for him.

And now this.

The day after Smith's press conference, Wallace, along with the rest of the automotive industry, was back in Detroit, essentially to walk through the same exhibits, and hear the same news briefs, at the show that opened just after L.A.'s. It was an odd ritual, doing everything twice, but it made its own sort of sense. Detroit drew more of the automotive press, which was based there, and was more of an industry affair. Also, Detroit had the Friday night black-tie dinner. Everyone who was anyone in the industry came to the Friday dinner.

That night, Bob Purcell and his wife found themselves standing near the Saturn exhibit where an EV1 was displayed, at one of those strange moments at a large gathering when the hubbub of conversation suddenly abates, like a sailplane hitting a patch of cold air. Purcell looked around, and there was Wallace, standing alone, examining the EV1.

"Hey John," Purcell said. "How's it going?"

Wallace nodded hello and smiled a sort of sad half smile. "Congratulations," he said. He gestured to the car with his glass. "I can't believe you're going to do it."

For an instant Purcell wondered if Wallace was being derogatory. He wasn't, though. He seemed—well, it was the oddest thing, Purcell thought later. He seemed happy for Purcell. Happy *someone* was making EVs happen at last.

"You take care, John," Purcell said, moving off with his wife.

"Yeah, you too, Bob," Wallace said softly. "Take care."

A week later, three of EV1's chiefs, along with a passel of engineers, set out for Lansing to begin an exercise never before done at GM. Maureen Midgley was there at the plant to greet them and to lead them over to the EV1 general assembly area. Filled in, the GA was still a light and airy place—no huge, oc-topal rails, no robots, just eight small workstations. At the first was an un-adorned EV1 body.

Ron Dork, the electrical chief, stood by Station #1 that first day, along with two of his engineers. They watched as a union worker began loading in the car's wiring harness. The craftsman worked slowly and deliberately from the technical specs the engineers behind him had drawn. At one point he held a wrench in one hand while having to pick up a bolt. "That's awkward, right?" the engineers asked. The union man nodded. The engineers took notes.

Each station would take a day. Eight stations, eight days, to make the first final production car: the first EV1 the team would feel was ready to be sent to market. Two cars would be assembled this way. Then a break, to refine the process. Then a faster build. Then a break. Then faster yet.

Mike Liedtke, the Data Keeper, had volunteered to oversee Station #3. Here the heat pump was put in, along with the charge port. Midgley had Sta-tion #4: chassis, suspension, and tires. On the fifth day, at Station #5, Jim Ellis watched as the car's propulsion system was installed. There was the in-verter, sleek and compact, fully debugged, its Band-Aids replaced by real de-sign changes, its EMI shielded at last. There were the batteries, and the motor. There was the work of nearly six years, by a team of hundreds. Six years of invention on demand.

When the work at Station #5 was complete, its craftsman got into the car and turned it on. No smell of carbon monoxide infused the air. No emissions at all. And so the worker did what no automotive assembly line worker had ever been able to do. He pushed the forward button, depressed the accelera-tor, and simply drove it to Station #6.

The future had arrived.

Changed Lives

))))

The car that so many hands had helped create had shaped its creators' lives, too.

By late fall of 1995, Alan Cocconi, the inverter wizard, was working intensely to outdo himself. His latest conversion, a four-seat Honda Civic with an urban range of 118 miles, had just been tested by the gasheads at *Road & Track* and declared "a whisper-quiet pocket-rocket capable of outgunning all but a handful of gasoline-engine performance cars." But rich actors, as he put it, had shown little interest in buying Honda conversions for $80,000 each, and so far, to his exasperation, no major carmaker had stepped up to license his technology. So Cocconi had decided to challenge GM head-on, with a two-seat high-performance EV sports car. A *ground-up*. He and his partners at AC Propulsion had hired a Detroit designer to adapt an existing body, and hoped soon to produce a prototype that might net him his first orders. "We could do the first cars in just four months," Cocconi declared, "and still beat GM."

With Impact, Alec Brooks and Paul MacCready had won guru status at GM, and were working on various projects, most prominent among them a hybrid vehicle. MacCready, always peering into his "cloudy crystal ball," was especially interested now in what he called "sub-cars," small, electric- or hybrid-powered vehicles that might be used by commuters between home and train station, or station and office; sub-cars might not be owned by their drivers at all, but rented at one spot, and dropped off at another, like airport luggage carts.

Back in July 1992, Don Runkle, Baker's one-time rival, had been moved from advanced engineering at the Tech Center to be general manager of

GM's Saginaw steering division. There he oversaw 14,000 white- and blue-collar workers, managed plants all over the world, and led a $3 billion operation. It was a far less glamorous post than his previous one, but a likely stepping stone to a senior vice presidency.

Among the princes, personal rivalries still burned, but the wars of turf had ceased, as corporate reshufflings erased the old lines of division.

A year after Hughes's EV unit had been absorbed by Delco Electronics, Rami Helmy had stopped worrying that giant DE would squash his little start-up. The matchup made sense: Hughes could take advantage of DE's economies of scale in ordering parts for its EV1 inverters, and so costs were coming down.

Delco Remy, too, had been submerged, its name changed first to AC Delco Systems, then to Delphi Energy and Engine Management. For Bill Wylam, the feisty battery chief who had tried so hard to knock Hughes out by making whole EV drivetrains, there was good and bad in that. A corporate heritage had been lost, which meant a lot to Wylam; swept out with it had been nearly all of his managers, some to other GM jobs, many to early retirement. Now the remnants of his battery team reported to the "virtual" company intended to serve as a roof over all GM EV products: Delco Propulsion Systems. The Hughes EV unit was under that roof, too, as was the EV activity at Delco Electronics. Wylam never had gotten his whole EV drivetrain; he did have the motor and batteries, and when Ovonic batteries got produced, he would have those, too.

Helmy and Wylam, along with Al Laubenstein of Delco Electronics, reported directly now to John Williams, the churchgoing planner and ex-manager of the USABC who had become the senior engineer at Delco Propulsion Systems. Williams still shuttled to Indiana each week from his home in Michigan and saw his wife only on weekends. No longer, though, did he have to roam the empty halls of a rented office building. The new headquarters of DPS was nearly complete, just a corporate-park block away in Indianapolis, affirming GM's commitment to EV components, and to DPS as the one roof over all others.

All of EV1's propulsion components would be managed by Williams and sold outside GM as DPS products. So would those of the S-10 EV pickup. Williams hadn't been given the business: the era of charters was definitely over. He'd had to bid for it, against Westinghouse and General Electric, against James Worden's Solectria, too. DPS had won the bid from its own parent, GM, because it had the best, most validated, most price-competitive parts. Williams, low-key and self-effacing, the easiest chief to overlook on the original EV platform, was becoming a powerful man.

Stan Ovshinsky, the Ovonic battery inventor, could hardly be pleased at having Williams, his old nemesis at the USABC, poised to oversee sales of

GM-Ovonic batteries. His more immediate concern, however, was prodding GM to take his batteries to production. It irked him intensely that GM had helped push the mandate aside, more so that CARB's august battery panel had found his batteries not ready for market. "I just hope I did the right thing," he sighed one day of his decision to join up with GM. "I wonder if I was being naive." Maybe GM had taken his cooperation with it as a sign of weakness rather than strength. Certainly it seemed not to share his own more entrepreneurial spirit—a can-do attitude, as he put it. But as the battery improved—soon, he vowed, an Ovonic pack would have 400-mile range*—the craziness would disappear, the bureaucratic foot-dragging, the fear.

Meanwhile, Ovshinsky had taken the best insurance policy he could. As of January 1996, Robert Stempel was the new chairman of Ovonic's parent company, Energy Conversion Devices. It was a company immeasurably smaller than his previous one, but in a broader sense, Stempel's stature had only grown. He was the acknowledged elder statesman of electric vehicles now, their most distinguished advocate. And after a fall that would have ended most executives' careers, his third act had just begun.

Among the original EV chiefs, there was pride and delight in EV1's happy ending, but exhaustion, too, and for some, nagging doubts about staying on a platform where further promotion was not possible, and where the unlikelihood of profits in the foreseeable future would continue to mean minimal bonuses.

Jon Bereisa, for one, had thought he'd be on to another program long ago. Instead, to his mortification, he had turned fifty on the platform, his eyesight increasingly troubled by the fluorescent lights. Innovation was his strength, so Purcell had put Bereisa on to the next vehicle, assigning a younger engineer, Ronn Jamieson, to see the EV1 to market. But Bereisa wasn't sure how long he wanted to stick around. Doing the second or third advanced car, as he put it, didn't hold the charm of the first. He might have preferred a promotion to some executive rank outside the EV platform, but in the Jack Smith era, the median age of senior executives had dropped to below fifty. "The trap of aging," Bereisa mused one day. "I don't see a future for me at GM, other than to stay where I am. And the thing is, I like the risk, but I like the reward, too."

Jim Ellis, at fifty-six, sometimes spoke as if he might retire after EV1. Thirty-five years, he reckoned, was a long enough time to be doing anything. Both Ellis and his wife were avid skiers and campers, and there were, as he put it, a hundred trips he wanted to take. But if the newly defined platform

---

* In May 1996, Ovshinsky would see his vision nearly fulfilled as a Solectrian Sedan driven by James Worden in the eighth annual American Tour de Sol achieved a range of 375 miles on a single charge of his Ovonic battery pack.

kept growing as he hoped, more like an inverted pyramid than any GM program of the past, he might be around longer than he expected.

For Bob Purcell, the seeming bottom-line GM finance guy, the last two years had worked a sea change. Learning to trust his team, to be borne along by their talents, had relaxed him. Seeing a close friend die, a male colleague in his fifties, had affected him, too. After more than a decade of pouring all his energies into GM, Purcell had determined to restore more balance to his life. He'd rekindled a long-dormant passion for playing guitar. Now when he went home at night, he picked up his electric bass, or his six-string, put on Cream or Jimi Hendrix albums, and played along.

For his forty-eighth birthday, Ken Baker had given himself a Harley-Davidson motorcycle called a "Bad Boy." It reminded him of his first years in Detroit, when he'd spent almost every warm-weather weekend in regional dirt bike races. As he'd begun his corporate climb in earnest, he'd sold his bike and spent weekends as a suburban family man. Over the last spring, he'd come home at the end of the workday, traded his suit for black leather riding gear, and gone for long rides on the rolling roads that snaked around the lakes of Bloomfield Hills. He liked the fresh air on his face; he liked being alone. And he wanted time to think.

By June 1995 Baker's mind was made up. Partly it was the sense of new beginnings that the EV program had instilled in him. Also, the two children he and Rosetta had raised were nearly grown. In the Bakers' marriage, not untypically, the closest bond had been not between parents, but parents and children. Now the Bakers' daughter was in college, doing better on her own, the son almost through high school. Anguished but resolute, Baker and his wife filed for divorce.

For Baker, always an emotional man, the next months had been the rockiest of his life. He'd put on weight, enough to have to haul out some of the old suits he'd never thought he'd have to wear again. He'd talked to lawyers, and hammered out terms. One day that fall, he'd gone riding on his "Bad Boy" to a favorite cider mill, garbed in black leather, and sat surrounded by families at picnic tables until his loneliness drove him away. Stopping at the house of old friends in Grand Blanc, he'd been introduced to an attractive female veterinarian, just divorced, who'd also just happened to stop by. The two began dating, and Baker's life began looking up again. Soon the extra weight was gone.

Often, in those tumultuous months, Baker's thoughts turned to his job. In the nearly two years he'd been a GM vice president, he'd done much to prove himself, setting R&D on a more aggressive, commercial track, positioning it to be the think tank for real products, not futuristic fantasies. Now the Advanced Technology Vehicles platform would report to him as well.

Sometimes it seemed enough. Sometimes being vice president seemed a lot less fun than he'd imagined it would be. Perhaps his expectations had been too keen: being vice president had meant, he'd somehow assumed, that life would finally be perfect, that all problems would be solved. Of course, they weren't. And being that much further removed from the real work of engineering that he loved had proved a mixed blessing as well.

Should he have stayed with Impact, he wondered? Taken the gamble it might be revived? Turned down R&D? Certainly, seeing someone else bring the car to market still stirred feelings of loss and regret. Yet given the choice again—at that time, in those circumstances—he would have made the same career decision. He was an engineer, and a dreamer of sorts, but also a corporate man. Allowed to rise in the ranks, he rose.

A different thought haunted him as he stood in his VP's office, looking out over the lake. Managing Impact—the job he'd so dreaded—had become the best time of his life. The greatest challenge. The most satisfying success.

What could equal it now?

Epilogue

))))

For GM, and for California, EV1's arrival marks the end of one struggle and the start of the next. Just as inventing the lightbulb set Thomas Edison on a long hard campaign to establish power grids for it, EV1 and other early electric vehicles now need an infrastructure of charging stations, private and public. They begin, of course, with the infrastructure Edison bequeathed, but high-voltage fast-charging systems must be added to it if the EV market is to grow; and the market must grow for costs to decline, as they can, to make EV prices competitive with gas cars.

Soon after GM's announcement, Southern California Edison took a first step. It unveiled Edison EV, a stand-alone business financed by Southern Cal's holding company to be GM's exclusive agent for Hughes inductive chargers in California. Credit for the idea goes to Diane Wittenberg, a plucky Southern Cal manager who spent her previous two years trying to shoot down Oilies' distortions in the press. On a 1995 visit to Michigan, Wittenberg asked Purcell and his chiefs how they expected Hughes chargers to be installed for EV1 customers. The chiefs hadn't thought about that.

"Well," Wittenberg said, "*I'll* tell you. As a new EV owner, you'll have to get quotes from two or more electrical contractors. Of course, it's a small job, so it'll be hard to get even one to come out to your house. When you do get a quote, you'll have to pull a permit from the local government. *Then* you'll have to get it installed. *Then* you'll have to get it inspected. *Then* you'll have to call the utility and get it energized."

The chiefs gave Wittenberg their blessing to set up a one-stop shop. Now when a customer buys an EV1, his Saturn dealer will put him in touch with

Edison EV—Diane Wittenberg, president—which will both sell him a 220-volt Hughes inductive charger and install it. Initial costs are high: $2,000 for the charger, $500 for installation. But GM and Edison EV expect them to drop sharply as their market expands, and few customers seem likely to content themselves with the 110-volt onboard charger that comes with the car: it still takes fifteen hours to recharge an 85 percent discharged pack, while the 220-volt charger does the job in three hours. For Ford and Chrysler, with no saleable EVs as yet, Edison EV is a real threat that could end the charger battle before it begins.

Ironically, as the Oilies were quick to observe, GM's announcement of EV1 came amid reports that California's air is officially two-thirds cleaner than it was in the 1960s. Despite the doubling of cars in the state, California air regulators have done such a heroic job of beating back smog—standard by tightening standard—that in 1995 the Los Angeles basin had only twenty-three days of modestly unacceptable air, compared to 120 in 1975. Unfortunately, L.A.'s air remains the worst in the nation—twenty-five times worse than that of any eastern city, ten times worse even than its neighboring California cities, which include nine of the ten worst-air cities in the nation. The state's air must get two-thirds cleaner than it is *now*. EVs, drawing current from California's grid of clean power plants, still represent the best single hope for cleaner air in the state.

California is the center ring, though as in any circus, two other rings vie for attention. In Europe, Peugeot can actually claim to have beaten GM to market—though just in France, with an electrified version of its small 106 city vehicle that will excite hard-core environmentalists and urban planners, but not many others. The 106's twenty nickel cadmium batteries give it a range of just 50 miles—though the car does have four doors—a top speed of about the same, and a 0–30 miles-per-hour acceleration of more than eight seconds. The car costs $17,500, but without batteries, which Peugeot plans to rent on a monthly basis, since a pack would double the car's retail price. Other European carmakers remain stuck in the prototype stage or, as with Nicholas Hayek's Mercedes/Swatch car, newly resigned to producing low-polluting gas-fueled versions of their EV designs until better batteries appear.

As for Japan, the big fear that Impact's engineers shared, of a surprise ground-up EV from Toyota, has proved groundless, at least for the near future. Within three months of GM's EV1 announcement, however, both Toyota and Honda declared plans to market four-passenger EV conversions in California starting in the spring of 1997. Both intend to use nickel metal hydride batteries; Toyota said its supplier would be Matsushita, currently being sued for patent infringement by Ovonic, while Honda acknowledged it had taken a financial interest in Ovonic and would be, as Stan Ovshinsky put it, an active partner. By the turn of the century, of course, Japan's Big Four may be able to marry American ingenuity to their own expertise in high-tech electronics and produce a second, far cheaper generation of EVs that knocks the Big Three out of the park. An EV isn't a computer, but the Japanese can probably produce one as well as the other, given about the time it takes to disassemble an EV1.

Outside the three rings lie realms of the world where no EVs are being made, yet which may have more effect on EVs than any other. In the last three decades, automobile ownership per capita in China has increased twentyfold; now even that rate is fast accelerating. If China puts as many cars per capita on the road as Japan already has, some 600 million will be added, doubling the number of cars in the world today. India, too, is modernizing at a dizzying clip. As the Third World's oil consumption grows, so will its output of carbon dioxide and other fossil fuel emissions—unless, just possibly, small and inexpensive electric vehicles come to the rescue. Already in Bangkok—no longer Third World but cursed for its progress with the world's worst traffic—electric buses and "tuk tuk" taxis are being tested. Peugeot is working hard on electric scooters. So are Stan Ovshinsky and Robert Stempel; already, Ovonic is exporting its nickel metal hydride powder to licensees in Japan, Taiwan, and China for EV scooter batteries. "Within the next five years," declares Ovonic's president Subhash Dhar, "there will be hundreds of thousands of EV scooters in those countries."

The air of developing countries is at stake. But that air is ours too, for better or worse. It girdles the same globe. After a year of blizzards, floods, and record heat, the consequences of fouling that air seem as clear as they did in the scorching summer of 1988, back when work on GM's Impact began. That was the summer NASA's James E. Hansen made household words of greenhouse warming in Senate testimony, and declared its imminence a 99 percent certainty. Cooler temperatures returned, and Hansen was dismissed as a doomsday sayer, with the loudest voices raised by a small, influential cabal of lobbyists for the Oilies.

Now even the United Nations's conservative climate council agrees the earth's temperature is rising. Almost certainly the rise is due to the ever-greater quantities of carbon dioxide spewed into the atmosphere by the burning of fossil fuels throughout this century. The rising temperature causes moisture to evaporate, and all manner of strange weather results. Over deserts, the sucking up of precious moisture causes droughts; over rainforests, torrential downpours; over snowpacks, snowstorms and arctic air that can migrate south to collide with warm, wet ocean fronts—prescription for a blizzard, if the ocean front hasn't already torn into the coast as a hurricane on its own.

So many measures will have to be taken to cut back on that burning, in so many countries, to have some effect. So many technological breakthroughs will be needed. So much going up against political powers, special interests, cynicism, and apathy.

One measure, though, has nearly emerged from those thickets. One measure is nearly here.

It gives hope—and a hell of a ride.

Appendix

))))

EV1 Technical Specifications

Body type: two-passenger, two-door coupe

Drive system: front engine, front drive

Drivetrain: computer-controlled, liquid-cooled 137-horsepower three-phase AC induction motor and propulsion inverter module

Power source: 1,150-pound battery pack of twenty-seven 16.8 kilowatt-hour, maintenance-free, recombinant lead acid batteries

Battery life: 25,000–30,000 miles

EPA range estimates: 70 miles city, 90 miles highway

Charging system: inductively coupled Hughes magnetic-field charger. Using standard 220-volt, 30-amp current, the Hughes charger takes the pack from 85 percent depth of discharge to full in three hours

Cost of Hughes home charger: about $2,000

A convenience charger is provided aboard the vehicle as a standard feature; using 110-volt, 12-amp current, it provides an 85-percent charge in 8–10 hours

Charging cost: about $1.90 for electrical current to fill 85 percent of the pack

Acceleration: 0–60 miles per hour in 8.5 seconds

Top speed: governed to 80 miles per hour

Trunk space: 10 cubic feet

Length: 169.8 inches

Height: 50.5 inches

Width: 69.3 inches

Wheelbase: 98.9 inches

Curb weight: 2,970 pounds
Drag coefficient: 0.19

Energy-efficient Features

- rigid welded and bonded aluminum alloy body structure
- polymer body panels
- electric motor-driven heat pump
- electrohydraulic speed-sensitive power steering
- electrohydraulic braking system with blended regenerative braking
- low-inflation tire monitor; high-voltage isolation assurance
- self-sealing, low-rolling resistance Michelin (P175/65/R14) tires and aluminum wheels

Standard Features

- double wishbone front suspension
- bucket seats
- AM-FM-CD-cassette audio system
- Electriclear windshield and solar glass
- dual-power outside mirrors
- side door defoggers
- daytime running lamps
- cruise control
- power door locks
- power windows
- keypad door entry and keypad vehicle activation (no key needed for either)
- remote release for trunk

Safety Features

- dual air bags and seat belts
- four-wheel anti-lock brakes
- traction control

Manufactured in Lansing, Michigan

Notes

))))

1: A Dubious Offer

This chapter, and those that follow, rely to a great extent on author's interviews with the characters mentioned. Interviews were conducted at the GM Tech Center in Warren, Michigan, as well as at GM's headquarters in downtown Detroit.

5   "After a decade as chairman, Roger Smith . . ." Maryann Keller offers the best review of the Smith years in *Rude Awakening*; there are sketches of Robert Stempel and Lloyd Reuss on p. 111, and longer ones in Keller's *Collision*, p. 28 ff.

2: Time and Again

The most exhaustive history of electric vehicles to date is surely Ernest H. Wakefield's labor of love, *History of the Electric Automobile*. Michael Brian Schiffer offers a lighter overview in *Taking Charge*; Bob Brant also offers a concise and detailed account in chapter 4 of his *Build Your Own Electric Vehicle*.

13   " 'You can't get people to sit . . .' " *Invention & Technology*, Fall 1990.

13   "So confident was Thomas Edison . . ." Of the several biographies that recount this chapter of the inventor's life, two are *Edison, a Biography*, by Matthew Josephson (Wiley), and *Thomas A. Edison: A Streak of Luck*, by Robert Conot (Da Capo).

14   The account of Sunraycer was aided by *Sunraycer's Solar Saga*, by Bill Tuckey, a commemorative volume commissioned by GM from the Berghouse Floyd Tuckey Publishing Group of Gordon, Australia.

15   "Among engineers, MacCready was legend . . ." This sketch is drawn from *Time*, June 11, 1990; *Reader's Digest*, August 1991; *Discover*, March 1992; and *The New York Times Magazine*, March 29, 1992.

18 For the account of the Impact concept car, interviews with principals were buttressed by several good press accounts: *U.S. News & World Report*, August 26, 1991; *Business Week*, October 21, 1991; "Here Comes the Electric Car—It's Sporty, Aggressive and Clean" by Mark Fischetti, *Smithsonian*, March 1992; "Really Cool Cars," by Lesley Hazelton, *The New York Times Magazine*, March 29, 1992; "GM and the Juicemobile," by Marla Cone, *Los Angeles Times Magazine*, June 21, 1992.

20 "Unfortunately, the science of lead acid . . ." See Wakefield, chapter 10.

23 "Cocconi labored over the inverter alone . . ." Reporting for this account was done first for *Men's Journal*, June–July 1994, for a profile of Cocconi titled "Hot-Wiring the Electric Autopia."

5: A Nemesis Known as CARB

50 "CARB . . . had come into being . . ." See Brant, p. 34.

52 "For all the improvements in hydrocarbons . . . vehicles still produced about half of them . . ." *Future Drive*, by Daniel Sperling, p. 44.

52 ". . . as the state's population grew from 29 million . . ." The 1992–93 Biennial Energy Report of the California Energy Commission.

52 ". . . the 74 million cars registered . . ." *The Keys to the Car*, by James J. MacKenzie, p. 12.

52 ". . . the state would have to expand its freeways . . ." 1992–93 CEC report.

52 ". . . the average freeway speed . . ." 1992–93 CEC report.

53 ". . . they drove 65 percent more miles . . ." *California Air Quality: A Status Report*, California Air Resources Board.

53 "A 1990 study would conclude . . ." Intergovernmental Panel on Climate Change. *Climate Change, the IPPC Scientific Assessment*. Cambridge University Press, 1990.

53 "Cars . . . contributed 25 percent of the country's man-made carbon dioxide . . ." *The Keys to the Car*, p. 12.

53 ". . . America's cars, trucks, and buses required roughly 8 million barrels . . ." *The Keys to the Car*, p. 7.

53 ". . . transportation's share had increased . . ." *The Keys to the Car*, pp. 7–8.

53 "Oil had come to account . . . for nearly half of America's $110 billion trade deficit . . ." "The Window of Opportunity," Electric Vehicle Development Corporation, February 1991.

54 ". . . the lobbyists themselves estimated that the world's reserves would last at least forty more years. . . ." Energy Information Administration. "1992 Annual Energy Outlook, with Projections to 2010," Department of Energy.

54 ". . . the world's population was due to grow from 8 to 12 billion by 2010 . . ." *The Population Bomb*, by Paul Ehrlich, Random House, 1968.

6: Framing the Picture

63   "Tragically, GM's new chairman acted . . ." *The New York Times, The Wall Street Journal*, et al, November 2, 1990. Also, *Comeback*, p. 305.

10: Low, Lower, Lowest

95   "Nine northeastern states . . . had chosen . . . to adopt the California mandate . . ." *The New York Times*, October 30, 1991.

11: The $2 Million Gamble

99   "Discreetly, one director . . ." *Collision*, p. 40.

99   "When Stempel balked at the finding . . ." *The New York Times*, April 6, 1992.

14: The Downward Slide

121   "After more than a week of feverish press speculation . . ." *The Washington Post*, October 13, 1992; *The New York Times*, October 26 and 27, 1992, et al.

15: Picking Up the Pieces

132   "One of the strongest prospects was BMW's E2 . . ." *Autoweek*, May 18, 1992; *New Scientist*, November 7, 1992.

132   "Volvo's concept hybrid supplemented . . ." London *Times*, December 4, 1992; *Motor Trend*, April 1993; *Road & Track*, June 1993.

133   "Mercedes-Benz had provided . . ." *The New York Times*, November 3, 1992.

133   "Renault . . . had the wackiest design . . ." *Autoweek*, October 19, 1992; *Automobile* magazine, December 1992.

133   "Hayek was Swatch Man . . ." *Smithsonian*, March 1992; *Autoweek*, September 7, 1992; *The Economist*, October 17, 1992. Good profiles of Hayek appeared in *The Wall Street Journal*, March 4, 1994, and in *The New York Times*, March 28, 1994.

139   "On January 22, 1993, lawyers representing the Big Three had persuaded a federal district judge in New York . . ." *Utility Environment Report*, February 5, 1993.

17: The Partners Square Off

149   "The talks raised the tantalizing possibility of federal research money . . ." *Automotive News*, March 1, 1993.

152   "In February, both GM and Ford had submitted proposals for $150 million in hybrid R&D funds . . ." *Automotive News*, March 29 and April 5, 1993; *New Fuels Report*, October 4, 1993.

152   "Amory Lovins . . . was not alone . . ." *Electricity Journal*, June 1993.

153 "A CARB study showed . . ." *Motor Trend*, October 1993. See also "What's the Charge?" a study of EV emissions benefits in Southern California, produced by the Environmental Defense Fund and the Natural Resources Defense Council (June 1994).

153 "But in Phoenix, Arizona, where 68 percent of the energy was supplied by coal plants . . ." Arizona Department of Commerce Energy Office.

18: Gentlemen's Agreement

161 "Under Jack Smith's leadership, GM in eight months . . ." *Fortune*, October 17, 1994; also, chapter 8 of *Collision Course*.

19: The Mandate Looms

164 " 'We have never had any plans to join in . . .' " *Detroit News*, September 10, 1993.

164 " 'There is absolutely no economic basis for electric vehicles . . .' " *The Wall Street Journal*, October 23, 1993.

164 "In July, the same New York district judge . . ." *The New York Times*, July 14, 1993.

168 "The carmakers had sought an injunction against the state, but on November 2 . . ." *The Wall Street Journal*, November 4, 1993.

20: A Covert Operation

The account of Stan Ovshinsky's life and career was helped by a long interview that appeared in Kenneth A. Brown's book *Inventors at Work*, as well as by profiles in *Discover* (November 1984) and *Corporate Detroit* (January 1993), and an hour-long television profile on *Nova* that was produced by WGBH-TV in Boston, Massachusetts, and aired on October 16, 1987.

21: Up from the Ashes

183 "Sensing the ambivalence . . ." *The New York Times*, January 28, 1994.

183 "In announcing the delivery of Ford's first Ecostar prototypes . . ." *Automotive News*, November 22, 1993.

184 "That winter, the oil companies' California lobbying arm . . ." *Los Angeles Times*, April 14, 1994.

185 "Yet even as these notes were sounded . . ." *Autoweek*, January 24, 1994.

185 " 'I do not understand the politics of the American manufacturers . . .' " *Automotive News*, March 14, 1994.

186 "The CARB regulators . . . took Cocconi's CRX for a ride . . ." *Autoweek*, June 29, 1992.

187 "That day, the Ozone Transport Commission . . . held a formal vote . . ." *The Wall Street Journal*, *The New York Times*, et al, February 2, 1994.

189 "A year ago, Volkswagen had pulled out of its EV joint venture with Hayek . . ." *The New York Times*, January 26, 1993.

22: Aiming High

198 "ECD has just declared its fifth consecutive year of losses . . ." Gannett News Service, December 27, 1994.

198 "NASDAQ had dropped ECD from its stock listings . . ." ibid.

198 ". . . the SEC, in June 1993 . . ." ibid.

23: A Horror of High Expectations

202 "Like the young Henry Ford . . ." A good profile of James Worden appears in *The New York Times*, March 6, 1994.

205 " 'On that window sticker for your . . .' " WUOM-TV, August 26, 1994.

25: A Company of Two Minds

222 " 'Who'll buy 'em?' " *Chicago Tribune*, April 16, 1994.

222 "A first incident had occurred May 2 . . ." *The New York Times*, June 4, 1994.

223 "Instead, it announced publicly that six carmakers had agreed to a conductive charging standard . . ." *PR Newswire*, September 8, 1994.

26: The Threshold

225 " 'Why should we rush about . . .' " *Automotive News*, December 5, 1994.

227 "It would be put out for sale by 1997 at $20,000 per car, declared James Worden . . ." *Business Wire*, December 2, 1994.

227 "It was at Anaheim that Mary Nichols of the EPA . . ." *Automotive News*, December 7, 1994.

27: Setbacks on Every Side

233 "In September, the International Trade Commission had voted . . ." *The New York Times*, September 5, 1994.

28: California Blinks

243 "Most were senior citizens who had begun the day . . ." *Los Angeles Times*, June 28, 1995.

246 "In early March, Weld offered a compromise . . ." *The Boston Globe*, March 7, 1995.

246 "The ultimatum, observed Trudy Coxe, among others . . ." *Automotive News*, July 10, 1995.

246 "At the local Omni hotel . . ." *Albany Times-Union*, August 23, 1995.

247 "The little California start-up was booming . . ." Stories on U.S. Electricar's boom and bust appear in *The Wall Street Journal*, March 23, 1995; also, *Automotive News*, March 27, 1995.

247 "Trying to save face, Wallace blustered . . ." *Automotive News*, April 10, 1995.

248 "One day, a flock of firemen came forward . . ." *Business Wire*, October 26, 1995.

248 ". . . the humbled governor bowed out . . ." *The New York Times*, September 30, 1995.

251 "The second came on November 21 . . ." *PR Newswire*, November 21, 1995.

251 ". . . CARB's chairman had officially asked the carmakers to propose alternatives . . ." *The Los Angeles Times*, December 7, 1995.

251 "During a CARB hearing . . ." San Francisco *Chronicle*, Sacramento *Bee*, December 15, 1995.

252 " 'Production capacity is not something to be taken lightly . . .' " *Los Angeles Times*, December 7, 1995.

29: The Dream Comes True

255 "For the fourth quarter of 1995 . . ." *GM News*, January 30, 1996; also *The New York Times*, February 6, 1996.

Selected Bibliography

))))

Brant, Bob. *Build Your Own Electric Vehicle*. Summit, PA: Tab/McGraw-Hill, 1994.

Brown, Kenneth A. *Inventors at Work: Interviews with Sixteen Notable American Inventors*. Redmond, WA: Tempus/Microsoft, 1988.

Cronk, Scott A. *Building the E-Motive Industry: Essays and Conversations About Strategies for Creating an Electric Vehicle Industry*. Warrendale, PA: Society of Automotive Engineers, 1995.

Ingrassia, Paul, and White, Joseph B. *Comeback: The Fall & Rise of the American Automobile Industry*. New York: Simon & Schuster, 1994.

Keller, Maryann. *Rude Awakening: The Rise, Fall, and Struggle for Recovery of General Motors*. New York: Morrow, 1989.

———. *Collision: GM, Toyota, Volkswagen and the Race to Own the 21st Century*. New York: Currency/Doubleday, 1993.

MacKenzie, James J. *The Keys to the Car: Electric and Hydrogen Vehicles for the 21st Century*. Baltimore: World Resources Institute, 1994.

Maynard, Micheline. *Collision Course: Inside the Battle for General Motors*. New York: Birch Lane, 1995.

Perrin, Noel. *Solo: Life With an Electric Car*. New York: W. W. Norton, 1992.

Schiffer, Michael Brian. *Taking Charge: The Electric Automobile in America*. Washington, D.C.: Smithsonian Institution Press, 1994.

Sperling, Daniel. *Future Drive: Electric Vehicles and Sustainable Transportation*. Washington, D.C.: Island Press, 1995.

Tuckey, Bill. *Sunraycer's Solar Saga*. Gordon, Australia: Berghouse Floyd Tuckey Publishing Group, 1987.

Wakefield, Ernest H. *History of the Electric Automobile*. Warrendale, PA: Society of Automotive Engineers, 1994.

Index

»»

ABOUT THE AUTHOR

MICHAEL SHNAYERSON is a contributing editor at *Vanity Fair* and a consulting editor at *Condé Nast Traveler*. He lives with his wife, the writer Cheryl Merser, and daughter on the east end of Long Island, New York.

ABOUT THE TYPE

This book was set in Electra, a typeface designed for Linotype by W. A. Dwiggins, the renowned type designer (1880–1956). Electra is a fluid typeface, avoiding the contrasts of thick and thin strokes that are prevalent in most modern typefaces.